the gap-year guidebook 2014

Editor: Jonathan Barnes

John Catt Educational Ltd

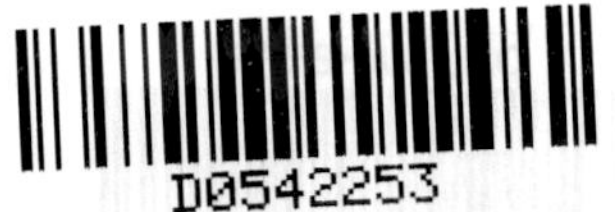

Published in 2013 by John Catt Educational Ltd,
12 Deben Mill Business Centre, Old Maltings Approach,
Melton, Woodbridge, Suffolk IP12 1BL

Tel: +44 (0) 1394 389850 Fax: +44 (0) 1394 386893
Email: info@gap-year.com Website: www.gap-year.com

First published by Peridot Press in 1992; Twenty-second edition 2014

British Library Cataloguing in Publication Data.

ISBN: 978 1 908095 93 0

Designed and typeset by John Catt Educational Limited
Printed and bound in Great Britain by Ashford Colour Press.

Contacts

Editor
Jonathan Barnes
Email: editor@gap-year.com

Distribution/Booksales
Tel: +44 (0) 1394 389863
Email: booksales@johncatt.com

Production - James Rudge

Advertising
Tel: +44 (0) 1394 389853
Email: info@gap-year.com

contents

contents ... continued

Your gap-year abroad

contents ... continued

Your gap-year in the UK

contents ... continued

Many thanks to all those who have given their time, advice and expertise to help us keep this book as up-to-date as possible. Thank you also to those who have shared their gap-year adventures with us.

Our front cover image was sent in by Laura Young, of Fakenham, in Norfolk. It was the winner of our 2013 gap-year Travel Photography competition.

Preface

Why gap-years are back in vogue...

Preface: gap-years are 'back in vogue'...

Richard Oliver, chief executive of the Year Out Group, introduces the 2014 edition and looks at the current gap-year market...

Gap-years are back in vogue with a significant increase in the number of people applying for projects reversing the downward trend of the past three years. While people of all ages now take time out and use the services of gap-year organisations, it is still those aged 18 to 24 that form over 70% of the gap-year market and of these the majority are school leavers. This is group that was most affected by the significant rise in tuition fees that was announced by the Government in 2010 and came into effect in 2012.

Such was the scale of the increase in 2012 that teachers, career advisers and parents understandably urged students to forego their plans for a gap-year and secure their place at university by 2011. The hiatus stretched into 2012 as school leavers were undecided about whether to go to university or straight into employment. A year on and the situation is much clearer. Students are considering their options more carefully and once again their advisers are encouraging them to at least consider the benefits of taking a gap-year.

The benefits of a gap-year

As each person's gap-year is unique so the reasons for taking it will be wide and varied. But while it is important to know why you are taking a gap-year, it is even more important to consider how it will benefit you in the medium and long term. It is the potential benefits that make all the effort to plan a suitable and worthwhile programme and to raise the necessary funds worthwhile.

Students who take a gap-year arrive at university refreshed and focused. They have a greater understanding of their place in the world having experienced different cultures and customs. This enables them to make a more considered contribution to their studies and university life in general. Some students may take time to readjust to academic life but this is more than compensated by their social maturity. In summary they are more likely to complete their chosen course and to succeed.

For graduates and school leavers going straight to university then a gap-year needs to be used to acquire or hone skills and gain experience that will enhance their CV and make them more attractive to employers. Financial awareness, communication and negotiating skills are gained during the fundraising process, which is an important phase of the gap-year experience. Assessing and managing risk, adjusting to and learning from different customs and cultures and learning a language are all skills that are valued by potential employers. But the main benefit comes from successfully initiating, researching, planning and executing a complex programme that builds self-confidence. This will come through in interview and help convince an employer that you will be able to make a positive contribution to their team from the outset.

Planning a gap-year

The key to a successful gap-year is to plan and research in as much detail as possible. This takes time. If you are considering a course then a few weeks' lead may suffice. But if you intend to do voluntary work or join an expedition then think in months rather than weeks. The *gap-year guidebook* will lead you through the detail.

Safety is an issue that needs to be assessed during the research and planning phase and kept in mind throughout your time overseas. The overwhelming majority of gap-year programmes pass off without serious incident; participants have a great time and arrive home safely. However, it is important to realise that all gap-year programmes contain an element of risk; the level of which will depend on the destination and the activity. One of the main advantages of using a reputable gap-year organisation is that it will provide you with ample pertinent information to indicate the risks involved and the steps they have taken to mitigate those risks. They will also be on hand to support you if things go wrong. But gap-year organisations expect their participants to play their part and take responsibility for their own actions. There is now a British Standard – BS8848:2014 – that covers adventurous activities, expeditions and fieldwork overseas, which includes most gap-year programmes. The standard is voluntary but all gap-year organisations should be aware of the standard and be able either to state that they comply with it fully or explain why not.

In conclusion...

The concept of taking time out from education or employment is no longer the province of the school leaver or recent graduate; it is open to all ages. The number of international participants, especially from the US, is increasing annually. A well-structured programme that demonstrates that the time out has been used wisely will enhance a CV, be fun and may change your life forever. But the basis of a successful programme lies in the initial research and planning that enables you to make an informed decision. This requires time and diligence. What better place to start than with *the gap-year guidebook*.

Why take a gap-year?

If you're reading this book, it's likely you've already decided to take a gap. But if you need any more convincing, then you might find some inspiring words on these pages. We asked a range of gap-year organisations (about whom you will find more information about in this book) what they believed the benefits were of taking a gap-year. Here are some of the best answers...

Kaya Responsible Travel

"We think the famous quote by Mark Twain sums this up quite well: 'Twenty years from now you will be more disappointed by the things that you didn't do than by the ones you did do. So throw off the bowlines. Sail away from the safe harbor. Catch the trade winds in your sails. Explore. Dream. Discover.' Students sometimes say to us that they think taking a gap-year is a waste of time and that they think they should just go and look for a job right away. However, the experiences that you have during that time can really change and shape your life and will give you great memories for the rest of your life – you don't want to grow up and regret not doing the things that you wanted to do.

"There are so many benefits to taking a gap-year both personally and professionally. On a personal level, not only is it great fun but taking a gap-year can equip you with so many skills that you can't get through studying. Skills such as team-building, decision-making, initiative, and communication skills are all skills that you are likely to develop through taking a gap-year. These are the type of skills that employers look for when recruiting so showing that you have these skills will make you more attractive to prospective employers. A recent survey carried out by Time Bank through Reed Executive showed that, among 200 of the UK's leading businesses, 94% of employees who volunteered to learn new skills had benefited either by getting their first job, improving their salary, or being promoted.

"Despite the professional benefits of taking a gap-year, I still believe that one of the main benefits of taking a gap-year is just the experience itself. Personally, after graduating, I spent six months in the Philippines working with street children. These six months were genuinely the best months of my life. It's the first time in my life when waking up at 6.30am to get ready for 'work' wasn't a chore! The local community were so friendly and welcoming and the children were just adorable. Those are life-long memories which are priceless!"

Gap 360:

"Your gap-year will give you better perspective in your life, meaning you'll be taking some truly life-changing experiences back home with you. These experiences will have a massive impact on your future, broaden your horizons and set you on the road to independence.

"A gap trip can be the time in your life when you learn the most about yourself, discover new avenues for your future and have the unforgettable experience of a lifetime. A gap-year is an open door for everyone, giving you a fresh perspective and a whole new lease of life so the question is not so much is a gap-year for you, but which gap-year is right for you?"

Projects Abroad:

"The first thing to say is that everyone is different and what's right for one person might not be right for you. Having said that, a gap-year does give you a wonderful opportunity to get away from your normal routine of education or work for an extended period of time – an opportunity that doesn't come around very often. Not only that but you can also use the time to travel the world, meet new people, learn new skills and get a fresh perspective on life.

"As long as you are using the time to do something constructive then you will gain a huge amount from a gap-year. It can make you more employable by enhancing your CV, but it also improves what employers call 'soft skills' such as teamwork, leadership and responsibility. Most of our volunteers say that they feel more confident after taking a gap-year and they also develop a love of travel and learning about different cultures that stays with them long after their gap-year is over."

The Dragon Trip:

"Visiting a foreign country opens your eyes to different cultures; many therefore return home with a new appreciation for their own country while gaining a broader worldview in the process. Remember, you only live once, so passing up a chance to travel is tantamount to passing up a life-altering experience.

"Foremost on the reasons to travel is that you discover a lot about yourself and how to cope in different situations. You can grow so much by travelling that you never could by being sat in a classroom or lecture theatre. Travelling for an extended period of time will no doubt bring about some challenges that take you out of your comfort zone, but overcoming this will make you stronger. Travelling really does provide people with a new perspective on life, this could be by not stressing over the little things, learning to fend for yourself or by discovering what aspects of life you really value. You will find your own path in life, rather than simply following the norm. You will realise how much fun you can have with new friends and promising to get out there and meet new people once back home is an invaluable trait. Another bonus is that there is absolutely nothing like being inspired by some of the great wonders of the world or discovering your own wonders.

"To be bilingual is becoming imperative in many everyday jobs as more and more companies are doing international business. It is possible that English may not be the worldwide international language within the next decade; this is likely to change to Chinese Mandarin. Immersion is the best way to learn a language so what better way than to have fun travelling whilst subconsciously developing a skill that could put you in a great position for your career.

"The main benefits of taking a gap-year are that you broaden your horizons; learn from others and make friends for life from all around the world (which means free holiday accommodation for years to come!). It enables you to learn numerous life skills in a year that can take decades to learn if you never travel or push the boundaries. This could be learning a language, learning how to save and budget but also discovering that money isn't the key to happiness and that there is so much more to life.

"Whether you know exactly what career path you want to follow and want to develop life skills to enhance this, or you are contemplating where your life is headed and need inspiration and time to think; travelling is a must. The knowledge acquired from traveling is invaluable. You'll be enriched on many levels, and meet some amazing people."

Raleigh International:

"There are so many reasons people might consider taking some time out of education or work. This experience can really help people gain perspective and realise what they really want from life."

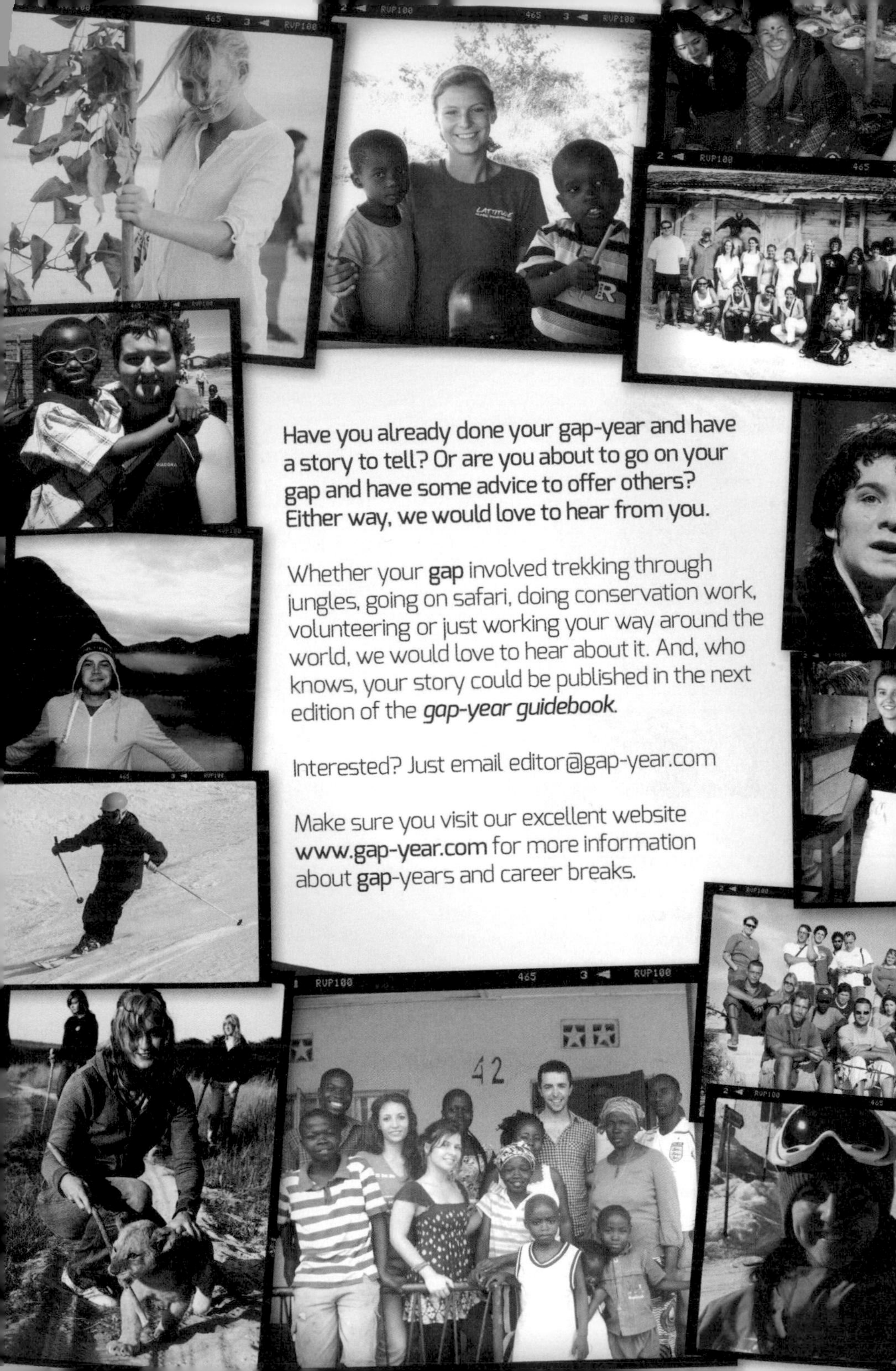
Have you already done your gap-year and have a story to tell? Or are you about to go on your gap and have some advice to offer others? Either way, we would love to hear from you.
Whether your gap involved trekking through jungles, going on safari, doing conservation work, volunteering or just working your way around the world, we would love to hear about it. And, who knows, your story could be published in the next edition of the gap-year guidebook.
Interested? Just email editor@gap-year.com
Make sure you visit our excellent website www.gap-year.com for more information about gap-years and career breaks.

Tips for travellers

Tips for travellers

For starters, what do we mean by gap-year?

Well, according to the Oxford Dictionary, a gap-year is defined as:

'a period, typically an academic year, taken by a student as a break between school and university or college education.'

Typically, yes, but we'd contend that a gap-year can be and is much more than that nowadays. It's certainly not limited to just students. Nowadays people travel to volunteer, work and study. You might be taking a year out from work, spending a redundancy pay-out or enjoying your retirement.

Don't think your break would have to be for a year either – it could be as long and short as you like, or can afford!

But the one thing all such trips have in common is the fact that they're all about taking time out of the normal routine to do **something different, challenging, fulfilling, memorable** – so that is our definition of a gap.

Who goes on a gap?

As we've just explained, anyone *can*. But who does?

It's estimated that 230,000 young people (teenagers and those in their early 20s), 90,000 people on career breaks and 200,000 retired people take a gap every year.

The Year Out Group, which represents 36 of the leading gap-year providers in the UK, say that about two-thirds of gap-years organised through its members are booked by those aged between 17 and 24.

Gap specialists Gap 360 say their biggest age group is 18-22, with 23-26 a close second. "Interestingly, about 50% are either school leavers, at university, or just leaving uni – and 50% are working or can't find a proper job," they told us.

But industry experts report that they are now seeing many young professionals taking extended career breaks, and even couples whose children have flown the nest taking the chance to go and see the world.

So the answer is people of all ages, all walks of life, able-bodied and disabled go on a gap.

Why should you take a gap?

There are as many reasons to take a gap as there are different opportunities on offer. You will have read some excellent examples in the preface to this book.

Time out before further study? A break from the daily work routine? A memorable experience? To give something back? To learn something new? A way to gain work experience that will boost your career prospects? All are valid reasons.

The benefits of taking a gap-year are considerable. Younger gappers who have taken a structured trip are likely to arrive at university refreshed and focused and research shows they are more likely to finish their chosen course.

And if you feel like you're fed up with the daily grind of a 9-to-5 job, a career break can help you get out of your rut. Working full-time for even just ten years means roughly around 20,000 hours of sitting in an office staring at your computer screen. A career break will help you gain new perspective on life and work and will be an experience you remember for the rest of your life.

Increasingly, young people planning a gap-year do so with improving their CV in mind and making sure they are more attractive to employers when they return. A well-planned gap-year that includes a work placement and learning new skills is likely to be of a huge benefit when you're back and looking for a job, particularly in tough economic times when work may be hard to come by.

Richard Oliver, chief executive of the Year Out Group, told us: "The job market is increasingly competitive especially for graduates. Almost every day there are stories in the media of employers complaining that young people do not have the necessary skills to take their place in the work force. Students are learning that if they take a gap-year they need to fill their time wisely, a point that Year Out Group has been making ever since it was launched 13 years ago.

"Consequently gap-year participants are choosing projects that will enable them to acquire new skills or hone existing ones and gain experience that will enhance their CV. For many this means they set their sights on paid work and internships, which can be found more easily nearer home. Many seem to overlook that volunteering is voluntary work and the skills and experience required to succeed in a paid job, such as teamwork, good communication, problem solving, thinking on one's feet, risk

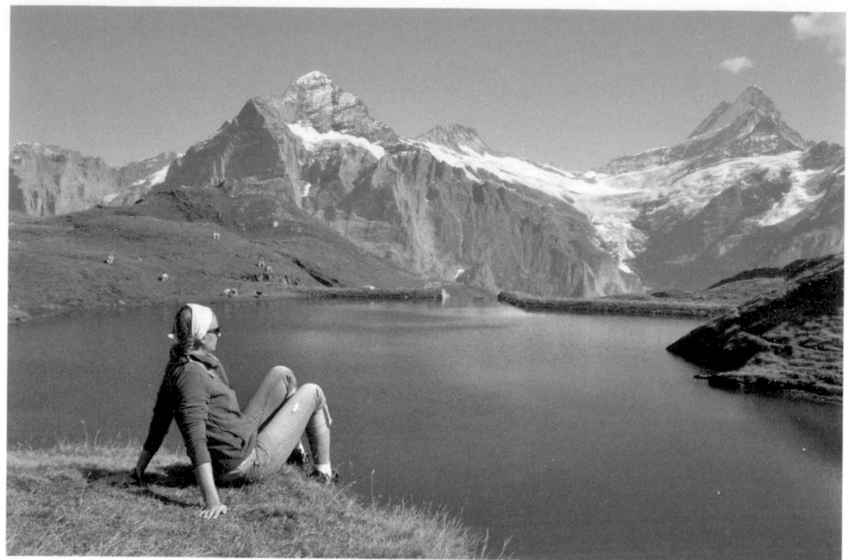

management, can be acquired just as readily as a volunteer. The advantage of doing this overseas is that it takes you out of your comfort zone, requires you to learn how to adjust to different customs and cultures and to open your mind to new ideas and opportunities. If it also lead to learning a language, so much the better."

Have tuition fees and the economy had an impact?

It's true that the uncertain economic times and the introduction of tuition fees of up to £9000 a year have made people think much harder about what they do and how they spend their money.

Gap-year organisations have reported tough times over the past few years, but the evidence coming out of 2013 is that business has really picked up. Gap 360 said the number of people sent on placements in 2013 was 100% up on the previous year.

"Many people predicted at the start of the recession that people would stop taking gap-years and doing overseas voluntary work", say our friends at Projects Abroad. "However, the number of volunteers joining our projects is continuing to grow year on year.

"Not everyone is choosing to commit to an entire year – many volunteers join a project during their long summer holidays or after university. On balance though, we still speak to plenty of people week in, week out who are planning ahead for their gap-year or career break, so we feel that the market is still going strong."

As we've already mentioned, with the traditional route of going straight to university after finishing A levels not proving as dependable as in previous years and a sluggish jobs market, more youngsters are considering vocational training or work experience on a gap-year abroad, allowing them to gain the hands-on experience that employers are looking for.

What's more, experts say the number of young professionals booking extended trips and work sabbaticals is still rising – up 30% in the past five years.

So, if anything, industry leaders are expecting to see more people taking a gap, despite the economy.

Planning your gap – the first steps

What do you want to do?

The beauty of the modern gap-year is the amount of choice and variety on offer: each is as unique as the individual participant, and each is an opportunity to create a tailored programme to meet their own personal ambitions.

You know your own personality, your interests, your strengths and weaknesses. Are you someone who likes to get stuck into something for a while – or do you want to be on the move a lot?

If you're not confident about coping alone with unfamiliar situations you might want a more structured, group setting. On the other hand if you know you need time away from the crowds, you're bound to want to build in some independent travel.

Voluntary work attracts the most placements and the greatest variety of projects, with placements available in nearly every country where gap-year providers operate.

Teaching is the most popular activity and is the ideal way to experience a country's culture and customs. When volunteering as an individual it generally follows that the longer the placement, the greater the benefit to both the volunteer and the host organisation.

Or perhaps you want to explore things you've always wanted to pursue but never had time? It could be anything from a spiritual retreat to meditation and yoga, art, photography, a new language or particular places and cultures.

Maybe you're particularly concerned about the state of the world and would like to do your bit environmentally or contribute to helping disadvantaged people? The possibilities are endless and many gappers end up constructing a programme that combines several elements.

Those with a full year at their disposal will perhaps have time for more than one activity, and might want to combine a structured element to their gap with some travel. The increase in cheap flights and wider access to previously unreachable destinations has made this even more possible.

Choosing the activity, destination and organisation most suited to the individual can be a difficult and time-consuming task. However, proper planning and research is crucial and will help ensure you get the most out of your time; a gap or career break can easily be wasted without planning ahead.

It is also important that you are aware of your responsibilities. Dropping out of a placement or programme before it has finished can be disruptive not only to you but also to others directly and indirectly involved.

A gap-year can also be used for spiritual reasons or for personal development and there are companies that specialise in emotionally and spiritually-enriching trips.

But don't worry if all this sounds a bit heavy: the planning and preparation stage can be almost as much fun as the trip itself. And of course, this is where *the gap-year guidebook* comes into its own...

my gap-year
Alice Riley

Alice Riley has recently returned from Tanzania where she spent five months as a volunteer English teacher with Oyster Worldwide...

Poring through travel brochures trying to plan the perfect gap-year, I eventually found Oyster Worldwide. Unlike other companies I looked at, they offered the opportunity to live as a local rather than a tourist.

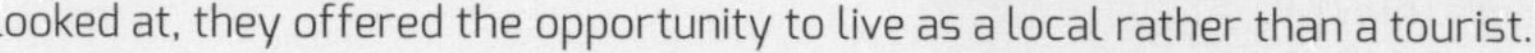

So from January 2013, I spent five months in Arusha, Tanzania. We lived in villages on the outskirts of the city. The house was basic but we soon became accustomed to bucket washes and cooking dinner by candlelight! In the villages we fully experienced Africa: banana plants, street food and children shouting "Mzungu!" (white person) everywhere we went. Everyone is really friendly and it's common to be invited round to a local's house for dinner, getting an insight into a completely different culture and a taste of traditional African food. The city provides some welcome home comforts like Western restaurants and incredible nightlife meeting other volunteers, but look out for the occasional Maasai in traditional dress!

During the trip there was never a dull week. A typical day would start with teaching English at a local primary school in the morning then, as the projects are designed to be flexible, we had most afternoons free. We used this time to get involved with a nearby orphanage, a centre for disabled children undergoing corrective surgery, or just spent the afternoon chilling in Arusha. Each week was packed with memories: new friends, canoeing in Lake Deluti, or visiting an African family living halfway up Kilimanjaro; experiences I will never forget.

On our first day of teaching my housemate and I walked to school holding hands both terrified with worst-case scenarios running through our heads. But we soon found there was nothing to worry about, and with practice my teaching skills improved! We were given a class each to teach their English lessons; I was teaching Class 5. My class contained 73 children aged 10-15. I taught various English grammar topics such as possession, apostrophes and adjectives. Their usual lessons involve primarily being sat in silence copying from the blackboard, so our job as volunteers was to try and make English more fun! For me this included drawing a lot of pictures which the children enjoyed copying, however the other teachers liked my drawings so much I had to draw their posters too! The big highlights of the trip included visiting the beach paradise Zanzibar. We went snorkelling, swam with turtles and experienced an amazing full-moon party. We also went on a four-day safari around the Serengeti and Ngorongoro crater where we saw all the Big 5!

I would recommend taking a gap-year with Oyster, especially to anyone considering Arusha! You meet so many interesting people, make lifelong friendships and experience things most people can only imagine.

For more information on Oyster, see **Chapter 6 - Volunteering Abroad** or visit **www.oysterworldwide.com**

Where do you want to go?

The Year Out Group's most recent research (for 2012/13) makes interesting reading and gives you a definite idea of gap-year strongholds. Here's the top 10. The 2011/12 positions are in brackets.

1. South Africa (1)
2. Canada (2)
3. Cambodia (20)
4. India (4)
5. UK (18)
6. France (13)
7. Thailand (5)
8. Australia (3)
9. Costa Rica (11)
10. New Zealand (7)

Here's Richard Oliver's thoughts on those figures:

"Once again **South Africa** tops the popularity poll. It continues to attract those taking a gap year whatever their age because it has a wide variety of activities and is seen as comparatively safe. It is a very popular tourist and business destination so there are plenty of flights which ensures competitive prices. In addition the exchange rate, though not as good as it was, remains reasonable. Activities include voluntary work with conservation in the many private game reserves being most popular. There are also many opportunities for teaching, sports coaching and care work.

"**Canada** retains second spot primarily because all the organisations offering winter sport activities (ski and snowboard instructor training and subsequent work plus a wide variety of jobs in the resorts) all seem to have their main centres in Canada where the snow levels can be relied upon.

"**Cambodia** has jumped into the top 10 as the country becomes more accessible to volunteers. Once again a wide variety of activities is available including teaching, care work and conservation projects. It is comparatively safe, the people are very warm and welcoming and once there the cost of living is low.

"**India** remains in fourth place. Voluntary work placements are as popular as ever but there is also an increasing number of internship placements available. These placements enable participants to acquire a valuable perspective on Indian customs, culture and business practices in this rapidly developing country. The skills and experience gained on these placements should significantly enhance a CV.

"It is a long time since the **UK** has been in the top 10. The Year in Industry offers a fantastic opportunity for those considering a career in business, especially in manufacturing and engineering, to experience a full year working in industry. Participants are offered training, mentoring and are paid. These placements often lead to the parent company sponsoring participants through university or offering further work experience in the vacations. A job offer on graduation is not unusual. The number of placements available has risen recently as host companies recover from the economic downturn. The UK has also become a destination of choice for students from a wide variety of countries to take up internships and to volunteer. Voluntary work includes acting as carers for disabled students who need support when attending university.

"**France** – there has been a surge in interest in improving language skills with French courses the most accessible. There are also opportunities to gain work experience.

"**Thailand** continues to be popular. It is a very popular tourist destination so there are plenty of flights and there are hundreds of volunteering opportunities especially in teaching, community and conservation projects.

"**Australia** and **New Zealand** have both dropped down the list this year but are still both in the top 10 so remain attractive to significant numbers of gap-year travellers.

"**Costa Rica** is the only country on the American continent in the top 10. Its popularity stems from the wide variety of activities available, comparative ease of access and its geographic position that enables gap-year travellers to on to South America or the States. South American countries are less popular than they were partly because there is political unrest in many of them but mainly because flights are expensive."

That gives you an idea of where others have gone. So where do you fancy?

If you want to visit several places you can let a cheap round-the-world ticket decide the framework for you. Otherwise you need to get your route clear in your mind.

Do you feel attracted to a particular area or to a particular climate? Unexplored territory or the popular backpacker places you've heard about? If you're unsure, try connecting with people who've been, through the many gap-year internet messageboards.

Heading for unknown territory off the backpacker routes in search of something more unusual will usually mean higher costs, perhaps a longer wait for visas and less efficient transport systems – therefore more preparation and travelling time. A bit of netsurfing, a check with any contacts who know a country and a chat with a travel agent will help you get a better idea of what this might mean.

Then there's the risk factor. Obviously family and friends will want you to avoid danger zones. The political situation in some places around the world is serious, unstable and can't be ignored.

Raleigh International

You want your gap travels to be stimulating, fun, to let you experience different cultures and meet new people, but do you really want to end up in the middle of a war zone with your life in danger? Foreign news correspondents and war reporters with large back-up organisations prepare properly, with proper insurance and safety and survival courses – and it makes sense for gappers too!

A good starting point is the Foreign Office website (**www.fco.gov.uk**) where you can find country profiles and assess the dangers and possible drawbacks to places you're thinking of. The FCO updates its danger list regularly as new areas of unrest emerge, but it's not, and never can be, a failsafe.

How long have you got?

Now you have at least a rough idea of where you want to go and what you want to do. The next step is to consider how long you might need to get it all in. How much time you can spare depends on *when* you're taking your gap.

That's going to be dictated by when you have to be back for starting university or college or, for career breakers, how much time your employer's prepared to let you have, or even whether you're willing to risk quitting your job for more gap time.

Lydia Rosling, of The Dragon Trip, which offers backpacking and volunteering opportunities in China, says that gaps are 'rarely the typical 12 months anymore':

"We are seeing 'gap-years' become extended gap experiences and the 'power gap'. Some think that one year is just not enough time to see everything they want and their trip is often extended, whereas 'power gappers' do a lot of travelling in a short space of time. This is usually during the long break between college and university, as well as during university summer breaks."

my gap-year
Charlie Gough

Following a successful nine months as a volunteer in London, Blue Ventures had offered me the opportunity to work at their field site in Madagascar for a year as a field scientist. Going out to Madagascar, and Andavadoaka for the first time I was understandably excited. Whilst I had a wealth of diving experience in the UK I hadn't yet seen a coral reef, and based on my reactions to seeing a sunken car, a tompot blenny, or even an old boot, most of the BV office was pretty certain my head would explode when I encountered a coral reef for the first time!

I was lucky enough to be joining Blue Ventures at a real time of change, with the integrated conservation programme growing to incorporate local management, education and even family planning! My first year, based in Andavadoaka, was incredible. First I had to learn all of the corals and reef fish, as a field scientist my job involved teaching volunteers how to identify all of these amazing creatures so that we can monitor them and see the effects local management is having on their populations.

Working as a field scientist was a fantastic experience, and I have since returned to Andavadoaka in many different capacities. While the projects have grown and the people changed, the atmosphere in Andavadoaka is still amazing, and it is the infectious happiness and enthusiasm of the expeditions staff and volunteers that makes it so great. In any single expedition you are likely to meet people from six different nationalities, ranging in age from 17 to 71 with a great variety of interests and experiences. Sitting at dinner you are rubbing shoulders with the BV conservation team, local staff, and other visiting researchers, all of which leads to some amazing conversations, as well as some extraordinary party nights!

Everyone is different and while Andavadoaka is definitely a place to chill out, I would urge anyone visiting to remember that life is not going to be handed to you while you sit in your hammock... you have to get up and get out on a pirogue (local sailing canoe), ditch the diving for a day (or even a few) and experience some of the amazing conservation work that is being carried out by the local communities in this remote region of the world. When you get home the best photos and memories are never of your lazy day in the hammock, or being underwater they are when you are surrounded by ten six-year-olds playing on the beach drawing pictures in the sand and learning Malagasy/teaching English, talking with a nahoda (village elder) about how fishing has changed since his day, or learning with one of the mama's how to cook bokoboko (small delicious donut balls) after a night of counting squelchy sea cucumbers. If you are going all that way, experience everything Madagascar and Blue Ventures has to offer!

For more information on Blue Ventures, see **Chapter 6 - Volunteering Abroad** or visit **www.blueventures.org**

We are hearing plenty of evidence that shorter placements of a few weeks rather than a few months are in increasing demand. Here, you need to consider what you want to get out of your gap, and whether you are getting value for money. University entrance tutors and employers will want to see how your gap made a real difference – they will be looking for commitment, determination to see a project through, planning ability, the ability to think on one's feet, to assess and manage risks, and to raise money and manage finances. If you've taken on a short placement just to 'tick the gap-year box', you may find you haven't really gained these skills at all.

You should also be careful of last minute bookings, says Richard Oliver "Not so long ago gap-year organisations would stop accepting applications several weeks before the departure date. In many cases gap-year placements were booked over a year in advance. Now the trend is to leave it to the last minute to book a place. This is often possible if you plan to take a course but when it comes to joining an expedition or volunteering if you leave it too late you should expect to be disappointed.

"The message is to book as far in advance as possible to avoid disappointment. It also gives you time to prepare yourself mentally and physically for the challenges you have set yourself."

Jon Arnold, of gap-year travel specialists Oyster Worldwide, agrees that it's wise to get sorted as soon as you can:

"We have seen that people are leaving the planning of their gap-year until much later in the year. Whereas most people a few years ago would book at least 12 months in advance, we are seeing that people are choosing to leave their options open until much later. In most cases this works fine, however we do increasingly find that projects are booked up or work permits have run out for particular countries by the time people make up their minds. Our advice is still to book as soon as possible.

"For 'traditional' gap-year students, taking a gap between A levels and university, I always suggest organising their gap-year in the summer holidays after their AS levels if they can. That way they can come back to their UCAS applications in September, deferring their entry and actually giving reasons in their Personal Statement as to why they are deferring by talking about their gap-year plans. The university admissions tutors are always keen to get applications from students that can show they are organised enough to have already made plans for their gap-year."

How much do you want to spend?

Estimates vary widely, but the average cost for a full year's **gap** is £5000 for young people, around £6000 for mature travellers and up to £9000 for career breakers.

Much depends on where you're going and what you plan to do, and these days, if you care about the planet, climate change and ethical travel, you need also to include the costs of carbon offsetting. It's important to do as much research as possible,and a good place to start is **Chapter 2 – Finance**.

Before you go, know where you're going

The more you know about your destination, the easier your trip will be: India, for example, is unbearably hot and humid in pre-monsoon April to June, Australia has seasons when bush fires are rampant and then there are the cyclone seasons in south Asia and rainy seasons in South America – and the consequent risk of flooding.

It's also worth finding out when special events are on. It could be very inconvenient to arrive in India during Diwali, when everyone's on holiday and all the trains are full! Similarly Japan – gorgeous in cherry blossom season but avoid travelling in Golden Week.

Check out **www.whatsonwhen.com** – it's a great site, that lists all sorts of events around the world.

Before visiting any country that has recently been politically volatile or could turn into a war zone, check with the FCO for the current situation. Logon to **www.fco.gov.uk** for up-to-date information.

Note: If you're from a country that qualifies for a Visa Waiver for the USA (and that includes UK citizens) you must now register online your intent to visit the USA and you *must* receive travel authorisation. Authorisation still doesn't guarantee you'll be granted entry and you may still be asked to go to the US embassy for an interview, but you have to go through the process before you can do anything else. You'll find the details here:

travel.state.gov/visa/temp/without/without_1990.html

If you're intending to visit for longer, or are planning to work, you will need the correct visa (see **Chapter 5 – Working abroad**).

Sort the paperwork

If you need to get yourself a passport for the first time, application forms are available from Post Offices or you can apply online. But remember: passport interviews are a new part of the process and are required by all applicants, aged 16 or over, who are applying for a passport for the first time.

You can call 0300 222 1000 to make an appointment or for other enquiries about this, but remember also that first time applicants can't use the fast track service.

There are 68 interview offices around the country and you have to go to the correct one for where you live – see the map on the IPS (Identity and Passport Office) website:

maps.direct.gov.uk/LDGRedirect/MapAction.do?ref=passportinterviewoffices

The standard adult ten-year passport currently costs £77.50 and you'll need your birth certificate and passport photos. It should take no more than a month from the time you apply to the time you receive your passport, but the queue lengthens coming up to peak summer holiday season.

You can use the Passport Office 'Check and Send' service at selected Post Offices throughout the UK or send it direct. The 'Check and Send' service gets your application checked for completeness (including documentation and fee) and is given priority by the IPS – they are usually able to process these applications in two weeks.

If your passport application is urgent and you're not applying for the first time, you can use the guaranteed same-day (Premium) service or the guaranteed one-week (Fast Track) service. Both services are only available by appointment at one of the seven IPS offices around the UK (phone the IPS Advice Line on 0300 222 0000), and both are more expensive (£128 for Premium, £103 for Fast Track).

The services are only available for renewals and amendments. And although you'll get a fixed appointment you'll almost certainly have to wait in a queue after this for your passport.

The IPS website is very helpful: **www.ips.gov.uk**

The FCO provided us with a checklist to help sort your travel documents:

- Check your passport is valid for the country you are travelling to – some countries require six months left to run after your return date to the UK so check this as soon as you can to allow plenty of time
- Keep your passport in a safe place while you're away, ideally in the hotel safe. Pack a photocopy of the main personal details and photograph page for ID purposes, so it's easier to replace if it goes missing
- If your passport does get lost, stolen or damaged while you are away, you'll need an Emergency Travel Document (ETD) issued by the Foreign and Commonwealth Office. It's important to remember that an ETD does not guarantee you entry to every country and will cost you time and money
- Make sure you've got the correct visa for the country you are visiting and allow plenty of time to research and prepare. Visit the Foreign and Commonwealth Office's travel advice page at **www.gov.uk/knowbeforeyougo** to read up on country specific travel advice, information and entry requirements

Leave someone in charge at home

Make sure you have someone reliable and trustworthy in charge of sorting things out for you – especially the official stuff that won't wait. Get someone you really trust to open your post and arrange to talk to them at regular intervals in case something turns up that you need to deal with.

my gap-year
Aliya Biggs

Aliya Biggs spent her gap-year before university volunteering in Vietnam with Projects Abroad...

Arriving in Hanoi airport I had no idea what to expect! I'd done some reading on Hanoi before I arrived but it didn't mention just how busy the city actually was; motorbikes everywhere! I was picked up from the airport from a member of the Projects Abroad team and driven to the office for my induction. This included detailed information on difficulties there could be adjusting to the local culture and homesickness.

I lived in shared accommodation with other volunteers who were from all over the world. One of the reasons I enjoyed my time in Vietnam so much was because of the amazing people I lived with for that month. Despite all of us speaking different languages and having different cultures we all got on so well and had so much fun!

I volunteered at the Hope Centre in a class of 15 children who were the oldest in the centre, ranging from 9-13 years old. The majority of the children had autism or some form of pervasive personality disorder, as well as three children who had Down's syndrome. The centre was well equipped and very clean. While the teachers worked with those who could read and write, I helped look after two children called Zim and Yung who were unable to do this. We played counting games, made shapes with lego and worked on coordination by playing with balls.

We did many different activities designed to help improve the children's physical abilities like balancing games, throwing balls into baskets and threading beads. These were my favourite lessons as I was able to play with all the children and really get to know them. The children even put on a play for the other children and staff!

One of the highlights of my trip was a weekend where I took an overnight train to Sapa with a group of other volunteers where we spent two days trekking through the mountains and rice fields, learning about the different ethnic minorities in Vietnam. We also went on an oriental cruise two day cruise round Ha Long Bay, one of the new Seven Wonders of the World.

On the weekends when we weren't travelling, we spent time visiting the many tourist sites in Hanoi. I went to the ethnic minority museum and the Old Quarter, where I spent hours exploring all the alleyways and shops. It's fair to say you can never get bored in Hanoi, there's always so much to see!

Leaving Vietnam was one of the hardest things I've ever done - I wished I could have stayed there longer. It was harder still saying goodbye to all the amazing and hopefully lifelong friends I made there. The experience has made me a much stronger person and made me even more determined to achieve my aim of becoming a psychologist. I can't wait to go back!

For more information about Projects Abroad, see **Chapter 6 - Volunteering Abroad** or visit **www.projects-abroad.co.uk**

However, there are some things you just have to do yourself, so make sure you've done everything important before you go. This particularly applies to any regular payments you make – check all your standing orders/direct debits and make sure to cancel any you don't need; and that there's money in your account for any you do need.

If you have a flat or house you're planning to sub-let, either use an accommodation agency or make sure someone you trust will keep an eye on things – it may be necessary to give them some written form of authority to deal with emergencies. There's more on all this in **Chapter 3 – Career breaks and older travellers**.

What to take

Start thinking early about what to take with you and write a list – adding to it every time you think of something. Here's a general checklist to get you started:

- Passport and tickets.
- Padlock and chain.
- Belt bag.
- Daypack (can be used for valuables in transit/hand luggage on plane).
- First aid kit: including any personal meds: split between day pack and rucksack.
- Notebook and pen.
- Camera.
- Mobile phone and charger.
- MP3 player – much less bulky than CDs.
- Money: cards/travellers' cheques/cash.
- Torch/candle.
- Sheet sleeping bag.
- Universal adapter.
- Pack of playing cards.
- Spare specs/contact lenses.
- Guidebook/phrasebooks – if doing several countries trade in/swap with other travellers en route.
- Spare photos for ID cards if needed.
- Photocopies of documents/emergency numbers/serial numbers of travellers' cheques.
- Clothes and toiletries *etc.*

Some of these checklist items will be more relevant to backpackers and people on treks, than to people on a work placement or staying in a family home. The list can be modified for your own particular plans.

Handy items

We asked gap-year veteran Becci Coombes, from GirlsTravelClub.co.uk, where you'll find gear, gifts and advice, for her top tips on packing for your trip:

my gap-year
Rohan Soni

University graduate Rohan Soni spent three-and-a-half months in Latin America with Kaya Responsible Travel...

I wanted to go to South America as I wanted to brush up on my Spanish, which I have largely forgotten since I learnt it at school! Peru and Ecuador sounded like really diverse countries with a lot to see, and I was intrigued by Belize because of it's British colonial past and combination of Caribbean and Latin American culture.

I chose to volunteer as I wanted to do something more meaningful than just travelling as a tourist. Volunteering allows you to get closer to the local people, their cultures and customs, and see how they really live. It's also a great way to make lasting friendships.

In Peru, I worked on the Animal Rescue Sanctuary project. As well as feeding and cleaning the animals, I helped to build new enclosures. I also showed tourists around the sanctuary to educate them about the importance of the conservation work.

I volunteered on the Fair Trade and Agroforestry Internship in the Amazon Rainforest, which is a fair-trade tea producer, in Ecuador. I worked in their charitable foundation and was involved in two projects. The first was an Economics project to find out the cost to a farmer of growing the tea, to ensure the price paid is fair. The second was to conduct surveys in the communities to find out what problems people face. This information would then be presented to a committee of farmers, who would decide how to spend a fund set aside for community development.

My final project was in Belize, where I helped to construct a sustainable home and organic farm for orphans, who are forced to leave the state-run system at age 16. The aim of the project is to provide a stable home and allow them to concentrate on studying or gaining skills for employment. I helped to build the roof which was really hard work in the hot sun, but rewarding to know that I have left something physical behind.

I really enjoyed all the projects, especially as I had the opportunity to try a variety of completely different things. I was fortunate enough to work with incredible people in all three projects and made friends who I'm sure I will keep it touch with. But the most gratifying thing was seeing the difference that the projects are making, and knowing that my effort was worthwhile.

For more information on Kaya Responsible Travel, see **Chapter 6 – Volunteering Abroad** or visit **www.kayavolunteer.com**

"The key to a well-packed rucksack is not to fill it up," Becci told us, "but leave plenty of room for your necessary holiday purchases. When you are packing, lay everything out you think you are going to need, then halve it, before halving it again!"

Here is a list of some handy items Becci has found useful that you might never have considered...

- **Dental floss**. Have you ever thought about how handy 50 metres of strong string (albeit minty-flavoured) all neatly packaged in a cute little box with a handy integral cutter could be? Many times I have used it for hanging mozzy nets, as an emergency bootlace, as a strong sewing thread, and it also makes a great washing line for drying your swimming gear.
- Forget those universal sink plug things; when you fill the sink up with water then try and actually wash something in it, the plug will either be knocked out by your vigorous sock-washing or just float about annoyingly as all your precious hot water drains away. A **squash ball** is much more useful; you can wedge firmly it into the hole and then use it to play squash afterwards.
- **Micropore medical tape** is marvellous stuff for the thrifty packer. Not only can you use it as an emergency plaster on blisters and little cuts, you can hold dressings on with it or put it on tiny splinters to yank them out of your thorn-ravaged flesh.
- **Clear ziplock bags** in different sizes. You can use them for storing wet swimming costumes; keeping those less-than-pleasant socks from tainting the rest of your gear, and also keep any maps nice and dry as you tramp through unexpected downpours looking for shelter.
- **Bin bags** also come in handy in many more ways than you'd think. Aside from using them for litter, you can always use one as a rucksack cover or an emergency poncho in a downpour; just cut a head hole and sit under it, keeping your arms nice and warm next to your body. Fill one with dry leaves as a mattress to insulate you from the ground damp as well; on one of our travel skills courses we stuffed them really full and used them as beanbags, and they were surprisingly comfy!
- I always make sure I've got a few **elastic bands** about my person as they are always being used for different purposes. Roll up your biggest items of clothing and secure with a couple of bands so they take up less space, and also put a couple round your flip-flops to keep them nice and tidy. Hang towels from trees by securing round one corner.
- I tend to keep my most useful bits and pieces in a **plastic lunchbox**, just because damp plasters/matches/Twixes aren't half as much fun as dry ones, and I have found the box very handy for all sorts of bits and pieces. Again, it can be used for collecting water from streams, as an ingenious receptacle for emergency cornflake consumption or, well, as a lunchbox.
- Lastly, and most importantly for us girls, my mum's top piece of travel advice is only pack **very good quality chocolate** with a high cocoa content, as it doesn't melt when it gets hot, it just bends!

There are other useful items you might want to consider. Water purifying tablets, for example, are great in an emergency, although they won't deal with all the possible waterborne parasites. Sometimes boiling water and adding iodine are also necessary. It's best to stick to bottled mineral water if available – even for brushing your teeth – but always check that the seal is intact before you buy. That way you will be sure it's not a mineral water bottle refilled with the local dodgy supply.

my gap-year
Dougie Critchley

Dougie Critchley, 18, from Perthshire, Scotland, travelled to Costa Rica and Nicaragua with Raleigh International...

I always wanted to do a gap year and follow in the footsteps of my siblings but I wanted to do something a bit different. Raleigh gives you the chance to do things that you would never get to try at any other time in your life. The memories that I have returned with aren't just a photo album, it is also about what I have learnt and how I developed as a person.

The water project we worked on in the village of Matapalo in Nicaragua was amazing. It is very rare that you get the chance to go somewhere so remote in a foreign country and be treated as one of their own. Living amongst a community who embraced us like family was overwhelming, they took me in like a son.

The village was one of many in Nicaragua without access to a clean and sustainable water source. This meant that families, mostly women, spent hours every day collecting water from the river. The water here was contaminated and detrimental to their health. Often girls in the family are kept back to help their mothers with chores like this, which prevents them attending school.

Together with the Matapalo community we worked hard on the project; to turn on the taps at the end and celebrate with them was very rewarding. We also did a lot of work to raise awareness of gender equality issues in Matapalo. This is a real problem in Nicaragua. We hosted children's activities which gave the women time to get away and talk together. This sounds so simple but it's something they never get the opportunity to do. I felt that this programme wasn't just about infrastructure. We had time to consider global issues and to help raise awareness and start discussions about other ways the community could find to strengthen its resources.

We did a trek on the adventure phase of our expedition. This was very tough but so rewarding. We walked 250km, from one side of Costa Rica to the other. We had to carry everything that we needed with us, including our food and drink. It really struck us that people across the world are constantly living within limited means and have daily struggles to access food and water. We didn't realise that trek would give us this sense of understanding; however it really put things into perspective for all of us and made us think about the meaning of social justice.

Getting the volunteers to think about the wider influence of their actions was a crucial part of the Raleigh experience. People from different parts of the world and from different backgrounds had different views on things; to get people to understand those views and to give them the opportunity to speak up in an open forum was really beneficial. I feel like I now have a global network, not just UK based friends.

Brilliant, fantastic, amazing – that's how I'd describe an unforgettable experience.

For more information about Raleigh International, see **Chapter 6 – Volunteering Abroad** or visit **www.raleighinternational.org**

Lifesaver Systems produces a bottle that converts even the nastiest stuff into drinkable water without the use of chemicals. It's not cheap but being ill through drinking bad water while travelling can be expensive or even life threatening.

Remember it's easy to get dehydrated in hot countries so you should always carry a bottle of water with you and drink frequently – up to eight litres a day.

Less is best

As airlines struggle with rising fuel costs, and diminishing passenger numbers, they are becoming increasingly inventive in dreaming up extra charges. Excess and overweight check-in baggage is one particularly fruitful area – and it's confusing as the rules vary from airline to airline. This makes it even more crucial to think very carefully about what you need to take – and what you could do without.

Basically, some charge per piece and others by weight, but that's not all. Some carriers limit you to one check-in piece, others, like BA, allow two. It can also depend on your route and your destination. Weight limits vary from as little as 20kg per bag to 30kg. Charges can even be different on outward and return journeys, with some carriers charging as much as £30 per kilogram over the permitted weight, or £90 per extra bag. It won't take much to wipe out all the money you've saved by searching for the cheapest available flights!

Inevitably if you fly business or first class the allowances are more generous but the above assumes that most people on a gap will be flying economy.

Packing tips

- Pack in reverse order – first in, last out.
- Heavy items go at the bottom.
- Pack in categories in plastic bags – easier to find stuff.
- Use vacuum pack bags for bulky items.
- Store toilet rolls and dirty undies in side pockets – easy for thieves to open and they won't want them!
- Take a small, separate backpack for day hikes *etc*. You can buy small, thin folding ones.
- Keep spares (undies, toothbrush, important numbers and documents) in hand luggage.
- Take a sleeping bag liner – useful in hostels.
- Take a sarong (versatile: can be a bed sheet, towel, purse, bag...)
- Travel towels are lightweight and dry fast.
- Remove packaging from everything but keep printed instructions for medications.
- Shaving oil takes less space than cream.
- Put liquids in squashy bottles (and don't carry liquids in hand luggage).
- Fill shoes, cups *etc* with socks and undies to save space.
- Tie up loose backpack straps before it goes into transit.

Now sit down and rationalise – cross off everything you don't really need. Pack enough clothes to see you through – about five changes of clothing should last you for months if you choose carefully. Don't take anything that doesn't go with

my gap-year Tamsin Clube

Tamsin Clube spent 3 months as a volunteer in Romania as part of her gap year with Oyster Worldwide. ..

With an ambition to travel and a passion for working with young people, I took on a project in Romania with Oyster Worldwide. The project was three months working with abandoned children in Romanian family homes in and around Brasov. Brasov is a beautiful place to live and work; the people are friendly and welcoming, there's a lot to do, and it really felt like home.

I quickly bonded with the other volunteers and our fantastic representative. Some of us became very good friends and have remained in close contact. Oyster Worldwide provided us with weekly language training, advice and tourism trips. They made every effort to help us explore and experience the Romanian culture, whilst also considering our wellbeing.

My role was to go and support the carers in three different family homes and one orphanage. The public transport is reliable and cheap, which made it easy to get to and from the placements. I mainly worked with disabled children and teenagers. There were big challenges, and some days I returned to our flat completely exhausted. It can be very frustrating to see how little these people have compared to us. However, it was so rewarding to see progress in the children. For example, seeing a child start to socialise or helping a child learn to walk. I built good relationships with the children and carers, and I still think of them often.

Over the months I learned some of the Romanian language, tried new foods and experiences, and met lots of wonderful people. The placements helped me to develop true compassion, patience and creativity. You need to be self-motivated, bursting with enthusiasm and prepared for surprises. My pockets were always filled with little toys and baby wipes!

My time in Romania was such a blessing. I didn't want to just do a project for the sake of it, I wanted to be a help and make a positive difference. I returned the following year, and I hope to again in the future.

For more information about Oyster Worldwide, see **Chapter 6 – Volunteering Abroad** or visit **www.oysterworldwide.com**

everything else and stick to materials that are comfortable, hard-wearing, easy to wash and dry and don't crease too much. Make sure you have clothes that are suitable for the climates you are visiting and don't forget that the temperatures in some dry climates can drop considerably at night!

You can find very lightweight waterproofs and thermals that can be rolled up easily.

Tip: remember most places have cheap markets, not to mention interesting local clothes, so you can always top up or replace clothes while you are travelling.

Relax, you can't prepare for every eventuality if you're living out of a rucksack. The best way to know what you need is to ask someone who's already been on a gap what they took, what were the most useful things, what they didn't need and what they wished they had taken.

Maps, directions and vital information

You won't need anything too elaborate: the maps in guidebooks are usually pretty good. A good pocket diary can be very useful – one that gives international dialling codes, time differences, local currency details, bank opening hours, public holidays and other information.

Take a list with you of essential information like directions to voluntary work postings, key addresses, medical information, credit card numbers (try to disguise these in case everything gets stolen), passport details (and a photocopy of the main and visa pages), emergency contact numbers in case of loss of travellers' cheques and insurance and flight details – and leave a copy with someone at home.

Another way of keeping safe copies of your vital documents (even if everything you have is lost or stolen) is to scan them before you leave and email them as attachments to your email address. However, it is well known that you shouldn't send sensitive information via email and it's not clear whether that advice also applies to attachments, given that they're all stored on a remote server, so you might prefer one of the many online secure data storage options, such as **www.omneport.com.**

Or you could even put it all on a memory stick, which has the advantage of being small and easy to conceal and carry.

Those of you with a smartphone or an MP3 player on to which you can download apps will be able to input a mass of information and effectively 'carry' maps, timetables, hostel finders, information lists, and photographs of your valuable documents with you in one small, slim device.

The FCO offers travel advice through social media updates and email alerts. You can subscribe to the alerts at **www.gov.uk/foreign-travel-advice**, selecting the country you are travelling to. Updates will also be issued via the FCO Twitter account @fcotravel and on their Facebook page: www.facebook.com/fcotravel.

Where to buy your kit

Some overseas voluntary organisations arrange for their students to have discounts at specific shops, like the YHA. The best advice on equipment usually comes from specialist shops, although they may not be the cheapest: these include YHA shops, Blacks, Millets and Camping and Outdoors Centres.

Rucksacks

Prices for a well-stitched, 65-litre rucksack can vary greatly. Remember, the most expensive is not necessarily the best, get what is most suitable for your trip.

A side-opening backpack is easier than a top-opening one. You can get all sorts of attachments but if you don't need it why pay for it? A good outdoor store should be able to advise you on exactly what you need for your particular trip. Most of these stores have websites with helpful hints and lists of 'essential' items.

You should be able to leave your rucksack in most hostels or guest houses, if you are staying for more than a day, or in a locker at the train station. Always take camera, passport, important papers and money with you everywhere, zipped up, preferably out of view.

Footwear

It's worth investing in something comfortable if you're heading off on a long trip. In hot countries, a good pair of sandals is the preferred footwear for many and it's worth paying for a decent pair, as they will last longer and be comfortable. If you're going somewhere cheap you could just pick up a pair out there but you're likely to be doing a lot more walking than usual, so comfort and durability are important.

Some people like chunky walking boots, others just their trainers, but it's best to get something that won't fall apart when you're halfway up a mountain. Take more than one pair of comfortable shoes in case they don't last, but don't take too many – they'll be an unnecessary burden and take up precious space in your rucksack.

Sleeping bags

Go to a specialist shop where you can get good advice. Prices vary widely and you can sometimes find a four-season bag cheaper than a one-season bag – it's mostly down to quality. You need to consider:

- Can you carry it comfortably and still have the energy to do all you want to do?
- Hot countries – do you need one? You may just want to take a sheet sleeping bag (basically just a sewn-up sheet).
- Colder countries: what will you be doing? Take into account weight and size and the conditions you'll be travelling in – you might want to go for one of those compression sacs that you can use to squash sleeping bags into. For cold countries, you need heat-retaining materials. You can usually – but not always – rent down-filled bags for treks in, say, Nepal.

First aid kit

Useful basics:

- Re-hydration sachets (to use after diarrhoea).
- Waterproof plasters.
- TCP/Tea tree oil.
- Corn and blister plasters for sore feet.
- Cotton buds.
- A small pair of straight nail scissors (not to be carried in your hand luggage on the plane).
- Safety pins (not to be carried in your hand luggage on the plane).
- Insect repellent.
- Antiseptic cream.
- Anti-diarrhoea pills (only short-term; they stop the diarrhoea temporarily but don't cure you).
- Water sterilisation tablets.
- Antihistamine cream.
- Your own preferred form of painkiller.

You can get a medical pack from most chemists, travel shops or online from MASTA (**www.masta.org**).

www.gapyeartravelstore.com also specialises in medical kits for travellers: the contents vary from sting relief, tick removers, blister kits, sun block and rehydration sachets to complete sterile medical packs with needles and syringe kits (in case you think the needle someone might have to inject you with may not be sterile).

my gap-year

Louisa Moore

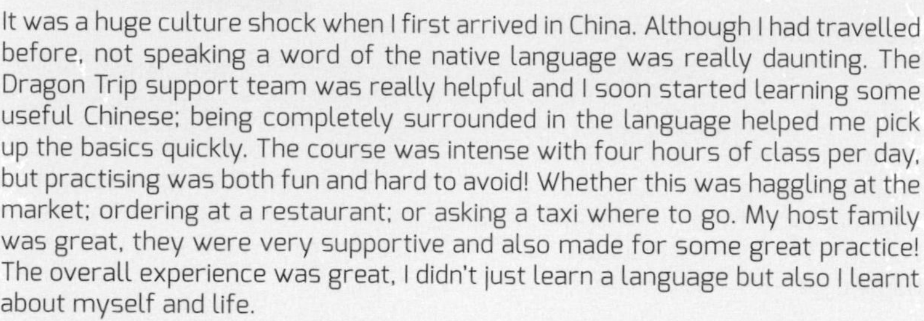

I have always loved to travel and after sixth form was my first opportunity to go abroad for a long time. I signed up for the Dragon Volunteer Trip because I wanted some purpose to my trip. I did the full four-month trip which consists of one month learning Mandarin, two months teaching children English in a rural area of China, with the final month spent travelling with a group around the country.

It was a huge culture shock when I first arrived in China. Although I had travelled before, not speaking a word of the native language was really daunting. The Dragon Trip support team was really helpful and I soon started learning some useful Chinese; being completely surrounded in the language helped me pick up the basics quickly. The course was intense with four hours of class per day, but practising was both fun and hard to avoid! Whether this was haggling at the market; ordering at a restaurant; or asking a taxi where to go. My host family was great, they were very supportive and also made for some great practice! The overall experience was great, I didn't just learn a language but also I learnt about myself and life.

At Hope School near Thousand Island Lake we jumped straight into teaching the children English. It was a challenge to keep the whole class motivated and actively learning in the classroom but I soon picked up some good techniques. Rural China can be very poor, but Hope School gives children in the area the opportunity to get a proper education which can help towards a more prosperous future. The kids were enthusiastic to learn which made the whole experience worthwhile because I knew that teaching these children English would give them a head start in life that they wouldn't have otherwise had. It was so rewarding for me at the end of the two months to see just how much they had improved.

I came to give something to the local community and hadn't expected to gain so much in return from the experience. The personal benefits of volunteering meant I developed as a person and learnt things about myself that I never would have otherwise.

Travelling in the final month of the trip was a lot of fun. We joined a group of 10 other backpackers and it was great to show off some of my Mandarin! Being on a planned trip meant we fit so much into the 25 days and didn't have to worry about booking transport etc. The guides were great and showed us the best local food but still gave us the freedom to do our own thing when we wanted.

In short, this trip was life changing. It has given me a new view on life and I have even decided to change my degree to now study Chinese. Having a HSK qualification in mandarin helped me massively in applying for the course at University. I have a new found passion in China and really believe this will put me in a good position to do business in the future. Incredible experience and value!

For more information about The Dragon Trip, go to **www.dragontrip.com**

You can also buy various types of mosquito net, water purification tablets and filters, money pouches, world receiver radios, travel irons and kettles. Not to mention a personal attack alarm.

Cameras

Picture quality on many mobile phones is now so good that you may not need to take a camera as well, especially if you're going to be uploading your pictures on to one of the many photo sharing websites now available.

If you do want the back-up of a camera, check with your local photographic dealer about what will best suit your requirements. Make sure you get a camera case to protect from knocks, dust and moisture and don't buy the cheapest you can find. Cheap equipment can let you down and you need something that doesn't have software compatibility/connection problems.

Here are a few other tips:

- Digital cameras use lots of power (especially if using flash). Take plenty of batteries with you or take rechargeable batteries and a charger (you'll save money in the long run but check they're usable in your particular camera).
- Don't risk losing all your photos. Back them up as you travel. Maybe visit an internet cafe occasionally and upload your best photos to a site such as Instagram or Photobucket. Upload them on to your Facebook site. Or even send them to your home email account.
- Don't walk around with your camera round your neck. Keep it out of sight whenever possible to reduce the risk of crime.
- Remember certain countries charge extra for using a camcorder at heritage sites, safari parks and monuments, but often they don't charge for still cameras.

Looking after yourself...

Health

Note: although we make every effort to be as up-to-date and accurate as possible, the following advice is intended to serve as a guideline only. It is designed to be helpful rather than definitive, and you should always check with your GP, preferably at least eight weeks before going away.

It's not only which countries you'll be going to, but for how long and what degree of roughing it: six months in a basic backpacker hostel puts people at higher risk than two weeks in a five-star hotel.

Before you go you should tell your doctor:

- Your proposed travel route.
- The type of activities you will be doing.

Ask for advice, not only about injections and pills needed, but symptoms to look out for and what to do if you suspect you've caught something.

Some immunisations are free under the NHS but you may have to pay for the more exotic/rare ones. Some, like the Hepatitis A vaccine, can be very expensive, but this is not an area to be mean with your money – it really is worth being cautious with your health.

Also, many people recommend that you know your blood type before you leave the country, to save time and ensure safety. Your GP might have it on record – if not, a small charge may be made for a blood test.

If you're going abroad to do voluntary work, don't assume the organisation will give you medical advice first or even when you get there, though they often do. Find out for yourself, and check if there is a medically-qualified person in or near the institution you are going to be posted with.

People who've been to the relevant country/area are a great source of information. Some travellers prefer to go to a dedicated travel clinic to get pre-travel health advice. This may be especially worthwhile if your GP/practice nurse does not see many travellers.

Here are some options:

www.welltravelledclinics.co.uk is a UK travel clinic company, and part of the Liverpool School of Tropical Medicine **www.e-med.co.uk** has a useful free travel service, which you can email for advice on immunisations, anti-malaria medication and what to watch out for.

www.fitfortravel.scot.nhs.uk

www.travelhealth.co.uk

Department of Health website:

www.nhs.uk/LiveWell/TravelHealth/Pages/Travelhealthhome.aspx

For safety advice try the Foreign and Commonwealth Office:

www.fco.gov.uk/travel

Another good idea is to register with an organisation such as Medic Alert, a non-profit-making charity providing a life-saving identification system for individuals with hidden medical conditions and allergies.

The MedicAlert service is particularly helpful for those who wish to travel. The MedicAlert emblem contains the international sign of medicine, and is recognised around the world. MedicAlert also has a 24-hour emergency number that can be accessed by medical personnel anywhere in the world and has a translation service in more than 100 languages. As a MedicAlert member, you wear a bracelet or necklet (known as an emblem) engraved with a personal identification number, main medical conditions and an emergency telephone number.

In an emergency, medical personnel have immediate access to vital information on the back of the MedicAlert disc. By phoning the emergency number, they can also gain further medical and personal information such as your name and address, doctor's details, current drug therapy and next of kin details.

Membership to the service, including a tailor-made emblem, starts at £19.95 plus the first year's membership at £25.

Accidents/injuries

Accidents and injuries are the greatest cause of death in young travellers abroad. Alcohol/drug use will increase the risk of these occurring. Travellers to areas with poor medical facilities should take a sterile medical equipment pack with them. Make sure that you have good travel insurance that will bring you home if necessary.

AIDS

The HIV virus that causes AIDS can be contracted from: injections with infected needles; transfusions of infected blood; sexual intercourse with an infected person; or possibly cuts (if you have a shave at the barbers, insist on a fresh blade, but it's probably best to avoid the experience altogether). It is not caught through everyday contact, insect bites, dirty food or crockery, kissing, coughing or sneezing. Protect yourself: always use condoms during sex, make sure needles are new and if you need a blood transfusion make sure blood has been screened, and don't get a tattoo or piercing until you're back home and can check out the tattoo shop properly.

Asthma and allergies

Whether you are an asthmatic or have an allergy to chemicals in the air, food, stings, or antibiotics, ask your GP for advice before you go. You will be able to take some treatments with you.

Allergy sufferers: if you suffer from severe shock reactions to insect bites/nuts or any other allergy, make sure you have enough of your anaphylactic shock packs with you – you may not be able to get them in some parts of the world.

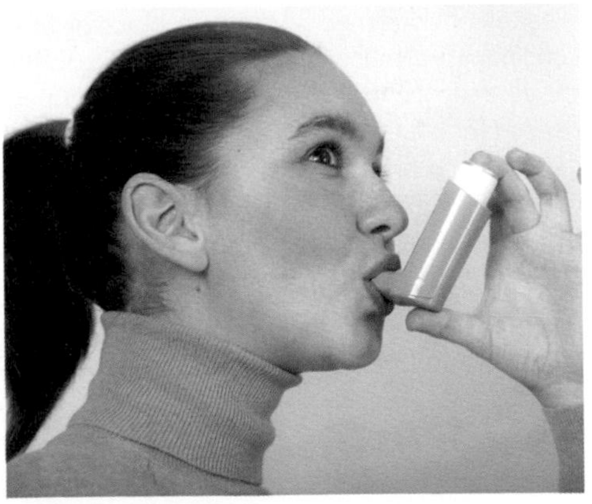

Chronic conditions

Asthmatics, diabetics, epileptics or those with other conditions should always wear an obvious necklace or bracelet or carry an identity card stating the details of their condition. Tragedies do occur due to ignorance, and if you are found unconscious a label can be a lifesaver. See **www.medicalert.org.uk** for information on obtaining these items.

You should also keep with you a written record of your medical condition and the proper names (not just trade names) of any medication you are taking. If you are going on an organised trip or volunteering abroad, find out who the responsible person for medical matters is and make sure you fully brief them about your condition.

Contraceptives

If you are on the pill it is advisable to take as many with you as possible. Remember that contraceptives go against religious beliefs in some countries, so they may not be readily available. Antibiotics, some malaria treatments, vomiting and diarrhoea can inhibit the absorption of the pill, so use alternative means of contraception until seven days after the illness.

Condoms: unprotected sex can be fatal, so everyone should take them, even if they are not likely to be used (not everyone thinks about sex the whole time). Keep them away from sand, water and sun. If buying abroad, make sure they are a known brand and have not been kept in damp, hot or icy conditions.

Dentist

Pretty obvious but often forgotten: get anything you need done to your teeth before you go. Especially worth checking up on are wisdom teeth and fillings – you don't want to spend three months in Africa with toothache.

Diabetics

Wear an obvious medical alert necklace or bracelet, or carry an ID card stating your condition (preferably with a translation into the local language). Take enough insulin for your stay, although it is unlikely that a GP will give you the amount of medication needed for a full year of travelling – three to six months is usually their limit, in which case, be prepared to buy insulin abroad and at full price. Ring the BDA Careline to make sure the brand of insulin you use is available in the particular country you are planning to visit. Your medication must be kept in the passenger area of a plane, not the aircraft hold where it will freeze.

Diabetes UK, **www.diabetes.org.uk**
Careline: +44 (0) 845 120 2960, weekdays 9am-5pm.
Email: careline@diabetes.org.uk

Diabetes UK produces a general travel information booklet as well as specific travel packs for about 70 countries.

Diarrhoea

By far the most common health problem to affect travellers abroad is travellers' diarrhoea. This is difficult to avoid but it is sensible to do the best you can to prevent problems. High-risk food/drinks include untreated tap water, shellfish, unpasteurised dairy products, salads, peeled/prepared uncooked fruit, raw/undercooked meat and fish. Take a kit to deal with the symptoms (your doctor or nurse should be able to advise on this). Remember to take plenty of 'safe' drinks if you are ill and re-hydration salts to replace lost vitamins and minerals.

If vomiting and/or diarrhoea continue for more than four to five days or you run a fever, have convulsions or breathing difficulties (or any unusual symptoms), get someone to call a doctor straight away. Seek advice on the best doctor to call; the British embassy or a five-star hotel in the area may be able to offer some advice here.

Eyes

Contact lens wearers should stock up on cleaning fluid before going, especially if venturing off the beaten track; but if you're going away for a long period it might be worth switching to disposable types so there's less to carry – ask your optician for advice.

Dust and wind can be a real problem, so refreshing eye drops to soothe itchy eyes and wash out grit can be really useful. If you wear contact lenses, your optician should be able to offer you a range of comfort drops which will be compatible with your lenses.

Also most supermarket pharmacies, plus travel and camping shops, sell plastic bottles of mildly medicated hand cleanser that dries instantly. They're small and light to carry and you only use a small amount each time so it's worth packing a couple. They're really useful for cleaning hands before putting in contact lenses if the local water supply is suspect. It's also worth making sure you have glasses as a back-up, as it's not always possible to replace lost or torn contacts.

If you wear glasses consider taking a spare pair – they don't have to be expensive and you can choose frames that are flexible and durable. Keep them in a hard glasses case in a waterproof (and sandproof) pouch.

Malaria

This disease is caught from the bite of an anopheles mosquito and mosquitoes are vicious and vindictive. Highest risk areas are tropical regions like sub-Saharan Africa, the Solomon Islands and Vanuatu (Pacific), the Amazon basin in South America and parts of Asia. There's no jab, but your GP will give you a course of pills to take.

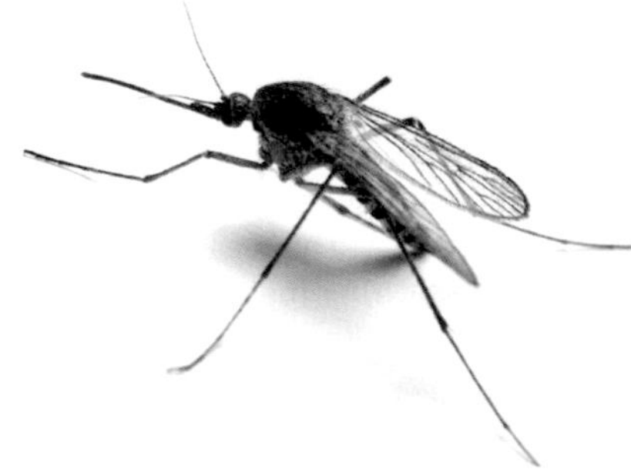

The most dangerous form of malaria is falciparum, which is particularly common in sub-Saharan Africa (places like Ghana, Gambia, DR Congo). It can cause liver, kidney, stomach and neurological problems and if left untreated, can be fatal.

One bite from a mosquito is enough. The parasite gets to your liver within 30 minutes and will reproduce there rapidly, infecting the blood stream. Once the parasites are in your blood stream you start to notice symptoms. Some versions can remain dormant in the liver, leading to repeat episodes of the illness.

The best protection is to try (as much as possible) to avoid being bitten. Here are tips for how:

- Use insect repellent, preferably containing either at least 30% DEET (diethyltoluamide), or extract of lemon eucalyptus oil.
- Keep your arms and legs covered between dusk and dawn and use a 'knockdown' spray to kill any mosquitoes immediately.
- Mosquito nets are useful, but they can be hard to put up correctly. It is often worth carrying a little extra string and small bits of wire so that the net can be hung up in rooms that don't have hanging hooks. Ideally the net should be impregnated with an insecticide, you can buy nets that are already treated from specialist shops and travel clinics.
- For some places, dual-voltage mosquito killer plugs are a good idea. *Holiday Which?* tested hand-held electric buzzers that claim to frighten off mosquitoes and found that they did not work on the anopheles mosquito.
- Another good idea is to spray clothes with permethrin – which usually lasts up to two weeks, although Healthguard has a product, called AM-1, which works for three months or 30 washes. Visit **www.healthguardtm.com** to find out more or call them on +44 (0)20 8275 1100.

The pills can be expensive, and some people, particularly on long trips, stop taking their pills, especially if they're not getting bitten much. Don't. Malaria can be fatal.

No one drug acts on all stages of the disease, and different species of parasites show different responses. Your GP, practice nurse or local travel clinic should know which one of the varied anti-malarials is best for you, depending on your medical history (*eg* for epileptics or asthmatics, for whom some types of anti-malarials cannot be prescribed) and the countries you are visiting. Visit your GP or travel clinic at least eight weeks before you go to discuss the options.

It's also worth doing a little research of your own before going to your GP or practice nurse. A useful website is **www.malariahotspots.co.uk** All the anti-malarial tablets have various pros and cons, and some of them have significant side effects. If you're going to an area where you have to use the weekly mefloquine tablets, MASTA recommends that you start taking the course two-and-a-half to three weeks before departure. Most people who experience unpleasant side effects with this drug, will notice them by the third dose. If you do have problems, this trial will allow you time to swap to an alternative regime before you go.

If you are in a malaria-risk area, or have recently been in one, and start suffering from 'flu-like' symptoms, *eg* fever, muscle pain, nausea, headache, fatigue, chills, and/or sweats, you should consider the diagnosis of malaria and seek medical attention immediately.

A traveller with these symptoms within several months after returning from an endemic area should also seek medical care and tell their doctor their travel history. The correct treatment involves the proper identification of the type of malaria parasite, where the traveller has been and their medical history.

Sunburn

Wherever your gap-year takes you, the advice from Cancer Research UK's SunSmart campaign is to enjoy your time in the sun safely. This means not getting caught out by sunburn which, as well as being unsightly, is a clear sign that skin cells have been damaged. Over time, this damage can build up and may ultimately lead to skin cancer.

So while everyone needs some sun in their lives, too much can be harmful. The facts are worrying – skin cancer is one of the most common cancers in the UK and the number of people who develop it is increasing faster than any other type of common cancer. Every year over 11,000 people are diagnosed with malignant melanoma – the most lethal type of skin cancer – and almost 2000 die from the disease. It is diagnosed in a disproportionately high number of younger people, being the second most common cancer in young adults (aged 15-34) in the UK.

And as well as causing skin cancer, too much UV can cause premature ageing, making skin look old and leathery before its time.

But the good news is that most cases of skin cancer can be prevented.

When you're out in the sun, the most important thing is to make sure you don't burn. Get to know your skin type and how it reacts in the sun. As a general rule, the lighter your skin, the more careful you should be.

When your risk of burning is high, often during the hottest part of the day, spend time in the shade, cover up with a T-shirt or a towel and regularly apply plenty of sunscreen (at least factor 15 – but the higher the better) to protect your skin.

Whatever your skin type the message is simple – don't let sunburn catch you out.

Anyone can develop skin cancer but some people have a higher risk and need to take more care, including those with fair skin, lots of moles or freckles, a history of sunburn or a family or personal history of skin cancer.

SunSmart is the UK's skin cancer awareness campaign, funded by the UK health departments. To identify your skin type, find out more about skin cancer, how to enjoy the sun safely, and the dangers of using sunbeds visit **www.sunsmart.org.uk**.

Tick borne encephalitis (TBE)

Ticks are second only to mosquitoes for carrying diseases to humans and immunisation is recommended for people who intend to walk, camp or work in heavily forested regions of affected countries between April and October when the ticks are most active. Your doctor or practice nurse can advise if you should have this immunisation for your travel destination.

We asked Tick Alert for their advice. Here's what they had to say:

"TBE is a viral disease contracted via the bite of an infected tick that is endemic in 27 countries in Europe. It leads to an annual average of 10,000 cases needing hospital treatment. Two in every 100 TBE sufferers will die from the disease."

TBE symptoms

TBE incubation is six to 14 days and at first can cause increased temperature, headaches, fever, cough and sniffles, symptoms similar to a cold or flu. The second, more dangerous phase of TBE can lead to neck stiffness, severe headaches, delirium and paralysis. There is no specific treatment for TBE.

How to protect yourself

- Use an insect repellent that is effective against ticks.
- Avoid wearing shorts in rural and wooded areas, tuck trousers into socks, or cover all exposed skin with protective clothing (though not always practical in summer).
- Inspect your skin for ticks and remove any found as soon as possible with fine-tipped tweezers or a tick-removal tool. If using a special tool, follow instructions for use. If you are using fine-tipped tweezers, grasp the tick firmly and as close to the skin as possible. In a steady motion, pull the tick's body away directly outwards without jerking or twisting. Make sure you get the tick's head out as sometimes the head can remain embedded.
- Also, avoid unpasteurised milk which may also be infected with the TBE virus in endemic regions.

Vaccinations

Ones to consider:

- Hepatitis (A&B).
- Japanese Encephalitis.
- Meningitis.
- Polio.

- Rabies.
- Tetanus.
- Tuberculosis.
- Typhoid.
- Yellow Fever.

Ask your GP for advice on vaccinations/precautions at least six to eight weeks before you go (some may be available on the NHS). Keep a record card on you of what you've had done. Certain countries won't admit you unless you have a valid yellow fever certificate.

Seeking medical advice abroad

You can expect to be a bit ill when you travel just due to the different food and unsettled lifestyle (painkillers and loo paper will probably be the best things you've packed).

While you're away:

- Keep a record of any treatment, such as courses of antibiotics, that you have when overseas and tell your doctor when you get back;
- Be wary of needles and insist on unused ones; it's best if you can see the packet opened in front of you, or you could take a 'sterile kit' (containing needles) with you; and
- If you don't speak the language, have the basic words for medical emergencies written down so you can explain what is wrong.

Is a gap-year safe?

Accidents can happen anywhere and so can earthquakes, floods, cyclones and other random events.

But there are some risks you can avoid by being alert, informed and prepared. You should take personal safety seriously and not put yourself in danger by agreeing to anything about which you have misgivings, just because you don't want to risk someone thinking that you're stupid or scared.

Tip: there's one rule: If in doubt – don't

The Foreign Office estimates that of the approximately 250,000 young people who take a gap each year, around 75,000 are prone to a reckless spirit that it calls the 'Invincibles'.

The FCO deals with an estimated 3.5 million enquiries, and supports around 85,000 Brits in difficulty each year. While support includes visiting those who have been admitted to hospital or arrested, to rescuing British citizens from forced marriages abroad, the FCO launched Know Before You Go because it had found that the most common problems it was being called in on were the most preventable ones, such as inadequate or no insurance or lack of proper medical precautions.

The FCO opened a new crisis centre in the summer of 2012 with 50% more staff, so it can respond to multiple crises at the same time. It is also introducing a new mobile registration system for British nationals caught up in a crisis, which will enable people to register with the Foreign Office by text message from their mobile phones.

The FCO has an online travel guide that you can find at:

www.gov.uk/government/news/plan-pack-explore-a-new-guide-for-travellers

While the FCO deals with all travellers, not only those on a gap, we agree with the message about being as prepared as possible before you go and that's what this guidebook is for.

We also recommend that you consider taking a gappers' safety course before you go, to teach you how to recognise danger (from people as well as natural disasters), and how to look after yourself in a bad situation – it could be the thing that saves your life.

What the experts say

Planning a gap-year can be a very exciting time. In order to get the most out of and enjoy it to the fullest you need to plan and prepare for every eventuality. Staying safe is the key to having a good time.

These days research comes in many different forms, books, websites, fairs and courses. Safety courses have increased in popularity in the last few years particularly with celebrities such as Ewan McGregor and Charley Boorman taking part and training before their high-profile motorcycle trips.

There are a number of different courses run by various companies across the country ranging from two hours to two days, the one thing they all have in common is that they are run by instructors with first-hand experience, a priceless tool.

Why attend a course? Why not? Attending a specialist gap-safety course can be a vital tool in the planning and preparation of your trip, increasing self-awareness and enabling you to recognise danger and get yourself out of tricky situations.

Most of the courses follow a similar format, covering:

Before you go – research, cultural differences, preparation, insurance, documents and money.

What to take – the clothing you will need, first aid kits, gadgets, electrical items, security of your belongings and tips on economical packing.

Over there – accommodation, food and water, transport, local authorities and awareness of a new environment and laws.

Medical Issues – emergency first aid, staying healthy, self-defence, climate, bites, bugs and vaccinations.

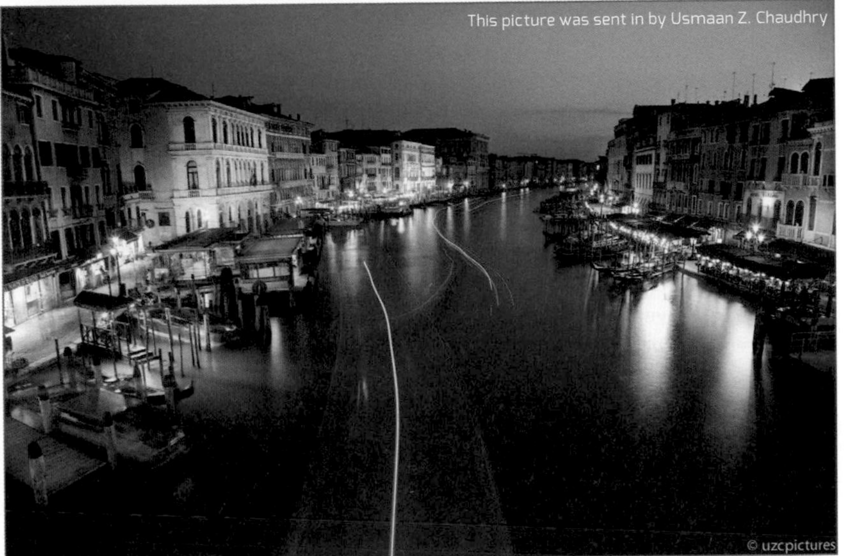

This picture was sent in by Usmaan Z. Chaudhry

Many of the courses will also run a 'for girls, by girls' session.

Make sure you know enough about what you want to do and where you want to go, talk to other travellers (there are many messageboards online). If you're travelling with an organisation, check them out; ask to speak to others that have done the same trip.

Ensure you have adequate travel insurance to cover everything you want to do including working both paid and voluntary plus any activities you have in mind to do.

Make sure you have copies of all of your documents, try an online document safe. Ensure you have telephone numbers of people to contact in an emergency; emergency medical assistance company, someone at home and if possible someone in the same country.

Travelling to unknown countries can be a great culture shock so a little preparation beforehand will ensure that you make the most of all of your opportunities without missing out.

Gap 360 offer free travel safety courses that will help you prepare for unexpected situations and teach you to travel safety. For more information, go to: **www.gap360.com**. There you also find some PDFs on a range of travelling topics.

The point is that as long as you have done all you could to be well prepared with travelling essentials and knowledge, then you should go for it!

Personal safety and security checklist

We've canvassed lots of opinion about this, and we've had lots of suggestions. We think the following, courtesy of Gap Aid, are among the most important:

- Don't drink too much or stay out too late, it is not like being at home and you will make yourself unnecessarily vulnerable.

- Hanging the 'Do Not Disturb' sign on your hotel door when you go out should help deter thieves.
- Having waterproofed documents (either laminating or in a secure plastic wallet), there is always a chance you will get caught in the rain or need to cross a river if trekking, this way your valuables and documents will stay dry.
- Walk with confidence and never use your guidebook, get out your map or start counting money in the street, find a café, sit and relax and read in peace, don't make yourself a target. Keep a small amount of change for food and drinks in a separate wallet so you don't have to keep going through your notes.
- If you have a 'weak' stomach avoid street stalls, eat in busy restaurants (where the locals are) and try and eat vegetarian if possible, although saying this salads can be some of the worst.
- If travelling alone, you are most vulnerable when you are sick (sometimes you feel like you have to travel that day) but our best advice would be don't. If you feel ill (like being drunk) don't travel and if you do make sure you are with another person you know well.
- Don't be afraid of approaching other backpackers – this is easier in non-western countries when you can generally tell who is a traveller and who isn't. Not only might you make new friends but also it's great to share experiences and good times as sometimes travelling can be very lonely.
- Talk to locals: the best way to get insight before you travel is to talk to trusted people who live there. Networks are springing up all over the place offering unique local insights based from food lovers, or culture vultures, try Tripbod: **www.tripbod.com**.
- Whatever happens, however bad – remember people are generally good and you will find people (other backpackers, locals, hostel owners etc) who will go out of their way to help you and make sure that you are safe and okay.
- If you are in trouble, whatever the local police tell you, contact the local British embassy or consulate – most of them are incredibly helpful and they will have dealt with situations like yours before and will know what you should do, make sure that you have several copies of their contact details to hand.

Tip: it can help to arrive with some local currency in notes and coins. You can often change travellers' cheques in banks at airport arrivals halls.

Remember, anyone can get lost. When you are on the road don't panic. Always agree meeting places before you go somewhere and play safe by having a back-up plan. Then if you don't turn up reasonably on time someone will be alerted to raise the alarm.

Before you do anything or go anywhere think about the consequences – this isn't about not having a good time, or being boring – it's about getting through your gap without taking foolish risks.

In many places, though, you'll find people are very hospitable and curious about you and you might find their unabashed and quite frank questions intrusive. While you have to be sensible about how much information you give, equally try not to be too suspicious about their motives. What feels like an invasion of your personal space,

or probing questioning, doesn't automatically mean anything sinister – remember the British in particular can be quite reserved so you'll notice the contrast. It's all a question of balance and courtesy.

Caroline's Rainbow Foundation is a charity set up to promote safety awareness for young travellers. They gave us some additional pointers, all worth emphasising:

- Leave copies of all your travel documents, visas, insurance policies and bank card details with someone back home. If you lose them or they are stolen it is easier to report if you have all the details to hand. If you can store them on the computer and email the images to yourself, you will always have the documents where ever there is internet. Lock your passport and travel tickets in a safe if possible.
- If you plan to work abroad find out if you need a work visa and get it before you leave. Some countries will not let you work while on holiday. Try not to be tempted by the offer of cash in hand; if caught you could easily be deported or even imprisoned.
- If you take regular medication ensure you have enough for your trip. Also keep a note of what it is in case you lose it. You may be able get hold of it in another country but this is not guaranteed. It may also be called a different name so try to have a note of the generic name of the drug rather than a brand name. Pharmacists can usually help with this. If taking a large amount of the prescription medication with you take a doctor's letter explaining what it is and why you need it. Easier than being mistaken for smuggling drugs.
- Try to learn a few simple phrases in the local language If you find that hard or you do not understand the dialects at least you should learn to recognise them when written down. Knowing what the sign is for a bus stop, cafe, phone, police or hostel could be very helpful, particularly when arriving somewhere at night.
- Try to book your first night's accommodation in a new location, especially if you plan to arrive after dark. Make sure you know where the place is, how far it is from your arrival point and the best to get there. Standing around with a map and large

rucksack is a give away that you are new in town and could attract unwanted attention.

- Try not to carry lots of money around with you. Lock it away in a safe if you can, Most hostels have a safe at reception. Remember you can be watched using a cash point or inside a bank.
- Remember items such as condoms are often inferior in quality, especially in places such as Africa and South America; if you think you might need them it's probably best to take your own that you know are safe.
- Be aware of the food and dietary habits in the country/countries you plan to visit. While sundried grasshoppers may not be your normal diet, you might want to be prepared to try new foods. Hygiene abroad, particularly in developing countries, may not be at the same as at home so be careful not to offend when offered food even if you think it looks raw or disgusting. If you do get a 'gippy tummy' make sure you drink plenty of clean, ideally bottled, water to ensure you don't get dehydrated.
- Local transport is usually very different abroad, especially in developing countries. You may have no choice but to travel on a bus with worn tyres, too many passengers, or no seat belts to avoid being left in a deserted location, but it is worth finding out if there are any other options. Try to sit near to the main door or by an emergency exit if possible. It may seem fun to hang off the bus or sit on the roof like the locals but realistically this could be very dangerous.
- While travelling from place to place try to lock your luggage if you can not see it and do not leave any valuables in it. Take all valuables with you regardless of mode of transport.
- Be careful where and how you take photographs. It's often not a good idea to take photos of anything official, or anything which could be connected to the military, such as airports or border checkpoints. This could attract unwanted attention or hostile behavior from the local people or officials.
- In hotel or hostel rooms, check that your windows and doors lock properly and keep them locked at night. Request a room that is not on the ground floor. Check the fire evacuation procedure from your bedroom in case of emergencies.
- Make sure that someone always knows where you are and when you can be expected to return. This is especially important in rural places where mobile phones may not work.
- Never leave your drink unattended – it could be spiked or stolen.
- If you are travelling in a hire car, keep the doors locked at all times, especially when you are stuck in traffic. Make a note of contact numbers for the rental company in caes of breakdown or theft. Be careful when parking you car as you may not be able to read or understand the parking rules. You do not want to return and find your car has been towed away.
- Nothing is worth more than your life. Money, cameras etc can be replaced, especially if you have insurance. If challenged do not put up a fight, letting go could save your life.

In-country advice...

Responsible travel, respect, behaviour and dress codes

Here's a quick checklist from the Foreign and Commonwealth Office:

- Familiarise yourself with your destination and its local laws and customs
- Learn some key phrases and words of the local language, this can make a huge difference to your trip and the reception you get and might help in an emergency
- Get a good guidebook and make sure you know about local laws and customs, especially those relating to alcohol and drugs. Your guidebook may also have the layout of the town or city you are visiting which can prove very useful!
- Book your first night's accommodation in advance. You're at your most vulnerable when you first arrive in a foreign country and are likely to be tired and uncertain of your surroundings
- Try to blend in to the local community – be conscious of any religious dress codes and dress accordingly. It's important to be respectful when you are visiting someone else's country
- Photographs – certain sites within a country can be sensitive, e.g. military bases, government buildings etc. Be mindful of what you are photographing. It's worth asking before you snap so as not to run into trouble or cause offence

Your first impression of some countries will be a swarm of people descending on you, pestering you to take a taxi or buy something – at night when you're tired from a long plane trip it can be quite scary. If you're not being met by anyone, check whether there's a pre-pay kiosk in the airport and pay for a ticket to your ultimate destination. That way the taxi driver can't take you on a detour since they won't get their money until you're safely delivered and your 'chit' has been signed.

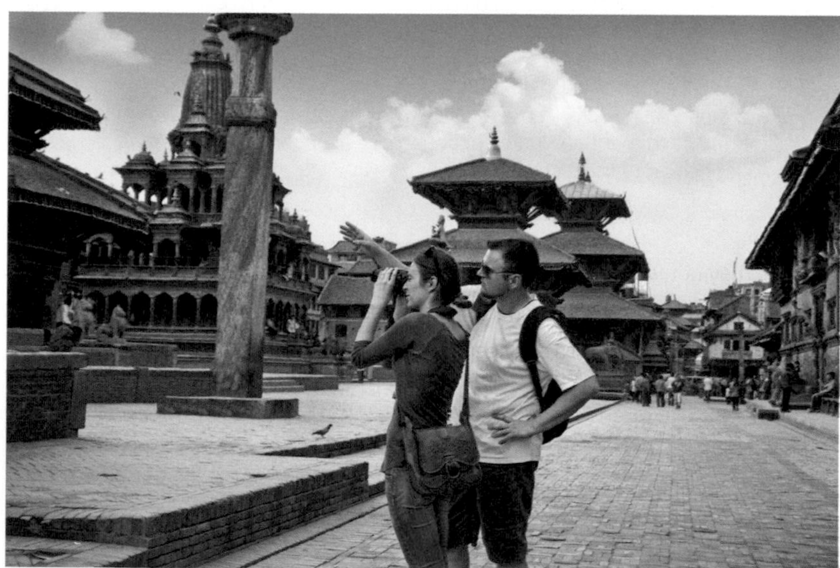

Some people advise that, if you arrive alone in the middle of the night (which is often the case on long-haul budget flights), it might be safer to wait until daylight before heading onwards. That's not a pleasant prospect in most airports, but it may occasionally be the sensible option.

In many countries of the developing world, where there are no social security or welfare systems, life can be extremely tough and leave people close to despair. That's likely to be even more the case, in the face of growing food shortages and escalating fuel and food costs as a result of the ongoing global recession. What may seem like a cheap trinket to you may be enough to buy them a square meal for which they are desperate enough to steal from you violently, so it is sensible not to wear too much jewellery.

Equally, wandering around discarding uneaten food is a particularly tactless thing to do, when large numbers of people may not know where their next meal is coming from.

Bear in mind that, in most places, even the so-called First World, rural communities are usually far more traditional and straight-laced than city ones and casual western dress codes and habits can offend.

If you don't want to find yourself in real trouble, do some research. Each culture or religion has its own codes of behaviour and taboos and, while no one would expect you to live by all their rules, as an ethical and responsible traveller, showing respect for the basic principles is a must as a guest in their country, not to mention being a sensible precaution if you want to stay safe.

Also remember that a country's native people are not just part of the landscape, they are individuals who deserve respect and courtesy, so if you want to take a photo of them – ask first, or at least be discreet!

These are the sorts of things you should bear in mind: in most Asian and African countries don't wear a bikini top and shorts in city streets if you don't want to attract the wrong kind of intrusive male attention. In any case an all-over light cotton covering will better protect you from sunburn and insect bites.

Men and women should dress modestly, particularly, but not only, in Muslim countries. Women especially should wear long sleeves and cover their legs. Uncovered flesh, especially female, is seen as a 'temptation' and you'll be more comfortable, not to mention finding people more friendly and welcoming if they can see you're sensitive to local customs.

You should also remember that, in Buddhist countries, the head is sacred and so it is unconventional to touch it.

Before entering temples and mosques throughout India and south Asia, you must remove your shoes. There are usually places at the entrances, where you can leave them with attendants to look after them. Women are also expected to cover their hair – and in Jain temples wearing or carrying anything made of leather is forbidden. Even in parts of Europe you'd be expected to cover your head and be dressed respectfully if you go into a church.

Open gestures of affection, kissing or even holding hands between married couples can be shocking to some cultures. This is particularly true of India, though it seems to be relaxing a little in the cities. However, you will often see men or boys strolling around hand in hand or with arms around each other's shoulders in India - don't misinterpret: they are friends, *not* gay couples!

Remember also, that if you are speaking English with a local inhabitant, they may not understand or use a word with the same meaning as you do. Particularly in the area of emotional relationships and dating, remembering this and understanding the local religion, customs and morality can save a lot of misunderstanding, misery and heartache.

Sitting cross-legged, with the soles of your feet pointing towards your companions, is another example of a gesture regarded as bad manners or even insulting in some places and actually if you think about it, it's pretty logical if you're in a place where people walk around less than clean streets either barefoot or in sandals.

Since daily life and faiths are often closely interlinked, it helps to know a little about the major philosophies of life in the countries you visit so, to get you started, here's some very basic info about some of the main belief systems out of the many hundreds around the world. We use the term belief systems because, arguably, some of these are closer to being philosophies of life than to religions or faiths in the sense most people would understand them:

Bahá'i

God: a single God known through God's creation and prophets.

Foundation text: Bahá'is believe that all religions are different approaches to faith in a single God. So no core text, but Bahá'ís believe in unity, equality and human rights for all. The founder, Bahá'u'lláh, taught that world unity is the final stage in the evolution of humanity. There is no conversion and no requirement for followers to renounce their previous faith. Bahá'i originated in Iran, and is the world's youngest, and widely considered to be its fastest-growing, religion.

Place of worship: can be anywhere, but there is a stunning modern, pink marble building, the Lotus Temple, in Delhi.

Holy day: the main one is 29 May, which commemorates the founder's teachings and his death on that day in 1892.

Shinto

The official religion of Japan, it has no specific God, no founder and no specific core texts.

Beliefs: a three-level universe; the Plain of High Heaven; the Manifested World; and the Nether World, but with the invisible worlds seen as an extension to the visible world. Kami (gods and spirit beings which include the ocean, the mountains, storms and earthquakes) allow believers to regard the whole natural world as both sacred and material. Ethics start from the basic idea that human beings are good, and that the world is good. Evil enters the world from outside, brought by evil spirits. Shinto has no moral absolutes and assesses the good or bad of an action or thought in the context in which it occurs: circumstances, intention, purpose, time, location, are all relevant in determining whether an action is bad. Harmony depends on the group being more important than the individual.

Place of worship: shrines: an enclosed sacred area with a gate, an area for ablutions and a main sanctuary. There is an emphasis on ancestral spirits and on the importance of gratitude for the blessings of the kami. There are many special prayers and rituals marking the various stages through life from birth to death.

Festivals: the main one is *Oshogatsu* (New Year) but there are festivals throughout the year marking spring and autumn as well as coming of age (*Seijin Shiki* or Adults' Day) and *Schichigosan* (when parents give thanks for their children's lives and pray for their future).

Taoism

God: *Tao* means 'the Way' and is a philosophy of living, but there is a concept of the Eight Immortal Beings (*Psa Hien*) who are the protectors of various aspects of life.

Core text: the *Tao Te Ching* (the Book of the Way, known in the West as the *I-Ching*) written by Lao Tzu.

Place of worship: everywhere – the Way is essentially a philosophy for living a life in balance.

Core beliefs: *Tao* is 'The Way' and the first cause of the universe, *Te* is the virtue of the person who lives in accordance with *Tao*. Taoists follow the art of *wu wei*, (ie to let nature take its course, but also to be kind to others because it will be returned) and the essential aim of Taoism is to achieve a world in equilibrium (a balance of Yin and Yang, the extremes of the universe such as the sun and moon, heaven and earth, chaos and order). There is no rigid division between body and spirit.

Mechanisms for achieving balance include meditation, breathing exercises, use of acupuncture, practising Tai Chi, and *Feng Shui*.

Confucianism

God: like Taoism, in China Confucianism is a philosophy for living life and therefore there is no concept of a God.

Place of worship: everywhere.

Core beliefs: based on the teachings of Confucius, who was a philosopher, moralist, statesman and educationist. The *Jen*, the essence of his teaching can be loosely translated as 'social virtue'. Like Taoism it strives for balance and harmony – by behaving towards others as one would want them to behave towards oneself. Confucius is believed to have met Lao Tzu and, by some accounts, to have been his disciple. His main concerns were with good order in human beings' principle relationships and with good government expressed in the values: *Li* (ritual, propriety, etiquette); *Hsiao* (love within the family, love of parents for their children and of children for their parents); *Yi* (righteousness); *Xin* (honesty and trustworthiness); *Jen* (benevolence, humaneness towards others); and the highest Confucian virtue, *Chung* (loyalty to the state *etc*).

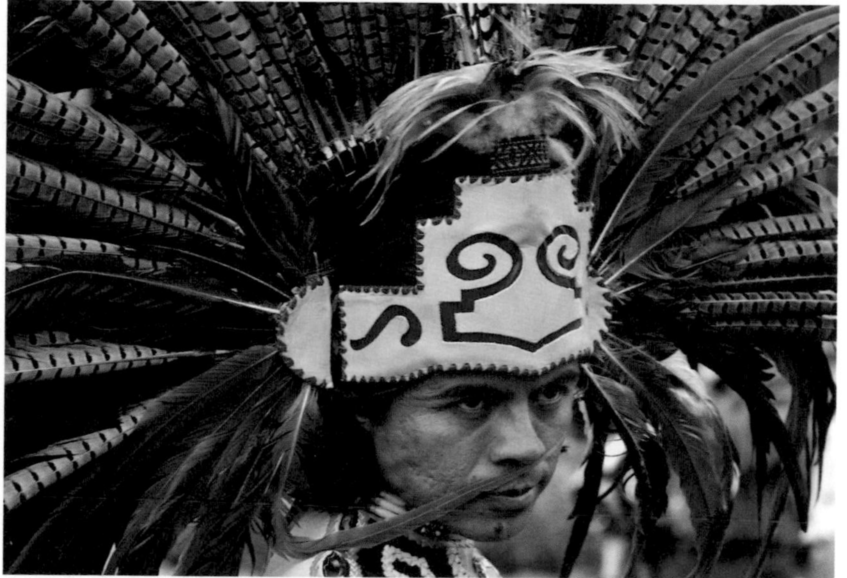

Shamanism

In Latin America, particularly the area around the Peruvian Amazon basin, the traditional holistic belief system is called shamanism though the shamanistic tradition is not found only in Latin America.

Within the shamanist system, as in other traditional systems around the world, diet is important for both physical and spiritual wellbeing. Shamans are found in many communities and act as a link to the spirit world, healing specific illnesses, both mental and physical, as well as officiating at important life moments, such as birth and death. Plants are the starting point for seekers of physical and spiritual health and the shaman will help select the one that is appropriate for an individual's needs.

Many shamans have expert knowledge of the plant life in their area, and a herbal regimen is often prescribed as part of the treatment. They often say they learn directly from each plant how to harness their effects and healing properties only after obtaining permission from its abiding or patron spirit. Each plant is believed to have a spirit and each is linked to treating a specific condition of the mind or body.

It's possible to join programmes in the Amazon basin but – a note of warning – there's a spiritual as well as dietary aspect to the treatment, sometimes using plants with hallucinogenic properties, which can be a test of mental strength and stability. Misuse and abuse of these powerful plant-based 'medicines' can have dangerous and even fatal consequences.

Humanism

Humanists are agnostic or atheist since they believe it is impossible to prove the existence of God and that it is possible to be good without the need for a God.

The essence of humanist practice is that it is about rational behaviour, rejecting both a supernatural being involved in human affairs and the idea of an afterlife.

Core texts: there are none, nor are there any declarations of faith. Humanists regard themselves as independent thinkers who have arrived at a set of moral and ethical values and behaviours, which are shared. They include accepting responsibility for one's actions and behaviour and that it is important to try to live a full and happy life and to help others do the same. They value human rights, freedom of communication, freedom from want and fear, education should be moral but free of bias from the influence of powerful religious or political organisations and that no doctrine, religious or political, economic or moral should be immune to critical scrutiny.

Zoroastrianism

God: Ahura Mazda.

Foundation text: the Avesta. There are few rules in Zoroastrianism, whose basic concepts are truth and purity and can be summed up as 'good thoughts, good words and good deeds'. Men and women are considered equal and with a responsibility for their own behaviour. The main thrust is to be the best one can be so there is a strong emphasis on education and on free will. Zoroastrianism is named after its founder the prophet Zarathustra and originated in Persia (now Iran). Many followers fled to India (where they are known as Parsis) following the Mongol invasion of Persia and its subsequent conversion to Islam.

Place of worship: Fire temple – the eternal flame is seen as a symbol of purity, but it is *not* worshipped. It is incorrect to call Zoroastrians fire worshippers.

Main festival: Noruz – New Year (around 21 March).

Islam

God: Allah.

Foundation text: the *Qur'an* transmitted by the Prophet Mohammed (the Messenger, Rasul, of God). It is customary when referring to the Prophet to add the words "peace be upon him".

Place of worship: Mosque. It is also a place of learning and teaching. The five pillars of Islam: *Shahada* (declaration of faith); *Salat* (prayers five times a day); *Zakat* (charity tax for the poor); *Sawm* (fast during Ramadan); and *Haj* (pilgrimage to Mecca).

Holy day: Friday.

Main festival: Ramadan – a month when Muslims fast from dawn to dusk.

Greeting: *As Salaam aleikum* (Peace be upon you); reply *Wa aleikum salaam.*

Prohibited food and drink: pork, alcohol.

Jihad: literally means struggle – it does not mean holy war, though the term has been inaccurately used in that way by many people, Muslim and non-Muslim. The struggle is primarily a personal one against one's own faults and weaknesses.

Judaism

God: *Yhwh* (pronounced Yahweh).

Foundation texts: the Old Testament of *The Bible* and the *Torah.*

The Talmud: an explanation of the *Torah*, teachings and discussions of Jewish scholars.

Place of worship: the Synagogue, also used as a place of learning and teaching.

Holy day: Sabbath (sunset Friday to sunset Saturday).

Main festival: Yom Kippur – the day of atonement when Jews must seek forgiveness from those they have wronged.

Prohibited food: pork.

Zionism: an international political movement launched in 1897, by Austrian journalist Theodor Herzl, with the aim of establishing, in law, a Jewish homeland in Palestine. To be a Jew is not automatically to be a Zionist.

Hinduism

God: Brahman – represented by the 'Om' symbol, the creator and destroyer of life and the universe. The multiplicity of other 'gods' such as Brahma, Vishnu and Shiva, (the Trimurti) Parvati, Kali, Durga and Ganesha, to name but a few of the many Hindu deities, represent different paths to follow reflecting the variety of human life and the sense of personal responsibility for one's own actions.

Foundation literature: the *Vedas*, the core text representing an oral tradition coming direct from God.

Main festival: Diwali is the main one but there are many more. Place of worship: temples to the many different deities are widespread and can be anything from tiny street shrines to huge, elaborately carved ancient monuments. People also have shrines in their homes. Many rivers, not only the Ganges, are also sacred.

Holy days: far too many to list. There is no specific day for prayer.

Prohibited food: beef (cows are sacred) but various peoples follow specific dietary requirements, from total vegetarianism through to eating of non-prohibited meats and fish, depending on the region they're from and their caste.

Essence of Hinduism: life is seen as an endlessly-repeating cycle of death and rebirth. Essentially the aim is to reach *moksha* and therefore release from the cycle of reincarnation. Karma is the accumulated result of a person's past action and determines the form in which they will be re-born. Dharma is the path of righteousness and duty, following which the individual can hope to improve their karma until they eventually reach *moksha*. This means that, as for other faiths, Hinduism is interwoven into the fabric of daily life and there is an emphasis on personal responsibility for one's behaviour, and therefore on modesty in dress and actions.

Buddhism

God: there is no name or central concept of a God. Buddhism is essentially a philosophy and a way of life leading to the goal of attaining nirvana – the release from the struggle to survive and from passion, aggression and ignorance.

Place of worship: although there are many shrines to the founder of Buddhism, Siddharta Gautama, he is not worshipped as a god nor is he seen as one. The nature of Buddhism does not require a place of worship and the *stupas* (characteristic round towers) are sacred buildings housing relics or the remains of a saintly person. There is, however, a tradition of monastic communities, particularly found in the foothills of the Himalayas, in Thailand and in Tibet.

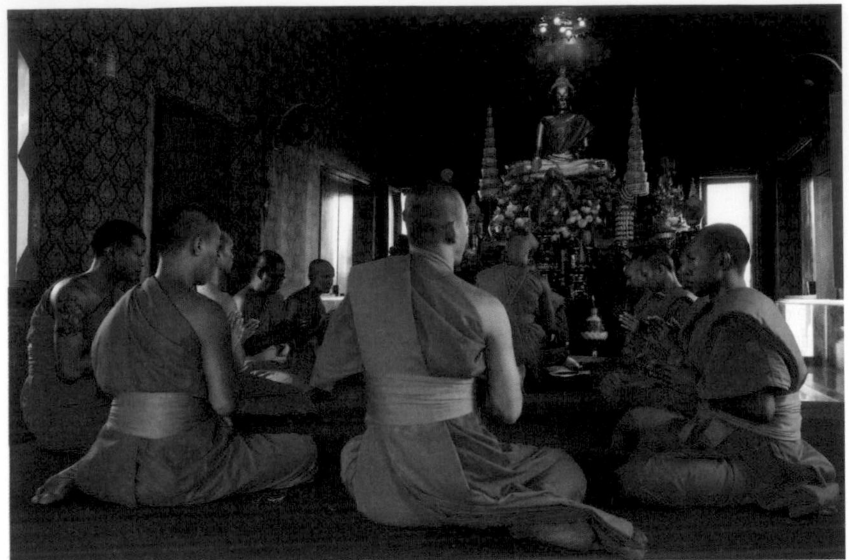

The essence of Buddhism: a philosophy for living summed up by the Four Noble Truths and the Noble Eightfold Path. The four truths were contained in the Buddha's first sermon and explain that suffering is part of life (the first truth) caused by the struggle to survive and by craving and aversion (second truth). That suffering can be overcome and we can become happy and free with more time to help others (third truth). The fourth truth is the way to achieve this – by following the Eightfold Path.

The Eightfold Path: Right View; Right Intention; Right Speech; Right Discipline; Right Livelihood; Right Effort; Right Mindedness; and Right Concentration.

Affirmation: Buddhists take five vows: to refrain from killing living beings; taking that which is not given; from sexual misconduct; from false speech; and from alcohol and drugs which confuse the mind.

Jainism

God: Jains believe in karma and there is no room in the belief system for a creator God. To follow the Jain faith is to follow a very rigorous and difficult way of life.

Place of worship: there are many ancient, beautiful and very ornate temples in India, particularly in Gujarat, but they are not quite places of worship in the sense generally understood.

The essence of Jainism: all beings, including inanimate objects, such as stones and earth, are alive and feeling. Consequently this is a strictly non-possessive and non-violent code of living.

Followers are divided into *sadhus* (monks), *sadhivas* (nuns), *shravak* (laymen) and *shravika* (lay women). The essence of Jainism is to strive for liberation of the self through right faith, right knowledge and right conduct (not unlike the Zoroastrian good thoughts, good words and good deeds).

The five great vows (*Maha-vratas*): right conduct includes truth, not harming any living thing, not stealing, chastity, detachment from people, place and material things. Jains wear only white, usually with a mask over the nose and mouth to avoid inhaling insects. They also carry a soft brush to sweep any place they plan to sit to avoid harming any living thing.

Main festival: *Paryshana Parva* (August/September), which ends with people wishing each other *Michhami-Dudakam*, meaning: 'Forgive me if I have done anything wrong or hurt your feelings knowingly or unknowingly.'

Sikhism

God: Sikhism recognises one universal God of all nations, who has no name.

Place of worship: *Gurdwara* – this is both a temple and a community centre, a symbol of equality and fraternity. Many *Gurdwara* community kitchens, known as *Pangat*, or *Guru-Ka-Langar*, produce a daily meal to feed thousands of destitute people in their neighbourhoods. It's a religion firmly rooted in the world and so encourages work, enterprise and wealth.

Foundation text: the *Guru Granth Sahib*. The essence of Sikkhism: the religion evolved in India at a time of considerable spiritual confusion, following the *Mughal* (Muslim) invasion into largely Hindu India. Sikkhism is open to anyone and is a faith rooted in optimism and in equal status, though with different roles, between men and women. Sikh unity and personality is based on the five Ks – *Kesha* (long and uncut hair); *Kangha* (a comb); *Kara* (a steel bracelet); *Kaccha* (special shorts worn as underwear) and *Kirpan* (the sword).

Prohibited: alcohol, tobacco, eating meat, and adultery.

Holy day: there is a daily service, called the *Granthi*, in the *Gurdwara* and Sikhs are expected to start their day with prayer, though they can visit the *Gurdwara* at any time of the day to pray. However what matters most is the way they live their daily lives.

Festivals: Vaisaki – harvest festival (around 13 April) and the celebration of the birth of the *Khalsa* (the brotherhood of those pure in word and deed).

For more information, or if you are interested in finding out about other religions, try: **www.bbc.co.uk/religion/religions**

Communication: Keeping in touch

Spare a thought for those you're leaving behind – friends as well as family. Not only will they be worried about your safety, but they may actually be interested in your travels – most are probably jealous and wish they could go too.

It's not just about keeping them happy: make sure you tell them where you are and where you are going – that way if something does happen to you, at least they know where to start looking. Backpackers do go missing, climbers have accidents, trekkers get lost; at least if someone is concerned that you have not got in touch when expected, they can then alert the police. If you've promised to check in regularly with close family *make sure you do*, especially when you move on to another country. Of course, if you don't stick to what you agreed, don't be surprised if the international police come looking for you.

While you probably can't wait to get away, you may be surprised how homesickness can creep up on you when you're thousands of miles away. Getting letters or emails can be a great pick-me-up if you're feeling homesick, weary or lonely, so, in order

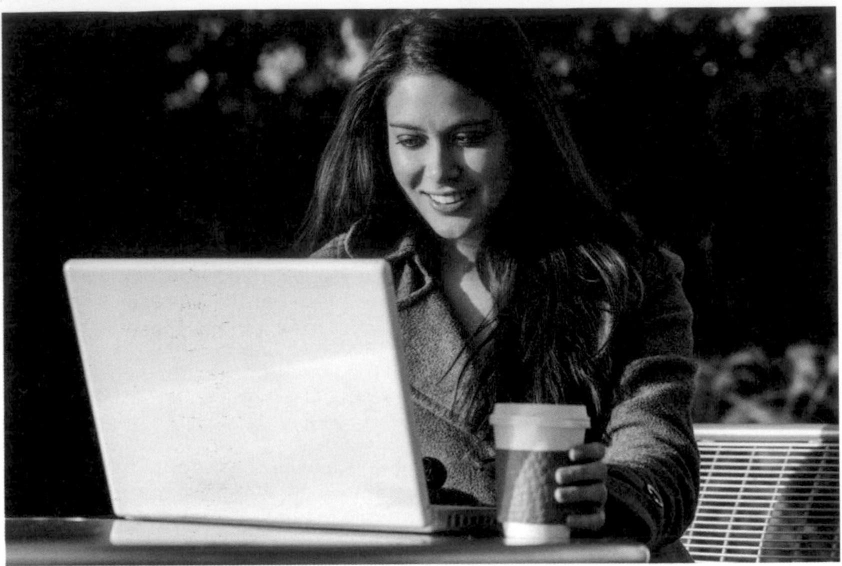

to ensure a steady supply of mail, distribute your address(es) widely to friends and family before you go. If you're not able to leave behind an exact address then you can have letters sent to the local Poste Restante, often at a main post office, and collect them from there. Also, parcels do usually get through, but don't send anything valuable.

Keeping a diary/sketchbook to record places, projects, people, how you're feeling and the effect things are having on you, can help when you get an attack of the homesick blues or just feel a bit down.

Mobile phone basics

Make sure you've set up your account to allow you to make and receive calls and text messages in all the countries you'll be travelling to (and emails if you've got a smartphone).

Try to limit use of your mobile to emergencies – they usually cost a fortune to run abroad as you pay for all the incoming calls at international rates too.

It's worth insuring the handset, as mobile theft is common and if it's the latest model, try not to flash it around.

If you are staying in one country for several weeks, consider getting either a cheap local mobile phone or a local SIM card for your UK mobile. Don't forget to alert friends back home to the new number. Local texts and calls tend to be very cheap and incoming calls from abroad are free, which avoids the massive charges when using your UK mobile.

Snail mail

Aerogrammes are a cheap way of writing from most countries. Registering letters usually costs only a few pence (or equivalent) from Third World countries, and is definitely worthwhile. Postcards are quick, cheap and easy – though not very private.

www.pc2paper.co.uk: This website allows you to send letters worldwide from the internet and store addresses in your account. You type your message and they then convert it into an actual letter and post it for you. The costs vary depending on weight and size.

Email

If you can get to a cybercafé or internet kiosk in an airport, hotel, university, office or home when you're abroad, you can simply log in to your mailbox (remember you'll need your user ID and password if these are part of the package). If you think getting to a cybercafé is going to be hard, there are always smartphones (you need to register your email address before you leave).

Thousands of cybercafés now sprinkle the globe, and internet connections can be difficult in Delhi but perfectly okay in Bolivia, so you'll probably find somewhere that you can email home at some point.

Internet cafés

Remember that internet cafés are much more than just a place to upload your latest batch of photos, check in with the folks at home and pick up the footie results along with your email.

In many places they're a lifeline for local people – to small farmers or traders, to families separated by war, poverty or natural disaster or a way of bringing education to children in isolated villages across the developing world – and, like any other kind of café, a place of crucial social interaction.

Equally if you are travelling independently and following your whims where better than to check with other backpackers for decent places to stay or get an idea of local customs and prices for food, transport, entertainment, whatever.

So even if you're travelling with the latest in e-technology it's worth taking your netbook or laptop to an internet café for a wi-fi hook-up. You'll get as much info from the people as you can from the machine!

Perhaps we should also include one note of caution – look for cafés with open spaces not curtained booths. Very often, particularly in very traditional societies where there is only minimal contact permitted between unmarried boys and girls, internet cafes with computers in closed booths are often male-only territory – and a place to check out the latest in 'adult' entertainment... not a good place to go if you're a female gapper just wanting to check her email and say hi to mum!

Online journals

Another easy way to keep everyone up-to-date is to set up a travel blog – as many people now do. On Facebook, your photos and comments will be available only to your 'friends' (unless you relax the privacy settings for a particular album) but there is the added advantage of being able to send messages and pictures to specific people without having to remember their email address, providing, of course, they too have a Facebook page.

Other sites you might like to check out are:

www.travelblog.org

www.offexploring.com

www.fuzzytravel.com

www.travoholic.com

And finally... back to earth

We've talked to enough people who've already taken a gap to know that returning home can be a shock to the system.

Returning to ordinary life takes time. It doesn't matter when you took your gap, you're likely to still go through the same sequence of feelings over the three months it generally takes to readjust.

How you respond, though, will depend on what you are returning to – if you went between school and university you might find yourself switching courses or storing up something else to explore later. Or you might be quite content to take up your course with renewed enthusiasm after a travelling break from study.

It's different again for people mid-career or over-50 mature travellers, but the pattern of adjustment is pretty much the same.

InterHealth, who provide a full range of health services and pre-travel health preparation, describe the feeling as 'reverse culture shock':

"Reverse Culture Shock is a common response experienced by people returning home from another culture. It can often be worse than culture shock as it's often unexpected. Returning home should be the easiest part of the trip, and sometimes it is, however, your trip may have changed you, your values and expectations. Sometimes it may be difficult to acknowledge that you have changed and home is still the same. Your family and friends may have unrealistic expectations of you. This may be hard on you but it will also be hard on them.

"You may feel a major loss upon returning home, almost as if you have been bereaved. There may also be a communication barrier between yourself and your family and friends back home. You may not be able to express the magnitude of what you have been through abroad.

"Your view of your home country may have changed in the light of your overseas experience, and you might find yourself rejecting some of your old values and ways of living. This may cause conflict between you and your friends and family who may be affected by your lifestyle change.

"You may try to re-adapt to your old lifestyle and re-connect with your old friends but find it hard to do so. Situations and relationships back home are bound to have changed in your absence; especially if you have been away for a long time. You may feel that you no longer belong and that joining in is hard.

"If you have returned home without an immediate plan for the future you may feel as though there is a lack of purpose to your life, which sorely contrasts to when you were abroad and perhaps carrying out an important role."

All of the above can leave you feeling isolated, anxious, or depressed. It is important to remember that you are not alone in these thoughts, and that things can be done to help.

Here are some tips form InterHealth to help you adjust:

- Prepare: prepare yourself before you go by learning more about reverse culture shock.
- Keep in touch: keep in touch with your friends and family while you are away.
- Give yourself closure: say a proper goodbye to your friends and colleagues.
- Take a break: when you get home, take at least a few days off.
- Write: writing can be a cathartic experience and can help order your thoughts. If you have experienced some life-changing or difficult events, write about them.
- Avoid indulgences and rash behaviour: avoid self-indulgence in alcohol, drugs, and food – these comforts make you feel good in the short-term but are guaranteed not to help your recovery process. Also try to avoid making rash decisions; you may feel bored and want to accept the first offer that comes your way, but it is best to be patient and let your emotional state settle.

"Usually you will settle down quickly, depending on certain factors such as the effectiveness of your coping strategies and the extent of your overseas experiences. The experiences from your international assignment are likely to become incorporated into your values and the way you live. You may find yourself drawing on them to inform your decisions and thoughts, and when advising others.

"If, after a few months, you have not settled after your return we recommend you talk to a trustworthy friend or a psychological health professional. You can email **phs@interhealth.org.uk** for further advice."

The length of time you've been away makes no difference to the feelings you go through on your return and even after six months you may still need time to adjust."

We've talked to people who've taken a two-week leave of absence from work through their company's charitable foundation and to people who've spent a year or more away. They all report coming back and finding themselves looking at everything through fresh eyes and questioning the importance of various aspects of homelife that they have previously taken for granted.

On average, it seems to take about three months between stepping off that last plane after a gap and getting back into life's routines. To start with, a commonly-reported phenomenon is the odd sensation of the body decelerating while the brain's still on the move. So, after the first three weeks of initial euphoria and sharing, be prepared to come down to earth with a bump.

What do you do now?

This one depends on what you had planned before you left and whether the option is still there – and if you still want to do it – once you're back.

Some people advise that, if you can manage it, putting aside some money for about three months of living expenses for your return, as part of pre-gap preparations, takes the pressure off if you're going to be job hunting. But, if taking time out isn't an option, don't panic.

If you already have work to go back to you may have to combine the post trip elation with a fairly quick return to the 'rat race'. And you'll need to think about how you interact with your colleagues. How much do you say about your trip? A spokeswoman for one major UK employer, which supports its staff in taking time out, and also has a foundation on whose projects they can do voluntary work, had this advice:

"When you are returning to work it is important to have a plan. Returning to work after 18 weeks or more can prove difficult on both a psychological and logistical level. Keep your line manager up-to-date with the timings of your return to work. This will ensure that they can factor you into their resource planning and also help you integrate back into the working environment.

"Do not rule out a degree of retraining when you return to work. Refreshing your skills will benefit most people in the work place, and, if you have been away from work for a long period of time, you should use the opportunity to familiarise yourself with new systems, procedures and practices.

"When you return to work take into consideration reverse culture shock. Whilst you might be keen to talk about your travels for many months to come, your colleagues may not be so keen to listen."

Karen Woodbridge, director of Suffolk-based Hornet Solutions (an Independent HR/ Employment Law Consultancy), also offers some important advice:

"Whilst you will quite rightly be very excited about your trip and all the anticipated adventures, it is worthwhile to take the time in advance to plan carefully your readjustment and return into the working world.

"If you have been fortunate enough to have been granted a leave of absence, it is vital that you take note of that old adage 'Out of sight, out of mind'. So plan before you go how you can stay in touch, which is so much easier now via the internet and the use of Skype.

"When you do return remember that your colleagues have been getting on with business whilst you've been away. There may even have been changes of personnel, for example your old team members or boss may have left the company. There certainly will be new alliances and different company politics. Don't expect people to remember that you were a 'star performer' before you left. That role may well be occupied by someone else now. People might also be jealous of your experiences for actually doing something they always dreamed of and this too can be a challenge.

"Therefore in many ways it will help if you think about returning to your old position as if it were a brand new job, ie expect things to be new, to have changed and realise that it will be up to you, once again, to find out how everything works and prove yourself even more capable of succeeding now because you bring all your old skills, competencies and experiences to the role plus all the new ones you developed whilst you were away. Realising you may face these challenges and planning how to overcome them will help you to more successfully integrate and adapt to your return at work."

If you have to start earning as soon as you get back and your old job wasn't kept open for you, you can always consider temporary work. These positions are often available immediately and can be flexible enough to enable you to carry on with your permanent job search. And you never know, once working in a company, opportunities often come up that you'd never have expected.

However, when looking for that new permanent role, Karen says: "Remember firstly that many jobs never get advertised so get in touch again with all your old contacts and see what jobs they know about and may even be prepared to recommend you for.

"When putting together a CV, think through all the new skills you learnt on your trip that will be invaluable to employers. Unfortunately many people use the phrase 'travelling' to cover gaps; they may be using this term to hide an unsuccessful job that ended in dismissal or possibly even time spent in prison! Consequently, recruiters can be cynical whenever they see 'travelling' on a CV so tackle this head on by highlighting how your trip has increased the contribution you can make to the role for which you are applying. This also helps make the travelling period seem genuine but remember, in a job search situation it's the benefits to the employer that will count, not how much fun you had!"

You'll find more useful advice on this in **Chapter 3 – Career Breaks and Older Gappers**.

Deciding what next

While getting back to 'normal' life, you've no doubt been trying to process everything you've learned from your gap experience.

How do you feel? What's changed? What's been confirmed? Where to now? Is there something new you want to do next as a result? How to go about it? You'll almost certainly still be in touch with friends you made on your travels, maybe even had a couple of after-gap reminiscence meetings. Others may still be travelling and keeping you restless!

You may also still be in touch with the projects you worked on. It's a fairly common feeling to want to keep a link to something that's been a life changing, learning experience. Is this you?

The best piece of advice on dealing with the consequences of any life-changing experience is to be patient and give it time. Nothing but time can make things settle into some kind of perspective and help you work out whether you are in the grip of a sudden enthusiasm or something deeper and more long-lasting.

Change of direction?

In time you'll know whether your urge to travel has also become an urge to keep the links with the communities you visited now you're back.

What level of involvement do you want? Is it going to be something local like fundraising – doing local talks, letters to newspapers – or are you seriously looking to change career?

If you have come back with the germ of an idea for a career change as a result of a volunteer placement, for example, there's nothing to stop you slowly exploring the options and possibilities.

Have a look at your CV. Try to talk to people working in the field you're considering moving into. Armed with some basic information, you could also consider talking through issues such as what transferable skills you have to add to your volunteer experience, what training you might need and how affordable it is, with a careers counsellor or recruitment specialist – preferably with an organisation that specialises in aid/charity or NGO positions.

Try these links:

www.totaljobs.com/IndustrySearch/NotForProfitCharities.aspx

www.cafonline.org

www.charitypeople.co.uk

www.peopleandplanet.org

To keep you going you should also never underestimate the power of synchronicity. You may find unexpected connections and information come your way while you're getting on with other things. If it's meant to be, you'll find ways to make it happen.

Please see the directory pages starting on page 273 for information on companies and organisations offering services and products to help you on your gap-year.

Finance

Finance

How much money will you need?

It all depends on what you're doing and for how long. As we've already mentioned in **Chapter 1**, it's estimated that the average gap-year for young people is £5000, while that goes up to £6000 for more mature travellers and £9000 for career breakers. The key word here is *average*, but it at least gives you a 'ball park' figure.

What do you need to pay for?

A gap needn't break the bank, but it helps if you start by making yourself a list of all the things you might need to pay for, and then research how much it all comes to. Then you can start looking at ways you can save some money by shopping around and keeping costs down. Here's a checklist to help you get started.

Before you go:

- Passport
- Visas and work permits (check the FCO website for the relevant embassy – **www.fco.gov.uk**)
- Insurance
- Flights
- Fees for placements/organised treks *etc*
- Special equipment if needed
- Vaccinations – they're not all free – and a travellers' medical pack

When you've gone:

- Accommodation (if travelling independently)
- Transport (if travelling independently).
- Food
- Entertainment
- Shopping – gifts and souvenirs
- Emergency fund

Avoiding those 'hidden' costs

The above list covers the absolute basics, but if you're not careful there are plenty of extra costs that could eat into your budget – ones you wouldn't necessarily think of at first. We asked our **Know Before You Go** campaign partners at the Foreign and Commonwealth Office for the benefit of their experience, and here's a checklist they have come up with to help save you money, and to avoid some common pitfalls:

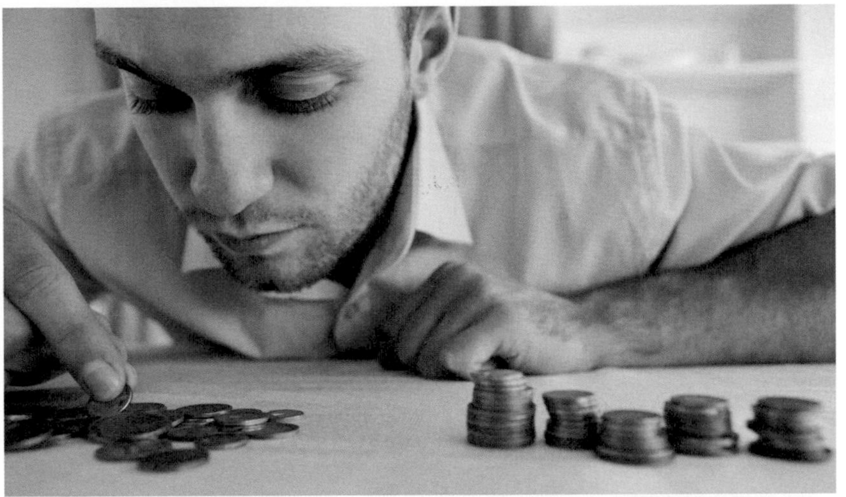

- Work out your budget before you go. Some pre-trip research will make it easier to work this out and try and stick to it. Think about how much you'll need on a daily basis – such as food, accommodation and any additional activities – and then work that out for the number of days you'll be away.
- Check the limits or cash available on any credit or debit cards you plan to take with you, as well as the validity and expiry dates so you don't get caught out overseas.
- Make sure you have made arrangements for any credit card bills to be paid while you are away to avoid your card being stopped. Consider giving someone the power of attorney to look after your financial affairs in the UK, while you're away.
- Notify your bank before you travel and inform them of the dates and countries you will be travelling through. Check your card/s can be used abroad and if any charges apply. Be sure to keep your cards safe, especially if you intend to use them throughout your trip
- Make a note of your credit / debit card details and the 24-hour emergency numbers and keep them separately.
- Take at least two cards, making one your emergency reserve, and make sure you know the PIN numbers for both debit and credit cards. Keep the emergency card somewhere safe.
- Make sure you have at least two forms of payment – take a mixture of cash (Sterling, Euros or US dollars), travellers' cheques and credit cards. Don't keep them together in one place in case you lose them or they are stolen. It's often better to over budget in case of emergencies.
- Jot down your travellers cheque numbers and an emergency telephone number for them should they get lost or stolen.
- Purchase a return ticket, or make sure you have enough money to buy one. It's worth noting that many countries will refuse you entry unless you have a return ticket.
- Always have some change in the local currency for when you arrive in case you need to make a telephone call. It is also advisable to have some local currency in small bank notes to catch a taxi or get something to eat or drink on arrival.

- Look out for local ATM machines. Today's global network means you can withdraw cash from machines in most places abroad. Be sure to check before use as costs may apply.
- Use a wallet for loose change and your day-to-day spending when carrying money around with you. Wear a secure money belt under clothing for your valuable documents and money.

Be aware that British consular staff can't pay your bills or pay for your journey home if you run out of money.

Raising the money

There's no doubt it's harder to raise money for gap travel in tougher economic times, when the competition for even low-skilled or part-time work is likely to be intense.

But, aside from the lucky few who can call upon major financial help from their families or wherever, most people will have to go out and earn the money, so it may be case of taking whatever is out there. It will be worth to pay for your 'once in a lifetime' trip.

There are other ways to raise some money however – auctions, fashion shows, garage sales and raffles could all help your cause and, with sites such as eBay, Facebook and Gumtree, it's easier than ever to sell unwanted possessions, however big or small. With a little imagination you could really lighten the financial load.

Sponsorship may be an option and local businesses may be interested if they think they can get some mileage out of it. You may able to get local media interested if you are doing something exceptional on your travels, and then you can give your business sponsors the free advertising they deserve.

Community groups, charities and religious organisations may well be interested in what you are doing and they may be willing to help in some way – particularly if you promise to give them a talk about your travels when you get back.

You could also apply for a grant. Have a look at the Directory of Grant Making Trusts. It is published each year and covers 2,500 grant-making trusts, collectively giving around £3billion.

If you are planning to do a training course during your gap-year, you may be eligible for funding via a Career Development Loan. A CDL is a deferred repayment bank loan to help you pay for vocational learning or education. The Department for Education pays the interest on your loan while you are learning and for up to one month afterwards.

You can get more info from the National CDL enquiry line: 0800 100 900; or by visiting the government website: **www.gov.uk/career-development-loans/overview**

Money savers

The International Student Identity Card (ISIC) gives you more than 40,000 travel, online and lifestyle discounts. It costs £9, is accepted in the UK and worldwide. There's also a 24/7 worldwide free call helpline for medical and legal assistance.

Many leading airlines also offer exclusive student/youth fares to ISIC (and IYTC) holders. Your travel agent can help you find the right one and advise if any age restrictions apply.

You can order your ISIC online at: **www.isic.org**

The card sees you right through the academic year: it's valid from each September, for up to 16 months, in other words until December the following year. You need to qualify for the year in which you'll hold the card:

- If you're a full-time student (15 hours weekly for 12+ weeks) at a secondary school, sixth form or further education college, language school, The Open University (60 points or more) or any UK university.
- If you've got a deferred/confirmed UCAS placement (then you can grab an ISIC for your year away).

If you're neither of the above, but under 26, you can get an International Youth Travel Card (IYTC) with a similar range of benefits. You can get the cards online at: **www.ISIC.org** or by phoning 0871 230 8546.

For budget flights and student discounts, you can check out the internet and we've included some hints in **Chapter 4 – Travelling and accomodation**.

If you're travelling independently, cut the cost of accommodation by: staying in the guest houses attached to temples and monasteries; camping or staying in a caravan park; as a guest in someone's home; sharing a room; or using budget hotels or hostels, but be careful to check for cleanliness and proper exits in case of emergency.

If you're a mature traveller, perhaps you could investigate a house swap for part of your time away, but see also **Chapter 3 – Career breaks and older travellers** for other ideas.

Buy second-hand: rather than spend a fortune on a backpack, do you know someone who's just returned from a trip and might be willing to lend or sell you any equipment they no longer need? Check the classified ads in your local paper, buy on eBay (or similar) or try some gap-year message boards.

Make sure that whatever you buy is in clean, sound condition, that the zips work, there are fittings for padlocks, and it's right for your body weight and height. If it's sound but a bit travel-worn, so much the better – you'll look like a seasoned traveller rather than a novice!

Money security

We've covered some of this in the FCO's checklist earlier in this chapter, but it's worth explaining a bit further. It's best to take a mix of cash, travellers' cheques, credit/debit card and travel money cards, and here's how best to take care of them:

Cash: carry small change in pockets, not big notes. Distribute it between a belt bag, day pack and your travel bag so you have an emergency stash.

Travellers' cheques: record serial numbers and the emergency phone number for the issuer in case of theft. You sign each one when you get them from the bank but then there's a space for a second signature. Don't sign this second box until you're cashing it – if you do and your cheques get stolen, they can be cashed and you invalidate the insurance cover. Only cash a couple of travellers' cheques at any one time – get a mix of larger and small change denominations. Often street traders and snack stalls, or taxis and rickshaws, won't have change for a large note and it makes you vulnerable – you seem rich.

Hotel currency exchanges are more expensive, local banks can take a long time and require ID. If you can find a Thomas Cook centre they're the most efficient and speedy we've found. Street rates can be cheaper but be very careful. A lot of street money changers are trading illegally – don't hand over the cheque until you have your money and have counted it.

Credit card: essential back-up. The problem with a credit card is losing it or having it stolen – keep a note of the numbers, how to report the loss of the card and the number you have to ring to do so.

Both Visa and Mastercard are useful, in an emergency, for getting local currency cash advances from a cash dispenser at banks abroad. Remember, if you're using your credit card to get money over the counter then you're likely to need some form of ID (*eg* passport).

If you are paying for goods or restaurant meals by using your card, you should insist on signing bills/ receipts in your presence and not allow the card to be taken out of your sight. This way you'll have no unpleasant surprises or mysterious purchases when you see your card statement.

Travel Money Cards: pre-pay travel cards are now a well-established alternative to travellers' cheques and can be used at an ATM using a PIN number. The idea is that you load them with funds before you leave, but beware – like credit and debit cards, most charge for every reload and for cash withdrawals. To find out more check out these two examples:

www.iceplc.com/cashcard
www.travelex.com

Wiring money

If you find yourself stranded with no cash, travellers' cheques or credit cards, then having money wired to you could be the only option. Two major companies offer this service:

MoneyGram – **www.moneygram.com**

Western Union – **www.westernunion.com**

Both have vast numbers of branches worldwide - MoneyGram has 180,000 in 190 countries and territories and Western Union has 379,000 agent locations in 200 countries and territories.

The service allows a friend or relative to transfer money to you almost instantaneously. Once you have persuaded your guardian angel to send you the money, all they have to do is go to the nearest MoneyGram or Western Union office, fill in a form and hand over the money (in cash).

It is then transferred to the company's branch nearest to you, where you in turn fill in a form and pick it up. Both you and the person sending the money will need ID, and you may be asked security questions so you need to know what the person sending the money has given as the security question *and* its answer. Make sure they tell you the spelling they've used and that you use the same.

There are now also smartphone applications for people to send money to each other. Barclays' Pingit allows its users to receive and send money, without charge, to anyone with a UK current account and a mobile phone number.

The service links users' current accounts to their mobile number. They can then 'Ping' money to another mobile phone number (the person receiving the money has to register with the service to access it). The service is protected by a passcode.

Older travellers with more assets will have specific financial concerns and perhaps more sources of funds than younger gappers, and we've included some detail in **Chapter 3 - Career breaks and older travellers**.

Sticking to a budget

Easier said (or written) than done, definitely, but you should at least try! For starters, you can get a good idea of costs before you go from a gapper who's been there recently. Messageboards are a good place to find such people. You can also get an idea of how far your money will go if you check an online currency converter like **www.xe.com**

As a general rule you'll find your money will stretch quite a long way in most of the less developed parts of the world, and once you're in-country you can find out fairly easily from other travellers/locals the average costs of buses, trains, meals and so on.

Having said that, the global recession and rises in oil and food prices have had an impact on most countries' economies. They've particularly hit costs in the less developed world and the signs are that it may take some time for things to settle down. As you're planning some months ahead of your trip it may be sensible to add a little extra for potential inflation when you're working out your minimum and maximum spend per day. The trick then is to stick to it.

Here are some tips:

Shopping: you're bound to find a zillion things that will make good souvenirs/gifts – best advice, though, is to wait. You'll see lots more wherever you are and the prices for the same goods in popular tourist and backpacker destinations will be much higher – and possibly of lower quality – than they will be in smaller towns and villages.

Do your buying just before you move on to the next destination, or return home, so you won't have spent too much money at the start of your trip, won't have to carry it all around with you and also by then you'll have an idea of what's worth buying and for how much. Another advantage of buying locally is that more of what you pay is likely to benefit the local community, and craftspeople, rather than the middle links in the chain.

If you buy souvenirs/gifts mid-trip, you could consider posting them home to save carrying them around with you but don't risk sending anything too valuable, and make sure you know what's permitted to send (and what's not) since you'll almost certainly have to fill in a customs declaration slip, which will be stuck to the outside of the parcel.

Bargaining: make sure it's the custom before you do, and try to find out roughly what it should cost before you start. Also try to look at yourself through local eyes – if you're wearing expensive jewellery and clothes and carrying a camera or the latest mobile phone you'll find it much harder to get a real bargain.

Whatever you do, smile and be courteous. The trader has to make a living, usually in pretty harsh economic conditions, and you're a guest in their country. Not only that, but if you're a responsible traveller then ethically you should be offering a fair price, not going all-out to grab a bargain you can boast about later.

Don't give the impression you really, really want whatever it is. Don't pick it up – leave that to the market trader, then let them try to sell it to you. They will tell how much they want and it's likely to be inflated, so you offer a price the equivalent amount below the figure it should be and that you're willing to pay. If they start the process by asking you how much you're willing to offer then mention that you've asked around local people so you know roughly what it should cost, before you name a price a little below what you're prepared to pay. From this point on it's a bit like a game of chess and it can be very entertaining – so don't be surprised if you collect an audience!

You might be told a heart-rending story about family circumstances or the trader's own costs, but you can counter that by saying that however much you like the item, you're sorry but it's outside your budget. Gradually you'll exchange figures until you reach an agreement. One technique is to pretend you're not that bothered and start to walk away, but be prepared for the trader to take you at your word.

Not getting ripped off by cabbies: find out beforehand roughly what the local rate is for the distance you want to go. Then it's much the same principle as bargaining in a market. It's generally cheaper not to let hotels find you a cab – they often get a rake-off from the fare for allowing cabbies to park on their grounds, so it will cost you more.

Agree a price before you get into the vehicle and if you're hiring a car and driver for a day (which can often work out cheaper especially if you're sharing with friends) usually you'll be expected to pay for a meal for the driver so make sure you agree that the price of a stop for food is included in the deal.

In India there's a system of pre-pay kiosks, particularly at airport exits, where you can buy a chit – a paper that states a fair, and usually accurate, price for the journey. The driver can't cash it until you're safely at your destination, can't charge you more than is on the chit, and it has to be signed – usually by your hotel/accommodation before it can be cashed. So you can be sure you'll not be taking any long detours to bump up the cost. It's worth asking whether there are similar systems wherever you are.

Tipping: it's a bit of a minefield and you need to find out what the fair rate is. A tip should be a thank you for good service, so, for example, if you're in a restaurant and there's already a percentage on your bill for service you shouldn't pay more, unless of course you feel your waiter deserves it! Remember if you over-tip you raise expectations higher than other travellers – and locals – may be able or willing to pay.

Finding and affording a guide: find out if there's a local scheme for licensing/approving guides and what the 'official permit' looks like. Nearly always there will be any number of 'guides' at the entrances to any interesting place you might want to visit. Some will be official – others will be trying their luck. You'll usually find out when you pay the entrance fee.

Insurance

It's important to take out comprehensive travel insurance, however long you are travelling for, and to check that it covers you for everything that you want to do while you are away. Should something go wrong while you are overseas, costs can quickly escalate with average prices ranging from £15,000 to over £100,000 (in Europe and America respectively) for treatment and re-scheduled flights back home.

"An emergency abroad can be extremely expensive," the Foreign and Commonwealth Office told us. "Medical treatment or returning to the UK could cost you thousands of pounds, unless you are adequately insured. We will do what we can to support people who require medical assistance but the FCO cannot pay their medical bills or fly them home."

Well, there a vast number of policies - and they all cover different things – so it's difficult to know which one to go for. But the basic things to check for are:

· Medical costs.

· Legal.

· Passport loss.

· Ticket loss.

· Cash loss.

· Luggage.

· Flight cancellation.

· Missed flights.

· Working abroad.

· Hazardous sports.

· Specific medical conditions.

Other things you should ask:

· Is there a 24-hour helpline?

· Can you cover yourself for an unexpected return home so that you can continue your gap later without losing your cover?

- Are there any special declarations you need to make on the health conditions of immediate family?
- Are there any conditions and requirements regarding pre-existing medical conditions?
- Are there any age restrictions or extra age-related costs on the policy? This is particularly important for mature travellers.

Some banks provide cover for holidays paid for using their credit cards, but their policies may not include all the essentials you'll need for a gap-year.

Banks also offer blanket travel insurance (medical, personal accident, third party liability, theft, loss, cancellation, delay and more). You may be able to get reductions if you have an account with the relevant bank or buy foreign currency through it.

Who to choose?

You don't have to buy a travel insurance policy as part of a travel package through a travel company and there is intense competition between insurance companies to attract your attention. It may be tedious but the best advice is shop around, check out the internet, talk to a broker and read the small print very carefully.

Medical insurance

If you're going to Europe you can get a European Health Insurance Card (EHIC), which allows for free or reduced cost medical treatment within Europe, should you need it. You can apply online: **www.ehic.org.uk** or there's an automated application service on **0300 3301350.**

If you need further help you can call Overseas Healthcare Team on 0191 218 1999.

Your card is valid for three to five years and should be delivered to you in seven days. The EHIC card only covers treatment under the state scheme in all EU countries, plus Denmark, Iceland, Liechtenstein, Norway and Switzerland. You can also pick up application forms at your post office.

However, the EHIC is not a replacement for a travel insurance policy. It only covers necessary care and won't cover things such as repatriation to the UK in the event of a medical emergency

Countries with no health care agreements with the UK include Canada, the USA, India, most of the Far East, the whole of Africa and Latin America.

Wherever it happens, a serious illness, broken limb, or even an injury you might cause someone else, can be very expensive.

Medical insurance is usually part of an all-in travel policy. Costs vary widely by company, destination, activity and level of cover. Make sure you have generous cover for injury or disablement, know what you're covered for and when you've got the policy read the small print carefully. For example, does it cover transport home if you need an emergency operation that cannot be carried out safely abroad?

Some policies won't cover high-risk activities like skiing, snowboarding, bungee jumping *etc* so you'll need to get extra, specific, cover and an insurance broker can help with this. Companies may also make a distinction between doing a hazardous sport once and spending your whole time doing them. Some insurance policies also have age limits.

If you have a medical condition that is likely to recur, you may have to declare this when you buy the insurance, otherwise the policy won't be valid. Also, check whether the policy covers you for the medical costs if the condition does recur, as some will not cover such pre-existing conditions.

Already covered?

If you're going abroad on a voluntary work assignment you may find that the organisation arranging it wants you to take a specified insurance policy as part of the total cost. You may also find you have a clash of policies before you even start looking for the right policy.

For example, if your family has already booked you a one-year multi-travel insurance policy to cover travel with the family at other times of the year, you may find you are already covered for loss of life, limb, permanent disablement, some medical expenses, theft and so on. These multi-trip policies can be basic as well as quite cheap, but it's essential to check the small print of what the policy covers as it's possible that there may be a clause compelling the insured to return to the UK after a short period of time.

Just like many of the 'free' insurance policies that come with bank accounts, many of these policies only cover for trips of up to 60 days at a time, at which point travellers had to return to the UK. In other words, great for a holiday or two or for a business traveller but no use at all if you plan to be out of the country for the whole year.

In this case you can start by finding out (through the broker or agent who sold you the policy) if any additional cover can be tacked on to your existing policy, though this can be expensive and most off-the-shelf policies won't do it. A specific gap-year or backpacking policy may be more appropriate and actually work out cheaper than trying to add stuff on.

Try to find a policy that doesn't already duplicate what is covered by an existing policy (they don't pay out twice), but some duplication is unavoidable and it's obviously better to be covered twice than not at all.

Making a claim

Read through the small print carefully before you travel and make sure you understand exactly what to do if you need to make a claim – most policies will insist that you report a crime to the police where this is possible (often within a certain time period), and that you send in the police report with your insurance claim. What you don't want to happen is to have a claim dismissed because you don't have the right paperwork to back it up.

Insurers won't pay you money unless you have complied with all their rules and many travel policies impose conditions that are virtually impossible to meet. For example, some policies demand that you report not only theft of items but also loss of items. Fine, but the police are likely to be pretty reluctant to write a crime report because you think you may have accidentally left your camera in the loo!

If you do have anything stolen and you have to get the local police to give you a report, it's a good idea to dress reasonably smartly when you visit them, be prepared to wait and try to be pleasant and polite no matter what!

The Foreign Office website (**www.fco.gov.uk/travel**) has a good page about insurance and is worth checking out for advice and links. In addition to a list of what your travel insurance should cover, which is similar to the one at the start of this chapter, it suggests the following extras, which are not always included:

- Legal expenses cover can be useful as it will help you to pursue compensation or damages following personal injury while you're abroad – very important in countries without a legal aid system.
- Financial protection if your airline goes bankrupt before or during your trip – given the state of the airline industry this may be worth serious consideration for at least the next couple of years.

A spokesman for the Association of British Insurers told us: "The vast majority of travel insurance claims are settled quickly. However, the best way to avoid potential problems is to read the policy before you go, and ensure that you fully understand what you are covered for, and the terms and conditions. If anything is unclear, contact your insurer.

"Take a copy of the policy with you and make sure you know how to claim, especially any emergency contact numbers that you may need."

Our friends at DU Insure added that it is worth noting the excess on your policy – something that is often overlooked.

"Almost all policies have an excess attached to different sections of cover. That amount is deducted from the claim, normally for each person covered and for each relevant section of the policy. If you make a number of claims whilst you are travelling this can add up so think about taking out an excess waiver so that you have to contribute nothing. It may cost a little more but could save you a small fortune."

You'll also need to let your insurers know about any existing medical conditions before you head off:

"If you don't declare a pre-existing condition, the entire policy will probably be invalidated. **If you are in any doubt, talk to the insurer before you buy**. Note also that, if you have an existing injury that is exacerbated by a second accident while you are travelling, cover for this may also be excluded."

What to do if you get an emergency call to come home

We all hope there'll be no family crises while we're away on our gap but it does occasionally happen that someone close is taken seriously ill, or even dies, and then all you can think about is getting home as quickly as possible.

We've talked to a couple of insurers about this and they reinforce our advice to *always* read the policy carefully before you set off on your travels.

Generally speaking, your gap-year travel policy ceases once you return home, but some insurers offer extra cover for one extra trip home (or more, up to four, but the price rises with each one) without your policy lapsing. In a backpacker/adventure policy of three to 18 months, one home return is in the region of £5 and four would be around £24 extra on your policy.

Most insurers are used to dealing with sudden early returns and have a 24-hour emergency assistance company to help you through the whole process.

You need to let them know anyway so you can set the ball rolling for claiming for the cost and they can deal with getting you from your gap location to the airport, or, if you have one, you can use the help of your placement provider's in-country reps, or even a combination of the two, so you don't have to deal with transport hassles when all you can think about is getting home quickly.

However, there are often restrictions. First off, your family emergency has to affect an immediate relative – so husband, wife, mum, dad, grandparents, sisters and brothers, children, grandchildren – but *not* aunts, uncles and other extended family. It has to be serious injury, illness or death of a relative – family feuds and divorces do not count!

If you have home return extra on your policy you're covered for one extra flight home; you're *not* covered for an additional flight back to resume your gap. But, if you have a return ticket, as most gappers do, the best way to go is to use your existing return, if the airline will reschedule, claim for it, then book another return flight. It's often cheaper to book a return flight than an extra one-way only.

If your ticket cannot be changed and you need to purchase a new ticket for your return journey, this can be arranged via a flight-ticketing agent or direct with the appropriate airline (subject to availability of flights and seats).

Websites such as Expedia and ebookers offer a wide selection of flights including single leg and one way tickets, which you can buy online and be allocated e-tickets, or collect them from the airline sales desk at the airport.

During peak travel or holiday times you might find the quickest way to get home may be to go to the airport and wait to pick up a 'no show' seat on standby.

Overall, say DU Insure, the key is to read everything carefully – and have reasonable expectations from your insurer.

"Travel insurance is intended to cover emergencies, not make life more comfortable. All insurers have their favourite examples of customers who have unrealistic expectations – the sort of people who try to claim for a massage because their legs are aching after a day on the ski slopes."

Please see the directory pages starting on page 279 for information on companies and organisations offering financial and insurance services for gappers.

Career breaks and older travellers

Career breaks and older travellers

What exactly do we mean?

You will read the terms 'career break' and 'sabbatical' a lot in this chapter. They will essentially refer to the same thing: stopping work for a period of time to do something new or different. You would generally consider a 'sabbatical' to be a period of time away from your job, with the agreement to return at the end of it. A career break, however, might mean cutting loose altogether – quitting your job and seeing what happens; maybe with the intention of starting a whole new career when you're back, or just a leap into the unknown. Either way, it's what we'd consider a gap, so this chapter looks at how to do it and what you'll need to think about.

An emerging trend

They may still be in the minority in the gap-year market, but the number of career breakers is definitely on the rise. Taking a month, six months or a year out of your workplace is an excellent way to add new skills to your CV, re-assess your career (or maybe your life!), or just to recharge your batteries or and get away from the routine.

There may be something you've always wanted to do or somewhere you've wanted to – and maybe now you're in a better position to afford it? Or maybe you want to 'give something back' after years in the 'rat race'?

You might have heard of the terms 'extravagapper' or 'flashpacker' to describe the more mature member of the gap community.

Extravagappers are thought of as newly-redundant city professionals with generous redundancy packages, who are taking the opportunity of a career break rather than plunge back into a possibly demoralising, recession-hit job market.

Flashpackers are those with backpacking with 'flash or style', who typically spend freely, or even excessively, for activities at their chosen destination.

These are caricatures, of course. People who take career breaks come from all sorts of backgrounds, and with varying degrees of affluence.

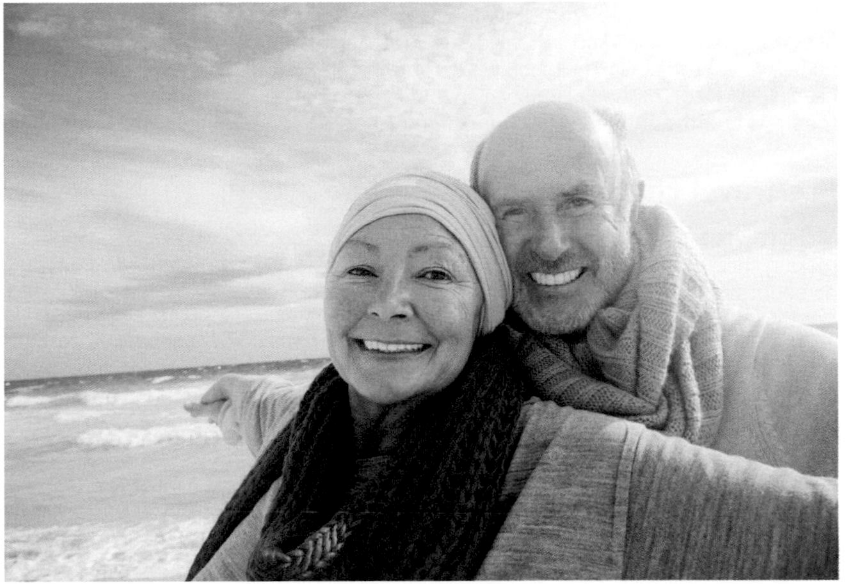

Taking a career break for one month to a year is the fastest-growing sector of gap-year activity and there's some anecdotal evidence that the global recession is increasing the numbers.

Around 90,000 people take a short sabbatical each year in the UK – in other words a 'gap-month'. It may be worthwhile considering something like this, or perhaps a longer trip if you've been made redundant or taken early retirement.

Several organisations that arrange places for people on overseas projects, have told us that more than half of their activity is now focused on helping place mature travellers and/or people who are taking a career break.

Raleigh International told us that, over the last 12 months, they have seen a 45% increase in the number of career breakers volunteering with them. They added: "We regularly hear stories about volunteer managers who return home to follow a completely different career path."

Lydia Rosling, of The Dragon Trip, who organise backpacking tours of China, reports a 'significant' increase in career breakers, mainly in their mid-to-late 30s – "people who are unhappy in their current job and have been working continuously with little reward. They want a break to put life back into perspective and possibly re-think their career".

People are living longer and are also a lot healthier well into old age. Many, therefore, feel they want to continue to use their skills in places where they will do some good.

This, coupled with the issues of the retirement age being put back and worries about inadequate pension provision, has also prompted many older people to think about extending their working lives and perhaps also pursuing a different career altogether.

Taking a gap, perhaps to volunteer in another country, is one good way of identifying skills, wisdom and knowledge gained over a working lifetime, that may be useful in another sector and this could lead to a new career.

Here's a great example from Kaya Responsible Travel: "We had one volunteer in her 40s who had worked in logistics for 20 years, but after joining our Marine Conservation project in Thailand, quit her job, did an A level in marine science, and is heading back to Thailand at the beginning of next year to join the team as an intern for a few months before seeking work in the area."

Pre-travel checklist

Older travellers generally have different considerations from younger ones when making their plans. These include the effects of taking a gap on careers, what to do about the house and mortgage, financial issues and whether or not to take the children, if this applies.

This list covers the extra responsibilities older people might have to consider. It only covers the basics of what you might have to organise – but we hope it will be a useful start for you to cherry-pick what's appropriate and no doubt add your own extras!

Work:

· Talk to your employer about sabbatical/career break options

Career break:

· What do you want from it?

· What do you want to do?

· Where do you want to go?

Finance:

· Paying the bills

· Mortgage

· Financing and raising money for the trip

· Insurance

· Pensions and NI contributions.

The house: Are you going to let it? If yes, you need:

· To talk to an accommodation agency

· Safety certificates

· Insurance

· To investigate tax exemption

Storage of possessions:

· What do you want to store? And can it be stored at home?

Children:

· Talk to the school(s) about taking them

· Find out about education possibilities where you're going

· If they're coming, how long will the trip be?

Safety precautions:

· Wills and power of attorney

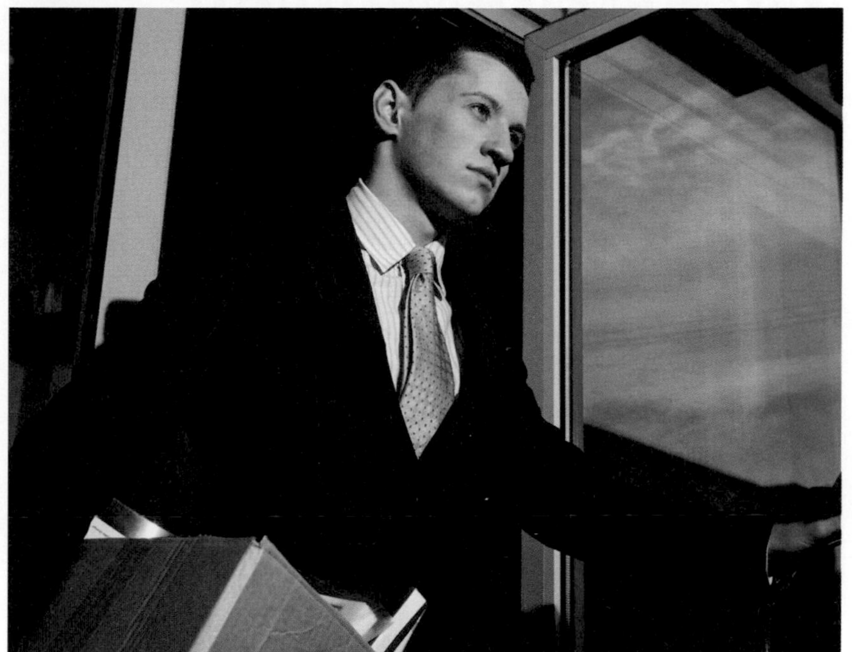

Arranging a sabbatical

There is no legal obligation on employers to offer employees sabbaticals/career breaks. However, they are often regarded as an important part of an employee's career development, and may be granted for a variety of reasons including study research travel or voluntary work which can often be related to the employee role.

Here's some useful things to know:

- Sabbaticals can help companies retain senior staff by giving them the chance to do something different, without leaving altogether.
- Employers who grant sabbaticals will usually attach various conditions to eligibility and what happens during the sabbatical.
- Sabbaticals are usually only available to employees at senior levels and those who have completed a specified number of years of continuous service.
- Some organisations do not even have sabbatical policies.
- Where an employer does grant sabbaticals, it must ensure that part-time employees are afforded the same benefits as equivalent full-time staff.
- Normally the employee will not receive pay or benefits for a sabbatical as the employee's contract is seen as suspended.
- It's important that a strategy for the return to work is agreed in advance of the sabbatical.
- The employer should take particular care to ensure that any guarantee of re-employment is worded clearly and unambiguously in order to avoid any disagreement or challenge at a later date.

What if you can't arrange a sabbatical?

Companies have no obligation to provide career breaks, so if you're turned down, you'll need to think about what to do. You may decide to resign. If not, you might want to consider how it will affect your future prospects there. It's a tricky one, and depends very much on both you and the company: your career goals, and their hopes and plans for you.

One option you might consider if you can't arrange a sabbatical and are wary of just quitting is arranging a job swap with someone from another country in a similar industry. You need to consider:

- Where do you want to travel?
- Do you speak a second, third or fourth language?
- Will you need housing?
- Do you need to be paid while away?
- How long do you want to be away for?

This may be easier in an international company where there may even be opportunities to transfer to the overseas office. Many such companies offer formal secondment programmes so it's always worth exploring these first.

If the above options are not possible, and you are prepared to resign, you could investigate whether your company might agree to guarantee you a job on your return.

Even if they don't guarantee a position for you, have regular contact with the key decision-makers whilst you are away by the occasional email *etc*. This will keep you in their minds and make it easier for you to approach them when you come back home, to see if they have any suitable job opportunities. Just remember, in job hunting, as in everything else, it's not *what* you know but *who*. So it's absolutely vital that you make the effort not to lose touch with your professional colleagues, networks and contacts whilst you are away. If you do, you'll regret it once you are back.

If you're not already signed up to LinkedIn, you might like to consider it. This website is the business world equivalent of Facebook. It's free to use and you can link to colleagues and business contacts and post recommendations about them and, importantly, get them to post recommendations about you.

You can even upload your CV, and indicate that you are open to job opportunities. It could also be useful to add your list of contacts gained *whilst* you're on your career break, thus adding extra value to your LinkedIn profile.

No sabbatical? Take your chances

If you're willing to quit and take your chances, what about finding work when the break's over?

What the jobs market will be like when you return is anyone's guess; however, you'll have a faster and more productive job search if you work at it before you leave.

Think now about the job you should be aiming for after the gap. Your gap is likely to develop new skills and ambitions so you might want something different from the current role.

In the various sections in the book, you'll discover the vast range of things you can do on your gap; the skills you can learn and the places you can visit. Whatever you choose, it's likely you'll be boosting your CV in a number of ways – and not always those you'd expect.

Olivia from AllAboutCareers.com told us: "The most surprising by-product of my travels was how it aided my job hunt after I returned. Travelling meant I could properly take time to think about the career I wanted when I got back, but it also helped in other ways. For instance, I had a job interview in which the interviewer had also travelled to Cambodia, and the small talk really helped ease me into the interview."

So, it's likely you'll return from your gap with a new skills, a new sense of purpose, and a clearer idea of what you want to do in the future.

Your target job identified, talk to the people who'll help you find future vacancies. Research the specialist recruitment consultancies in that sector (*eg* Google them), then ask to talk to consultants with at least two years experience of recruiting for the jobs that interest you. You want to know those consultants' best guesses about the likely state of that jobs market a year from now, what skills employers are most likely to look for in candidates and so on.

Stay in touch with the most useful of these recruitment consultants (*eg* by sharing snippets of your gap news with them). Keeping yourself at the forefront of their minds puts you on the inside track for news about developments in the jobs market. Similarly, stay in touch with ex-colleagues, university tutors and careers service advisors – they will often have huge networks for you to tap in to.

It's also a good idea to plan your career break around the natural hiring cycles of your industry. Recruitment activity tends to fall in December and early January, the Easter break and the weeks that coincide with the school summer holidays, for example. It may be harder to find jobs in these periods. The busiest times for recruitment tend to be the early spring and autumn.

Do update your CV before you go, ensuring it's ready for your return to employment. It's a good idea to keep it available on email so you can send it to interested parties while you're away, if an opportunity presents itself.

Finance

You've talked to your employer, perhaps also worked out what you hope to do – there are plenty of organisations to help you plan your chosen activities in the various sections in this book. The next crucial question is finance.

Obviously the amount of money you'll need depends on where you want to go, what you want to do, and how long you want to be away. At this point, drawing up a rough budget for how much it will cost would be a good idea. (See **Chapter 2 - Finance**, for a checklist). Once you have this it's worth talking to your building society or bank to see whether they have any schemes that can meet your needs.

While banks often have student and graduate advisers who can advise on what to do about everything from travel insurance to suspending direct debits and deferring loan payment, they don't seem yet to have reached the stage of having advisers *specifically* for career breakers. They are, however, increasingly aware of the trend to take a career break and may well be able to use their experience of advising younger gappers to help you think the finances through.

One recent survey amongst older people in the UK revealed that a large majority are extremely pessimistic or fearful about the quality of their lives in old age. A significant number were taking the view that, if their old age was going to be so grim,

why not have one last adventure? Consequently, they were using annuities and equity release or lifetime mortgages to unlock money from their homes to boost their retirement income and pay for such adventures.

This might seem like a good plan. However, there have also been many reports of schemes offering to buy people's homes and allowing them to rent them back for their lifetimes, only for them to be evicted after a few months or to find 'hidden charges' that meant they saw little money at the end of it. So beware! Read the small print *very* carefully.

Some companies offer lifetime mortgages, where you can release the value of your home and live in it without paying anything until you die, when the company will recover its money from the sale of the home.

Individual circumstances vary and if you feel you are 'asset rich but cash poor' it may be tempting to consider such options. You should only consider such a scheme with a reputable company and if the scheme includes protection against negative equity. We would strongly advise that if you are thinking of doing something like this you consult an independent financial adviser.

Maximise your funds: the chance for a good clear out

Is the garage crammed, are every drawer and cupboard stuffed? Is it all 'file and forget' or 'might come in handy' but never has? Admit it, you're one of those people who hasn't touched any of this stuff for years and you've kept saying you'd do a massive clearout.

But the more you add over the years, the more daunting it is and the easier it is to put off. We all do it. And how much houseroom do some of us give to all that stuff our children insist they have no space for but have sentimental attachments to?

Preparing for your year out is the perfect opportunity to de-clutter your life. Have a look at what you need to get rid of and turn into funding for your gap. Consider

raising some cash by selling items through online auction sites, such as eBay, holding a garage sale or a car boot sale.

You'll create space to store your precious items (the things you want to keep but not leave lying about), you'll add some cash to your travel fund, and you'll come back to a well-organised home. Also, if you've decided to let your home empty (more of this later on) you'll need less rented container space – and save yourself some money.

Imaginative fundraising

If you've already settled on the kind of project you want to do and it involves raising a specific sum, as volunteer projects often do, you can hold fundraising events to help you raise the cash – the options are as limitless as your imagination!

You have an untapped resource where you work – you could try asking for a contribution from your employer. It's good PR to have a link with someone doing something for a worthy cause.

If your employer agrees, what about baking cakes to sell at coffee time or holding competitions (guess the weight/number of objects in a container) or even asking colleagues to sponsor you? Even simple things like putting all those irritating bits of small change that weigh down pockets, and cram purses, into a large pot or jar can mount up surprisingly quickly.

Pensions and National Insurance contributions

If you have an occupational pension and are taking a sabbatical you should check with your employer to see if they offer a pension 'holiday' and what that might mean to your eventual pension, but it might be possible to stop or reduce your payments while you are away. If you have been with the company less than two years, it might be possible to arrange a refund of pension contributions.

For the state pension you might want to look at two issues: during the time you're away, you will be officially classified as living abroad and you won't be paying NI. However, you should check what that will do to your contributions' record and how it might affect your eventual state pension.

You can find out if there are gaps in your record by calling the HMRC (HM Revenue and Customs) helpline (0845 915 5996) and for more information. People living abroad should call: 0845 915 4811.

Once you have that information it's worth talking to the DWP (Department for Work and Pensions). They have a help and advice service (Tel: 0845 606 0265) and you can find out what you can expect by way of state pension. A DWP adviser told us that, from 2010, to get the maximum state pension both men and women will have to have paid NI for at least 30 years.

However, another useful fact, if you're likely to reach retirement age during your gap and can afford it, is that there's an incentive for deferring your state pension. For every five weeks you agree to defer, you get 1% added to your eventual pension. After a year, you can either take that as a taxable lump sum or have it incorporated into your regular pension payments. You can defer for more than a year and continue to add this interest to your eventual state pension.

The Directgov website also has a useful page on pensions for people living abroad: **www.direct.gov.uk/en/BritonsLivingAbroad/Moneyabroad/DG_4000013**

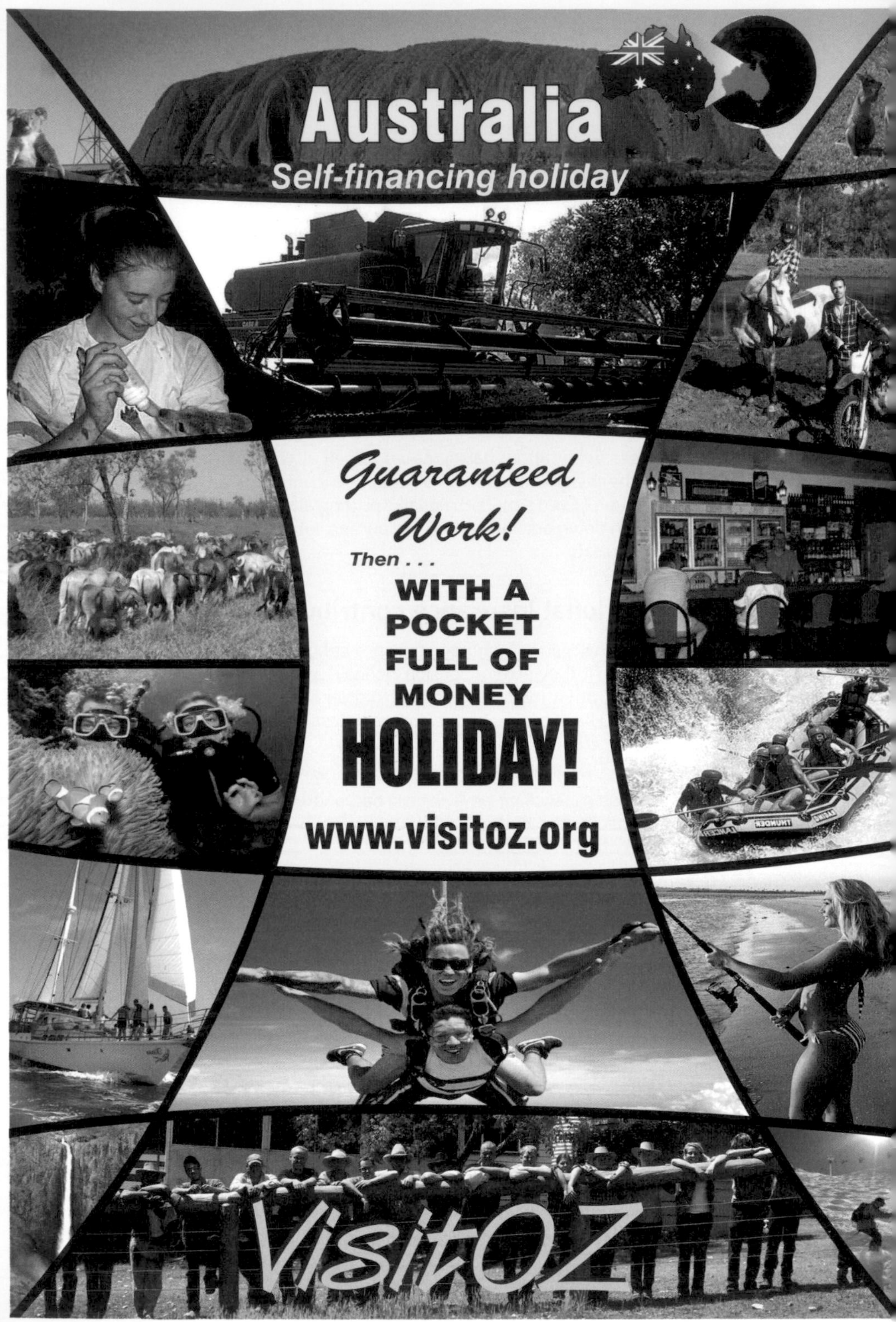
Australia
Self-financing holiday
Guaranteed
Work!
Then . . .
WITH A
POCKET
FULL OF
MONEY
HOLIDAY!
www.visitoz.org
VisitOZ

Earning on your career break

It may even be possible to part-fund your career break by using your skills on volunteer and other projects.

United Nations Volunteers sometimes pay modest living or travel costs, for people with the skills they need for particular volunteer projects.

Have a look at their website: **www.unv.org/how-to-volunteer.html**

If you wanted a 'taster' before taking the big step of leaving the country, UNV also has a scheme for online volunteers, where you can become involved in worthwhile projects, using your computer in your spare time, at home:
www.onlinevolunteering.org/en/vol/index.html

There are also organisations that can help with funding for specific projects: the Winston Churchill Memorial Trust (WCMT) is one of them. It provides grants for people wanting to travel abroad and work on special projects that they cannot find funding for elsewhere and, crucially, then use the experience to benefit others in their home communities. Applicants must be British citizens, resident in the UK and must apply by October each year.

The Trust awards travelling fellowships to individuals of all ages wanting to pursue projects that are interesting and unusual. Categories cover a range of topics over a three-year cycle. Roughly 100 are awarded each year and they usually provide funds for four to eight weeks.

The Trust emphasises that fellowships are *not* granted to gappers looking to fund academic studies, attend courses or take part in volunteer placements arranged by other organisations.

The advice is to study the WCMT website for examples of projects that have been funded, as they are very wide-ranging and will help you come up with your own ideas.

To find out more you can contact the Trust at:

29 Great Smith Street, London SW1P 3BL
Tel: +44(0) 207 799 1660
Fax: +44(0) 207 799 1667
Email: office@wcmt.org.uk
www.wcmt.org.uk

Tax issues

If you go to live or work abroad, and become non-resident in the UK, you might still have to pay UK tax – but *only* on your income earned in the UK (savings, dividends, rental income *etc*). If you do need to pay, you may need to complete a self-assessment tax return.

This website explains the tax implications for all the circumstances in which you might be abroad, whether temporarily or permanently. It's particularly useful if you're thinking of renting out your home:
www.direct.gov.uk/en/BritonsLivingAbroad/Moneyabroad/index.htm

What about the house?

Some mortgage lenders may allow a payment holiday of up to six months without affecting your scheme.

Another option might be to rent out your house. You may need to check terms and conditions for subletting with your mortgage lender, but it can be a good way of covering the mortgage costs while you are away.

As it is your home and you need to be sure it will be looked after while you are away, the above reinforces our advice that, if you decide to rent, it's worth using an accommodation agent to take care of things and make sure you comply with all the regulations.

It would also be wise to check with the Inland Revenue to see whether you are eligible for a tax exemption certificate (on your rental income), which should be given to the accommodation agent.

When letting a house there are some rules to abide by and some safety certificates you must have if you're going to take this route. Another must is to tell your insurance company what you're planning.

Another possibility is a house swap

Obviously you'd have to be careful in arranging this and in satisfying yourself that you're happy with the people you're planning to swap with, but we've found a number of agencies that can help you.

The following arrange holiday swaps in many countries around the world and have plenty of advice on how to go about it. You have to sign up as a member to access some information:

www.homelink.org – annual membership is £115. It has regional websites in 30 countries and has been operating for 50 years.

www.intervac.co.uk – annual membership is £49.99.

www.homebase-hols.com – annual membership is £29.

Household contents: storage

Two things to think about if you really want to clear your house before renting:

· Do you really want to add this to your list of 'things to do' before you go?

· Can you afford it?

You would need a 20ft container for the contents of an average house. Most containers are 'self-service' so you would have to pack, move and unpack yourself and therefore need to add the costs of van rental and transport to the container rental costs.

You would also have to arrange your own insurance, but normally you can extend your household contents insurance to cover property on secured sites.

National removals and storage companies also provide container storage on managed sites and can sell you the packing materials and boxes you might need as well. Prices vary according to the distance from the storage site, size of container and length of time and some self storage companies do not charge VAT on household storage, but others do. It is worth bearing in mind that storage alone for a year would come to over £1000.

But remember, on top of that you have to add the packing, loading, removal and unloading costs at each end of your career break. On average the process can cost £300-£400 more than an ordinary house move and prices vary depending on whether your dates fall into peak season for house removals – such as children's school holidays and the peak times of year for house sales.

What about the kids?

There's some evidence that another growing trend is for families to take a gap together, particularly while the children are young.

While it's virtually impossible to get reliable figures, there's a lot of anecdotal evidence from gap providers.

Sarah Brown, of Kaya Responsible Travel, told us: "We've also had an increase in interest from families who want their children to see the 'real world' and really experience new cultures. One family even joined us in the Galapagos for six weeks as part of a year-long trip."

Phil Murray, director of gapadvice.org, says he has been asked about whether it's advisable to take children on gap-years: "The view is that as long as the children are safe, have access to medical facilities and their education development is not harmed, family gap-years can have very beneficial outcomes. Children are exposed to a variety of mind-broadening situations and their overall development can be very positive."

He adds that some gap-year companies might have a minimum age limit of eight years and that it's important to clear the break with the children's school.

my gap-year
Jean Ashbury

Retired teacher Jean Ashbury travelled with The Book Bus to a school in Rajasthan to help support learning English as a foreign language...

White cranes lined up on the school wall and eyed their insect breakfasts in the cow manure below. In the field beyond, camels the colour of dark chocolate foraged in the tops of acacia trees. Beside them, I could see the corkscrew horns of endangered black bucks and skittish chinkara deer (Indian gazelles) as they grazed in the scrub beside nilgai antelopes. In the playground a cow headed towards a classroom. And in the rafters above my head swifts flitted back and forth nest-building with twigs and scrap.

I sat on the steps outside a classroom with Haseena tucked in the crook of my arm. "Baloo," she said in Hindi and pointed to the cover of the story book in my hand. "Yes. A bear," I replied. "Yes yes," she said dismissively. "B-e-a-r ... bear."

I was at Haseena's school in a small village in Mandore near Jodhpur in Rajasthan. Four Book Bus volunteers and I were working on a pilot project to support learning English as a foreign language, and we were using favourite stories that British children read. Our aim was to teach with stories children enjoy instead of setting dry vocabulary and grammar exercises.

The school, big enough for a hundred pupils, was typical of the five we visited: low brick buildings, exteriors painted with the colours of the Indian flag, basic classrooms with blackboard and chalk, no resources to speak of, benches and desks for older children, and floor blankets for the younger ones.

After a prayer to Saraswati, the goddess of knowledge, the eager crowd of pupils and parents welcomed us with singing, dancing, and handshaking fit for celebrities. At the school, teachers draped marigold garlands round our necks, daubed vermilion tikkas on our foreheads and placed brown sugar on our tongues. Then there was more dancing. And speeches to show how much they valued our presence as 'ambassadors of English'. We stood looking sheepish with our canvas shopping bags full of pencils, crayons, paper, string, glue, scissors, sticky paper, story books...

After a tentative start, I fell into the days like the idealistic young teacher I used to be making resources every evening and discussing with my friends the nitty-gritty of the next day's plans. Every morning, a cheeky child would wink at me during prayers, but stand to attention to sing the national anthem and I'd wonder about that mischievous gene all children seemed to have.

"Kal milenge," said Haseena as she waved at the jeep taking us away from school.

"See you tomorrow," I said, and suddenly felt impatient for the morning.

For more information about The Book Bus, see **Chapter 6 - Volunteering Abroad** or visit **www.thebookbus.org**.

Whether to take the children out of school is really up to you as parents. Much will depend on the length of time you plan to be away and the point your children are at in their education.

Essentially you need to balance the effects of taking a child out of school against the benefits of the 'education' they will get from seeing something of the world. You also need to think through health and medical issues, but that may mean nothing more than carrying essential medical supplies with you, as all travellers are advised to do when travelling abroad.

It's also possible that you can get your child into a local school for some of the time they are away, or you can organise some basic study for them with the help of their school while you are travelling.

The official view from the Department for Education is that, ultimately, it is down to the parents, but that they should talk it through with their child's school or local authority.

It is crucial that it's cleared with your child's school and headteacher, who has to authorise it, if you don't want to face court action by the local authority and a possible hefty fine for taking a child out of school during term time. But parents who have done it, even with very small children, say that it has been a very worthwhile experience and brought them closer to their kids. A few gap organisations are now providing family gap volunteer placements.

Safety precautions

You will find a great deal of advice on all aspects of planning your gap in **Chapter 1 – Tips for travellers**, as well as in-country advice and what to expect when you get back. Tips for travellers is relevant to all travellers, whatever their age. We also cover the importance of getting the right kind of travel insurance and the questions you need answered in **Chapter 2 – Finance**.

But there are some other issues that perhaps might be more important for older travellers to consider. You almost certainly have more in the way of assets than someone straight from school or university – things like a house, insurance and pension schemes; valuable personal property.

In the unlikely event of something going wrong, it makes sense to ensure your affairs are in order and to have someone you trust authorised to take care of your affairs until you can do so for yourself. It will make things that much easier for those back home, who may be coping with the trauma of a loved one in hospital overseas, if they have some idea of how you want your affairs to be handled.

You should consider two things – making a will and possibly appointing someone with legal power of attorney.

Making a will

Points to remember when making a will:

- It doesn't have to be expensive.
- It can be amended later if your circumstances change.
- You can make it clear what you want to happen to your property.
- It prevents family squabbles.
- It allows you to choose executors you can trust.

You should:

- Give yourself time to think.
- Use a professional, preferably one experienced specifically with will preparation.
- Make sure you can update it without large additional charges.
- Make sure there's an opt out from executor or probate services if you don't need them – by the time the will is needed, which could be many years away, it may be that someone in the family, who was too young when you made it, who can deal with it.

Power of attorney

Many people choose to make an informal arrangement with a family member to take care of things at home while they're travelling, but if you were to need someone authorised to pay bills at home or liaise with your travel insurance company, it might make sense to have a proper, formal arrangement in place before you go to give them the authority to act on your behalf.

You might be able to arrange with your bank to add them as a signatory to your account, in case it should be necessary, as long as you feel comfortable that the person you choose will make the right decisions about your money if you can't.

A more secure way is to appoint a power of attorney, but be warned it's a lengthy process, which can take up to five months to process. Until the documents are properly registered, whoever you appoint cannot act for you.

There's no fast track procedure on compassionate grounds and the Public Guardians' Office website says: "If there are no problems with the LPA (Lasting Power of Attorney) or application, we are typically returning the registered LPA in around nine weeks from the date of receipt. If there are any problems with the LPA or application, we are currently informing the applicant within two weeks of receiving the application."

Getting it right when there are at least 30 pages of forms per person is no joke; and, if you're a couple, each one of you has to fill out a set. So to avoid delays and mistakes (with possible charging of repeat fees) it makes sense to get professional advice from a specialist.

The process is administered by the Office of the Public Guardian, which charges a fee of £150. But compare that with having someone professional look after your property and personal welfare. It can cost as much as £1500 for a couple. To find out more about the new legislation go to: **www.publicguardian.gov.uk**

Please see the directory pages starting on page 283 for information on companies and organisations offering trips and opportunities for career breakers and older gappers.

Travelling and accommodation

Travelling and accommodation

Getting about

Planes

The internet is invaluable when searching for ticket information, timetables, prices and special offers, whether you're travelling by air, sea, train or bus.

Because the internet gives customers so much information to choose from, travel companies have to compete harder to get your business. The internet shows you what flexibility is possible, so you could find your decision-making turned upside down.

When booking flights, have a look at special offers for round-the-world tickets first, find out how far in advance you can book, and then plan your destinations to fit.

If one of your destinations has a fixed arrival and departure date – for example if you're signed up for a voluntary project – you could try asking for a route tailor-made for you using the prices you find on the web.

Make sure you check out the company making an offer on the web before you use internet booking procedures (does it have a verifiable address and phone number?). Remember, under EU law companies must publish a contact address on their website. So, unless the company in question is a household name, or you are able to locate a legitimate address via another source, think twice before handing over your hard-earned cash.

It's important – as ever! – to read the Terms and Conditions to see what you're paying for and whether you can get your money back before you agree to buy – just as you would outside the virtual world.

What to watch out for

Once you've booked a flight online, especially if you do it through an agent such as **www.lastminute.com**, rather than direct with the airline, you may have to pay extra fees for rescheduling, not to mention date restrictions if you need to change the date. Unless you have a good, solid reason for cancelling – and most airlines define such reasons very narrowly – you also risk losing the money you've paid.

As we mention in **Chapter 1**, increasingly airlines are covering their additional fuel costs and taxes by adding charges for different services, like inflight baggage storage, airport duty, seats next to each other (if you're not travelling alone). You need to have your wits about you when you're going through the online booking forms as these extras can add a substantial amount to the final total, making that budget deal significantly more expensive than you originally thought (up to £100 at best and almost equalling the flight cost at worst).

Remember, the ads usually say 'flights *from* £XXX' and that's your clue to watch out for extras.

Bargain flights: scheduled airlines often offer discount fares for students under 26 so don't rule them out. Other cheap flights are advertised regularly in the newspapers and on the web. All sorts of travel agents can fix you up with multi-destination tickets, and student travel specialists often know where to find the best deals for gap-year students.

It's worth checking whether a particular flight is cheaper if you book direct with the airline – and if you are using a student travel card you may find that you have to do it this way to get the discount, rather than using one of the budget deal websites.

Above all, travel is an area where searching the internet for good deals should be top of your list – though it works best for single-destination trips rather than complex travel routes.

Lydia Rosling, of The Dragon Trip, which offers backpacking trips to China, also has some extra advice: "Plan to change your plans. Make sure your flight dates are flexible for a minimal cost. You may well want to extend your trip if you fall in love with China – and there is a large chance you will!"

Trains

Travelling by train is one of the best ways to see a country – and if you travel on an overnight sleeper it can be as quick as a plane. India's train network is world-famous and an absolute must experience! But don't think you can't use trains in other parts of the world. What follows is just a taster.

my gap-year
Tom Locker

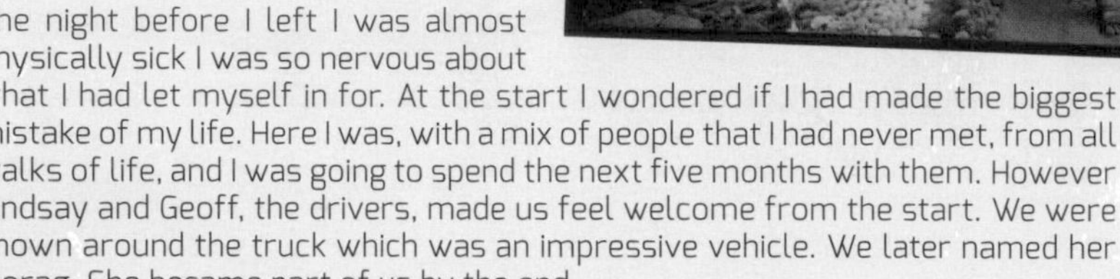

Tom Locker went on an overlanding adventure in Africa with Dragoman after leaving university...

The night before I left I was almost physically sick I was so nervous about what I had let myself in for. At the start I wondered if I had made the biggest mistake of my life. Here I was, with a mix of people that I had never met, from all walks of life, and I was going to spend the next five months with them. However Lindsay and Geoff, the drivers, made us feel welcome from the start. We were shown around the truck which was an impressive vehicle. We later named her Morag. She became part of us by the end.

We travelled across the desert with a local guide, Achmed. It got so hot at times that Morag would overheat so Geoff or Lins would have to put the heating on full to cool the engine. Not comfortable at 50C! To cross the sand we had to deflate the tyres but would still get bogged down. You would feel Morag lurch and we would all jump out. Teamwork was natural. Some would dig behind the wheels while others removed the sand mats. They would go under the wheels and we would repeat this until Morag hit firmer ground. This is when I started to bond with the others.

The desert was a moving place to be. We would camp next to great sand dunes that we would climb in the evenings to watch the sunset in silence. After, we would build a fire and have supper, with some cold beers from Morag's fridge.

It was the wild camping I loved. Something which sounds so scary to do in Africa actually became a highlight. Each night when we had finished supper, we chatted around the campfire, played some drinking games, and went to sleep. I gave up with the tent quite early on in the trip and just slept under the stars in my sleeping bag, my clothes as my pillow. This is how I slept for the whole trip.

In towns we would leave our camp and head into the centres, visiting bars and trying out our local language skills. Everyone we met seemed to be happy and content. The children would swarm around you with flashing smiles. We got lost in the souks, ate in the night markets, bartered for souvenirs – I come from rural England and had never experienced anything like it.

One of my fondest memories was when we came across an isolated beach dotted with palm trees and a sparse camp site. We were the only people there and it was paradise. We took a vote and stayed there for a few extra days (overlanding gives you the ultimate in flexibility as you are kind of your own bosses). The night swimming was special. The sea was full of fluorescent creatures. When you ran your hands through the water it would light up so you can imagine what swimming was like. We were sorry to leave.

I can honestly say that this trip was by far the best experience of my life. Far and away the best decision I have ever made!

For more information about Dragoman, visit **www.dragoman.com**

Inter-railing – Europe and a bit beyond

If you want to visit a lot of countries, one of the best ways to travel is by train on an InterRail ticket. With InterRail you have the freedom of the rail networks of Europe (and a bit beyond), allowing you to go as you please in 28 countries.

From the northern lights of Sweden to the kasbahs of Morocco, you can call at all the stops. InterRail takes you from city centre to city centre – avoiding airport hassles, ticket queues and traffic jams, and giving you more time to make the most of your visit. Passes are available for all ages, but you need to have lived in Europe for at least six months.

Overnight trains are available on most of the major routes, saving on accommodation costs, allowing you to go to sleep in one country and wake up in another.

Supplements apply so ask when you book. You will have to pay extra to travel on some express intercity trains or the Eurostar. Most major stations such as Paris, Brussels, Amsterdam and Rome have washing facilities and left luggage.

The InterRail One Country Pass can be used for the following countries:

Austria, Belgium, Bulgaria, Croatia, Czech Republic, Denmark, Finland, France, Germany, Great Britain, Greece, Hungary, Italy, Luxembourg, Macedonia (FYR), Netherlands, Norway, Poland, Portugal, Republic of Ireland, Romania, Russia, Serbia, Slovakia, Slovenia, Spain, Sweden, Switzerland and Turkey.

The alternative choice is the InterRail Global Pass, which is valid in all participating InterRail countries. Available for several lengths of travel, it is ideal for gappers wanting to explore several, or even all, European countries in their year out.

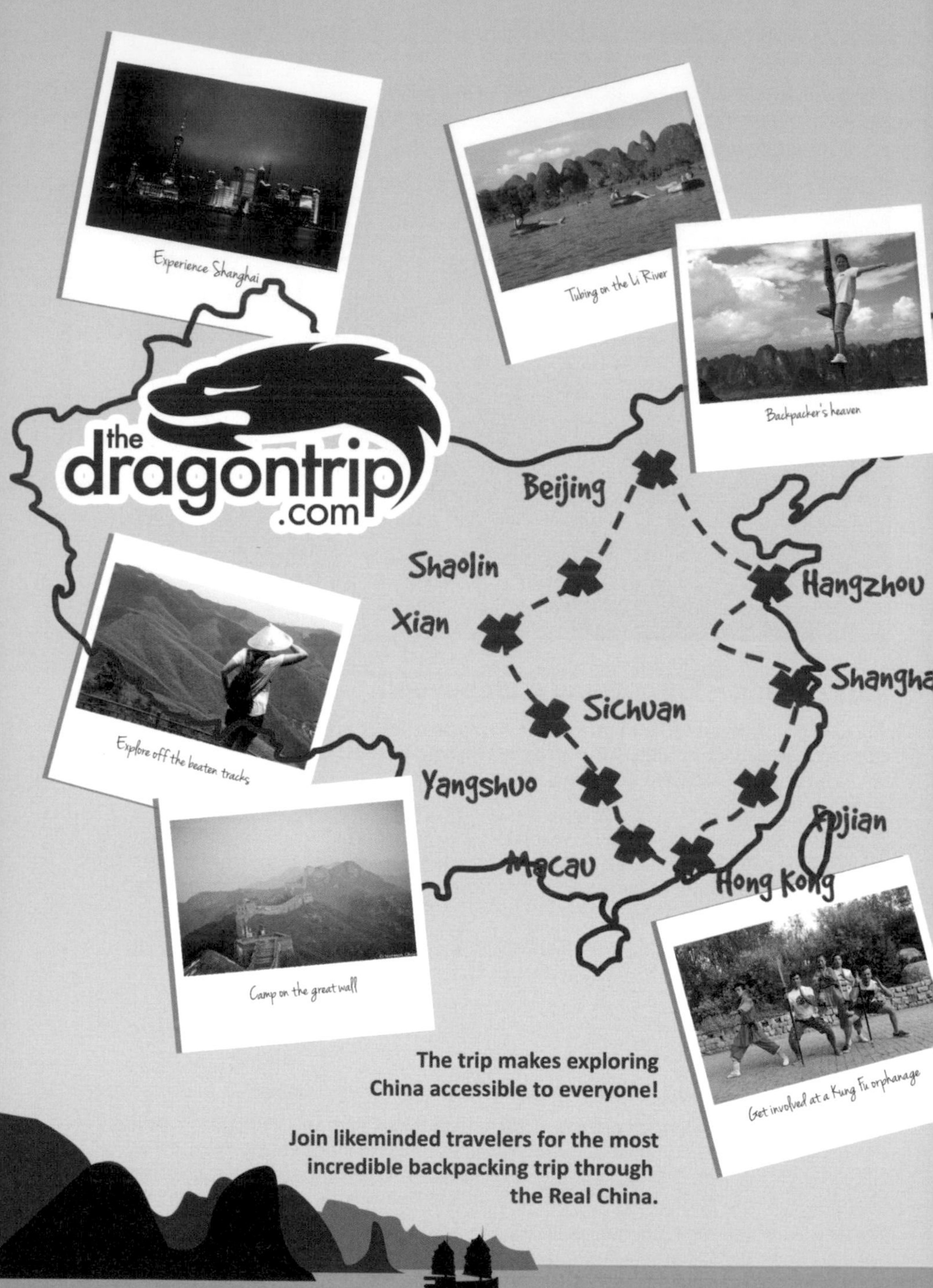

Experience Shanghai
Tubing on the Li River
Backpacker's heaven
the dragontrip .com
Beijing
Shaolin
Hangzhou
Xian
Shangha
Sichuan
Explore off the beaten tracks
Yangshuo
Fujian
Macau
Hong Kong
Camp on the great wall
Get involved at a Kung Fu orphanage
The trip makes exploring
China accessible to everyone!
Join likeminded travelers for the most
incredible backpacking trip through
the Real China.

One Country Pass prices

Second class prices vary by the country and range from £33 (under 26)/£51 (over 26) for three days in one month, to £74/£116 for eight days in one month in Bulgaria; to £181/£289 in France.

Belgium, The Netherlands and Luxembourg are combined as the InterRail Benelux Pass. For Greece you have the option to order a Greece Plus Pass, which includes ferry crossings to and from Italy.

Global Pass

For second class travel, over 22 continuous days, prices range from £276 (under 26) to £414 (over 26) and are valid from five days to one month. For further details on prices and how to buy an InterRail pass, visit their website: **www.interrail.eu.**

Eurostar

The Eurostar train is a quick, easy and relatively cheap way to get to Europe. You can get from London to Calais from £69, and the trains are comfortable and run frequently. Tickets can be purchased online at **www.eurostar.com**, in an approved travel agency, or at any Eurostar train station.

Trans-Siberian Express

If you're looking for a train adventure – and you have a generous budget to play with – what about the Trans-Siberian Express? You could do a 14-day Moscow-Beijing trip. Do this as a 'full-on' or a 'no-frills' package.

You can also choose from a range of other trips lasting from nine to 26 days. On top of this you will need some money for food and drink, visas, airfare *etc*.

For China, Russia and Mongolia you'll need to have a visa for your passport to allow you into each country. Contact each relevant embassy to find out what type of visa you will need (*ie* visitors or transit). It's probably easiest to arrange for all your train tickets, visas and hotel accommodation through a specialist agency, about six months before you leave. Your journey will be a lot easier if you have all your paperwork in order before you leave – although it will cost you more to do it this way.

The trains can be pretty basic, varying according to which line you're travelling on and which country owns the train. On some trains you can opt to upgrade to first class. This should give you your own cabin with shower, wash basin and more comfort – however, although you'll be more comfortable, you may find it more interesting back in second class with all the other backpackers and traders.

If you're travelling in autumn or winter make sure you take warm clothes – the trains have rather unreliable heating. If you travel in late November/December you may freeze into a solid block of ice, but it will be snowing by then and the views will be spectacular. Travelling in September will be warmer and a bit cheaper.

If you want to read about it before you go, try the *Trans-Siberian Handbook* by Bryn Thomas. It's updated frequently and it has details about the towns you'll be passing through, and includes the timetables.

There are several websites you can look up, but **www.trans-siberian.co.uk** is one of the best out there. For cheaper options you could also try Travel Nation, which has a useful page of FAQs on the Trans-Siberian Moscow to Beijing rail trip: **www.travel-nation.co.uk/trans-siberian-train/faqs.htm**

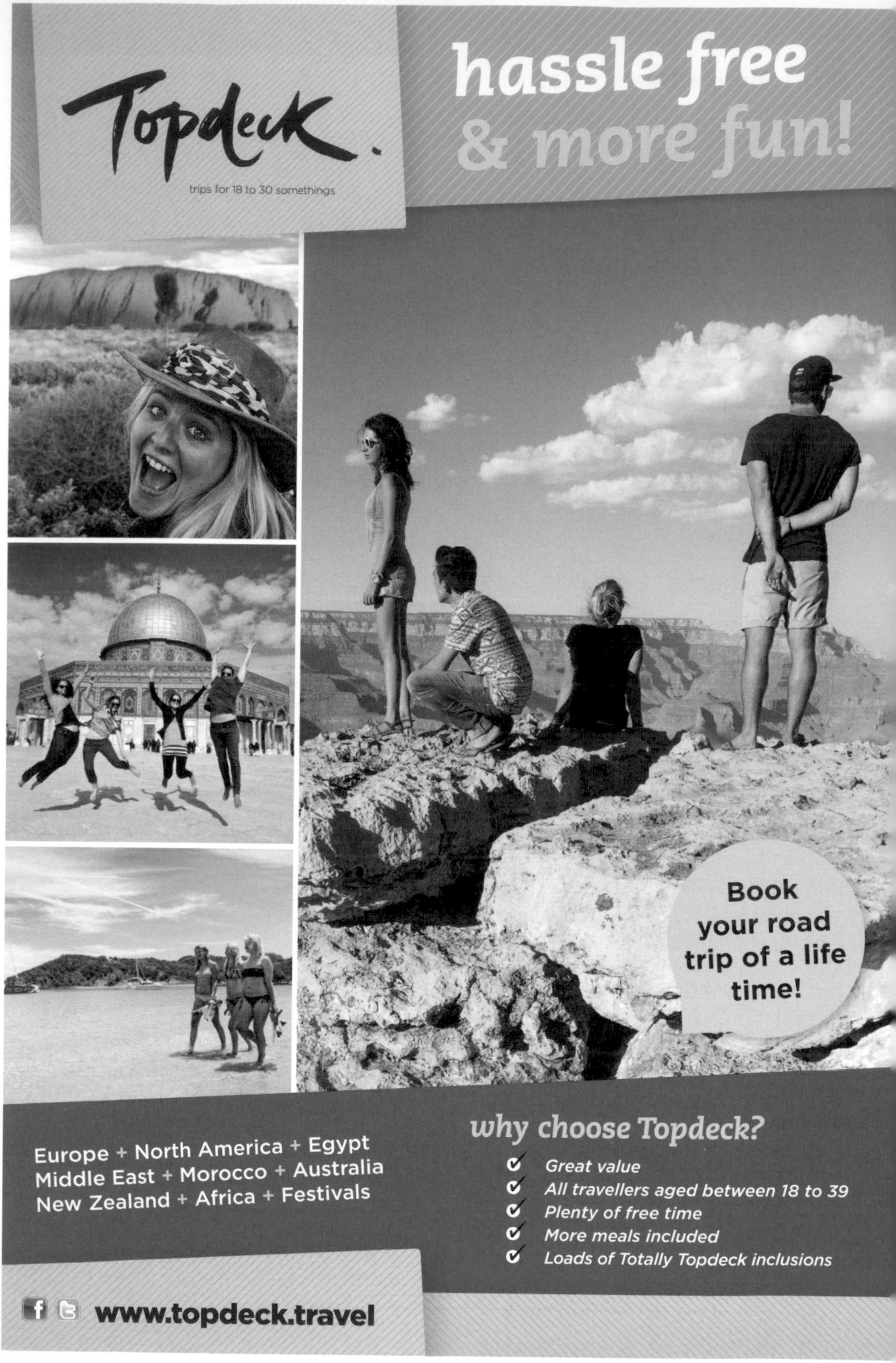
Topdeck.
trips for 18 to 30 somethings
hassle free
& more fun!
Book your road trip of a life time!
Europe + North America + Egypt
Middle East + Morocco + Australia
New Zealand + Africa + Festivals
why choose Topdeck?
Great value
All travellers aged between 18 to 39
Plenty of free time
More meals included
Loads of Totally Topdeck inclusions
www.topdeck.travel

India and the rest of the world

Tell anyone you're going to India and you'll invariably be told you must try a train journey. Indian trains are the most amazing adventure – with all sorts of extras - like a meal included in the price on the Shatabdi Express intercity commuter trains, or the vendors who wander the length of the train with their buckets of snacks, tea or coffee, calling their wares "chai, chai, chai" as they go.

But Indian trains get booked up weeks or months in advance, especially if you're planning to travel during any major public festival like Diwali, which is a national holiday. You need a seat or berth reservation for any long-distance journey on an Indian train; you cannot simply turn up and hop on. Bookings now open 90 days in advance. Reservations are now completely computerised and a tourist quota gives foreigners and IndRail pass holders preferential treatment. Go to: **www.irctc.co.in**

There's also a unique reservation system. After a train becomes fully booked, a set number of places in each class are sold as 'Reservation Against Cancellation' or RAC. After all RAC places have been allocated, further prospective passengers are 'wait-listed'. When passengers cancel, people on the RAC list are promoted to places on the train and wait-listed passengers are promoted to RAC.

If you want to try your hand at organising your own train travel in India you can get a copy of the famous Trains at a Glance from any railway station in India for Rs 35 (50p) or you can download it as a PDF from: **www.seat61.com/India.htm**

But beware, it contains every train timetable (94 in all) for the sub-continent and it's very long.

Trains get booked up days, even weeks in advance so be sure to book ahead, **www.cleartrip.com** is an excellent, secure site to do this through.

The Man in Seat 61 is possibly the most incredibly comprehensive train and ship travel website ever. It literally covers the world from India to Latin America, Africa and south-east Asia. It's not only about times, costs and booking, it goes into some detail about the kinds of conditions you can expect.

It's written by Mark Smith, an ex-British Rail employee and former stationmaster at Charing Cross. He has travelled the world by train and ship and it's a personal site run as a hobby, so he pledges it will always remain freely available: **www.seat61.com**

Buses and coaches

Getting on a bus or coach in a foreign country, especially if you don't speak the language, can be a voyage of discovery in itself. UK bus timetables can be indecipherable, but try one in Patagonia!

Get help from a local you trust, hotel/hostel staff, or the local police station if all else fails. In developing countries, locals think nothing of transporting their livestock by public transport, so be prepared to sit next to a chicken! That said, some buses and coaches can be positively luxurious and they do tend to be cheaper than trains.

The 'Old Grey Dog'

Greyhound buses have air conditioning, tinted windows and a loo on board, as well as a strict no smoking policy. Greyhound offers Hostelling International members a discount on regular one-way and round-trip fares. They have a Discovery Pass, which

my gap-year Vicki Milne

Vicki Milne went backpacking to China with The Dragon Trip...

Travelling China with The Dragon Trip was an incredible experience and one I will never forget. I am not the sort of person who usually does tours and have travelled in Europe on my own, but I signed up to The Dragon Trip mainly because of the language barrier.

The team had a really exciting 25-day trip that's designed for backpackers who want to experience the 'real' China; travelling on public transport and eating the local cuisine. The guides were such great fun and had an action packed plan for each day but were also totally flexible to suit us. They enabled us to experience more than just touristy areas with English translations.

Travelling with a group of 12 people from all around the world made the trip even more cultural, I learnt a lot from them and made some awesome friends.

After entering mainland China from Hong Kong we got a night bus – a bus with fully flat beds which surprisingly rocked everyone to sleep even through the driver's constant horn beeping! To wake up in Yangshuo, one of the most beautiful places I have ever seen, was magical. Karst peaks jut into the landscape for as far as you could see - it was like something from *Avatar*! The rest of the trip did not let me down, every day there was so much to see from beautiful scenery to buzzing cities and from ancient farming techniques to ultra modern technology and skyscrapers; no corner of Chinese culture was left undiscovered. Some of my most memorable moments were waking up to sunrise on the Great Wall, bamboo rafting in Yanshuo, watching Panda's eating bamboo for breakfast and one particularly epic night out with the group in Shanghai!

In total we travelled 5607km around China and the vast majority of this was done on night trains, which left the days available for exploring! Although night trains were a culture shock at first, it soon became the place where we could look forward to the best sleep.

The guides also became invaluable friends who taught us about Chinese culture, showed us the best food which varied in the different regions and they came most useful helping me bargain at the markets!

For more information about The Dragon Trip, visit **www.thedragontrip.com**

allows seven, 15, 30 and 60 days unlimited travel. There's the usual 10% discount for ISIC and Euro 26 ID cardholders (go to **www.discoverypass.com**).

The bus company operates outside America too, with Greyhound Pioneer Australia (**www.greyhound.com.au**) and for South Africa there's Greyhound Coach Lines Africa (**www.greyhound.co.za**). Check out their websites or contact them for information about their various ticket options.

See also **www.yha.com.au** (Australia) and **www.norcalhostels.org** (USA).
Greyhound Lines, Inc
PO Box 660691, MS 470, Dallas, TX 75266-0691, USA
Tel: 214-849-8966;
www.greyhound.com

Student gappers could also check out **www.aboutistc.org** (International Student Travel Confederation) for useful information and advice on special travel deals and discounts – planes, trains, coaches and ferries. Other useful sources of information are:

www.statravel.co.uk
www.thebigchoice.com/Travel

Touring

Travelling as part of a tour – usually as part of a group of like-minded gappers, on a coach especially fitted out for the task – can prove a fun, action-packed adventure. It doesn't have to mean chugging around the tourist sights, staring at the wonders of the world passing by your window. A tour can mean anything from full-on adventure trips across the desert to smaller, more intimate tours along a specific theme, such as vineyards or culinary hotspots.

Booking a place on a tour can be a great way to meet new people and shouldn't be dismissed just because some backpackers see it as 'the easy option'. If you do your research and book with the right company, you'll find yourself with a small bunch of like-minded people and a tour leader who should know your destination's history and culture inside out.

A good leader will also have contacts in the local community and can get you into local hotels and restaurants – leaving you to enjoy your travels rather than worrying about finding a place to sleep the night.

Scout around for long enough and you'll find a tour to suit most tastes, from smaller groups of travellers who are serious about getting off the beaten track to meet the locals and experiencing their way of life, to younger, noisier groups looking for a fun, sociable way to explore a country or region.

Overlanding

Overlanding involves travelling in groups on a rough-and-ready truck. Vehicles come fully equipped with a kitchen and tents – perfect for both seasoned backpackers and first-timers. Companies such as Oasis Overland and Dragoman have vast experience in offering such trips.

We asked Oasis Overland to help us explain more:

"Overlanding is, not surprisingly, all about journeying overland and taking the time to experience the places you are passing through. These are adventurous trips that

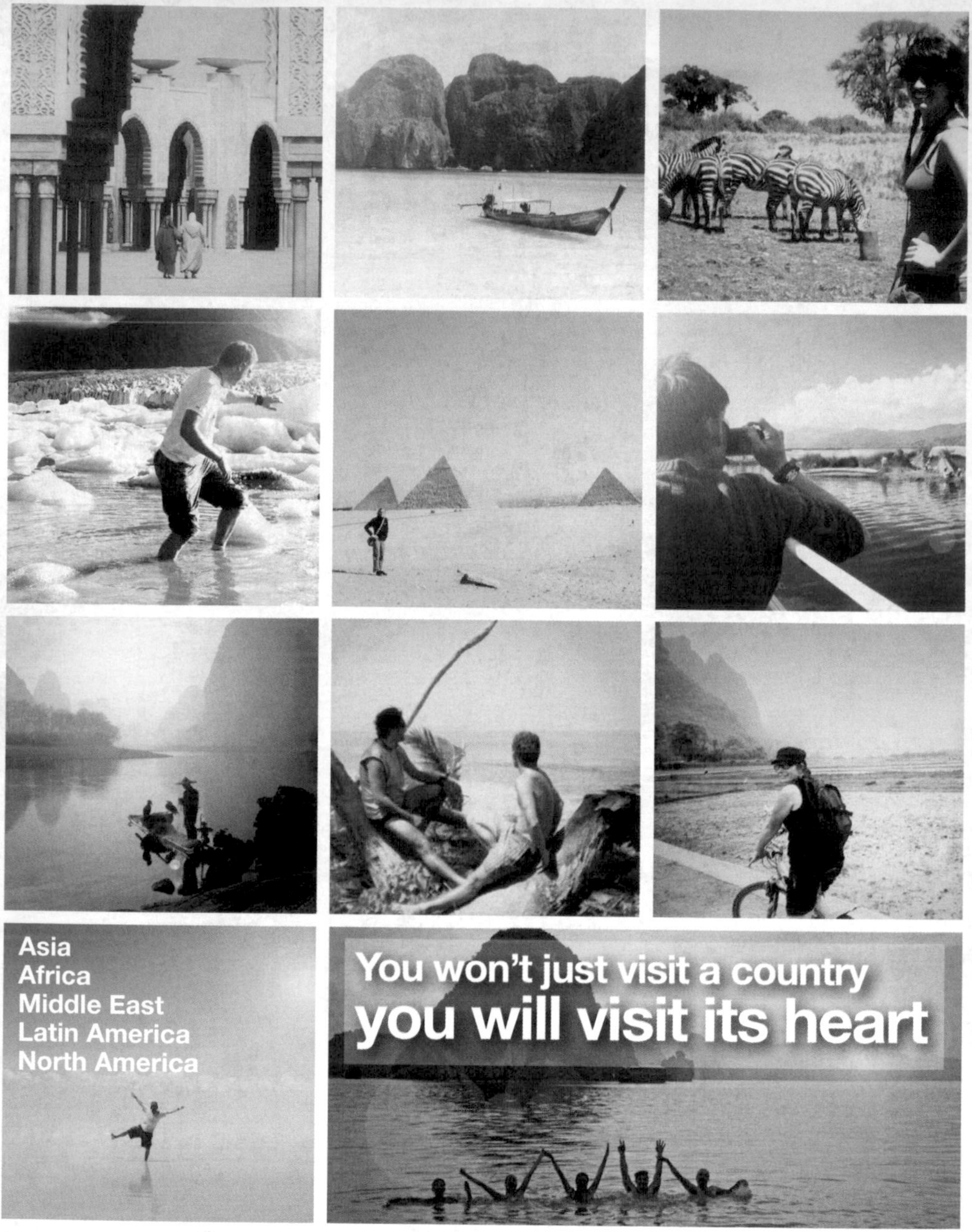

often go off the beaten track. It usually involves travelling in a truck that's been converted to carry passengers and along the way you camp or stay in hostels. Overland trucks are usually self-sufficient carrying tents, cooking equipment and food and everyone in the group mucks in with cooking, shopping at local markets, collecting firewood and setting up camp. There are overlanding opportunities around the world."

Why overlanding?

Some places can be difficult or expensive to get to under your own steam and an overland trip can provide a cheaper, hassle-free way of getting there. Being on a self-sufficient truck can mean that you get to stop and spend a night in the Sahara Desert or on the Altiplano, instead of passing through to the next town. Overlanding is a good option if you don't want to travel on your own or are apprehensive about being away from home for the first time as you're travelling in a group.

Benefits of overlanding

As well as the usual benefits of travel (broadening your horizons and your mind, learning self-sufficiency) by the time you finish your overland trip you will have gained great experience of team working as well as living with a group of people in close quarters and generally learning consideration for others. Overland trips are not hand-held holidays – you may have to organise your own flights and accommodation before joining the trip as well helping with the day-to-day running of the trip which will prove your organisational skills. Great stuff for your CV!

Practical skills you may pick up include camp craft (where not to pitch your tent, fire lighting *etc*, cooking for a large group of people) and languages in Spanish or French speaking parts of the world.

Oasis Overland, The Marsh, Henstridge, Templecombe BA8 0TF
T: +44 (0) 1963 363400
E: info@oasisoverland.co.uk W: www.oasisoverland.co.uk

Come and join us on one of our overland adventure trips and we promise to take you to some of the most awesome and spectacular places in the world. We believe overlanding is one of the most inspirational and rewarding forms of travel that you will experience in your life!

If you dream of travelling through Africa, South America, Central Asia and the Middle East, then look no further than Oasis Overland. Our trips are always adventurous, sometimes unpredictable and not your average package holiday.

* Adventures range from 8 days to 38 weeks
* Travel by custom-built expedition truck
* Stay in campsites, hostels or out under the stars
* Get involved - campfire cooking, shop at local markets, collect the firewood

Along the way you can hike the Inca trail in Peru, come face to face with Mountain Gorillas in Uganda, trek the Tien Shan Mountains in Kyrgyzstan or bungy jump at Victoria Falls - to name just a few!

We have been specializing in providing overland adventure travel for more than 14 years and our reliable, friendly and personal service is why our travellers come back year after year!

There are plenty of opportunities to step outside your comfort zone on an overland trip. For many, just travelling to a new country with a group of 20 strangers is an adventure in itself but if that isn't enough, on a longer expedition you may spend the day digging the truck out of a huge, muddy pothole or carrying sandmats for the truck to drive over in the desert and then camp out in the bush with only a bucket of water for a shower!

Car

Another popular option is to travel by car. It means you have somewhere to sleep if you get stuck for a bed for the night, you save money on train fares and you don't have to lug your rucksack into cafés.

If you are considering it, you need to know the motoring regulations of the countries you'll be visiting – they vary from country to country. Check that you are insured to drive abroad and that this is clearly shown on the documentation you carry with you.

The AA advises that you carry your vehicle insurance, vehicle registration documents and a current tax disc in the car and, of course, take your driving licence with you. If you still have an old paper licence you might want to consider getting it updated to a photo licence before you go, but make sure you leave enough time for this – the DVLA isn't known for its speedy processing.

It is also advisable to take an International Driving Permit (IDP) as not all countries accept the British driving licence. In theory you don't need one in any of the EU member states, but the AA recommends having an IDP if you intend to drive in any country other than the UK – and it's better than getting into trouble and being fined for driving without a valid licence.

An IDP is valid for 12 months and can be applied for up to three months in advance. The AA and RAC issue the permits – you must be over 18 and hold a current, full, UK driving licence that has been valid for two years. You'll need to fill in a form and provide your UK driving licence, passport and a recent passport-sized photo of yourself, which you can take to a participating Post Office. Be warned, you need to allow at least ten working days for processing, so don't try and do this at the last minute.

The AA website has loads of info about the permit, and driving abroad in general, and you can download the application form here: **www.theaa.com/getaway/idp/motidp002.html**

It's a good idea to put your car in for a service a couple of weeks before you leave and, unless you're a mechanic, it's also worth getting breakdown cover specifically for your trip abroad. Any of the major recovery companies such as the AA, RAC or Green Flag offer this service. Remember, without cover, if you end up stuck on the side of the road it could be an expensive experience.

The RAC recommends taking a first aid kit, fire extinguisher, warning triangle, headlamp beam reflectors and spare lamp bulbs. These are all required by law in many countries and make sense anyway. **www.rac.co.uk**

The Foreign and Commonwealth Office has put together a handy road tool at **www.fcowidget.com**, which allows you to select your chosen country and be directed to the local regulations for your trip.

And here are the FCO's key tips for driving abroad:

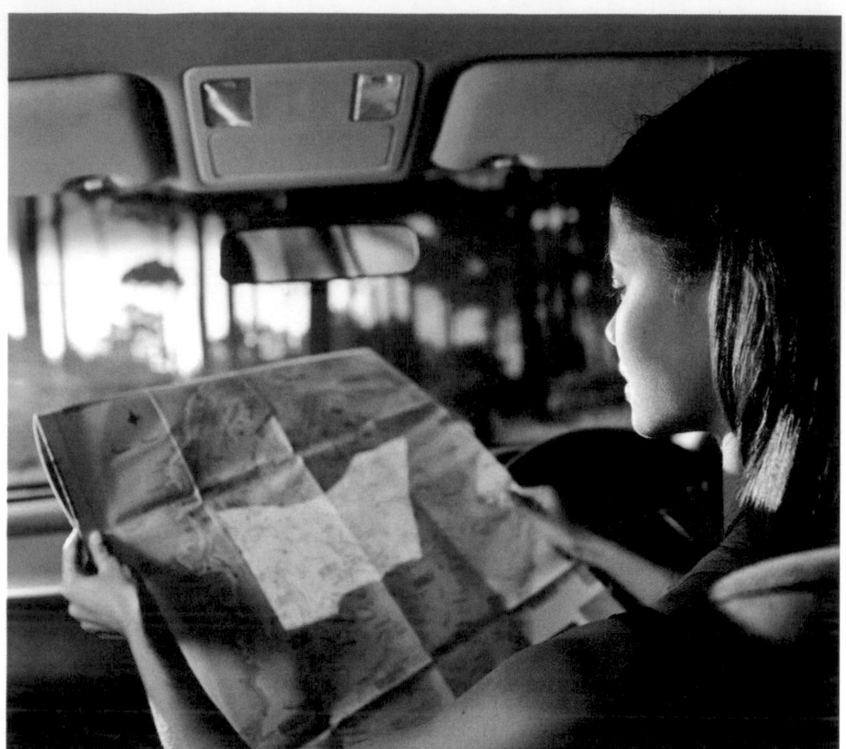

1. Research – research the driving regulations for the country you will be driving through and check your insurance policy to ensure you are covered for breakdown recovery, medical expenses and driving overseas.

2. Prepare – prepare for driving abroad, research the regulations of what you are required to carry in your vehicle and ensure that your own or hired vehicle adheres to these. Remember these are often very different to the UK.

3. Once on the road – expect the unexpected, drive with confidence and always wear a seatbelt. Be safe, don't drink and drive, don't overload your vehicle, don't use your mobile, or get behind the wheel when tired.

Unless you're a very experienced driver, with some off-road experience, we wouldn't advise hiring a car and driving in many places in the developing world. South-east Asian, south Asian, South American and African roads are often little more than potholed tracks, and you really have to know what you're doing when faced with a pecking order decided purely by the size of your vehicle and the sound of your horn – not to mention negotiating wandering livestock, hand-pushed carts, overloaded local buses and trucks, and pedestrians with no road sense whatsoever.

But often you'll find you can hire a car and a driver pretty cheaply for a day or two and then you'll be an ethical traveller contributing to the local economy.

In Australia, buying a cheap car to tour the country at your own leisure is a popular option. But attempting to drive around Australia in an old Ford Falcon or some clapped out old campervan is definitely a challenge.

Ships and boats

If you want to get to the continent, taking a ferry across to France or Belgium can be cheap – but why not sail free as a working crew member on ships?

Before you leave the UK, contact the head offices of shipping companies to find out the procedures and how to book a passage from a foreign port.

Or how about getting to grips with the rigging on a cruise yacht? There are numerous employers and private vessel owners out there on the ocean wave who take on amateur and novice crew. In this way you could gain valuable sailing experience and sea miles. You can also make some useful contacts on your way to becoming a professional crew member. And have the time of your life.

Then there's the 'Classic Sailing' gap-year challenge. If you're over 18, in good health and have a sense of adventure, you could join other amateurs helping an expert crew to cross the ocean in a beautiful tall ship (be it a brigantine or a schooner): from the Azores to Bermuda to Charleston, South Carolina. Learn the ropes and find your sea legs! Find out more at: **www.classic-sailing.co.uk**

Hitch-hiking

Hitch-hiking more or less died out after its heyday in the late 1960s and 1970s – partly out of safety concerns and partly as more and more young people became car owners. But with the onset of the recession it's become a regular feature of the travel pages in many national newspapers.

It costs nothing, except being a friendly and courteous passenger, and losing a bit of time waiting around for a ride, but you need to know what you're doing – and you need to know that in some countries it's illegal and that the usual sticking-your-thumb-out signal used in the UK is considered extremely rude in some countries.

There are no hard and fast rules about getting a lift, but above all you do need to think about your safety if you're going to try it – we wouldn't advise hitching alone for either men or women but on the other hand, if there are more than two of you, you might have trouble persuading a driver to stop.

If you are going to try it, make sure you know the basics. There are two useful websites:

www.hitchwiki.org/en
www.digihitch.com

Motorbike tours

If you're a keen biker and want to include your bike in gap travel plans, there aren't many places you couldn't go. There's an excellent website by UK couple Kevin and Julia Saunders who are double Guinness Book of Records winners for their bike expeditions around the planet. The site offers plenty of advice as well as the opportunity to join expeditions with guides and team leaders: **www.globebusters.com**

Bicycles

If you're feeling hyper-energetic, you could use your pedal-pushing power to get you around town and country. This is really popular in north Europe, especially Holland, where the ground tends to be flatter. Most travel agents would be able to point you in

the right direction, or you can just rely on hiring bikes while you are out there – make sure you understand the rules of the road.

With a globally growing 'green awareness', there's been a real surge in promoting cycling in the UK and abroad. Weather and terrain permitting it's a wonderful way of seeing a city, or touring a region, be it Portugal, Sweden, Provence, Tuscany...

But why confine it to Europe? There are many places where bicycles can be hired and it's a great way of getting around.

You can also participate in some amazing gap-year programmes, such as cycling to raise sponsorship for worthwhile charities and community projects worldwide. But charities aside, just get on your bike and enjoy a closer contact with nature and its vast range of spectacular scenery – getting ever fitter – for example, the USA's Pacific West Coast, Guatemala to Honduras, the Andes to the glaciers of Patagonia, Nairobi to Dar es Salaam, Chiang Mai to Bangkok, the South Island mountains of New Zealand...

Take a look at:

www.responsibletravel.com for cycling and mountain biking holidays; also:

www.imba.com (the International Mountain Biking Association)

www.cyclehire.co.nz/links.htm (independent cycle tours in New Zealand and worldwide links.)

Sustainable travel

Global warming, climate change and the world's depleting energy resources continue to be a serious concern, regardless of the economic climate, and increasingly people want to know how to be environmentally friendly on their gap travels. Nowhere is this likely to be more of an issue than in the types of transport you choose.

If you're hoping to travel to several destinations, time is inevitably an issue, so it may not be practical to avoid air travel altogether, but there are ways you can minimise your carbon footprint.

If you're concerned about global warming, and want to do your bit, you can pay a small 'carbon offset' charge on your flight. If you want to know more try:

www.co2balance.com

The site has a calculator so you can work out how much to pay for journeys by car, train or air. It also has some simpler options – for example £50 will offset one long-haul one-way flight from London to Australia. Your money goes towards sustainable development projects around the world and there's a complete list of all current projects on the website.

They are all managed by co2balance, but are also all independently validated and verified by international standards organisations. Projects include providing energy efficient woodstoves in east Africa, wind power in India and renewable energy projects in China.

The UK's Green Traveller website includes a list of the top ten fair trade holidays worldwide and lots more advice if you want your travel to be as environmentally friendly as possible: **www.greentraveller.co.uk**

To find out more about sustainable and responsible travel you could also look at the website of the International Ecotourism Society, which has a lot of tips for responsible travel both en route and in-country: **www.ecotourism.org**

Another option for responsible travellers is to make the journey part of your gap, if you have time; for example, plan a rail route with stops along the way allowing you time to explore.

Ethical travel

Thinking about the best way to get to and from your destination is one thing, but ethical travel means much more than that.

We asked Tourism Concern to explain further: "Tourism is an enormous industry and affects the lives of millions of people. Environments can be wrecked by irresponsible and unregulated diving, climbing and other outdoor activities.

"Communities have been forcibly removed from their land to make way for tourism developments across the world, from Africa to Australia. Water used for swimming pools, golf courses and twice daily power showers can dwindle supplies for the local populations. Exploitation of local workers is a problem usually invisible to a visitor's eyes. When you start to look more closely, the issues can seem overwhelming, but the good news is that with the decisions you make today and while you're away, you are taking big steps to ensure that your trip benefits everyone."

Here are Tourism Concern's ten tips for ethical travelling:

1) Be aware: start enjoying your travels before you leave. Think about what sort of clothing is appropriate for both men and women. If the locals are covered up,

what sort of messages may you be sending out by exposing acres of flesh? But use your guidebook as a starting point, not the only source of information. Once you've arrived, find out what's going on by talking to locals, then have your own adventures.

2) Be open: something may seem bizarre or odd to you, but it may be normal and just the way things are done to 'them'. Try not to assume that the western way is right or best.

3) Our holidays – their homes: Ask before taking pictures of people, especially children, and respect their wishes. Talk to local people. What do they think about our lifestyle, clothes and customs? Find out about theirs.

4) Giving constructively: giving sweets or pens to children encourages begging. A donation to a project, health centre or school is more constructive.

5) Be fair: try to put money into local hands. If you haggle for the lowest price, your bargain may be at the seller's expense. Even if you pay a little over the odds, does it really matter?

6) Buy local, behave local: look at the environment you're in, try to eat locally sourced foods and buy locally produced goods. Think about resources, don't shower for 20 minutes at a time in an arid zone, just because you might at home.

7) Ask questions: write a letter to your tour operator or venture manager about their responsible tourism policy.

8) Think before you fly: use alternative forms of transport where possible. The more and further you fly, the more you contribute to global warming and environmental destruction. Consider flying long-haul less often but staying longer when you're there.

visit: www.gap-year.com

9) Discover Tourism Concern: a charity that campaigns against exploitation in tourism and for fairly traded and ethical forms of tourism. Their website has a wealth of information on action you can take to avoid guilt trips. **www.tourismconcern.org.uk**

10) Be happy: by taking any, some or all of these actions you are personally fighting tourism exploitation. Enjoy your guilt-free trip!

Accommodation

Traditionally, hostels are the first option that springs to mind, whenever gappers or backpackers are looking for cheap accommodation.

Today there is a range of hostels available, which offer clean, safe and reasonably priced accommodation, some even have 'luxury' extras, such as internet connection, games rooms and laundry facilities.

However, safety can still vary widely and gappers often rely on *Rough Guide* or *Lonely Planet* guidebooks, or the word-of-mouth recommendations from other backpackers to find a suitable one.

Use your common sense and always check where the fire exits are when arriving at a hostel, because it's too late to look if there's already a fire and you're trying to get out of the building.

If you do find you're staying in a basic, no frills-style hostel, it's wise to make sure there's some ventilation when you have a bath or shower – faulty water heaters give off lethal and undetectable carbon monoxide fumes and will kill you without you realising it as you fall gently to sleep, never to wake up again.

Use your instincts – if you think the hostel's simply not up to scratch and too risky, go and find another one.

HostelBookers are one of the largest providers of hostels in the world, with over 20,000 youth hostels and cheap hotels on their books in over 3500 destinations around the world.

Here's what they told us:

"From the cosy comfort of your own bedroom at home, venturing into a hostel and bunking down with fellow travellers can seem a tad daunting. But with a little bit of know-how you can find hostels that tick all your boxes when it comes to meeting new people, stretching your budget and discovering amazing local sights. Aside from sussing out hostel facilities and location, on **HostelBookers.com** you can read guest reviews and ratings of hostels in over 3500 destinations – nothing beats learning from past guests' experiences.

"You can find hostels in all sorts of places; in the countryside, on the beach or in the very heart of a bustling city. If you're keeping to a tight budget, opting for a hostel a little out of town might prove cheaper than a hostel in the city centre. But be sure to weigh up travelling costs – perhaps the hostel has bikes for rent which would be a cheap and zippy solution for getting from A to B. Choosing to stay in neighbourhoods just outside the city centre might give you a more authentic experience than staying close to the tourist sights, and you're bound to stumble up on local eateries or student haunts if you find yourself in the university district.

"To see if your hostel really offers good value and not just a cheap price tag, be sure to check out the list of facilities on offer. Starting with the basics, find out if towels and linen are provided free of charge. Next, look for a free breakfast and whether the hostel provides free wi-fi access or internet kiosks.

Hostelbookers.com, 52-54 High Holborn, Holborn, London WC1B 6RL
T: +44 (0) 207 406 1800
E: support@hostelbookers.com W: www.hostelbookers.com

HostelBookers - the perfect choice for your gap year trip

If you're looking for a fun, sociable and cheap place to stay on your gap year HostelBookers.com will find it for you. We've got 23,000 properties in 3,500 destinations worldwide, ranging from campsites to boat accommodation to tree-houses, stationary planes, budget hotels and of course, amazing hostels.

With a range of prices and room set ups you'll definitely find somewhere to suit your budget. Of course, HostelBookers.com is the only independent hostel booking website with NO BOOKING FEES too, so the price you see is the price you pay.

We're 8.7% cheaper than our closest competitor - in fact we're so confident our lowest price guarantee means that if you find one of our properties cheaper elsewhere on the internet (using the same dates and booking conditions) we'll refund DOUBLE the difference.

Join over 100,000 travellers on HostelBookers' Facebook page http://www.facbook.com/hostelbookers or sign up to our monthly newsletter and you'll be the first to hear about our latest competitions, offers and news.

Wherever the next stop on your gap year is, make sure to book with HostelBookers to guarantee a great value experience that will leave you with more money to spend on the sights and activities with the new friends you're bound to make.

"If you are hoping to meet people on your travels, there are certain things to look out for when choosing your hostel. Most importantly, it needs a lounge area. This is where guests are likely to congregate and relax after a busy day of sightseeing.

"Next up, a hostel with a bar will usually prove more lively and here you can begin your night on the town and perhaps find out how other guests intend to spend their evening.

"Lots of hostels organise events such as bar crawls, free meals or trips to comedy clubs. These are not only geared to budget travellers but are also great ways to get chatting to other guests.

"Be sure to ask staff about things to do in the area. They are likely to be either keen travellers or locals themselves so you might be directed to more authentic bars, music events and all the places of interest your guidebook left out. Similarly, sharing your experiences with guests might reveal a few things to avoid or must-see places.

"Storing your possessions should be a priority, especially if you are sleeping in a dorm room. Ask if the hostel provides private lockers and if it is necessary to bring your own padlock and key – you can usually buy these at the front desk but bringing your own will save money.

"An increasing number of luxury hostels are equipped with secure key card entry to the rooms and you can find out if there is a 24-hour reception or CCTV cameras onsite.

"Quiz staff about the surrounding area and what is the safest way to travel to and from the hostel at night if you intend to stay out until the early hours. 'No curfew' seems to be standard hostel policy today but it is still worth checking in advance.

"If you are not happy about staying in a mixed dorm, an increasing number of hostels offer female-only dorm rooms – some boasting treats such as slippers, full-length mirrors and a free glass of bubbly in the evenings.

"Most hostels now offer both dorm-style and private rooms, some with en suite facilities so couples and families can find suitable accommodation too, although prices are a little higher."

Camping

If you're on a budget camping or caravanning can be worth considering though they're not options for some parts of the world and, particularly with camping, you need to think about whether you really want to carry all that extra equipment.

Many campsites are replacing tents with huts; usually they're in places close to areas where you can hike. You'll get a bed in a hut and use of other facilities so you only need a sleeping bag or sheet sleeping bag – no need to carry a tent.

Caravans, campervans and places to park them

Renting a caravan or travelling under your own steam with a camper van is another possibility – they call them motorhomes in the USA and it's easy to see why. They do have the advantage of giving you a secure place to leave your stuff and of not having to carry it all on your back but they're plainly not an option everywhere in the world. Check out these websites:

www.campingo.com/campsite.html
www.internationalcampingclub.com
www.eurocampings.co.uk/en/europe
www.rentocamp.com
www.allstays.com/Campgrounds-Australia
www.familyparks.com.au
www.takeabreak.com.au/caravanparks.htm

Temples and monasteries

Temples and monasteries are also an option worth exploring. The main consideration for deciding to stay in a monastery or temple guesthouse, should not be your budget, though there's no denying that it's affordable for the budget traveller. Indeed for anyone wanting some place to be able to relax and not be constantly on guard, or if you're seeking a peaceful sanctuary and simplicity, religious guesthouses are ideal.

Some places prefer that you have *some* link with their faith, even if only through a historic extended-family link, but there is a strong tradition of offering refuge, safety and peace in any religious community that isn't a closed order.

Historically, the religious communities and monasteries of many faiths have provided hospice and hospital services to their surrounding communities. Much of our early medical knowledge developed from here too.

Changing economics have also meant their costs have risen and many temples and monasteries have had to be practical about raising income for their communities and for the upkeep of buildings, whose antiquity makes them costly to maintain. Most are therefore open to guests regardless of faith.

Having said that, if you are considering this option, be prepared for rooms and meals to be simple, facilities to be austere and for the community to be quiet at certain times of the day. There will be daily rituals to the life of the community and, like anywhere else, it's only polite to respect their customs. Obviously it's not an option that would suit some gappers.

But a chance to think, to recharge the spiritual batteries, to learn more about oneself or a particular faith, maybe to learn yoga or meditation, is what some gappers are looking for and it can be worth considering this option as part of a gap programme.

Hotels

If you've been on the move for several weeks and careful with the budget, you can find your spirits are flagging from coping with the often spartan conditions in budget hotels, hostels and the like.

A couple of days of comfort in a good hotel can be a worthwhile investment as a tonic, to give you time out to sort your stuff, get some laundry done, have a decent shower and sleep in a clean, comfortable bed before you set off again.

Most hotels around the world use the familiar one to five-star rating system, where five is luxury and one is likely to be a fleapit! But the symbols used can be anything from stars, diamonds and crowns to keys, suns, dots, rosettes and letters.

As with most things in life you get what you pay for, but prices will vary wildly depending on whether you're in peak tourism season or off-peak, currency rates and the costs of living in the country you're visiting, so you may be pleasantly surprised by the rates in some of the better hotels and find you can stretch your budget without reaching breaking point.

But equally, hotel ratings are done by human beings, and they can vary wildly depending on who did them and which search engine you might have used. The best advice is to look for reviews or ratings from ordinary hotel guests who have actually stayed in the hotel – and slept in the beds!

There are several sources of independent information. Most of the travellers' guidebooks have lists of hotels within the different price ranges, but you have to bear in mind that, particularly in the tourism and hospitality industries, things can change between the time of printing and when you arrive.

If you want to check out a hotel while you're travelling, try this website:

www.tripadvisor.com

What makes this site special is that it's all written by travellers from their own experiences and it pulls no punches. There are millions of posts on just about every place or topic you can think of, covering destinations all over the world – including some that might surprise you, like the Middle East, (Saudi Arabia, Jordan, United Arab Emirates to name a few).

Useful websites for last-minute and affordable accommodation are:

'Bargain Rooms' – **www.roomauction.com** – you pay below the standard room rate by making the hotel a discreet offer, 'bidding' for the room.

www.laterooms.com – discount hotel rooms in UK and abroad; the low prices are genuine as they would rather see their rooms let out than not at all.

If you also have concerns about ethical tourism, whether it is the hotel's environmental impact or the conditions of its workers, the Ethical Consumer website has a report on these issues, which is downloadable as a PDF from:

www.ethicalconsumer.org/FreeBuyersGuides/traveltransport/hotels.aspx

Couch Surfing

This is the ultimate in finding free accommodation and, although there were safety concerns when this service first started, it's now had more than a million satisfied customers. But this not-for-profit organisation has a philosophy that's about more than that – it's about creating friendships and networks across the world.

Here's what they say on the safety issue:

"CouchSurfing has implemented several precautionary measures for the benefit of its surfers, hosts, and community. Every user is linked to the other users he or she knows in the system, through a network of references and friend links. In addition to the solid network with friend link-strength indicators and testimonials, we have our vouching and verification systems."

There's a lot more information on their website that should answer all your questions: **www.couchsurfing.org/about.html**

Please see the directory pages starting on page 285 for information on companies and organisations offering travel and accommodation services.

Working abroad

Working abroad

Working abroad is a great option if you desperately want to go overseas, can't really afford it and the bit you have managed to save won't cover much more than air fare.

It's one of the best ways to experience a different culture; you'll be meeting locals and experiencing what the country is really like in a way that you can't do as a traveller passing through. Most jobs give you enough spare time, in the evenings and at weekends, to enjoy yourself and make friends.

You don't have to be tied to one place for your whole gap-year – you can work for a bit and save up for your travels. That way you can learn more about the place and get the inside information from the locals about the best places to see before you set off.

You cover at least some of your costs, and, depending on what you do, the work experience will look good on your CV – but even if you're only doing unskilled seasonal work, prospective employers will be reassured that you at least know *something* about the basics like punctuality, fitting into an organisation and managing your time.

An internship with pay is a good way to get work experience if you already have an idea about your eventual career and will help in those early stages of the problem that affects many young people – when employers want experience but won't take you on so you can get it.

Jon Arnold, of Oyster Worldwide, who send people overseas to get paid jobs on their gap-years, told us: "Earning money on a gap-year is a very popular thing to do. A gap-year is a chance not just to flip burgers in your local burger restaurant or stack shelves in your local supermarket, you can go overseas and get a far more worthwhile experience.

"Paid work overseas looks fantastic on your CV. Not only does it show that you can immerse yourself in a new country, make friends and live away from your family, but it also shows that you can hold down a paid job, get to work on time and live on a budget."

Older gappers, too, may find that, despite the current global economic problems, their skills and experience are in demand, particularly in developing countries.

Key questions to get started

What kind of work do you want to do? There are some suggestions in this chapter but they're only a start.

- Is it to help pay your way on your gap?
- Is it to get work experience/enhance your CV?
- Where do you want to work? (Don't forget to check **www.fco.gov.uk** for country info.)
- What skills and experience do you have?

It doesn't have to be work experience or education, don't forget hobbies and interests. If you can ride a horse, dance, draw, paint, or are good at a particular sport, you could use any of those skills as a basis for finding work.

Planning ahead

Choosing your destination

There are some jobs that always need to be done, whatever the state of the world, and if you're just looking at ways of funding your travel you could look for seasonal farm work.

In most cases, gappers intending to do seasonal work outside the EU need to have a job offer in order to get a visa. If you should find that, when you get there the job is no longer available, you can try elsewhere – but we would advise you to have a back-up plan before you set off on your travels (*eg* contacts, an emergency fund, names of companies that specialise in work overseas).

If you are a UK citizen, or hold an EU (European Union) passport, you can work in any other EU member country without a visa or work permit and there are countless jobs available to students who can speak the right languages. Not all European countries are EU members – go to the European Union website to check: **www.europa.eu**

Speaking English is always an advantage for jobs in tourism at ski resorts, beach bars and hotel receptions and if you have a TEFL (Teaching English as a Foreign Language) certificate there's always the option of teaching.

You could try using message boards to find out what other gappers have done and what it was like. If you want to be more adventurous and venture outside Europe, then check the Foreign Office website – **www.fco.gov.uk** – for the list of countries they consider are simply too dangerous to even go to.

Getting your paperwork sorted

Before you go, you should:

- Check whether you need to set up a job – you may need a confirmed work offer before you can get a work permit and visa – try **www.gap-year.com** for contact lists and more advice, or refer to the internship and graduate opportunities section in the directory of this guidebook.
- Check on the work permit and visa regulations for the country you plan to work in and make sure you have the right paperwork before you leave. Remember, you don't need a work permit or visa if you're an EU citizen and planning to work in an EU country.
- Check if there's any special equipment or clothing you'll need to take, *eg* sturdy boots and trousers for manual jobs, reasonably smart clothes for office internships *etc*.
- When you're getting your insurance, remember to check that you'll be covered if you're planning on working. Working can invalidate a claim for loss or damage to your belongings on some travel policies. If in doubt, ask.
- Make sure you understand all the regulations and restrictions. You can get into serious trouble if you work without the necessary documents – you don't want to be deported during your gap-year! The best place to get information is the relevant embassy in London - there's a link on **www.gap-year.com** to the Foreign and Commonwealth Office website, where you will find links to all embassies.

Our friends at Gap 360 provide a series of PDF downloads covering things you'll need to get sorted before you go. You can find them at **www.gap360.com**

Finding a job

Finding a job may take time and effort. The more places you can send your CV to, the greater the chances of you getting a job. You can also register with international employment agencies but make sure you know what the agency fee will be if you get employment.

To find short-term jobs try:

www.transitionsabroad.com
www.pickingjobs.com
www.anyworkanywhere.com
www.overseasjobcentre.co.uk

If you use an agency, always insist on talking to someone who has used it before – that way you'll really find out what the deal is.

Do a search to see if there's a website for a particular area you want to go to and then send or email your CV, with a short covering note, to any interesting local companies. Don't expect to be flooded with replies. Some companies are simply too busy to respond to every enquiry, though it always helps to enclose a stamped addressed envelope. It's also true that you may get lucky and have exactly the skills or qualifications they're looking for. Some companies will also advertise vacant posts on specialist employment websites, which often have an international section. You can register with the sites too, usually for free.

Tell everyone you know, including relatives and your parents' friends that you are looking for a job abroad – someone may know someone who has a company abroad who can help you.

Check the local papers and shop window notices. Lots of jobs are advertised in the local papers, or by 'staff wanted' notices put up in windows. So if you get there, and hate the job you've got, don't put up with it, or come running home – see if you can find something better. It's always easier to find employment when you're living locally.

Over the next few pages we've listed ideas on types of employment, and any companies we know about, that offer graduate opportunities or work experience, can be found in the directory. Always ask an employment company to put you in contact with someone they have placed before – if they say no then don't use them: they may have something to hide.

Au pairing

Being an au pair is a good way to immerse yourself in a different culture, learn a new language and hopefully save some extra cash. You don't need any qualifications to be an au pair, although obviously some experience with children is a bonus. However, au pairing is a hard job and a big responsibility and you may well have to pass the equivalent of a Disclosure and Barring Service (DBS) check.

In return for board, lodgings and pocket money, you'll be expected to look after the children and do light domestic chores like ironing, cooking, tidying their bedrooms and doing their washing, for up to five hours a day (six hours in France or Germany), five days a week, as well as spending two or three evenings a week babysitting. If you are asked to work more than this then technically you are not doing the work of an au pair, but of a mother's help (which pays more).

Remember that an au pair is classified as 'non-experienced', and you should never be left in sole charge of a baby. If the family gives you more responsibility than you can handle say so. If they don't stop – quit.

Finding an au pair agency

It may be safest to look for a placement through a UK-based au pair agency. It's also better for the prospective family abroad, since they will be dealing with an agency (possibly working together with an agency in the family's own country) that has met you, interviewed you and taken up references; they will want reassurance before they trust you with their children.

What you should check:

- Does the agency you use have connections with another agency in the country where you'll be working?
- Can they give you a list of other local au pairs so you'll have support when you're out there?
- Take time finding a suitable family. The fewer children the better, and you should expect your own room.
- What is there to do in your free time? You don't want to spend every weekend in your bedroom because you're stuck in the middle of nowhere.
- Do you get written confirmation of the hours, duties and pay agreed?
- The number and address of the local British Consulate – just in case.

Check that the au pair agency is a member of either the Recruitment and Employment Confederation (which has a website listing all its members and covering au pair employment in many countries) or of the International Au Pair Association (IAPA), which has a list of its registered agencies in 38 countries around the world:

International Au Pair Association
WYSE Travel Confederation
174 Keizersgracht
1016 DW, Amsterdam
The Netherlands
Tel: +31 (0)20 421 2800
Enquiry: inquiry@iapa.org
www.iapa.org

There are, of course, perfectly good agencies that do not belong to trade associations, either because they are too small to afford the membership fees, or because they are well-established and have a good independent reputation.

You can also find information on au pair work worldwide by using the internet. Registration is usually free and your details will be matched to the families around the world that have registered on the site and that meet your specifications (but make sure you talk to both the agents, here and abroad, and the prospective family before you make your final decision).

However, if you are considering organising an au pair placement independently, you should be aware of the risks:

- High probability of unsuitable au pair or host family candidates.
- Absence of a written contract.
- Little or no experience in the au pair industry.
- Lack of professionalism or financial stability.
- Non-existent standards or guidelines.
- Insufficient references and/or medical certification.
- Danger of document falsification.
- No rematch policy (secondary placement) if the initial placement is unsuccessful.
- No local support during the placement.
- Limited understanding of national au pair and visa regulations.

Remember also that au pair agencies operating in the UK and sending au pairs abroad cannot, except under specified circumstances, charge for finding you a placement.

If you have a complaint against a UK agency it's best to take it up with the Department for Business, Enterprise and Regulatory Reform's (BERR) Employment Agency Standards Helpline, Tel: +44 (0) 845 955 5105. It operates Monday-Friday 9.30am to 4.30pm.

Au pairing in Europe

There are EU laws governing the conditions in which au pairs can work:

- You must be 17 or over.
- You must provide a current medical certificate.
- You should have a written employment agreement signed by you and your host family; conditions of employment must be stated clearly.
- You should receive (tax exempt) pocket money.
- You should have enough free time to study.
- You should not be asked to work more than five hours a day.
- You must have one free day a week.

This is now the accepted definition for au pair jobs in the EU, but not necessarily in other countries. Some countries have different local rules.

Take a look at **www.conventions.coe.int/treaty/en/Treaties/Html/068.htm** for the details of the European Agreement and any local variations.

It's important to complete all the necessary paperwork for living and working in another country. Most agencies will organise this for you, and make sure the legal documents are in order before you leave. You should listen to any legal advice you are given by the agency you use. Many also now require written references, police checks and other proof of suitability – which is as much a protection for you as it is for the parents of the children you might look after.

Here's an example. Most French agencies require a set of passport photos, a photocopy of your passport, two references (preferably translated into French), and your most recent academic qualifications, as well as a handwritten letter in French to your prospective family, which tells them something about you, your reasons for becoming an au pair and any future aspirations.

The agency may also ask for a medical certificate (showing you are free of deadly contagious diseases *etc*) dated less than three months before you leave, and translated into French. Au pairs also have to have a medical examination on arrival in France.

The French Consulate advises you to check that the family you stay with obtains a 'mother's help' work contract (*Accord de placement au pair d'un stagiaire aide-familiale*). If you are a non-EU citizen you are expected to do this before you leave for France, but British au pairs do not need to.

Au pairing in North America

Being an au pair in the USA is well paid. You'll receive $195 a week (£125 approximately), have your flight paid for, free health insurance, free food and lodging with your own room in the family house. You also get two weeks' holiday and a chance to travel for 30 days at the end of the year.

Many American families need childcare help because both parents work. Childcare is very expensive in the USA and so a highly effective network of agencies has developed to supply international au pairs to US families.

The US Government regulates the au pair programme and in order to obtain the required J-1 au pair visa you must go though a local UK agency. The requirements are quite strict:

- Be aged 18-26.
- Be educated to minimum GCSE standard.
- Speak English well.
- Have no criminal record (including cautions) and obtain an enhanced CRB check.
- Have a minimum 200 hours of babysitting experience with non-relatives.
- Be able to drive and swim.
- Have no visible tattoos!

You also receive a $500 credit towards the college course of your choice.

The US Department of State website has all the up-to-date legislation on au pairing in the US. See: **exchanges.state.gov/jexchanges/programs/aupair.html**

If you enjoy being with children, this is a great option for a year. UK agencies include:

www.gap360.com
www.culturalcare.co.uk
www.aupairinamerica.com

EduCare

If you want to combine au pairing with some study, EduCare places people with families who have school-aged children and who need childcare before and after school hours. Au pairs on the EduCare scheme work no more than 30 hours per week in return for roughly two thirds of the rates paid to au pairs.

You must complete a minimum of 12 hours of academic credit or its equivalent during the programme year (financed by the host family for up to US$1000).

Internships and paid work placements

- Are you at university?
- Are you a new graduate?
- Are you looking for work experience to land your dream job?
- Want to spend a year in another country?

Taking an internship abroad – either as part of a university course or not – is a good way to boost your CV, as well as getting away for a year and doing something useful.

Richard Oliver, of the Year Out Group, told us: "There is steadily increasing demand for paid work placements overseas and many Year Out Group members now offer these.

"Paid work has always been popular as students seek to top up funds for the next stage of their travels. But in the current economic climate gaining work experience has become an important consideration when planning a gap-year and many gap-year organisations are now in a position to help secure suitable placements."

However, he warned: "Those choosing such placements should not expect to earn a fortune as most of the work is low-paid."

Some careers, the media for example, are extremely tough to get into, so using your gap-year to get relevant work experience may be a good plan. You'll have the benefit of something to put on your CV and also get an idea of what the job is actually like. Internships are not usually open to people pre-university. Many international companies offer internships but if you're thinking of the USA you should know:

1. Internships in the USA can be difficult to get without paying for the privilege, unless you have personal contacts within the organisation you hope to work for.

2. The USA has a strict job-related work permit system and won't hand out these permits for jobs that American nationals can do themselves.

3. The USA authorities also need to be convinced that the work experience offered provides an opportunity to the UK student that he or she cannot get back home.

If the companies listed in our directory can't help you, try these websites:

www.cartercentre.org
www.summerjobs.com (enter internships in the search box)
www.internshipprograms.com
www.internabroad.com/search.cfm
www.transitionsabroad.com/listings/work/internships/index.shtml

Before you sign up, make sure you're clear just what your placement will involve. An internship should mean you are able to do interesting paid work related to your degree studies, current or future, for at least six months, but increasingly, even on some of the internship websites listed above, the distinction between a voluntary (unpaid) placement and an internship is becoming blurred so you may have to search for a while – or be creative and try a direct approach to companies in the fields that interest you.

Sport instructors

If you're already a qualified instructor in skiing, sailing, kayaking, diving, football, or any other sport for that matter, there are many places all around the world where you can use your skills – and many personal benefits.

For example, Colin Tanner, of SITCo, who offer ski and snowboard instructor training in New Zealand, told us: "Working as a snowsports instructor means that you will meet a wealth of different people, from different parts of the world and with many different expectations and goals.

"One of the things a snowsports instructor must do is listen to the person you are teaching, adapt your lessons to suit the individual and develop fantastic and efficient communications skills – these are all fantastic skills that you can take forward, and apply to any area of life."

Typical summer seasons run from the end of April to the beginning of November and winter seasons tend to run from the end of November until the end of April. That provides an opportunity for all-year round work, although it's worth noting that recruitment normally starts five months in advance.

Here are a few websites worth having a look at:

Skiing:
www.ifyouski.com/jobs/job/description/instructor
www.jobmonkey.com/ski/html/instructors.html

Football:
www.deltapublications.co.uk/soccer.htm – soccer coaching in the USA

General Sports:
www.adventurejobs.co.uk
www.campjobs.com

Skiing doesn't have to be in European resorts, don't forget there's the US and Canada, but there are also ski resorts in the foothills of the Himalayas! For diving jobs you can go pretty well anywhere there's water and water sports.

Football's popular throughout Africa and Latin America, and there are now several football academies in India looking for help to spread the message of the 'beautiful game'.

But whichever sport is your passion, you can use it as part of your gap-year plan.

We have much more on the opportunities available for teaching and playing sport abroad in **Chapter 8**.

Teaching English as a Foreign Language (TEFL)

TEFL is one of the most popular ways of earning (and volunteering) when you travel, but you need to have a recognised qualification and it does help in getting a post abroad. It also has the advantage that, if you were thinking of teaching as a career, it's a good chance to find out if you like it before you begin your teacher training.

The two best-known British qualifications are:

· TESOL (a certificate from Trinity College, London).

· CELTA (Cambridge University certificate).

The USA has its own qualification and there are many private schools and colleges who offer their own certification. There are a great many colleges around the UK

CONVERSATION ASSISTANT PROGRAMME

CAPS is a programme designed for young people who would like to spend a year in Spain helping in a School as Conversation Teaching Assistant.

You will have all your bed and board paid for and receive an allowance every month.
Once in Spain accommodation, food and travel to and from the school is paid for. Also each assistant will receive an allowance of 200€ every month.

If you want to:

- Get professional teaching experience for your CV.
- Get personal enrichment and the experience of living abroad.
- Be part of a school with the support of a host family and a professional organization.
- Learn a new language and culture

CAPS is your programme!!

PROGRAMME DESCRIPTION

As **Conversation Assistant** (CA) you will be assigned to an infant, primary, secondary or technical school, mainly in Catalonia and Valencia regions. You will assist with classes of children between the ages of 3 to 16.

The CA will **assist the teacher**, and their specific responsibilities will be principally focused on reinforcing and **improving the speaking ability of the students in English**. The CA will help in the school **25 hours/week** from Monday to Friday

Possible tasks you could be given under the supervision of the teacher include:

-Conversation practice- Help in the language laboratory & audiovisual rooms.
- Help with oral exams.
- Explaining the culture of your own country.
- Stimulation of student's speaking skills.
- Playing English games, reading, songs.
- Help with linguistic questions.
- Help in other subjects apart from English such as science, art, sport.
- Preparing displays, complementary material, and conversation activities.

Accommodation: The CA will live with a host family during their time in Spain, family details will be sent prior to your arrival in Spain. The CA will have their own room and will be given breakfast and evening meals during the week and full board at weekends and on school holidays.

MORE BENIFITS WHEN THE CA IS ON THE PROGRAMME:

- **Travel insurance cover** in Spain in case of accident or death to the CA or caused by the CA to a third party is provided.
- **Help in learning Spanish and Catalan** (For CA's in the Catalonia region) through a distance learning course.
- Have the s**upport** from a serious and professional organization.

HOW TO APPLY

You can request more information and our application form to enroll by sending us an email
caps@hometohome.es

that offer TEFL courses but, ideally, you should check that the certificate you will be working for is one of these two.

It is worth doing your TEFL training within an accredited training centre, as most will help you find a placement once you qualify and face to face training can be more beneficial. One word of warning, if you were hoping to get a job with one of the many well-known language schools around the world, some will insist that you undertake your TEFL training with them first. It's always worth checking this out, and deciding how you wish to use your training, before you sign up for a course.

How to find TEFL work

The availability of work for people who can teach English can vary, particularly outside the EU. In most countries it is possible to give private lessons. As stated before, if you wish to work for a language school or academy, find out what their requirements are before you begin your training.

Most professional employers will expect you to have had some teaching practice before they will employ you. You should also find out more about the country you hope to find work in before you go. The contact details of the relevant embassies in the UK can be found on the FCO website – **www.fco.gov.uk** – and you should be able to obtain up-to-date details of visas, salaries, qualifications needed and a view about the availability of work in your chosen country. Rates of pay and conditions of employment will vary greatly from country to country and will most likely depend on your own education, training, experience and expertise.

In the UK, TEFL jobs are advertised in:
The Times Educational Supplement.
The Education Guardian.
In the education section of *The Independent.*
The EL Gazette.

www.eslbase.com/jobs
www.cactustefl.com
www.eteach.com
www.english-international.com
www.esljobfeed.com

You could also check out the various 'blacklists' that have appeared on the internet in recent years. These list schools to avoid or watch out for. These are informal sites run by people with experience of TEFL teaching. They should be a good place to find out about language schools around the world and whether or not it's worth your time pursuing a vacancy there.

The most popular destinations for TEFL teachers are China, Hong Kong, Japan, Thailand and, of course, Europe. As the EU grows, so does the demand for English teachers, and the advantage of securing a job within the EU is that the UK is a member. This will give you some protection and should involve far less paperwork than if you applied to work further afield.

In China, you are more likely to find work in a private school, rather than the state schools system, as the latter is controlled by the Department of Education in Beijing.

Hong Kong is an obvious choice as it was once a British Colony and English is a second language for nearly everyone there. The added advantage for those with no Chinese language skills is that all the road signs, public transport and government

Leiths List, Agency for Cooks, 16-20 Wendell Road, Shepherd's Bush, London W12 9RT
T: +44 (0) 1225 722983
E: info@leithslist.com
W: www.leithslist.com

If you would like to earn money during your gap year or whilst at university, cooking jobs can offer a flexible short term solution. Leiths List, Leiths School of Food and Wine's agency for cooks, can help place you in a suitable job at the right level for your ability and experience.

Once qualified from a reputable cookery school contact Leiths List and they will be able to place you in a cooking job suitable for your skill level and availability. From jobs lasting a few days, a week or weekend, to a longer term placement we have roles both in the UK and abroad which can fit around your travel plans.

Leiths School of Food and Wine run a 4 week course (the Essential Certificate) starting in August each year which teaches all the necessary skills to be able to cook for families in holiday homes or chalets. The more advanced Leiths Diploma in Food and Wine is a one year professional training course which many choose as an alternative to university if they wish to pursue a full time career in food. For more information see the 'cookery courses' section of this book.

Earning money through cooking is not necessarily restricted to your year off as Leiths have many under and post graduates who find work through Leiths List on a regular basis during their university holidays. Being able to cook is a skill for life that you can turn to when you wish to earn money at short notice, or even as a filler while looking for a more permanent job position.

"Being at university means that you have to fend for yourself. The Leiths Essential Certificate qualification has ensured that I can cook meals for not just myself but my whole house. Leiths has also taught me to cook healthy food, whilst sticking to a reasonable budget. During the holidays there are always jobs available, which is useful when cash-flow as a student is difficult!" Diana Cheal, graduated from Leiths 2007

For further details please view our website www.leithslist.com. Contact us on 01225 722 983, or email info@leithslist.com.

information are in English as well as Chinese and most of the shops, agencies and essential services (such as police, doctors *etc*) employ English speakers.

There is also a daily English language newspaper, *The South China Morning Post* and it may well be worth checking their online jobs section for vacancies:

www.classifiedpost.com.hk/jshome_en.html

If you want to take your skills and use them in Japan you should check out **www.jet-uk.org**. This is the Japanese Government's website for promoting their scheme to improve foreign language teaching in schools. You do have to have a Bachelor's degree to qualify though. The *Japan Times* (which is online) also lists job vacancies in English: **www.jobs.japantimes.jp**

There is a great demand for English speakers in Thailand and so if you are taking your **gap** in that country, and wish to earn money whilst there, TEFL could well be the answer, particularly as you will be unable to find work in a country where foreigners are forbidden from taking most unskilled occupations. The *Bangkok Post* lists job vacancies, including those for English teachers, in their online jobs section: **www.bangkokpost.net**

CAPS is an excellent programme designed for young people who would like to spend a year in Spain helping in a school as a conservation teaching assistant. You will have your bed and board paid for and receive an allowance every month. For more information, see the CAPS advert on page 138or go to: **www.hometohome.es/caps/eng/assistants.html**

Teaching English in private lessons

If you decide to supplement your income in-country by giving private lessons, you can put notices in schools, colleges, newspapers and local shops but there are some basic safety precautions you should take:

1. Be careful how you word your ad – *eg* 'Young English girl offering English lessons' is likely to draw the wrong kind of attention.

2. If you arrange one-to-one tuition, don't go to your student's home until you've checked out how safe it would be.

3. Equally, if you're living alone, don't give classes at home until you've got to know your student.

4. Arrange classes in public, well-populated locations, which will also help as teaching aids (coffee bars, restaurants, shops, markets *etc*).

5. Make sure you're both clear about your fee (per hour) and when it should be paid (preferably these should both be put in writing).

Usually, you'll be inundated by friends of friends as word gets round there's an English person willing to give private lessons.

Cookery

Cooking jobs are available abroad as well as in the UK, particularly during the summer months. Gaining some cooking skills is a great way to boost your CV and opens up new possibilities.

Alison Cavaliero, who runs Leiths List, an agency that supplies quality cooks for short or long-term vacancies, told us: "Families often look for a young person to

help *eg* during the long summer months – animal/child-friendly and an ability to drive are good skills combinations along with basic cooking skills to provide all-round household support. Some families have holiday homes abroad and in the traditional English holiday locations so there can be a chance to get to know a new area.

"Most employers feel more confident about hiring someone if they have a cooking qualification as they will need less direction – and we have been told by students who have cooking skills that they tend to get better paid jobs than their friends who don't."

Seasonal work in Europe

Working in Europe offers endless possibilities – from fruit picking to hospitality and tourism, leading nature trips to teaching English (for more on this see our TEFL section above). Some non-EU members need work permits so you should check the regulations in the country you want to go to.

Companies offer a variety of roles working with children at locations across the UK, France and Spain for as little as 12 weeks, to a maximum of ten months with the option to return the following year.

Jobs on offer include children's group leaders, activity or watersports Instructors, French-speaking tour leaders or administrators and Spanish-speaking roles. Non-guest-facing roles include support team positions: catering assistants, chefs, drivers, retail, housekeeping and maintenance. Some roles do not require qualifications or previous experience – in fact there are opportunities for a comprehensive training programme including apprenticeships and coaching awards so you may even have the opportunity to gain an additional qualification for life at no cost to yourself.

To find other short-term jobs try:

www.oysterworldwide.com/projects/paid-work
www.transitionsabroad.com
www.pickingjobs.com

Seasonal work in North America

Probably the most popular seasonal job for gappers in the US is working on a summer camp. The US has strict regulations on visas and work permits but summer camps are a well-established way of working for a short time.

US work regulations are very complicated, and specific, and this is one time where it would help to use a placement organisation to help you through the paperwork, but make sure you check out the small print about pay, accommodation and expenses.

"Each year thousands of young British and European students apply to join the summer camp programmes in the US as counsellors, advanced skill counsellors or 'campower' as the support team is called," says Richard Oliver, of the Year Out Group. "Programmes can only be arranged with specialist organisations."

If you don't fancy summer camp there are lots of other possibilities, from working on a ranch to cruise ship jobs. Have a look at: **www.jobmonkey.com**

It covers all sorts of work from fishing jobs in Alaska, to working on a ranch, to casino and gaming clubs and cruise work. But check with the US embassy to make sure you can get a visa or a work permit for the job you fancy. See: **www.usembassy.org.uk**

There are plenty of opportunities for working holidays in Canada, most commonly at hotels and restaurants, and ski and summer resorts.

Jon Arnold, of Oyster Worldwide, pointed out that Canada has a limited supply of work permits – 5,350 for 2013. These are released in batches and they tend to run out very fast, so it's very important to plan ahead. "Canadian work permits are generally released between January and March," Jon told us. "In order to be eligible you need to be 18 at the time of applying so this is worth bearing in mind.

"Working in a country like Canada for up to 12 months is an excellent way to spend your gap-year. There is so much to get involved in all-year round and the experience certainly won't do your CV any harm."

Visitoz, 16 Richmond Road, Taunton, Somerset TA1 1EW
T: 07966 528 644
E: will@vistoz.org
W: www.visitoz.org

A guaranteed job in Australia!

If you like to work hard, play hard and have fun - this is the job for you. Every day is different, every job is different, the scenery is constantly changing and the friends you make will be yours for life. What Visitoz is offering is not a boring, same every day, lifestyle, but something you have never experienced before - the Real Australia. You will learn skills that you never thought you would need and become very self reliant and sure of your ability to tackle almost anything. For Gap Year people, this is the best way to grow up - enjoy a secure environment, a secure job, earn money and spend it how you wish - you will go to University a much more interesting and confident person.

What is Visitoz offering?

You will go to a guaranteed properly paid job 9 days after arriving in Australia.

* Meet and Greet at Brisbane International Airport and one night in central Brisbane

* Three nights at the beach resort to get over jet lag and meet up with the others on the programme that week, have some sun, sea, sand and surf with your new friends from all over the world.

* Five nights on the farm for the introductory training. Ride horses and cross country motorbikes, work with cattle on foot and on horseback, drive and operate tractors, learn general farming skills and lots about farm and outback safety.

* Choose a job, anywhere in rural Australia, doing what you want to do where you want to do it - it could be on a farm or station, in rural hotels, pubs & resorts, or with rural childcare and teaching.

* On your 9th day in Australia start the journey to the job of your choice.

So - you have saved all this money - what are you going to do with it?

The jobs can last from 2-6 months. After that have a holiday, enjoy more of the sun, sea, sand and surf which you first experienced in your jetlag recovery days - but what about visiting one of the cities or taking a tour? There will be lots of ideas for you to ponder while the money is piling up! Just before you run out of money call Visitoz again for your second, third or fourth job - as required. The Visitoz jobs will also qualify you for the second Working Holiday Visa.

Programme Fees and costs:

$2299 Australian dollars. A deposit of $500 guarantees you a place. The balance of $1799 is only due 30 days before departure. If booked with the UK office the price is in pounds with a deposit of £100. If you plan to come between July and November please book very early to avoid disappointment.

We look forward to welcoming you to our farm and our country.

VISIT THE REAL AUSTRALIA AND GET PAID DOING IT!

Seasonal work in Australia and New Zealand

Periods of working and travelling in Australia and New Zealand are a very popular option and you can do everything from fruit picking to helping Amnesty International. However, you don't have to stick to the traditional backpacker temporary work – fruit picking, bar work or call centres. If you have a trade, IT skills or a nursing qualification they're also good for finding work.

David Stitt, of Gap 360, which specialises in overseas work programmes, said those in Australia were proving particularly popular, with the going pay scale AU$20-$25 (about £12-£15) per hour.

Australia has a well worked-out system to allow you to work and travel. It's called the working holiday visa. You can qualify for any specified work and UK passport holders can apply online. Specified work is work, whether paid or unpaid, in certain specified industries or postcodes – for more details have a look at:

www.immi.gov.au/visitors/working-holiday/417/specified-work.htm

The main points are:

- You must be between 18 and 30.
- It costs around £90 (AU$195). The charge is non-refundable.

You will also be required to have a health certificate before you apply for your visa.

What you can do:

- Enter Australia within 12 months of the visa being issued.
- Stay up to 12 months.
- Leave and re-enter Australia any number of times while the visa is valid.
- Work in Australia for up to six months with each employer.
- Study or train for up to four months.

Australia
Self-financing holiday
Guaranteed
Work!
Then . . .
WITH A
POCKET
FULL OF
MONEY
HOLIDAY!
www.visitoz.org
VisitOZ

To find out more go to:
www.immi.gov.au/visitors/working-holiday/417/eligibility-first.htm

Or call the High Commission in the UK:
Australian High Commission,
Australia House, Strand, London WC2B 4LA
Tel: 020 7379 4334
www.australia.org.uk

To find seasonal work try:
www.visit.org
www.seasonalwork.com.au/index.bsp
www.workaboutaustralia.com.au

Successful applicants should allow about three weeks to find work, although it may well come quicker than that. The average rate of pay for temporary staff us at about A$15 to A$21 an hour, enabling a good standard of living that can help fund travels.

Visitoz

New Zealand has a similar working visa scheme for either 12 or 23 months – and also a health certificate requirement. To qualify you must:

1. Usually be permanently living in the United Kingdom – this means you can be temporarily visiting another country when you lodge your application.

2. Have a British passport that's valid for at least three months after your planned departure from NZ.

3. Be at least 18 and not more than 30 years old.

4. Not bring children with you.

5. Hold a return ticket, or sufficient funds to purchase such a ticket.

6. Have a minimum of NZ$350 per month of stay in available funds (to meet your living costs while you're there).

7. Meet NZ's health and character requirements.

8. Satisfy the authorities that your main reason for going to NZ is to holiday, not work.

9. Not have been approved a visa permit under a Working Holiday Scheme before.

The regulations for British subjects are very clearly laid out on the NZ Government website:

www.immigration.govt.nz/migrant/stream/work/workingholiday/unitedkingdomworkingholidayscheme.htm

And here are a few websites to check for seasonal work in New Zealand:

www.picknz.co.nz
www.seasonaljobs.co.nz
www.backpackerboard.co.nz/work_jobs/seasonal_jobs_new_zealand.php

Help with applying for a working holiday visa

Individuals can apply for working holiday visas themselves or use an agency to prepare the paperwork for you. UK agencies for this include:

www.gap360.com
www.bunac.co.uk
www.visabureau.com
www.realgap.com

If you are not British you should check the websites to see if your citizenships allows you to obtain the visa.

The sort of work that you can obtain is not restricted, but in most cases you are only allowed to work for the same employer for six months. The idea is that it is a holiday being supported by working, rather then work being the prime reason for travelling.

Please see the directory pages starting on page 303 for information on companies and organisations offering working abroad opportunities.

6 Volunteering abroad

Sponsored by

Using education to fight poverty

The Book Bus is brilliant and like all the best ideas, the concept is simple: we bring together reading mentors (you!) and primary school classrooms in Africa, India, Ecuador and the Galapagos. In the UK we are supported by authors and publishers (one of the charity trustees is Quentin Blake) who provide the books and our task is to read with children and bring the stories to life. So if you like working with children, enjoy books and have an imagination that can conjure up the excitement and imagery hidden within words, then the Book Bus could be for you.

The Book Bus believes that education is the long-term solution to poverty in the developing world. Our literacy projects help disadvantaged children develop their reading skills, improve their education and increase their understanding of the world around them.

Book Bus projects can be found in the following places:

- Victoria Falls, Zambia
- Luangwa Valley, Zambia
- Blantyre, Malawi
- Rajasthan, India
- Puerto Lopez, Ecuador (Spanish speaking)
- Galapagos Islands, Ecuador (Spanish speaking)

The work is the same in each destination, except that in Ecuador the children speak Spanish, which makes this the ideal opportunity to learn or improve your language skills. We have teamed up with a language school in Quito, the capital, and they provide one-to-one tuition, with family-stay accommodation, for just £316 (1 week, full board including tuition)

What will you be doing?

Book Bus volunteers visit schools every morning from Monday to Friday and inspire children to discover the joy of reading. We use assisted reading techniques and arts & craft activities (guidance provided by the fulltime Book Bus leader) to bridge the gap between learning to read and the living, breathing story.

Afternoons are free to explore the area and prepare for the next day. Week-ends are the ideal opportunity to visit the local region and because the Book Bus is so popular locally, you are welcomed wherever you go.

How long? We ask for a minimum commitment of 2 weeks; there is no upper limit.

How much? £749 for 2 weeks plus 100 US$ per week local payment.

What else can I do? The Book Bus in Ecuador and Galapagos combines really well with the Galapagos conservation project: www.ventureco-worldwide.com/the-galapagos-islands/galapagos-conservation-project

Suggestion: 2 weeks language school + 2 weeks Book Bus + 2 weeks Galapagos conservation project.

Find out more: www.thebookbus.org

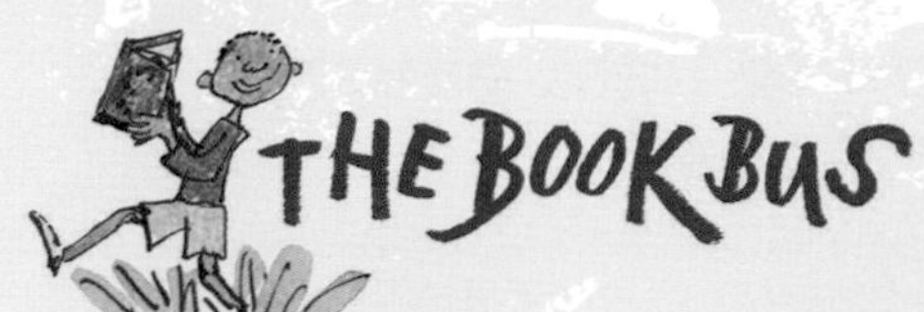
THE BOOK BUS

Volunteering abroad

Raleigh International

Voluntary work abroad can be one of the most rewarding ways to spend all, or part, of your gap-year. You could find yourself working with people living in unbelievable poverty, disease or hunger. It can be a humbling and hugely enriching experience and it can make you question all the things you've taken for granted in your life. It's no exaggeration to say it can be life-changing.

Some people who have done it have ended up changing their planned course of study at university or even their whole career plan. Year Out Group's members, who are all gap providers, report that volunteering is the top gap choice among all age groups and had risen by 20% in the last full year for which they carried out research.

Teaching and working with children are the most popular options and interestingly women gappers outnumber men, and women are also more likely to choose volunteering and expeditions rather than courses or cultural **exchanges.**

Who goes volunteering?

It's clear from speaking to gap providers that students on gap-years still make up most of the market, but the picture is changing.

Our friends at Kaya Responsible Travel, who offer volunteering opportunities in more than 20 countries, told us: "The age range of our volunteers is getting wider and wider. Where once volunteering was seen only for students on their gap-year from university, we now also have a lot older volunteers such as career breakers or retirees who want to do something exciting and new. We tend to find that the career breakers and retirees have specific skills such as business development, social work, marketing, or healthcare *etc* and would to use these skills to make a difference.

"2013 also saw a real surge in interest from 16 and 17-year-old volunteers. For us, it's really great to see that volunteering is on people's radar before they even reach university. We only have a handful of projects that can accept under 18s but where we can, we try to make volunteering accessible to as wide an audience as possible."

Projects Abroad, who have been offering volunteering abroad placements for more than 20 years, agreed: "The majority of our volunteers are in the 'traditional' gap year age bracket of between 17 and 23. However, over the past few years we have seen increasing numbers of career breakers and retired people choosing to go away with us.

"We are also recruiting a lot of 16-year-olds who can take part in our summer 2 Week Special projects, which are structured group trips for 16-19 year-olds. These younger volunteers want a shorter project that gives them a taster of what it's like to volunteer overseas before later taking part in a full gap-year before or after university."

Why volunteer?

We think Jon Arnold, of Oyster Worldwide, answers this question rather well:

"Volunteering overseas does not only help you but hopefully it helps others as well. Whether you are on a traditional gap-year or a career break, there is so much you can achieve by volunteering overseas.

"You can't expect to eradicate Third World poverty in a three-month volunteer trip but I really believe people can make a really positive impact on a few people's lives. Whether it is teaching someone to read or inspiring a group of kids to learn English and further their own career prospect, you can leave knowing you have helped them. You have changed their lives.

"Volunteering abroad also makes you more of an interesting person to speak to. If you can bring examples of your overseas volunteering into your CV, when you had to use team work, leadership, determination etc, then you will stand out from the crowd and hopefully be invited for interview.

"I speak to lots of people who tell me the stories from their gap-years, even years down the line. It is the people who have volunteered whilst living and immersing themselves in a small community that often have the best stories to tell. It is those memories that stick out to them and not necessarily the fact that they've travelled around and ticked off a tourist spots from their bucket list."

There's no denying that the economic situation has also added to the need for volunteers, with organisations like the UN reporting that it has affected approximately 40% more of the world's most vulnerable people.

So volunteer help is likely to be even more needed and appreciated. Voluntary work abroad can also give you wonderful memories and a new perspective on the world.

On an organised voluntary project you often live amongst the local community and tend to get closer to daily life than you do as an independent traveller. By taking part in an organised voluntary work project you can learn about a different culture, meet new people and learn to communicate with people who may not understand your way of life, let alone your language.

You will come away with an amazing sense of achievement and (hopefully) pride in what you have done. Career breakers have also found that a volunteer gap has

not only been a satisfying experience but given them new ideas and attitudes too. A structured volunteer placement can also give a new dimension to the skills you can highlight on your CV.

This is particularly important considering the current job market, say Kaya Responsible Travel, and something that many students think about before they choose their volunteer gap-year:

Kaya Responsible Travel

"Many students are choosing projects based on what skills they might be able to learn to help them gain employment after they've graduated.

"Last year, we had just as many volunteers join us on healthcare projects as on projects working with wildlife or teaching children, the regular favourites. In the past many of our enquiries sounded something like, 'I'm looking for something to do in my summer holidays and would like to work with animals.' Whereas now, most enquiries are much more specific such as, 'I'm studying environmental science and would like to get some experience in the field. Can you suggest anything?'"

Richard Nimmo, from Blue Ventures, who arrange marine conservation expeditions in some of the most pristine environments in the world, told us that many of their volunteers use the experience to flesh out their academic knowledge with some real practical experience:

"As well as all the soft skills that can be gained from a meaningful time away, a marine conservation expedition is the perfect way to get a head-start in a career in the field of marine biology and conservation by learning from top scientists about ecological monitoring techniques, species identification, as well as learning about Blue Ventures' unique integrated approach to conservation natural resources.

"The science aspect of the expeditions brings a whole new element to Scuba diving and even those who have been diving for years say that being able to identify and understand what you're seeing in the water suddenly makes it even more enjoyable! Diving every day means you can really get stuck into learning diving as a new skill or improving any existing qualifications."

Our friends at the National Union of Students told us that they believe volunteering abroad can prove a life-changing experience for gappers.

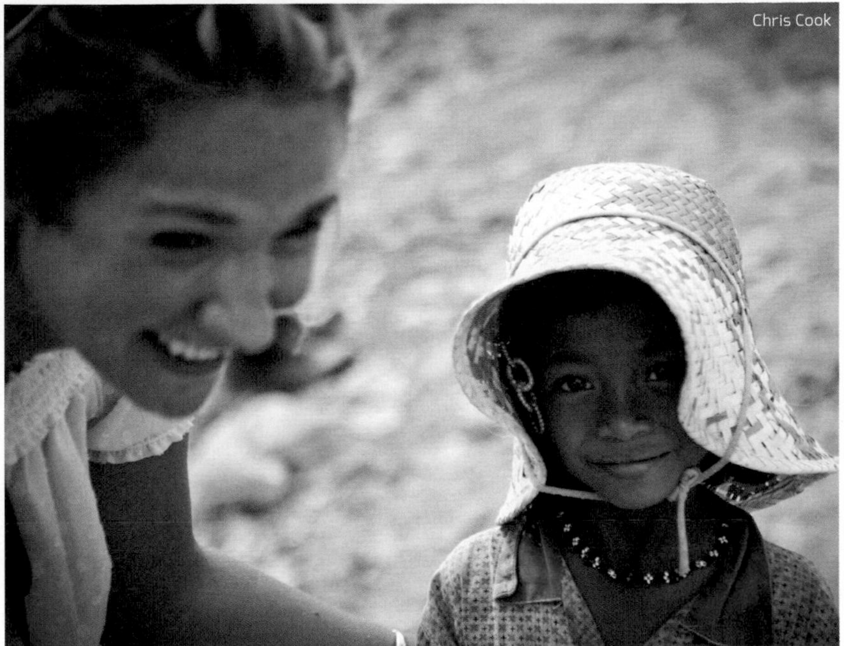

Chris Cook

"One way of using a year out is to see at as a break, a way to re-think your options, take some time to do the things you always wanted to do, or do things to open up doors and acquire skills you don't necessarily get in the classroom. Volunteering can be a rewarding and useful way to gain some skills and make beneficial contacts and you might want to get some valuable work experience in a field that interests you.

"If you do decide to volunteer abroad you should be careful about which organisations you support. Look for projects that emphasise learning and you can learn much from the communities in which you will live and work with.

"The most rewarding projects will not necessarily be most the glamorous but will be the ones where you really feel benefited a community in a way that simply sending money would not have."

Being realistic, voluntary work can be tough. You may be out in the middle of nowhere, with no western influence to be seen; food, language – the entire culture is likely to be totally different from what you're used to and there might not be many English speakers around: so you may have to cope with culture shock or feeling lonely, isolated and homesick at first, but if you stick with it you'll usually find those feelings will go as you get more involved in what you're doing.

Steffi Collaco, 21, applied to do law at Bournemouth University but decided to reconsider due to the fees involved. After working on projects with Raleigh International she realised she wanted to be a teacher.

She says: "I was inspired by children I worked with and motivated by meeting people from all over the world on Raleigh; they had a certain fire in their bellies and were very inspiring. I wanted to feel like that. I haven't been to university yet, but each step ahead of me is now more targeted. I feel more motivated because I know that I'm doing exactly what I want to do, having had time out to think about my options."

Are you going for the right reasons?

This is an obvious but often overlooked question, according to Nick Adie, of Lattitude Global Volunteering:

"It is a sad fact of life that there are many opportunities available for young people to volunteer on the proviso of gaining experience for their own benefits or because it 'fits in' with a wider plan to travel.

"If volunteers are not going with the primary view that they can help others, then they can actually be causing damage to a community for the purposes of furthering their own development. Simple steps can be taken to ensure you are volunteering responsibly; such as going with a reputable organisation such as a charity, volunteer for a decent period of time and ensure it fits in with the community – such as term times.

Oyster Worldwide

"Undoubtedly taking a gap-year enhances the important transferable skills that many graduate employers are looking for. These can be anything from organisation, to teamwork and leadership to communication – I am sure anybody who has been travelling will have demonstrated these skills at some point!

"Taking a gap-year is a great opportunity to develop these skills but it is important not to go simply because it does. Gappers must go because they want to go, volunteers must volunteer because they want to, not because it represents a check on the CV. It may be cynical to say but many gap-year opportunities that are little more than glorified holidays are sold with this in mind and it waters down the true value that can be attained from a productive gap-year. More now than ever it is down to the maturity of the gapper to know what they are doing and if it really has any value to a future career as well as what that cost may be to somebody else."

Jon Arnold agrees: "It is not just about developing yourself but also helping others. You've got to make sure though that you are immersing yourself into the project and not seeing it just as something to tick off your 'bucket list'.

Kaya Responsible Travel, Arch 28, North Campus Incubator, Sackville Street, Manchester M60 1QD
T: +44 (0)161 870 6212
E: info@kayavolunteer.com W: www.kayavolunteer.com

Join a volunteer project that makes the most of your skills and interests with Kaya Responsible Travel. With over 200 projects in 24 countries across Asia, Africa and Latin America, Kaya can identify a project that is right for you.

Sign up to projects from 2 weeks to 12 months, working with local people on issues affecting their communities and environments.

Kaya conservation initiatives include wildlife sanctuaries, breeding programs and habitat research, marine conservation on coral reefs, fair trade sustainable agriculture, reforestation and many other projects improving and protecting the environment and animals of the world.

Community initiatives include work with English teaching, child-care, sports development, women's empowerment, building, cultural restoration, all areas of health, therapy and medical work, as well as assisting in country specific issues, such as human trafficking in Thailand and HIV education in Africa.

Kaya have volunteers from 18-80 (and younger volunteers on selected projects), from all around the world, joining projects all year-round, travelling as individuals, with friends, groups and even as a family, and Kaya can help match each volunteer to a project that is right for them.

With a world of choice, you can make a world of difference on your travels, whilst discovering the real cultures in the heart of local communities. Contact the Kaya placement advice team or visit www.kayavolunteer.com to find the best project for you.

Kaya Responsible Travel

"We've noticed an increasing hedonism amongst some young people. They want to take a gap-year but they want to cram everything they can into the time, often to the detriment of the projects themselves.

"This has seen an increase in the number of organisations seizing on a money making idea and offering shorter and shorter volunteer programmes. There comes a point when people need to ask whether they are actually making a positive contribution or just getting involved to 'tick a box' to say they've 'taught in a school' on their gap-year and actually doing more harm than good.

"For people who really want to make a difference and learn about a whole new culture, you have to stay on the project for a significant period of time, ideally 3-6 months. You can't expect to make as much of a positive impact in a short 2-4 week trip for example.

"These people understand and have the conviction to make a real difference on their gap year by immersing themselves on the projects and their new life to truly get the most out of the whole experience."

What would you like to do?

There are a huge amount of options, as you'll see in this chapter and the directory section, so you need to make sure you find the best fit for you.

Here's some more advice from Kaya Responsible Travel:

"Really think about what you would like to get out of it. With so many options to chose from, making a decision about which volunteering abroad project to take part in can be quite tricky. At Kaya alone we have over 200 projects in 24 countries, in a range of sectors, from wildlife and environmental conservation to community,

Raleigh International

health and education work. By taking a bit of time to consider some questions about what is important to you, and getting advice from a placement advisor, you can start narrowing down those options and identifying a project that is the best match for you.

"We also encourage volunteers to do as much independent reading as possible. Looking at some pictures on Google images or checking out the Lonely Planet guide is a great way of getting yourself accustomed to the area that you will be staying in."

Raleigh are a leading charity provider of expeditions and volunteer projects abroad. They believe there are a huge amount of skills to be learned on the wide number of projects available to the interested gapper. They told us:

"Once you've made the decision to volunteer abroad, it's important to always do your research. There are lots of organisations that you can volunteer abroad with but you need to find the right one for you. Find out what you'll be doing, where your money will go, what support you will get and make sure this fits in with your own goals.

"With most volunteering opportunities, you'll find that you are taken well out of your comfort zone into incredibly challenging environments. You could find yourself in charge of a team of young volunteers in a managerial, decision-making and problem-solving role. Or you could be working with grass roots NGOs, devising an environmental project plan and gaining valuable insights into the development sector.

"Whatever you choose, volunteering abroad can help you gain experience in team-building, coaching, logistics, operations, multimedia or middle-management. With youth and sustainable development charity Raleigh International, you'll benefit from a two-week intensive 'Volunteer Manager' induction programme focuses on problem solving, analysing risk, project planning, leadership training and logistics. The real fun begins with the arrival of an army of young 'venturers' who provide the muscle-power for the programme – and whose development and welfare are overseen by the Volunteer Manager team for the next ten weeks.

blue ventures

discovery through research

Blue Ventures, Omnibus Business Centre, 39-41 North Road, London N7 9DP
T: +44 (0)20 7697 8598
E: info@blueventures.org W: www.blueventures.org

Want to dive on coral reefs? Explore marine life in tropical waters? Book a Blue Ventures expedition and join our international volunteers in exploring the underwater world!

Choose an expedition to either **Madagascar** or **Belize**. You'll dive in stunning marine environments, learn to identify a vast array of fish and corals, and contribute to valuable conservation research alongside marine scientists while living with local communities in a beautiful tropical setting.

We're an award-winning marine conservation organisation, and we help coastal tropical communities build skills and knowledge to protect the marine environments on which their livelihoods depend.

- Become a PADI Advanced Open Water diver, and take optional further courses (such as Rescue Diver and Divemaster).
- We've been running expeditions to the Indian, Atlantic and Pacific oceans since 2003. That's a decade of experience in providing you with adept skills and a safe, environmentally responsible trip.
- We employ highly skilled experts and a passionate team so you can expect top quality training with plenty of personal guidance.
- Rest assured, we take your wellbeing seriously with our dive protocols, risk assessments and rigorous safety checks.
- We've won 20 major awards to date, including 'Best Volunteering Organisation' at the British Youth Travel Awards in 2012 and the Virgin Holidays Responsible Tourism Awards in 2010 as well as the Buckminster Fuller Challenge in 2011. We've also been recognised by the United Nations and National Geographic.

Get in touch to find out how you can help and join an expedition today!

"We want volunteers with an open mind, commitment and a desire to change their world for the better. It's not for everyone so it's important that people understand what they're getting into before they sign up. Volunteers live and work in very basic conditions, collecting and purifying their own water, potentially digging their own toilet and living in close conditions with each other and local communities. All volunteers go through extensive training and are guided by a team of volunteer managers and our country staff.

"Before embarking on any trip, people should do their research, think about what they want to get out of their time out, ask a lot of questions and go with the organisation that most suits them. People coming with us tend to want a structured programme, working together in a team, with set objectives and guidance from project managers. For us it's really important that volunteers, local communities and project partners all work together and that all projects have a genuine, positive and sustainable impact.

"Volunteering overseas is also a great way to gain a deeper understanding of the culture of a country and to explore areas that you wouldn't get to see on the usual tourist route. And volunteer work can help you become clearer about your values and career goals. You'll return refreshed with a CV-packed full of new skills, not to mention a whole new set of friends and experiences."

Current trends

The most popular voluntary work activity, according to Richard Oliver of the Year Out Group, is working as a teacher or teaching assistant.

"Teaching placements may include sports coaching, teaching assistants, pastoral care outside the classroom or taking a class. They are an excellent way to learn about a people, their customs and culture especially if you live with a local family.

"However such placements really should be for a minimum of a term and preferably longer as it will take you most of the first term to find your feet and become effective.

Volunteer Maldives

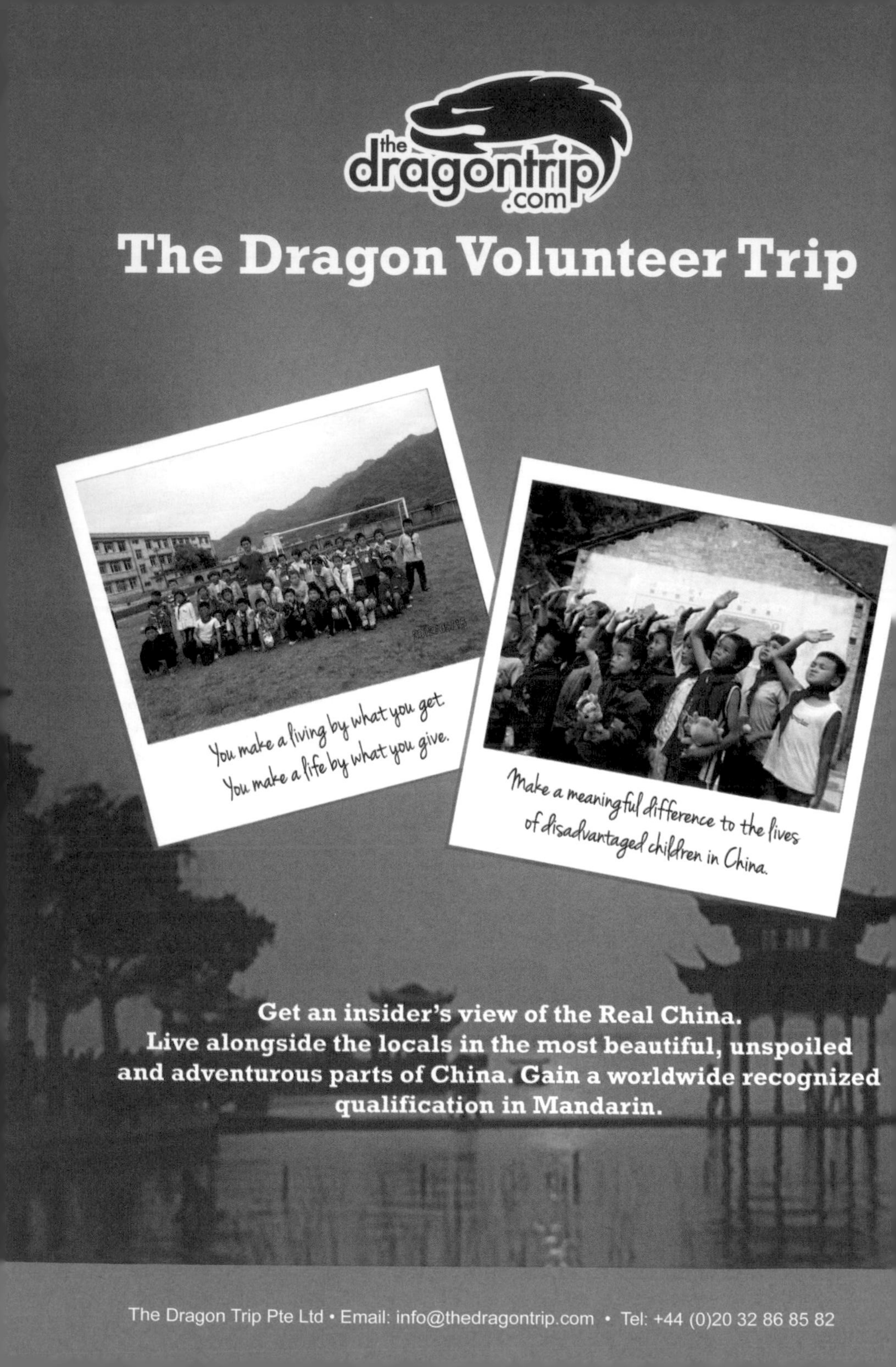
the dragontrip .com
The Dragon Volunteer Trip
You make a living by what you get.
You make a life by what you give.
Make a meaningful difference to the lives of disadvantaged children in China.
Get an insider's view of the Real China.
Live alongside the locals in the most beautiful, unspoiled and adventurous parts of China. Gain a worldwide recognized qualification in Mandarin.
The Dragon Trip Pte Ltd • Email: info@thedragontrip.com • Tel: +44 (0)20 32 86 85 82

If you can stay for the school year and see the seasons through the rewards will be even greater."

Voluntary work on community and conservation projects also remain popular. Community projects, such as building a school room or a dam, vary in type and length and tend to be done in teams and be of shorter duration than teaching or caring placements.

Conservation projects usually last a few weeks and should provide an excellent insight into aspects of conservation that only hands-on experience can provide.

For the first time this year, Year Out Group have drawn up a top 10 table for the most popular destinations for volunteers. Here are the results:

1. South Africa
2. Cambodia
3. Thailand
4. India
5. Ecuador
6. Kenya
7. China
8. Nepal
9. Sri Lanka
10. Fiji

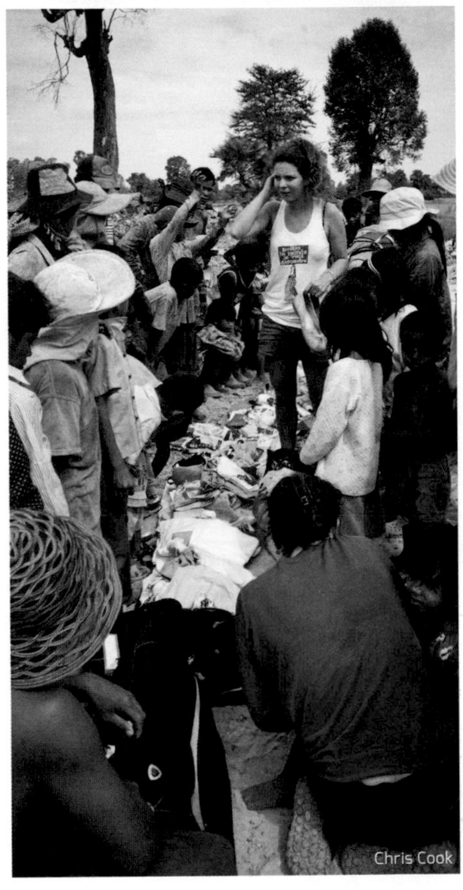
Chris Cook

The top four are the same as you will have seen in **Chapter 1** for all gap-year destinations. Otherwise, here are Richard Oliver's thoughts on the popularity of other countries:

"**India** and **Nepal** have always been popular. **Sri Lanka** is a great destination but fell out of favour as a result of the civil war with Tamil rebels in the north of the country. The war ended a couple of years ago and confidence has returned.

"The Orient is gaining in popularity. **Thailand** has been in the Top 10 consistently but has now been joined by **Cambodia**, **China** and **Fiji**. China, as one of the fastest developing country in the world, offers exciting opportunity for volunteers especially those with TEFL qualifications. Once again experience of China's customs and culture combined with an understanding of how business is conducted should provide a valuable addition to anyone's CV.

"Fiji offers a variety of activities including teaching and conservation and community projects. It is a long way away and flights are expensive but this is more than compensated by the experience the country offers."

Here are some thoughts from Projects Abroad: "The most popular projects are care and medicine and healthcare placements. A lot of volunteers are looking to either

Worldwide Experience,
Ashley Adams Travel (UK) Ltd, Guardian House,
Borough Road,
Godalming GU7 2AE
T: +44 (0) 1483 860 560
W: www.worldwideexperience.com

Worldwide Experience gives conservation enthusiasts the opportunity to become part of one of our exciting projects. We have a number of conservation experiences around the world which have all been carefully formulated by the Worldwide Experience team with the emphasis on environmental and educational conservation.

Our projects range from conservation based placements on some of Southern Africa's top game reserves, wildlife rehab centres, marine conservation and community-based projects and recently have signed up an Equine project in South Africa. Most of our projects run all year round which gives our volunteers the flexibility to start and end on dates that best suit them. Whether you want to go for just two weeks or three months, we ensure that you will get the best experience whilst making a difference on your placement of choice. None of our experiences, except our Vets Go Wild project, require any previous experience or qualifications, all you need is a passion for the experience you have chosen.

The Eco Schools Challenge gives schools and colleges the opportunity to travel as a group to one of our projects on a tailor made experience. We will ensure that the requirements and ambitions of the group are met, allowing for the group to have a hands-on experience by creating an outdoors classroom. Students will become a part of life changing experience through conservation education and an eye-opening cultural exchange.

The famous Vets Go Wild programme is based on a big five game reserve in the Eastern Cape. Veterinary students get the opportunity to work side-by-side with one of South Africa's leading wildlife vets Dr William Fowlds. The programme is designed for third year veterinary students, who have a passion for wildlife conservation and education with the main emphasis on academic training and practical experience. It will also count towards their extra mural studies, if from the United Kingdom.

Our Adult Gap experience allows for the more mature traveller to participate on some of our projects. We will carefully guide you in the right direction to place you in a project that we feel will best suit your expectations and requirements.

The Bear Grylls Travel Preparation Course is a one-day course aimed at students or mature travellers who are traveling abroad for the first time. From basic travel safety, accommodation, water purification, general knowledge of you environment and medical advice all learnt from Bears' travels around the world.

Worldwide Experience is a fully bonded tour operator so all our clients are fully protected as required by ABTA and ATOL which allows us to organise all your air travel requirements right from our office. Worldwide Experience caters for any adventure enthusiast and guarantees a life changing experience. All accommodation, meals and internal transfers are included.

help local people in disadvantages communities or to gain practical experience before starting a university degree. These two types of project give them the perfect opportunity to do so."

Nick at Lattitude Global Volunteering said there had been a huge increase in demand for outdoor placements in the past year, with many programmes booked up well in advance:

"Medical placements, particularly those working in Red Cross hospitals in Japan continue to be popular and as a result we have expanded our availability of these types of placements, not just in Japan but we have also introduced healthcare placements in Malawi too."

One exciting new development – and one that comes highly recommended by the NUS – is the government-funded International Citizen Service (ICS) programme.

It seeks to put young people at the forefront of the fight against global poverty and over the next three years 7,000 young people from the UK will work in partnership with young people in developing countries, on projects to fight poverty where help is needed the most.

The scheme follows a hugely successful pilot year and aims to offer a transformative experience for 18-25 year olds. The programme is designed to deliver three outcomes: to have a real and lasting development impact on sustainable development projects; to help the volunteers both from the UK and from developing countries learn key life skills such as teamwork, leadership, communication and project planning: and to instil in these volunteers a life-long commitment to development and to becoming active citizens, engaged in their communities back in the UK.

Only you can decide what's most important to you, it depends on whether you're more into plants, animals and the environment, in which case you'd be happier on a conservation project. If you're a people person you might do something that helps disadvantaged people, whether they're children, adults, and disabled or able-bodied.

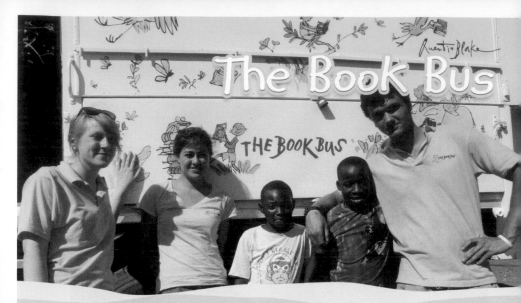

Whichever you feel is right for you there's a huge range of companies and types of voluntary placements to choose from.

Even if you are straight from school or university and haven't yet had much experience of work-related skills you shouldn't underestimate the skills and qualities you may have, and take for granted, that can be far less accessible to disadvantaged people in places where such things as access to education or to communications are not universally available.

Volunteer Maldives

How much time do you want to spend?

This is about how committed a volunteer you want to be. Would you feel more satisfied spending two weeks on a building project providing homes for people displaced by a natural disaster? Or are you the kind of person who wants to get stuck into a long-term project, where the results you see will be more gradual?

Because voluntary work is so popular with gappers, commercial companies offering volunteering packages exist alongside the more traditional not-for-profit organisations and the idealism associated with voluntary work, though still there, has come under some commercial pressure.

Some companies offer two to four-week holidays combined with some voluntary work, but equally there are many organisations still committed to the idealism of volunteering, offering placements from a few months to up a year or more.

However, you may not want (or be able) to offer more than a few weeks or months of your time, so the combined holiday/short volunteering option might be for you. There's no point in committing yourself to a whole year only to find that, after a few weeks, you hate it and want to go home early. The two-to four-week option may also be a good 'taster' experience to help you decide whether to commit to something more long-term.

Global Volunteer Projects, 7-15 Pink Lane, Newcastle-upon-Tyne NE1 5DW
T: 0191 222 0404
E: info@globalvolunteerprojects.org
W: www.globalvolunteerprojects.org

With Global Volunteer Projects you can teach conversational English in schools, help in orphanages and work with animals on conservation projects. You can also gain useful work experience in hospitals and clinics on our medical programme or work at newspapers, magazines, radio and TV stations on our media and journalism work experience placements.

The placements we offer are flexible and start every week on Friday with a comprehensive induction by our overseas staff. Our dedicated teams will support you during your stay, meeting you at the airport, taking you to the project site, helping you settle in to your accommodation and making sure that everything runs smoothly during your stay with us.

The placement duration is flexible, with most choosing a one to three month placement. This means that the projects can be done as part of a year out or during the summer vacation months.

All projects include either a basic language course or a culture course in those destinations where English is widely spoken.

Volunteers are located together in groups and live in either group 'hostel type' accommodation or with local families.

Placements are available in Cambodia, China, Ghana, India, Mexico, Romania and Tanzania.

Applications are accepted throughout the year.

For more information:

Call: 0191 222 0404

Email: info@GlobalVolunteerProjects.org

Visit: www.GlobalVolunteerProjects.org

So, it's a good idea to be honest with yourself about what you want – there's nothing wrong with wanting to travel and have a good time. But, whatever you choose, make sure you are clear about what you will be doing *before* you sign up and part with your money.

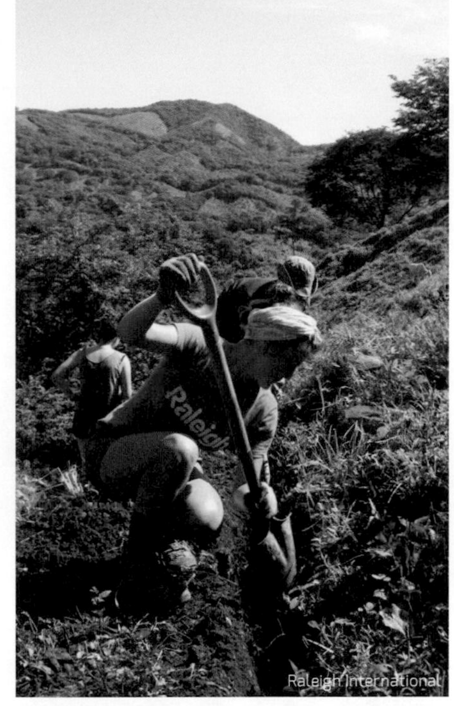

Raleigh International

When to start applying

Applications can close early, particularly for expeditions and conservation projects needing complex funding or for those tied in with international government programmes. If you'd like to go on one of these projects, planning should start about a year ahead, usually in the autumn term of the academic year.

Others can be taken up at very short notice. In fact, some organisations can take in applications during the August period (when you are getting A level results or going through clearing), and book you on a project that starts in September. If you don't have much time before your gap starts (maybe you didn't get the grades you expected, or you've made a last-minute decision to defer university for a year, or your company has offered you a sabbatical or made you redundant) it is always worth contacting a voluntary organisation about a project you're interested in. They may have had a last-minute cancellation.

Stiff competition

As more people are becoming motivated by the almost daily media reports on poverty in the developing world and on various global threats to the planet's climate, ecology and environment, to go out and do something, the competition for places can be fierce. Companies can afford to be picky – you may find you have to prove to them that you should be selected to go before they will accept your money!

They have a point. Increasingly NGOs and volunteers are trying to make sure both sides benefit from the experience, so placement organisations put a lot of effort into checking and briefing as well as getting you out there and providing in-country support. If you can't stick it, everyone loses out – including the person who could have been chosen instead of you.

What is the cost?

It varies hugely – some companies just expect you to pay for the air fare – others expect you to raise thousands of pounds for funding. It can be hard to combine raising money with studying for A levels or with work, but there are a lot of ways to do it.

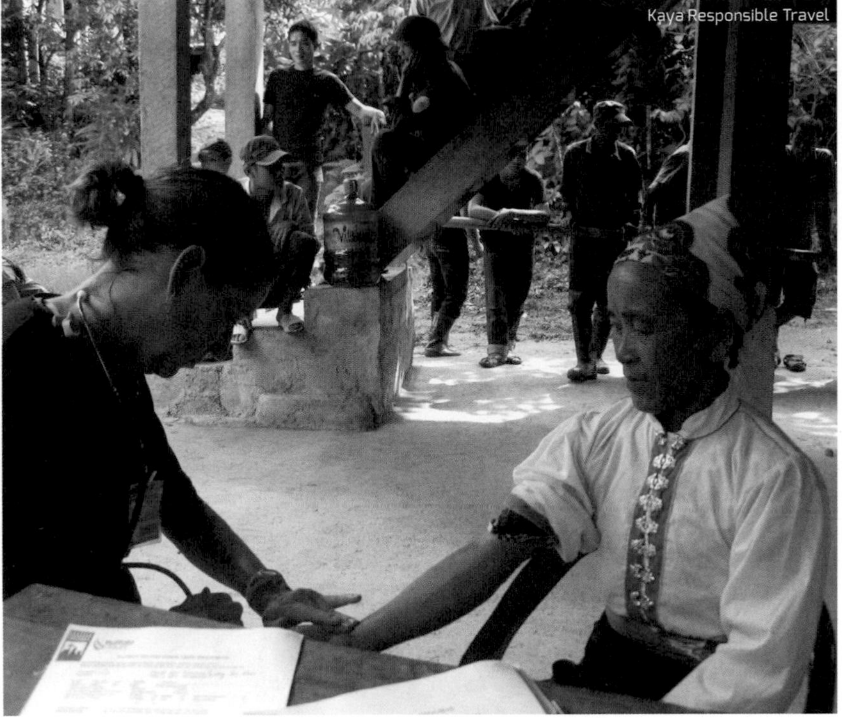
Kaya Responsible Travel

As usual, the earlier you start, the easier it will be. The organisation that you go with should be able to give advice, but options include organising sponsored events, writing to companies or trusts asking for sponsorship, car boot sales, or even just getting a job and saving what you can.

If approached, many local newspapers will do a short article about your plan if it's interesting enough – but it's better to ask them during the quieter news spells, like the summer holiday months, when they'll be more likely to welcome an additional story.

The last resort is to go cap-in-hand to your parents, either for a loan or a gift, but this can be unsatisfying and they may simply not be able to afford it. If your parents or relatives do want to help, you could ask for useful items for Christmas or birthday presents – like a rucksack.

Career breakers will have different considerations. There's more on this in **Chapter 3 - Career breaks and older travellers**, but if you work for a large organisation it's worth asking whether they have any links to projects, or run their own charitable foundation, which might offer placements to employees.

What to expect

Placements range from a couple of weeks to a whole academic year, but most provide only free accommodation and food – a very few provide pocket money. You'll need to be resourceful, be able to teach, build, inspire confidence, communicate and share what you know. Physical and mental fitness, staying power and the ability to get on with people are essential.

The Humanity Exchange, 324 East Oak Street, Fort Collins CO 80524
T: +1 778 300 2466
E: admin@thehumanityexchange.org W: www.thehumanityexchange.org

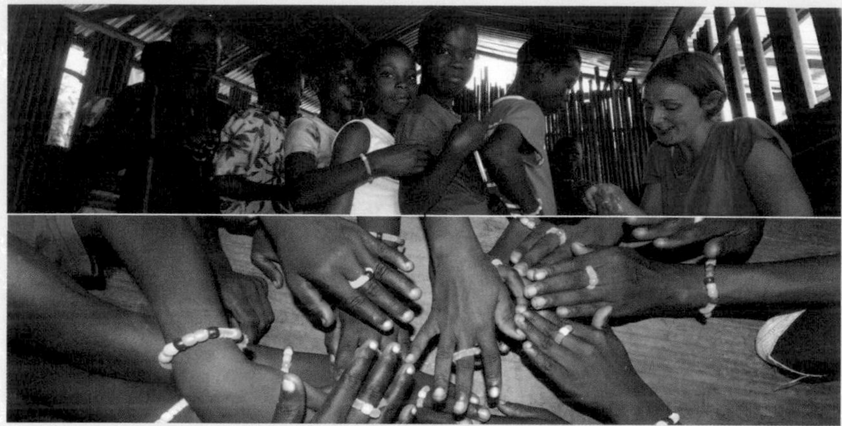

The Humanity Exchange works at grassroots level with NGOs, charities, schools and orphanages in developing world countries, arranging volunteer placements for independent travellers.

With projects in Benin, Cameroon, Ghana and Columbia, The Humanity Exchange work with communities off the beaten track who can benefit from the help of volunteers in community development initiatives such as adult education, teaching in schools, nutrition, HIV education, youth engagement and farming.

You can also learn a language whilst you work, with French classes in Benin and Cameroon and Spanish classes in Columbia to chose from - so you can develop your CV whilst helping the development of communities in some of the world's poorest countries.

Projects are available from 2 weeks to 12 months, but with low-cost project fees, volunteers at The Humanity Exchange often participate for a number of months and become a real part of the community. For those looking to work in the field of development, The Humanity Exchange offer projects that provide real experience at a grassroots level.

To become a Humanity Exchange volunteer, visit www.TheHumanityExchange.org to check out your project options or contact us to get advice on the best placement for you.

Are there ethical concerns?

The debate continues about the ethics of volunteering, and covers a variety of issues:

- Is it environmentally sustainable?
- Does it really benefit the people or is it creating a dependency culture?
- What's the 'benefit balance' between volunteer satisfaction and the community being helped?

Fair Trade Volunteering (**www.fairtradevolunteering.org**) has been created and established by leading volunteer organisations and advisors in the travel industry to enable volunteers to make a choice as to which volunteer experience they would like to have, and to give organisations wishing to provide FTV projects guidelines, help and support to be able to deliver them.

The 'volunteering industry' has in the past few years become just that – an industry, with different organisations giving different levels of importance to the benefit for the projects, the experience for the volunteer and the profit for the company. Just as the Fairtrade Foundation has helped the consumer to be able to make an informed decision when buying coffee, bananas and chocolate *etc*, Fair Trade Volunteering is looking to do the same for volunteering placements.

Here's what they told us: "Our belief is that short periods of volunteering can be positive, but only really if they are part of a longer partnership with the project, and combined with financial support above and beyond the volunteer's contribution, to ensure the work done can be continued throughout the year. Organisations that are approved by Fair Trade Volunteering not only ensure that the cost of the volunteer (and their work) is covered, but that there is also a financial premium given to the project to ensure their work can be further supported above and beyond the work done by the volunteers.

Chris Cook

volunteer maldives
maldives island adventure
Paradise Uncut
The Real Island Discovery Experience
2 weeks to 12 months placements & programs available for individuals or groups.
info@volunteermaldives.com
info@maldivesislandadventure.com

Volunteer Maldives

"Added to this, they must also show a long-term partnership with their projects, ensuring that the work done by the volunteer and the funds being sent are part of a longer term set of objectives. This means a volunteer who is only able to commit to a short period at a project is able to see that their contribution, both financial and physical, is part of a bigger picture that is making a genuinely positive difference.

"At the end of the day, it is up to the consumer to decide. By buying non-Fairtrade coffee, you are not necessarily doing a bad thing, you are still helping to provide a living for the people who make it. If you do buy Fairtrade however, it is because you are willing to pay the premium which Fairtrade ensures for its workers. The same holds for Fair Trade Volunteering."

Tourism Concern, meanwhile, is an independent, non-industry based UK charity that fights exploitation in tourism. They believe that it is vitally important for volunteer organisations to demonstrate that they have attained a recognised level of responsibility in the way they recruit volunteers, find placements and manage the volunteering process, and they have developed the Gap Year and International Volunteering Standard (GIVS). International Volunteering Organisations in the UK are now being assessed under GIVS and Tourism Concern advises you look for the GIVS kitemark in order to ensure that you sign up to worthwhile and rewarding placements.

GIVS assesses organisations on eight key principles:

1. **Purpose:** achievable objectives that have been identified by host partners and communities.
2. **Marketing:** marketing and imagery that is consistent with good practice.
3. **Recruitment:** fair, consistent and transparent recruitment procedures.
4. **Pre-placement Information:** clear and accurate information on the sending organisation, their partners, programmes and volunteer placements.
5. **Pre-placement training:** appropriate preparation, training and induction.
6. **Volunteer support:** ongoing support appropriate to the placement and volunteer.

7. **Risk Management:** ensuring protection, safety and well being of volunteers and those they work with.
8. **Monitoring & Evaluation:** ongoing monitoring and evaluation in order to improve performance and ensure work remains relevant.

For more information go to **www.tourismconcern.org.uk**

Here are some easy steps to follow from Tourism Concern to help you be a more ethical traveller – and your experience will be richer as a result.

1. **Your holiday, their home:** your travel destination is a place where people live; people who may have different values and sensibilities to your own. Opening your mind to new cultures and traditions is part of the joy and adventure of travelling. Be respectful but don't be afraid to ask questions. Getting to know the local people is the best way of learning about a place.
2. **Switch off and relax:** whilst your visit may provide some economic benefits to local people, it can also use up scarce natural resources. Water is in short supply in many tourist destinations, and one tourist can use as much water in one day as 100 people in a developing country would in a year. Keep this in mind when using water or electricity on holiday.
3. **Keep children smiling:** it is best never to give anything directly to children (not even sweets) as they may think there is no need to go to school (and hassle other travellers). Donating to a local school, hospital or orphanage will have a lasting impact. Tragically more than one million children are sexually abused by tourists every year. Help protect children by telling your hotel manager if you see something suspicious.
4. **Haggle with humour:** try to keep your money in the local economy; eat in local restaurants, drink local beer or fruit juice rather than imported brands and pay a fair price when you're buying souvenirs and handicrafts. Bargaining can be great fun, so haggle with humour – but remember that if you bargain too hard, sheer poverty might make a craftsman accept a poor price just so that he can feed his family that day. Pay what something is worth to you.
5. **Support Tourism Concern:** Tourism Concern – 'the voice of ethical tourism' – is a UK charity that campaigns against exploitation in tourism and for fairly traded and ethical forms of tourism. The website has a wealth of information on action you can take to avoid guilt trips. **www.tourismconcern.org.uk**

Some other points worth emphasising

Big organisation or small specialist? You might feel safer going with a big voluntary organisation because they should be able to offer help in a nasty situation. Experience is certainly important where organisations are concerned. But often a small, specialist organisation is more knowledgeable about a country, a school or other destination.

Size and status have little bearing on competence. A charity can be more efficient than a commercial company. Conversely a commercial company can show more sensitivity than a charity.

There are few general rules – talk to someone who's been with the organisation you're interested in. Organisations vary as to how much back up they offer volunteers, from virtually holding your hand throughout your stay and even after you come back, to the 'sink or swim' method.

visit: www.thebookbus.org

You need to know yourself if you're going to get the most out of your volunteering **gap**. If you feel patronised at the slightest hint of advice then you might get annoyed with too much interference from the organisation.

Though do bear in mind that they probably know more than you do about the placement, what sort of vaccinations you're going to need, what will be useful to take with you, and how to get the necessary visas and permits. Equally if you're shy or nervous it might be as well to go with an organisation that sends volunteers in pairs or groups. There's nothing wrong with either type of placement – it's about choosing what's right for you.

Talk to a few organisations before you decide which one to go with – and, probably even more useful, talk to some previous volunteers. They'll be able to tell you what it's really like; don't just ask them if they enjoyed it, get them to describe what they did, what they liked and why, what they didn't like and what they'd do differently.

Remember, wherever you're sent, you can't count on much. Regardless of the organisation, you will be going to poor countries where the infrastructure and support services can be minimal – otherwise why would they need volunteers?

Expect to be adaptable. Regardless of the reputation of the voluntary work organisation you choose, or the competence of voluntary work coordinators in a particular country, it's about your skills and human qualities and those of the people you'll be with so there's bound to be an element of chance as to whether the school you are put in, for example, really values you or whether you get on with the family you stay with. It's worth checking first what training is given and what support there is in-country, but be aware that you may not get what you expect – you need to be adaptable and make the most of whatever situation you find yourself in.

Safety first

If you're going with a good organisation they shouldn't send you anywhere too dangerous – but situations change quickly and it's always worth finding out for yourself about where you're going.

Check out the Foreign Office's travel advice pages on **www.fco.gov.uk.** The Foreign Office site also has lots of advice on visas, insurance and other things that need to be sorted out before you go, and advice on what to do in an emergency abroad. There's much more on all this in **Chapter 1 – Tips For Travellers**.

Also, make sure you have proper insurance cover and that it is appropriate for where you're going, the length of time you'll be away and for any unexpected emergencies.

Please see the directory pages starting on page 309 for information on companies and organisations offering opportunities to volunteer abroad.

my gap-year Joseph Dax

Joseph Dax, an A level student at Tavistock College in Devon, was so inspired by The Book Bus idea that he duly volunteered and headed off for two weeks in summer 2013 to Zambia to play his part in encouraging local children to get reading...

Have you ever been attacked by a crocodile? My trip to Livingstone, Zambia as a Book Bus volunteer left me with a very lasting impression! Camping in the grounds of 'Grubby's Grotto', an old colonial residence, myself and the other volunteers set off early each morning, trundling down winding dusty roads and tracks in the trusty (but rather bumpy) Book Bus.

With one of my groups of children, we read together the book 'I really want to eat a child' about a deluded baby crocodile named Achilles.

Afterwards, they all made their own crocodiles from cardboard, which subsequently ate me alive! Still hungry, the newly created crocodiles then proceeded to chomp on all the pencils and bits of paper they could find around the table until break-time when they escaped onto the playground to eat all the other children. Joking aside, the children loved reading about Achilles and the creative task really helped them to engage with the story. I would like to think that it contributed to helping them improve and enjoy reading a little bit more than before.

As a child, I had an insatiable appetite for reading, and I still do. It is a cliché, I know, but a passion for reading really can open the door to a world of opportunity. I believe that the journalist AC Grayling aptly describes the opportunities of literacy: "to read is to fly; it is to soar to a vantage which gives a view over the wide terrains of history, human variety, ideas, shared experience and the fruits of many enquiries".

As the aeroplane began its ascent from Livingstone airport I could see an aerial view of the awe inspiring Victoria Falls thundering away in the gorge below, with the mighty Zambezi River gliding into the horizon. This got me thinking about Grayling's metaphor and, it was then that the significance of increasing literacy in the developing world and the importance of The Book Bus's work started to sink in.

PS. I did meet some 'real' crocodiles on a riverbank; thankfully I was not eaten alive by any of them!

visit: www.thebookbus.org

Learning abroad

Sponsored by

E·S·L
LANGUAGE TRAVEL

Languages will make the world yours!

Preparing for a gap-year is probably one of the most exciting things to do; making plans, creating your travel itinerary, learning about the places you are going to visit and so much more! Far away from your daily grind, this unique time of your life will be given rhythm by a single keyword: freedom.

Expressing yourself in the language(s) spoken in the country(ies) you plan to visit will help you to bring your whole gap-year experience to another level. Being able to interact with people, order your meal in a restaurant, understand information boards or read reviews in a museum will definitely make you feel like a local.

Starting your gap-year with a few weeks of language study in full immersion will allow you to start your experience smoothly. During a language course, your skills will be trained daily, which will ensure fast and long-lasting progress. Moreover, the international environment provided by the school will be ideal to meet people from all over the world and even maybe future fellow travellers. Programs offered by specialised agencies include accommodation in addition to the language course. Most of the time you can choose to stay with a host family for a truly authentic experience or in a residence to benefit from more independence.

The flexibility of those programmes makes it interesting for anyone, whether you want to learn the language for one or two weeks or for a whole year. The duration of your course is completely up to you, to best suit your needs and projects.

Should you have a bit of time ahead of you, it might be worth considering an exam preparation course. Those courses lead to an official certificate, which is recognised worldwide. This represents a tangible achievement that will be useful back home to prove your language level and that will surely stand out in your CV.

Other options for a more long-term stay are internships or volunteer work as offered by ESL – Language Travel, a leading study-abroad agency. Ideal to build strong linguistic skills, you will be able to give a professional dimension to your experience. After a couple of course weeks, you could join a company for an internship or volunteer in support of the local community. This is an efficient way to put into practice your knowledge and to add another valuable line to your CV.

If you would rather emphasize local culture and fun, dozens of courses such as French + surfing, Spanish + tango or Italian + cooking are also on offer.

Come on and take the next step: when you can speak another language, the world is yours!

E·S·L
LANGUAGE TRAVEL

Learning abroad

While your gap-year will inevitably be about personal growth, because of all the new things you experience and see you could build on this by using it as an opportunity to combine living and studying abroad.

This might not seem appealing if you've just 'escaped' from a period of intense study and exams, but consider this:

- The learning doesn't have to be goal-oriented or laden with exam stress, you could learn a new skill and gain a qualification.
- You could pursue an interest, hobby or passion you haven't had time for before.
- You'll be able to explore and enrich your knowledge in your own way, rather than following a curriculum.
- You could also find you've added another dimension to your CV.
- You'll meet like-minded folk and have a lot of fun.

These are some of the things you could do: learn a language in-country, do a sports instructor course, music or drama summer schools, explore art, music, culture and learn about conservation. If you're not jaded with study or are at a time of life when a postgraduate qualification would be useful, and a career break possible, you could go for an academic year abroad. Another option for those of you who want to try to earn while you travel is to do a TEFL course.

Here's a good weblink for courses abroad: **www.studyabroaddirectory.com**

An academic year abroad

A good way of getting to know a place and its people in depth is to spend a whole academic year at a foreign school, either in Europe, the USA, or further afield. One possibility is an academic year before university:

- French Lycée
- German Gymnasium
- School in Spain
- Spanish-speaking school in Argentina

The most relevant EU education and training programmes are Comenius, Erasmus and Leonardo. For more information see:

Comenius: **www.britishcouncil.org/comenius.htm**

Erasmus: **www.britishcouncil.org/erasmus**

Leonardo: **www.ec.europa.eu/education/lifelong-learning-programme/doc82_en.htm**

A scheme called Europass provides trainees in any EU country with a 'Europewide record of achievement for periods of training undertaken outside the home member state'. So it's important to ask the school: "Is this course recognised for a Europass?"

visit: www.esl.co.uk

University exchange

If you want to spend up to a year abroad at a European university as part of the European Union's Erasmus (EuRopean community Action Scheme for the Mobility of University Students) scheme, you'll need to have some working knowledge of the relevant language – so a gap-year could be the time to start, either studying overseas or in Britain. Information about Erasmus courses is usually given to students in their first year at university.

To apply for Erasmus you must be an EU citizen. When you spend your time abroad, you continue to pay tuition fees or receive loans or grants as if you were at your university back home.

There's more information on: **www.britishcouncil.org/erasmus**

The scheme is also open to teaching and non-teaching staff at higher education and HE/FE institutions, as long as your home higher education institution has a formal agreement with a partner in one of the eligible countries. It must also have an Erasmus University Charter awarded by the European Commission.

Postgraduate MA/visiting fellowship/exchange

Several universities in the UK have direct links to partnership programmes with others around the world, but if you want to widen your search, the Worldwide Universities Network (WUN) is a good place to start looking for exchange, overseas study and funding for research projects. It's a partnership of 16 research-led universities from Asia, Australasia, Europe and North America.

WUN's Research Mobility Programme funds a period of study overseas, for senior postgraduates and junior faculty, to establish and cultivate research links at an

ART HISTORY ABROAD

Art History Abroad (AHA), The Red House, 1 Lambseth Street, Eye IP23 7AG
T: +44 (0)1379 871 800
E: info@arthistoryabroad.com W: www.arthistoryabroad.com

Cultivate your mind with AHA: a journey which will last you a lifetime

'Incomparable to any other gap year'

What Inspiring journeys the length of Italy with expert tutors, seeing and discussing many of the world's greatest achievements in art, architecture and sculpture. Learn how these fit into the greater picture of Western Civilization and find like-minded friends as you travel. Most importantly, have fun doing it.

When Six week courses starting in October 2013 and January, April and August 2014, and two-week courses starting in July and August 2014. New three month semester in London, Paris and Italy from September 2013 and September 2014.

Where Cities famous for art, music and food: Venice, Verona, Florence, Siena, Rome, Naples, Sicily and many more...

Why Discovering art with AHA is an experience which will last you a lifetime.

'I know that AHA has inspired me more in such a short time than my 14 years at school and I will be making every effort to return to Italy for many years and to try and recapture the magic and glory of our time. I feel incredibly lucky to have had such a breathtaking experience and made such firm friends, both students and tutors. I really feel that AHA is incomparable to any other gap year and I genuinely couldn't think of a better way to have spent mine.'

Student, Early Summer Course 2012

institutional and individual level between the partners in Europe, North America, south-east Asia and Australia. It is also intended to encourage the personal and academic development of individuals early in their research careers.

Check out: **www.wun.ac.uk/about**

Arts and culture

Art

If you want to go to art school, or have already been, no matter which art form interests you, travelling and soaking up the atmosphere is a good way to learn more and give you ideas for your own work. It's also a great opportunity to add to your portfolio.

You don't have to be an art student or graduate to enjoy the beauty of art and artefacts produced by different cultures. Most courses listed in this guidebook are open to anyone who wants to explore the arts in a bit more depth. For example, have a look at the courses offered by Art History Abroad: **www.arthistoryabroad.com**.

Culture

It's a cliché, but also true, that travel broadens the mind and you'll absorb much about the culture of the places you visit just by being there. However, if you want to develop your understanding in more depth, maybe learn a bit of the language and discover some of your chosen country's history, then you could go for the cultural component of some of the language courses listed in the directory.

Alternatively, you might like to try something like The John Hall Venice Course, which gives an insight into Western culture and achievements and features time spent in London, Venice, Florence and Rome. To find out more see their advert on page XX or visit **www.johnhallvenice.com**.

JohnHall Venice

John Hall Venice,
9 Smeaton Road,
London SW18 5JJ
T: +44 (0)20 8871 4747
E: info@johnhallvenice.com
W: www.johnhallvenice.com

The **John Hall Venice Course** is an epic gap year experience and one that you will never forget. It is a nine-week introduction to some of the finest and most thought-provoking achievements in the Western World, from the Classical past to today.

There are lectures and visits by a team of world-class experts and the course includes not only painting, sculpture and architecture but also music, world cinema, literature and global issues. There are also practical classes in studio life drawing and portraiture, as well as classes in photography, Italian language and cookery.

The course consists of a week in London, six weeks in Venice, a week in Florence and a week in Rome. The heart of the experience is Venice - to be in the historic and uniquely beautiful city of Venice, living more like a resident than a tourist, is a life-changing experience.

Students come from schools around the world - the UK, America, Africa, Europe and Asia, creating a cosmopolitan collegiate atmosphere that leads to friendships and connections for life.

There are many privileged private visits throughout the Course. There is an unforgettable night visit to St. Mark's in Venice, plus unique private visits to the Uffizi in Florence and to the Sistine Chapel in Rome.

The John Hall Venice Course gives a foretaste of a university style of living and learning. It will leave you with not only some lifelong friendships, but also a totally new awareness of what European civilization is about, and with a seriously improved CV.

Design and fashion

Every year, when the new season's collections are shown on the world's fashion catwalks, it's clear that the designers have 'discovered' the fabrics, or decoration or style, of one region or another.

So for those with a passion for fashion a gap-year is a great opportunity to experience the originals for themselves. Wandering the streets in other countries, and seeing how other people put their 'look' together, can be an inspiration.

Then there's the opportunity to snap up, at bargain prices, all kinds of beautiful fabrics that would cost a fortune back home.

But if you wanted to use part of your gap to find out more about fashion and design you could also join a fashion summer school in one of Europe's capitals, like the ones listed on this website:

www.learn4good.com/great_schools/fashion_design_career_courses.htm

Or why not India? The country's National Institute of Fashion Technology in Delhi runs summer schools for fashion stylists – here's the link: **www.nift.ac.in**

Met Film School

Film, theatre and drama

If you're thinking of a short course in performing arts, the USA is one of the most obvious places to go – most famously the New York Film Academy, which has a very useful page for international students:

www.nyfa.edu/admissions/international_student.php

The Academy runs summer schools in London, Paris, Florence, Colombia, China, Japan and South Korea.

Met Film School run courses at their studios in Berlin, incorporating writing, producing, directing and editing.

You can find out more at: **www.metfilmschool.de**

For a wider search try: **www.filmschools.com**

Or how about New Zealand? Try: **www.drama.org.nz**

If you want dance as well, the world's your oyster. You can learn salsa in Delhi (as well as in South America) and the traditional Indian Kathak dance in the USA. Here's a good place to start looking:

dir.yahoo.com/Arts/Performing_Arts

And then, of course, there's Bollywood. There are courses in film direction, cinematography, sound production and editing at the Film and Television Institutes of India, in Pune (south-west of Mumbai), which runs a number of courses for overseas students: **www.ftiindia.com**

Met Film School

Music

Whether you're into classical or pop, world music or traditional, there are vibrant music scenes all over the world.

From the studios that have sprung up in Dakar, the West African capital of Senegal, to the club scenes of Europe, to more formal schools, check out the opportunities to combine your interest with travel and maybe learn to play an instrument, if you don't already, or another one if you do.

We've checked online for short music courses, since the UNESCO site no longer offers a directory, and although there are plenty out there, it's a case of searching by location.

Here's one for all UK summer schools, including music:

www.summer-schools.info

Or how about helping out in a rock centre in Chennai, India?

www.unwindcenter.com

Media and journalism

Although the print media has been suffering from the global recession there are, of course, other options.

You may want to get into media/journalism but you're not the only one, so do thousands of others and the competition is intense. The skills you'll need could include media law, shorthand, knowledge of how local and national government works and, not least, the ability to construct an attention-grabbing story!

To get a job you may need to do more than gain a media studies degree or have on-the-job training in a newsroom.

It's, therefore, always a good idea to demonstrate your commitment and a gap is a good time to do this. You can try contacting your local paper for a work experience placement, though don't expect to be paid!

Plus, if you search the internet there are plenty of internships in newsrooms – many of them in India, where there's still a lot of attachment to local and national newspapers.

We Googled 'journalism placements and internships' and found possibilities around the world.

These websites may also be useful:

www.tigweb.org/resources/opps
www.internews.org

Photography

Travelling offers you the chance to develop your skills as a photographer – after all almost everyone takes pictures to remember their travels. But if you've always dreamed of turning professional, it's a chance to practice.

You could be innovative by contacting a local newspaper or magazine and asking if they'll let you accompany one of their photographers on assignments. You won't be paid but you'll learn a lot and it might give you pictures to add to your portfolio.

Languages

You learn a language much more easily and quickly if you're living in the country where it's spoken, but there's more than one reason to learn a new language. There's more to a language than just words: most language courses will include local culture, history, geography, religion, customs and current affairs – as well as food and drink.

Gemma Rescorla, director of Live Languages Abroad, told us: "Learning a language abroad is a life skill by which you can reap so many rewards. Not only is it an amazing feeling to be able to communicate with someone in their own language, it also: improves your cultural awareness; enhances your learning ability, increases your confidence; helps your career prospects; gives you a taste for travel; and the opportunity to make life-long friends from all around the world."

Think laterally about where you want to study. Spanish is spoken in many countries around the world, so you could opt for a Spanish course in South America, rather than

Spain, and then go travelling around the country, or learn Portuguese in Brazil, where it's the main language, or perhaps French in Canada.

Be aware though that if you learn a language outside its original country you may learn a particular dialect that is only spoken in a specific region of the country as a whole. It may even be considered inferior by some people (or not understood) elsewhere in the country.

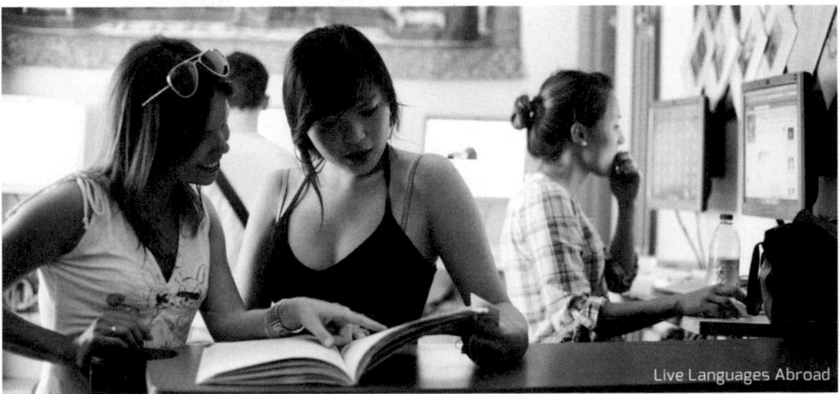

Live Languages Abroad

Finding the right place to learn

Universities often have international summer school centres or courses for foreign students, or there's the popular network of British Institutes abroad. And there are hundreds (probably thousands) of independent language colleges to choose from, either directly or through a language course organiser or agency in the UK.

The advantage in dealing with a UK-based organisation is that, if something goes wrong, it is easier to get it sorted out under UK law.

Choosing a course provider

There are a number of companies that you can choose to take your language course with. Do make you get as much information from them as possible before making your choice.

We would like to recommend ESL Language Travel, sponsor of this chapter. You can find out about their courses at: **www.esl.co.uk**

Live Languages Abroad also offer some excellent options. Their website can be found at: **www.livelanguagesabroad.co.uk**

These pages are also worth at look:

www.europa-pages.co.uk – for language courses in European countries.
www.ialc.org (International Association of Language Centres)

Living with a family

If enrolling on a language course sounds too much like school, another way of learning a language is staying with a family as an au pair or tutor (giving, say, English or music lessons to children) and going to part-time classes locally.

Language courses

Courses at language schools abroad can be divided into as many as ten different levels, ranging from tuition for the complete beginner to highly technical or specialised courses at postgraduate level. The usual classification of language classes, however, into 'beginner' or 'basic', 'intermediate' and 'advanced', works well. Within each of these levels there are usually subdivisions, especially in schools large enough to move students from one class to another with ease.

When you first phone a school from abroad or send in an application form, you should indicate how good your knowledge of the language is. You may be tested before being allocated your class, or you may be transferred from your original class to a lower or higher one, as soon as they find you are worse or better than expected.

Different schools will use different methods of teaching: if you know that you respond well to one style, check that is what your course offers. Foreign language lessons are often attended by a variety of nationalities, so they are almost always conducted in the language you are learning, forcing you to understand and respond without using English. In practice, however, most teachers can revert to English to explain a principle of grammar if a student is really stuck.

The smaller the class the better, though the quality of the teaching is most important – at more advanced levels, well-qualified graduate teachers should be available. Language schools and institutes show a mass of information, photographs and maps on their websites, so it's easy to find out if the school is near to places that interest you, whether it's in a city centre or near a coastal resort. The admissions staff should be happy to give you references from previous students.

In the directory, you'll find some of the organisations offering language opportunities to gappers, from formal tuition to 'soaking it up' while you live with a family. We've split the organisations according to the languages they offer: Arabic, Chinese, French, German, Greek, Indonesian, Italian, Japanese, Portuguese, Russian and Spanish. Here's a quick look at each:

Arabic

Arabic is the language in which the *Qur'an* is written and, although there are translations into the local languages of Muslims around the world, there's also a lot of argument about the way they're translated. This has led to differences about what Islam means.

It's all a matter of interpretation of the roots of words and what's more there are two main versions of Arabic: Fousha – Modern Standard Arabic; and Aameya – Egyptian Colloquial Arabic.

Chinese

As Chinese enterprises become global, the language is becoming a popular choice in UK schools, with as many as 400 state schools now offering lessons.

There are two main dialects. Cantonese is the language of most Chinese people living abroad, from Singapore to Europe and the USA. Cantonese is also spoken widely in the Guangdong and Guangxi provinces of mainland China and in Hong Kong and Macau.

Mandarin is the official language of government, international relations and much education in China is undertaken in Mandarin. It is the more formal language and most students are advised to learn it.

Both languages are tonal (the same sound said in a different tone will change the meaning of a word) and therefore can be quite difficult for English speakers to learn. The different tonal pronunciation, vowels and consonants effectively turn Mandarin and Cantonese into two different languages, although both use the same written characters. There are many, many other Chinese dialects, including Hokkien, Hakka, Wu and Hui.

You can find course information at: **www.mandarinhouse.cn/chinesecourses.htm**

It has a choice of 12 different courses in Chinese, including one for expatriates, in Beijing or Shanghai.

French

Languages have changed over time as they have been introduced to other parts of the world from their home countries and then developed in their own directions. Then there are the local dialects. French covers French as it's spoken in France, but then there's also Swiss French, Belgian French and Canadian French.

There's a busy French community in the UK, a large French Lycée in London and more than one teaching institute run by French nationals, so there are plenty of opportunities to carry on developing your French language skills when you return to the UK.

German

German has many very strong dialects (particularly in Austria, Switzerland and much of south Germany), and it is important to bear this in mind if you want to study German academically, or use it for business, in which case you may need to be learning and practising *Hochdeutsch* (standard German).

Many universities in Germany, Austria and Switzerland run summer language schools for foreign students.

Contact:

German Embassy
23 Belgrave Square
Cultural Department
London SW1X 8PZ
Tel: +44 (0) 20 7824 1300.

Their website has a section on studying in Germany: **www.london.diplo.de** There's also a lively German community in the UK and many courses run by the Goethe Institut (**www.goethe.de/ins/gb/lon/enindex.htm**). So, there are plenty of opportunities to carry on practising your German when you get back.

Greek

The thoughts of the great philosophers such as Socrates and Aristotle, upon whose ideas the foundations of western values were built, were written in ancient Greek.

Democracy, aristocracy, philosophy, pedagogy and psychology are just some of the many Greek terms that are part of our culture and language.

Modern Greek is spoken by ten million Greek citizens and by about seven million others spread around the world. The Centre for the Greek Language is a good starting point: **www.greeklanguagecentre.co.uk**

Indonesian

Based on the Malay trade dialect, Bahasa Indonesia is the national language of the Republic of Indonesia. In a country of more than 230 million people, who speak over 580 different dialects, having a national language makes communication easier, in much the same way as Hindi does in India.

There's no general greeting in Indonesian; there are different words specific to the time of day. But it's said to be an easy language to learn and Indonesia is such a popular backpacker destination it's likely to be worth making the effort. Here's a web link to get you started: **www.expat.or.id/info/bahasa.html**

Italian

Schools vary from the very large to very small, each with its own character and range of courses in Italian, Italian culture, history, art, cooking and other subjects. As in language schools across most of Europe, the language is often taught in the morning with extracurricular activities in the afternoon. If you want to do a course from March onwards it is advisable to get in touch with them at least two months in advance, as courses and accommodation get booked up early.

Most schools can fix you up with accommodation before your trip, either with a family, bed and breakfast, half-board, or even renting a studio or flat. If you're part of a small group, you might prefer to arrange accommodation yourself through a local property-letting agent, but this can be tricky unless you have someone on the spot to help.

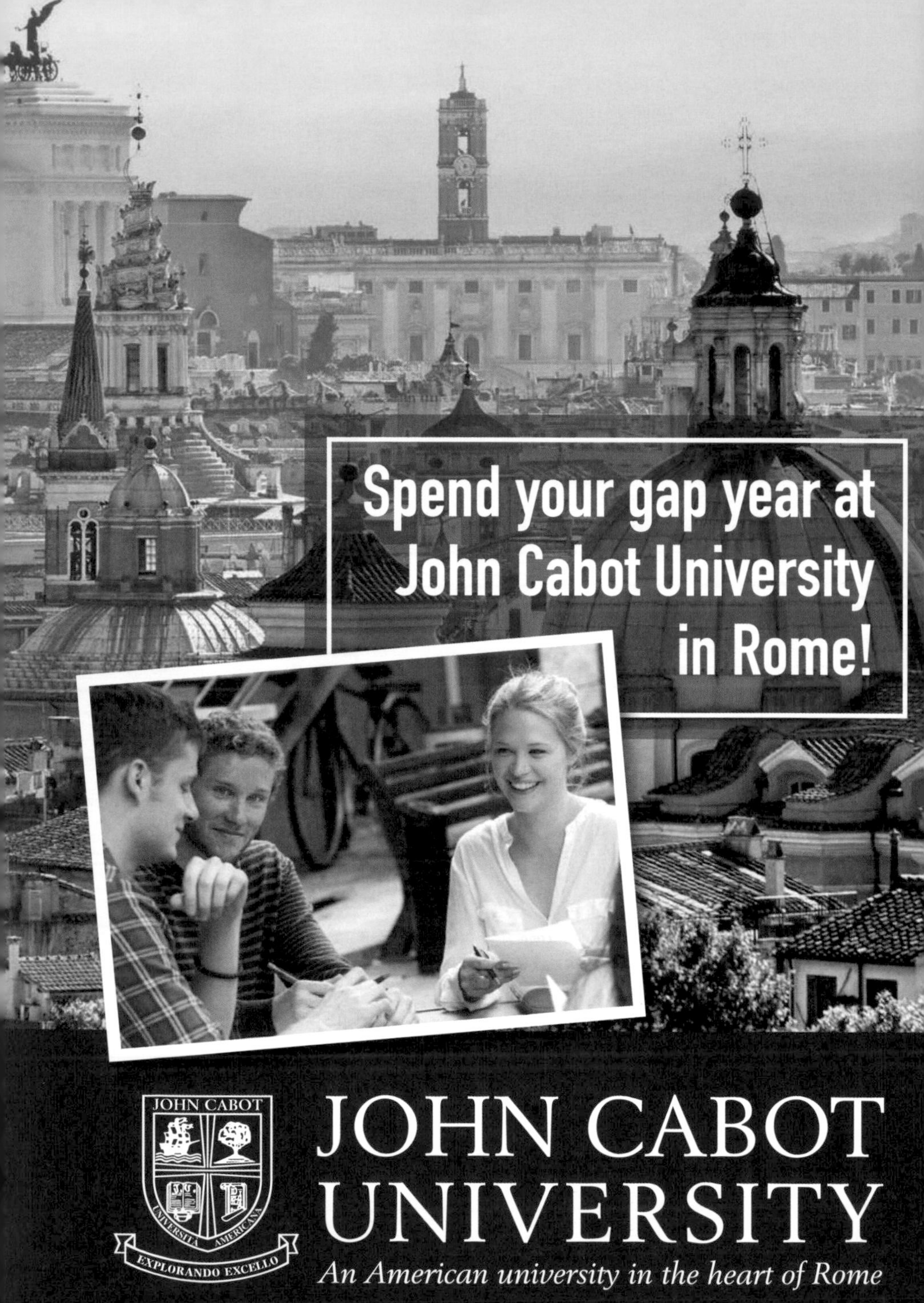

admissions@johncabot.edu • Apply now! • www.johncabot.edu

Japanese

If you can get to the Japanese Embassy in London you can look up a comprehensive guide in its large library called Japanese Language Institutes (based in Japan). The library also has material on learning Japanese and stocks Japanese newspapers including the English-language *Japan Times*, which runs information on jobs in Japan.

There's information about studying in Japan on the embassy website, with guidance on the type of visa you will need if you want to teach English as a foreign language or do other types of work there.

Japanese Embassy, 101-104 Piccadilly, London W1J 7JT
Tel: +44 (0) 20 7465 6500
www.uk.emb-japan.go.jp/en/embassy

Portuguese

You don't have to go to Portugal to learn Portuguese – it's the main language of Brazil too, so if you're heading for Latin America on your gap, try: **www.esl.co.uk/en/learn-portuguese-in-brazil.htm**

Russian

We suggest you check with the Foreign & Commonwealth Office before making any plans to travel to Russia to study.

That said, both ESL and Live Languages Abroad offers Russian language lessons in Russia:
www.livelanguagesabroad.co.uk/category/russian/russian-in-russia
www.esl.co.uk/en/learn-russian-in-russia.htm

Spanish

Spanish is the third most widespread language in the world after English and Mandarin Chinese. Over 400 million people in 23 countries are Spanish speakers – Mexico and all of Central and South America (except Brazil) designate Spanish as their official language.

Forms of Spanish can also be heard in Guinea, the Philippines and in Ceuta and Melilla in North Africa. But if you go to a language school inside or outside of Spain, you will probably be learning formal Castilian.

For information about universities and language courses, try:

Spanish Embassy, Education Department, 20 Draycott Place, London SW3 2RZ
Tel: +44 (0) 20 7727 2462
If you want to learn it in Latin America try:
www.expanish.com
www.spanish-language.org

CAPS is an excellent programme designed for young people who would like to spend a year in Spain helping in a school as a conservation teaching assistant. It's a great way to improve your Spanish. For more information, go to: **www.hometohome.es/caps/eng/assistants.html**

my gap-year

Alex Wolfson

Alex Wolfson went to Rouen to learn French with ESL Language Travel...

It's 8.45am on a crisp clear morning; I've walked across the Norman city of Rouen as the banks of the Seine come to life on Monday morning and I'm sitting in a classroom being asked about University, in French, by one of the friendly teachers at ESL's school in Rouen.

This isn't my French course itself; it's the placement test, which is done orally without gap-fill or grammar exercises. I struggle as I try to work out the French word for 'dissertation'! I do manage to communicate that my degree was in medieval history, and that being able to see Normandy, an area rich in the history of my period, is a reason I'm here. The teacher asks all the new students, from all over the World different questions to keep us on our toes. Afterwards we shown around the school and then placed in classes. Ellen, an American, and I are in Benedicte's class joining seven students who have already spent some weeks at the school. Over the next few weeks we will get to know each other much better. Benedicte asks us to sit apart so we don't speak to each other in English.

Benedicte's theme for the week is art. All the exercises are based around this topic. This throws me a little, as I don't even know how to talk about impressionist paintings in English! However, our teacher stresses that the important thing is to learn about the French language through the theme of discussing artists associated with Normandy. The week's lessons will conclude with a class visit to the Musée des Beaux-Arts in the centre of Rouen. Each week is based around a different topic. We look at a whole range of topics including Norman history, French politics, cinema and sustainable development; a topic that is very relevant to ESL.

The school offers a range of activities including visits to historic Rouen, Monet's house at Giverny, a gig by a local band, a visit to a cider brewery and (my personal highlight) a Norman cheese-tasting afternoon. This means I get to know the town itself and the region, and get the chance to meet lots of other students from other classes.

My accommodation in Rouen is excellent. I stay with a charming retired couple who have plenty of time to chat in French in their garden or over dinner. Monsieur tells me all about his vintage motorbike and his amateur racing days, while Madame tells me about her love of the South Coast of England! They take time to show me around Rouen and see the open-air market where we can pick up some fantastic local cheeses, recently made crepes, pates and ciders.

My stay in Rouen is a huge success and I'd recommend a language course abroad as part of a gap-year; my French is now a real skill I can now use in the workplace, I have spent time in a beautiful part of France that is not too touristy, and I have had memorable times with the people I have met there.

visit: www.esl.co.uk

John Cabot University

Multi languages

There are companies offering courses in many different languages. When you're getting references, make sure they're not just for the company – but specifically for the country/course you're interested in.

TEFL

Recent research has revealed that within the next ten years roughly half the world will be using English, so there's never been a better time to do a TEFL course. Like having a sports instructors' certificate, a TEFL qualification is useful if you want to earn a little money for expenses on a gap and it's a passport that will get you into many countries around the world and in close contact with the people. For more information on getting a TEFL qualification go to **Chapter 5 - Working Abroad**.

Please see the directory pages starting on page 329 for information on companies and organisations offering opportunities for learning abroad.

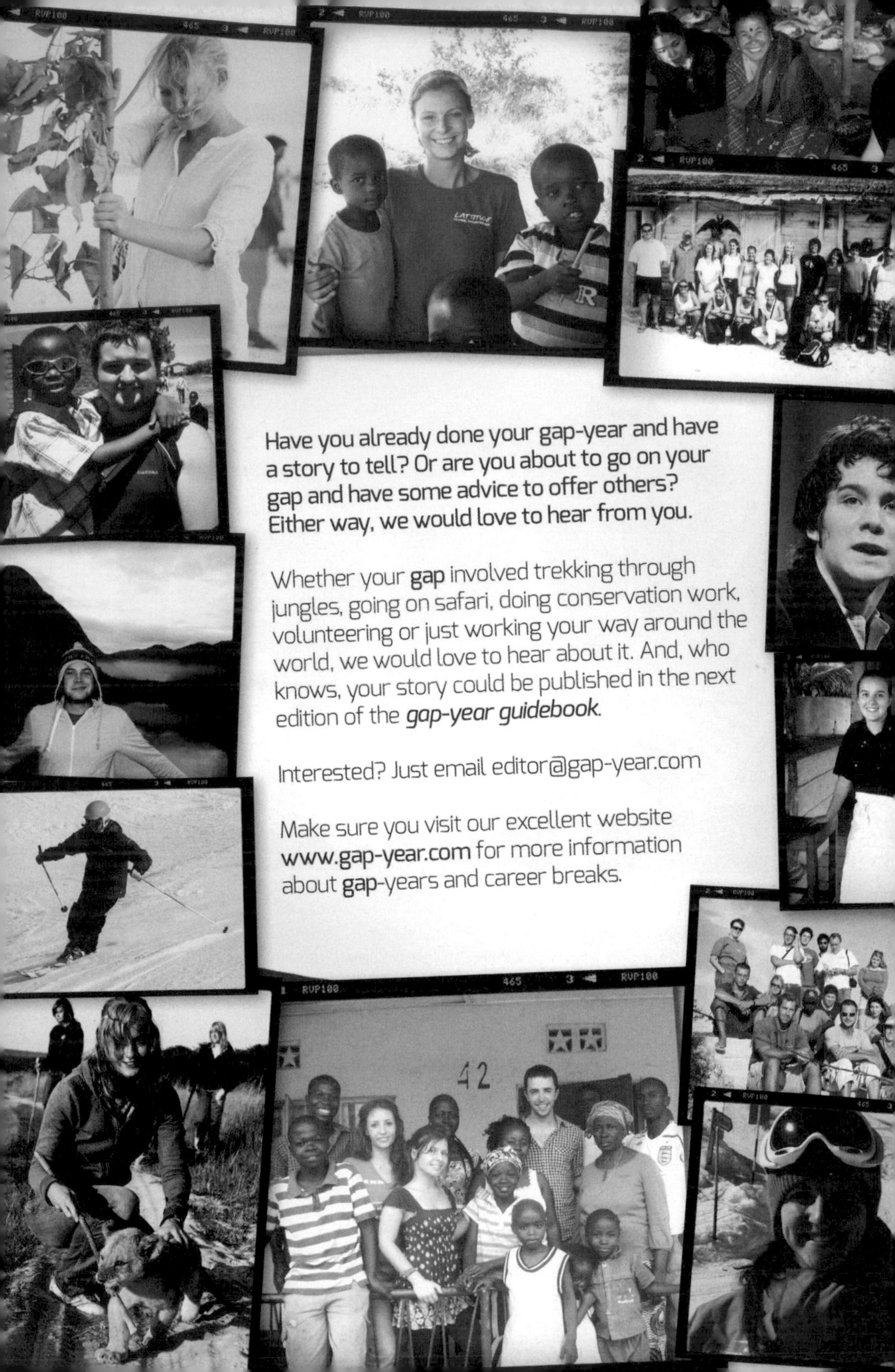

Have you already done your gap-year and have a story to tell? Or are you about to go on your gap and have some advice to offer others? Either way, we would love to hear from you.

Whether your **gap** involved trekking through jungles, going on safari, doing conservation work, volunteering or just working your way around the world, we would love to hear about it. And, who knows, your story could be published in the next edition of the ***gap-year guidebook***.

Interested? Just email editor@gap-year.com

Make sure you visit our excellent website **www.gap-year.com** for more information about **gap**-years and career breaks.

Sport

Sport

Travelling abroad doesn't mean that you have to stop playing the sports that you love – sports coaching projects are also a great way to give something back to a community on a gap-year or career break abroad. If you are looking to join a sports volunteer project, there are many different projects and destinations available.

Lots of companies offer you the chance to live, play, train and coach many different sports all over the world. Whether your chosen sport is football, cricket, rugby, netball, tennis, sailing or even polo, you can use your skills to enrich the lives of others by becoming a volunteer coach or use your time to improve your own skills for a career in your chosen sport.

And a sporting placement abroad can seriously boost your personal development – showing your commitment, teamwork and leadership skills to prospective employers.

So whether you want to use your football skills to become a coach teaching children in South Africa, join a cricket club for the season in Australia, experience the challenge of playing rugby in New Zealand or learn how to sail and dive in Thailand, there is definitely a placement out there for you.

Anne Smellie, of Oyster Worldwide, told us: "Many people are involved in sports as part of their daily lifestyles, and this passion is increasingly becoming an important part of the gap-year.

"Making a difference and doing something important on a gap-year has always been key, and this is ever more so the case.

"Making a genuine contribution to lives of young kids in poorer countries, all whilst playing the sports that you love, is an experience that is second to none. It looks fantastic on your CV, gives you some real employability skills, surrounds you in another culture – and is a lot of fun."

Training to be an instructor

There are many options to consider, but three of the most popular and well-established areas for gap-year students are skiing, snowboarding and scuba diving.

There are well-established routes for training as a professional and choices of courses tailored to gap-years. Specialist gap-year training companies will take care of all organisation and train you through national governing body sports coaching qualifications.

Colin Tanner, of SITCo, who offer ski and snowboard instructor courses in New Zealand, said: "If you are looking to do a ski or snowboard instructor course, then there are lots of options out there and the best course for you will be the one that suits your schedule. Just remember that as well as the northern hemisphere courses which are all December – March, there is also a great option in the southern hemisphere where winter is June – October.

"If you are a mad keen snowsports enthusiast then you can get the most out of your gap-year by training for your qualifications in the southern hemisphere and then be qualified and ready to work a season in the northern hemisphere. You can live the dream of the eternal winter!"

The British Association of Snowsport Instructors (BASI) is the official UK organisation with responsibility for the training and grading of snowsports instructors and provides official BASI Gap 10-week courses through its licensed ski school providers, ICE and New Generation, that operate in the world's premier ski resorts – Val d'Isere, Courchevel, Meribel and La Tania.

Once qualified as a level 2 ski instructor, your most likely first job would be teaching at a resort ski school. There is plenty of employment for newly qualified instructors, as long as you arrange your work visa in advance.

With a season's experience you are likely to be more in demand as an employee. Italy, Switzerland, Germany, Austria, Croatia, Spain, Andorra, USA, Canada and Japan are among the countries with established ski industries in the northern hemisphere.

Your opportunities in France can still be limited, though. The French snowsports authorities have traditionally made it difficult for non-French nationals to work in the Alps.

Laura Turner, from the Altitude Ski and Snowboard School, told us the biggest problem for a new instructor looking for a job is the lack of experience – and so any opportunity to gain experience should be grabbed with both hands.

"Initially one of the best ways is to apply to ski schools is for part-time work during the busy holiday weeks of Christmas/New Year, half-term and Easter. Do a good job, be helpful, be available whenever asked, professional at all times and it might then lead to more work. There are also several companies such as Interski in Italy who bring school groups out from the UK and often need extra instructors for a couple of weeks.

Dive Pro Africa

"Other things that help your CV stand out from everyone else's are: having a qualification and experience teaching in another sport and having a second language that you can teach in and knowing the resort you are applying to. Showing an interest in developing your instructor qualification further by doing some of the modules for the next level, *eg* the common theory for the BASI level 3, can also help."

"For those who wish to work as an instructor as a career as opposed to just for their gap-year, there are also now many further courses which can help you get your foot in the door.

"Joining one of these courses is another ideal way of getting work on a part-time basis whilst also giving yourself a whole season to prove to a company that you would be worth employing full-time in the future."

In the southern hemisphere New Zealand is famous for its mountains, but don't overlook Australia, which has several winter resorts too. Some schools in Australia and New Zealand employ new instructors from early season hiring clinics: you are expected to attend a short period of in-house training and if you measure up you get a job.

The instructor lifestyle is hard work but a lot of fun, although entry-level jobs are not too highly paid. On the plus side, you work on the sea or the slopes and have plenty of time to improve your own skills and enjoy your favourite sport.

Watersports instructor courses are also amongst the most popular for those interested in learning a new sport on their gap-year. In addition to diving, you will also find plenty of courses to qualify you to teach windsurfing, yachting and sailing, canoeing, kite surfing, kayaking – any activity on or around water, you can teach!

my
gap-year
Duncan Crawford

I studied sound engineering at The Academy of Contemporary Music in Guilford between 2003 and 2005, and after that I went on to work in the music industry.

I was lucky enough to work on the TV show *Only Fools and Horses*, and with recording artists Skunk Anansie. After a few years in the sound engineering industry I decided to take some time out to explore my other great passion of the outdoors and the mountains.

In 2009 I enrolled in the SITCo Ski Instructor Training Courses at Coronet Peak in New Zealand. Through SITCo I trained for and passed my NZSIA Level 1 and Level 2 ski instructor qualifications. As well as meeting some great lifelong friends, the SITCo course has set me on a new life path, in the outdoors, mountains and tourism industry.

Being trained in strong people skills and having a love for the outdoors, I have since gone on from SITCo to work as a ski instructor at Coronet Peak Snowsports School, and then also as a lead guide with New Zealand's Mount Cook Glacier Explorers.

For more information about SITCO, go to **www.sitco.co.nz**

Getting a job

Once you have earned your qualification, the world is your oyster for potential jobs.

We asked Colin Tanner, from SITCo, for his advice. He told us: "In order to get a job then employers (ski schools) will be looking for a number of things – a qualification, personal skills and experience.

"Taking part in a course will help you towards the qualification. The personal skills are an important part of instructing, and your own personal skills will get developed through any course from experienced trainers. Actual teaching experience is the hard part to get, but once you get your foot in the door you will be away. Sometimes you just need to look to some of the smaller resorts for your first job, gain some experience and then apply to the big glamour resorts.

"When writing your CV, adapt it to the business; your people skills and your presentation will be as important as the number of A levels. Such things as previous experience of teaching the local kids football team *etc* will be good to show you are a 'people person'."

Make sure you write a good covering letter with your CV. This is particularly important for jobs overseas where an interview might not be practical.

If you do have an interview, make sure you ask about the things that matter to you – terms and conditions of service, accommodation, feeding arrangements, insurance and equipment requirements, days off, daily routine, annual leave, flights home, *etc*. And don't forget about money – how do you get paid? Are what are the career opportunities? Is there a job specification available?

Here are some thoughts from Mark Slingo, of Dive Pro Africa, who offer scuba diving instructor courses in Kenya and Tanzania:

"Our Go-Pro internship packages to scuba diving instructors all include workshops to assist our new PADI instructors in finding employment after they finish their training.

As well as making personal recommendations to our vast worldwide network of scuba diving contacts, we provide a CV building workshop, a website design and social media marketing workshop to help our instructors promote their services and introduce all divers to the various online portals where they can search for jobs in scuba diving. We provide references for any potential employers and offer Instructor continuing education programs for instructors who want to be able to teach more and make themsleves more employable. These include PADI Specialty Diver Instructor courses, handicapped diver instructor courses and IDC Staff Instructor courses.

"The best advice we could give newly qualified instructors looking for work following passing their instructor exam is to make themselves as presentable as possible. If they have extra skills such as extra languages spoken or previous management, or transferable skills experience such as customer service or engine maintenance then these should all be mentioned. They should not fall into the trap of thinking that the skills they have could not necessarily help out in finding a job in scuba diving. We try to ensure that our interns leave with as many diving and first aid skills as possible, so anything else they can bring to the table can only be of benefit. Above all be keen and willing to talk about diving to anyone, anywhere anytime. Enthusiasm rubs off and is a trait that all dive schools look for."

Our friends at Oyster point out that there are some ski instructor courses that you can sign up for, safe in the knowledge that you will have a guaranteed job for the rest of the season, such as their course in the Canadian resort of Whistler.

"On arrival, you take a four-week course to gain your CSIA Level 1 instructor qualification and then begin working for Whistler Kids as an instructor for the rest of the season," they told us.

"This is not any old job, it's a job that comes with enormous responsibility – looking after other people's children on a mountain! This not helps with your own personal development but also shows future employers a lot about you as well."

For more information on this course, have a look at:

www.oysterworldwide.com/gap-year-in-canada-whistler.php

ALTITUDE**FUTURES**
INSTRUCTOR COURSES

Altitude Futures - Gap Course Verbier, Case Postale 55, 1936 Verbier
T: +44 7539 071166
E: info@altitude-futures.com W: www.altitude-futures.com

8 Sport

Altitude Futures Ski and Snowboard Instructor Courses

Altitude Futures run official BASI ski and snowboard instructor courses in Verbier, Switzerland.

Our winter Gap programmes offer an intensive 10 weeks of training geared towards developing your personal skiing or snowboarding skills and also training you to become a fully qualified ski or snowboard instructor.

When you book a course with Altitude you benefit from an experienced and established training programme run by instructors for instructors.

The Altitude Futures Gap Year Programme is famous for:

* 100% satisfied gap students
* Highest pass rates in the Alps
* Up to 50% off skis, boots and boards
* High quality accommodation
* Over 200 hours of on snow coaching
* Video debriefs and lectures
* Work experience with Altitude Ski School
* Gain your BASI level 1 and 2 licence
* Job opportunities after the course

Altitude Futures Coaching Team

Altitude Ski and Snowboard School employs top qualified coaches and trainers from Britain, Switzerland, Canada and Sweden. This depth of knowledge and experience makes Altitude the premier provider of instructor training in the Alps.

'The Altitude Futures gap students are the most successful and strongest group I have ever been within 16 years of being a BASI trainer.'

Andy Lockerbie - BASI Trainer & previous CEO of BASI

Coaching sport as a volunteer programme

There are hundreds of sports-based volunteer programmes available, from coaching cricket to underprivileged children in India to coaching football in inner cities in the UK.

Gap-years can be spent doing practically every sport you can think of, from hockey to netball and from basketball to football. There's also a range of countries you can go to. The benefits are obvious, says Anne Smellie:

"You can coach your favourite sports, from football to rugby, from netball to hockey and from cricket to swimming to deserving kids in some of the world's poorest areas.

"These kids do not have the opportunity to enjoy sports in an environment that we are used to here – and they are desperate for your help. As well as giving them an environment in which to play and learn games, they also learn motivation, team work and enthusiasm which is tough to get elsewhere."

Oyster Worldwide

As a sports-coaching volunteer, you will have the opportunity to help build communities through sport. For example, in working with a local football academy in Ghana, you will be able to establish relationships with young players who often have a fantastic talent and profound love of the game – but have been unable to progress because of a lack of physical training, emotional guidance and financial support. Giving them the opportunity to develop both their skills and their character can be a life-changing experience. Even without formal coaching qualifications, you can offer them constructive advice and new ideas on tactics, skills and their mental approach to training and competition, simply by arriving with enthusiasm, imagination and a general understanding of the game.

Development may not simply be about coaching. It may also involve education to understand how and why their ideas count, perhaps even some time as an English language teacher. On the best placements, you'll find yourself contributing to community development, in sport and beyond.

"It is hard to put into words how moving it is to teach these kids, who have so very little, the enjoyment of sports," Anne says.

"To see them progress with each session is an amazing experience, and you will work through that with them; from the frustration of not understanding something the first time, to the joy of being able to learn a new trick or a skill. These sports sessions give each child a moment of happiness and release, which is one of the greatest things that you could give someone."

The attributes you need depend on the activity you go for. If it involves teaching kids, you'll obviously need to have empathy with children, and if it involves a lot of hardcore activity, you'll need to be reasonably fit and resilient.

my gap-year
Emma Wolton

Emma Wolton spent her ski season in Whistler Blackcomb with Oyster Worldwide where she became a qualified ski instructor and had a guaranteed job teaching kids to ski…

Working a ski season had been on my to-do list for several years, so the opportunity to work in one of the best ski resorts in North America, work with kids and become a qualified ski instructor seemed to good to be true – but it wasn't! I took my gap-year with Oyster Worldwide and headed out for the winter to the top Canadian resort of Whistler Blackcomb with 23 other 'Oysters'.

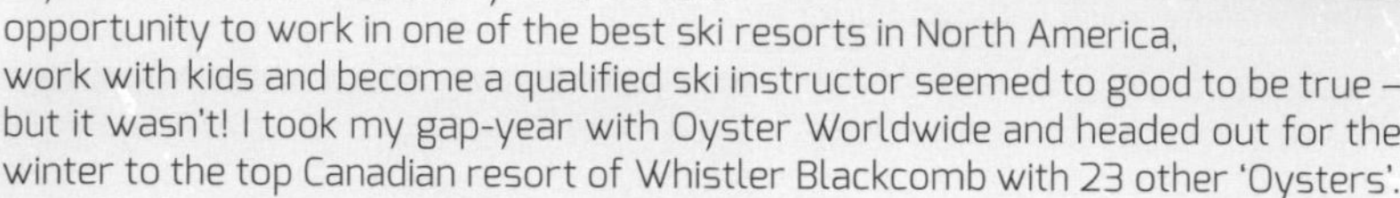

Before work officially started, we all got geared up; buying our very own sets of skis and boots that we would come to know very, very well in the next four-and-a-half months, as well as getting acquainted with life in the village.

After our training we were let loose on the mountain and found ourselves responsible for making skiers out of the little people in our charge. I started out by teaching the 'never-evers' (kids that hadn't skied before), but by the end of the season was teaching kids who could ski blue runs in parallel, almost better than me!

Our days started early with a morning meeting at 8:15am before the kids piled in. We'd then entertain them for a bit and give them a snack. Then we got out and began the skiing using our silliness, imaginations and fun as much as possible to keep the kids' attentions and keep them having fun on their holidays! The day wound up at around 3.30pm leaving time, in the second half of the season, for a run or two before the lifts closed.

I worked with the kids that came to ski school for a whole week. I really liked this as I got to know the kids well and found out what did and didn't work for them.

We were all staying in staff housing which was at the first stop up the gondola into the mountains making for the best commute to work you could ever imagine. Who can say that they got to ski into work each morning!? I stayed in a flat with three other girls from Oyster who became some of my closest friends. Everyone shared a room, with two bedrooms, a living room, kitchen and bathroom in a flat – pretty similar to university halls of residence if not a bit nicer!

Not only did I have a great time in Whistler, I also gained a qualification that looks great on my CV – I'm officially a CSIA Level 1 Ski Instructor! Overall I had an amazing time and would highly recommend it to anyone thinking of doing a ski instructor course or a ski season abroad. It was a fantastic placement. We had really good preparation and it was great to have Tory, our rep, out there in case anything happened. I made some brilliant friends, lived and worked in another country and improved my skiing so much.

For more information about Oyster, visit **www.oysterworldwide.com**

Even if the sport has nothing to do with your future career path, it will boost your CV. Better still, if in an interview you can make an energetic case for why you did it, it will make you stand out above others who have sat around on their bums in the summer. It can only impress a future employer.

In the developing world, sport is often more than just competition or idle pastime. Often sport can have a real impact at the heart of communities, and play a pivotal role in the health and prosperity of the people.

Playing sport

More and more people are looking to take a sports gap-year with a purpose, so they are using their time out to play a season of sport abroad: for example cricket in Australia, or rugby in New Zealand or South Africa.

Placements on these 'academy programmes' will usually mean you are matched with a club abroad at a suitable level for your standard, for whom you play at the weekends whilst perfecting your game throughout the week with coaching, fitness training and sports psychology from local coaches.

You may be set a specific training regime to stick to, which might include things like:

- Gym fitness work and flexibility training.
- Sport-specific fitness training.
- One-on-one sessions to develop specific skills.
- Video analysis.
- Group training sessions with other academy players.
- Club practice sessions.
- Sessions with players of a higher standard, perhaps even professionals.

Of course, you don't have to be looking at improving your skills to a semi-professional standard. You can also use your gap-year to take up a completely new sport. Perhaps you are interested in learning jiu-jitsu in Brazil, or polo in Argentina – you can certainly find placements to cover most sports in a huge range of countries.

Xtreme sport

Taking a gap-year gives you a once in a lifetime opportunity to do something amazing – the things that you just can't do at home and are likely to never forget. To some adventurous types, this means really exciting stuff, activities and adventures that get the butterflies going and gives you very sweaty palms.

There are companies that organise adrenaline-pumping activities in various locations around the world. These include adventures that really test your metal on a gap-year can have positive consequences when you return home.

That could mean bungee jumping or skydiving, scuba diving, swimming with whalesharks in Thailand or learning to surf in Australia. It would certainly pay to book before you go – you can organise things in-country but why take the chance of missing out? Also bear in mind that such activities are expensive - so make sure you have planned your budget in advance.

There is also merit in the idea of taking a qualification in an extreme sport – which might even help you stay for longer in certain countries.

The New Zealand Skydiving School, for example, teach a Diploma in Commercial Skydiving with graduate employment rates exceeding 95%. Careers available upon completion of this course include parachute packing, manifesting, video editing, and freefall camera. With further time in the industry many graduates continue on into dropzone management, tandem masters, and skydiving instructors.

Please see the directory pages starting on page 347 for information on companies and organisations offering sporting gap-year opportunities.

Working in the UK

9 Working in the UK

Why work on a year out?

If you're not working to raise money for gap travel and you've just finished school or university, you might want a break from study and take a deep breath or two for a while. But even though work doesn't seem too appealing, just try going through the complex claiming procedure for the Jobseekers' Allowance and then living on it for a few weeks, and you'll soon see that working has its advantages.

But there are plenty of much better reasons to use a gap for work:

Saving money for university

Going to university is an expensive thing to do. Today, the vast majority of graduates are heavily in debt and this burden will be with them for many years to come.

Graduate debt is rising sharply as temporary jobs dry up and tuition fees, rent and travel costs increase.

Studies suggest students typically spend £5000 a year on living expenses, including nearly £2000 on rent, £750 on bills, £700 on groceries, £700 on socialising, £400 on travel and £500 on books, equipment and field trips.

With tuition fees rising to a maximum of £9000 a year, total debt for a three-year course could break the £50,000 barrier. That said, there are big variations between regions and universities.

Even so, earning just a little bit now could really help your bank balance in the future.

Showing commitment

If you're attracted to a career in popular professions like the media, medicine and law, which are incredibly competitive and hard to get into, it could well prove necessary to grab any experience you can, paid or unpaid. It might make all the difference down the line when you have to prove to a potential employer that you really are committed.

Work experience

Another consideration is the frequency with which people applying for jobs report being rejected at interview 'because of a lack of work experience'. A gap is a great time to build up an initial experience of work culture as well as getting a foot in the door and getting recognised; in fact many students go back to the same firms after graduation.

Not sure what you want to do?

If your degree left you with several possible options and you couldn't face the university final year/graduate 'milk round' or you're undecided what career direction you want to head in, then a gap could be a great time to try out different jobs and to get a feel for what you might want to do in the future.

Whatever your reasons for working during a gap, you should start looking early to avoid disappointment.

visit: www.gap-year.com

Writing a CV

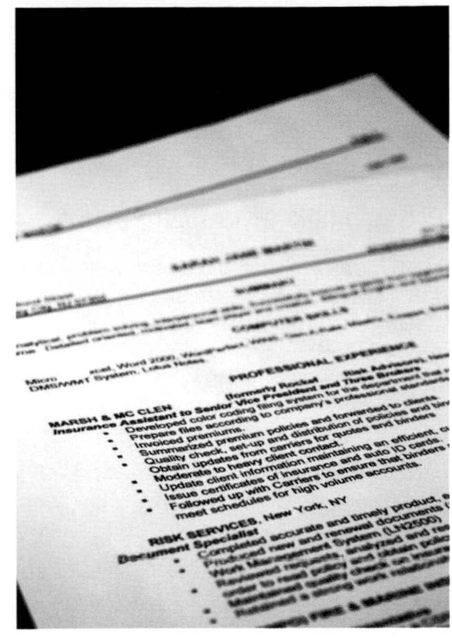

Fashions change in laying out a CV and in which order you arrange the various sections.

The advice is that a CV should be no more than two A4 pages and also that it should be tailored to the sector you're applying for.

The thing to remember is that employers are busy people, so they won't have time to read many pages, especially if they're trying to create a shortlist of maybe six interviewees from more than 100 applications for just one job.

If you're at the start of your working life, there's a limit to how much tailoring you can do. A good tip is to put a short summary of your skills, and experience to date, at the top so the recruiter knows what you can do. It can either be a bullet point list or a short paragraph, but remember that it's essentially your sales pitch explaining why you're useful to the company. It should only be a short summary of what's contained in the sections that follow.

There are a number of online CV-writing advice sites and templates that can help you, but do check for any fees before you start.

Here's a selection:
https://nationalcareersservice.direct.gov.uk/advice/getajob/cvs/Pages/default.aspx
www.alec.co.uk/cvtips
www.soon.org.uk/cvpage.htm

Here's a list of headings for the details your CV should include:

- Personal details: name, address, phone and email. You do not have to include gender, age, date of birth, marital details or nationality nor send a photograph, in fact some employers actively discourage photos for fear of being accused of bias in selecting people for interview.
- Short skills paragraph or key skills bullet points (see above).
- Work experience and skills: in order with most recent first. You can include part-time working that you've combined with education, as well as any voluntary work you've done, but if neither is directly within the job sector you're applying for, you need to focus on the transferable skills you got from it *eg* familiarity with office routines, record keeping, filing, if you've been in an office, or people skills if you worked in a shop.
- Achievements: have you been on any committees? (student council?), organised any events or fundraisers? Again, concentrate on what you learned from it, such as organisational skills, persuading companies to donate prizes for a raffle, planning catering and refreshments.

- Other skills: such as the Duke of Edinburgh's Award Scheme, workshops you've attended, hobbies *etc*.
- Education: again most recent first, with subjects studied and grades.
- References: you usually need two, one of them a recent employer, the other from school or university, though on a CV you only need to say 'references can be supplied'.

Getting the job

How do you get that first job with no prior experience? What can you offer?

The key is creativity. Show the company you're applying to that you can offer them something that nobody else can and do this by giving them an example. Be creative: If you're applying to an advertising firm, for instance, then mock up some adverts to show them.

Want to go into journalism? Write some sample articles and send them to local newspapers. Write to the editor and ask whether you could volunteer to help out in the newsroom to get a feel for the environment and the skills you'll need – a kind of extended work experience to add to what you should have had via school.

You could try this with companies in other fields you're interested in. Be proactive and persevere. It will show you have initiative and commitment and whatever your eventual career it will also help you to learn the basics of acting professionally in a professional environment.

Do the research: Whatever your chosen field, find out about the company and show your knowledge about the industry. If you are going for an industry, such as medicine or law, then showing that you are more than competent and willing is all that you can really do. Saying this, you have to make sure that you stick out from other applicants.

Contacts

In the directory of this guidebook we list some companies that specifically employ gap-year students or offer graduate opportunities. But take this as a starting point – the tip of the iceberg – there are hundreds of other companies out there waiting to be impressed by you.

Research is crucial. Tailor your approach towards that specific company and never just expect to get a job; you have to work at it. The general rule is that nobody will call you back – be the one who gets in contact with them.

Job surfing

You don't get the personal touch from a website that you do by going into a local branch and getting advice, or registering face-to-face, but recruitment websites are really useful if you know what you want to do and you have a 'skills profile' that one of their customers is looking for. Some of them are aimed at graduates and students, others at a general audience, others at specific areas of work (IT, for example).

Here are a few to start with:

Student summer jobs

www.activate.co.uk

(This one contains gap-jobs, summer jobs, internships and jobs for new graduates.)

Graduate careers:

www.milkround.com

jobs.guardian.co.uk

General vacancies:

www.reed.co.uk
www.jobsite.co.uk
www.monster.com

(Good for jobs in UK, but also Europe and across the world.)

www.fish4jobs.co.uk
www.gumtree.com

Technology specialists:

www.agencycentral.co.uk/jobsites/IT.htm

(This site has a list of IT specialist recruiters.)

Finance – FT jobs site:

www.ft.com/jobsclassified

On spec

If you can't find what you're looking for by using contacts, advertisements, agencies or the internet there is always DIY job hunting. You can walk into shops and restaurants to ask about casual work or use a phone directory (*eg Yellow Pages*) to phone businesses (art galleries, department stores, zoos...) and ask what is available.

Ring up, ask to speak to the personnel or HR manager and ask if and when they might have jobs available and how you should apply. If they ask you to write in, you can do so after the call. If you go in, make sure you look smart.

Remember, opportunities in the big professional firms are not always well publicised.

Temporary jobs (except agency-filled ones) are often filled by personal contact. If you have a burning desire to work for an architects' or lawyers' firm, for example, and you find nothing advertised, you could try making a list and phoning to ask if work is available.

Think about people you might already know in different work environments and ask around for what's available.

Banking: approach local branches for work experience. Also, try: **www.hays.com**

Education: most educational work experience is tied in with travelling abroad, to places like Africa or Asia, mostly to teach English. However, there are ways of gaining experience back home in England.

A very popular way is to see if the school that you have just left would like classroom helpers, or perhaps they need help in teaching a younger sports team. The key to this is to ask around and see what might be available.

But remember, for any work with children you will have to have a DBS (Disclosure and Barring Service) check. These were previously known as CRB (Criminal Records Bureau) checks. For more information, see: **www.gov.uk/disclosure-barring-service-check/overview**

As well as straight teaching, any experience with children can be very useful, so try looking at camps and sports teams that may need help – there are a few contacts for camps within the Seasonal Work section.

Legal and medical: it's well known that studying for these two professions is lengthy and rigorous, so any amount of work experience could prove very useful. There's plenty available, but lots of competition for the places so you need to start looking early.

Nearly all NHS hospitals look for volunteer staff. So, if you can't find a worthwhile paid job, just contact the HR manager at your local hospital.

Try also: **www.jobs.nhs.uk** (for all NHS jobs)
www.lawgazettejobs.co.uk (for law jobs, including trainee positions)

Media, publishing and advertising: working on television or the radio is a favourite and it is no surprise that, because of this, the media is one of the hardest industries to break into.

Work experience is highly recommended. Many companies are very willing to try out gap-year students as trainees, as raw talent is such a limited commodity they want to nurture it as much as possible – plus it's cheap.

There are many websites dedicated to media jobs, but a good place to look for publishing vacancies is **www.thebookseller.com**

Theatre: many theatres provide work experience for gap-year students, so it's definitely worthwhile contacting your nearby production company. This industry recognises creativity and application probably more than any other, so starting out early and fiercely is the only way to do it.

Try also: **www.thestage.co.uk/recruitment**

Internships

Graduates cannot rely on the safety net of the traditional internship or graduate job this year. A survey by the Higher Education Statistics Agency last year found that nearly one in 10 students were believed to be unemployed six months after graduating from UK universities. Applicants for jobs are expected to have more skills, better grades and some form of industry experience as a minimum. In such turbulent times it is essential to make your CV stand out and rise above the competition of the near 400,000 graduates leaving the UK's 168 universities every year.

Rajeeb Dey, founder of Enternships, a company which connects students with entrepreneurial work experience and full-time roles, told us: "Remember that the workplace is becoming increasingly competitive. Gaining work experience from an early age is essential and you're never too young to start.

"One of the most important pieces of advice I was given while being an intern was: 'Do not just follow directions. Think about why you are doing what you are doing'. This is such an important point: the education system doesn't always prepare us to think for ourselves. So entering the world of university, where you are given far less direction in how to manage yourself and your time (and not to mention your money!), taking initiative and being entrepreneurial in your outlook can be a culture shock for some. Nevertheless it is essential.

"One of the most important benefits of an 'enternship' is that enterns are given the opportunity to build this skill and also their own self-confidence. This means that not only is an enternship before university an impressive addition to your CV for when you leave university, it will also equip gap-year students with skills they will need while at university, and help them to get the most out of time that will seem to fly by.

"You should take every opportunity to develop new skills and gain experience; do not think that the only time to get work experience will be the summer holidays of your penultimate year at university. Times have changed – you need to get more proactive about the world of work; take every opportunity you have to do short-term work placements."

Check out **www.enternships.com** for ideas about some of the opportunities that are out there.

There's also some good information at: **www.allaboutcareers.com/careers-advice/internships**

Interviews

Once your persistence has got you an interview, you need to impress your potential employers.

Attitude – confidence and knowledge are probably top of the list for employers, so that is what you must portray, even if you're a bag of nerves and haven't got

a clue. They want to know you're committed.

Dress – make sure you are dressed appropriately (cover tattoos, remove nose piercings *etc*, don't show too much flesh, have clean and brushed hair – all the stuff that your teachers/parents tell you and really annoys you). If you're going for a creative job (advertising, art, *etc*) then you can probably be a little more casual – when you phone the secretary to confirm your interview time and venue, you can ask whether you'll be expected to dress formally. Alternatively, you could go to the company's offices around lunchtime (usually 1pm) and have a look at how people coming out are dressed.

Manner – stand straight; keep eye contact with the interviewer and smile. Be positive about yourself – don't lie, but focus on your good points rather than your bad ones.

Be well prepared to answer the question: "So, why do you want this job?" Remember they'll want to know you're keen, interested in what they do and what benefit you think you can bring to their company.

Gap-year specialists

If you would like to get a work placement from a gap-year specialist, the contacts listed in the directory sections in this guidebook are a good starting point for organisations to approach.

Another option is the Year Out Group, the voluntary association of gap specialists formed to promote the concept and benefits of well-structured year out programmes and to help people select suitable and worthwhile projects. The group's member organisations are listed on their website and provide a wide range of year out placements in the UK and overseas, including structured work placements.

Year Out Group members are expected to put potential clients and their parents in contact with those who have recently returned. They consider it important that these references are taken up at least by telephone and, where possible, by meeting face-to-face.

Year Out Group
Queensfield
28 Kings Road
Easterton
Wiltshire SN10 4PX
Tel: +44 (0) 1380 816696
www.yearoutgroup.org

Gap-year employers

In the directory we've listed companies that either have specific gap-year employment policies or ones that we think are worth contacting. We've split them into three groups: festivals, seasonal work and graduate opportunities and work experience.

This isn't a comprehensive list, so it's still worth checking the internet and your local companies (in the *Yellow Pages*, for example).

Festivals

Whether musical, literary or dramatic, there are all kinds of festivals taking place up and down the country every year. You need to apply as early as possible, as there aren't that many placements. Satellite organisations spring up around core festivals; so if you are unsuccessful at first, try to be transferred to another department. The work can be paid or on a voluntary basis. Short-term work, including catering and stewarding, is available mainly during the summer. Recruitment often starts on a local level, so check the local papers and recruitment agencies.

It's also worth having a look at this site: **www.festaff.co.uk/jobs-at-festivals**

Seasonal and temporary work

A great way to make some quick cash, either to save up for travelling or to spend at home, is seasonal work. There are always extra short-term jobs going at Christmas: in the Post Office sorting office or in local shops. In the summer there's fruit or vegetable picking for example. There's a website that links farms in the UK and worldwide with students looking for holiday work: **www.pickingjobs.com**

Another option, if you have reasonable IT skills, is to temp in an office. July and August are good months for this too, when permanent staff are on holiday. You can register with

local job agencies, which will almost certainly want to do a simple test of your skills. Temping is also a great idea if you're not at all sure what sector you want to work in – it's a good chance to find out about different types of work.

Pay, tax and National Insurance

You can expect to be paid in cash for casual labour, by cheque (weekly or monthly) in a small company and by bank transfer in a large one. Always keep the payslip that goes with your pay, along with your own records of what you earn (including payments for casual labour) during the tax year: from 6 April one year to 5 April the next. You need to ask your employer for a P46 form when you start your first job and a P45 form when you leave (which you take to your next employer). If you are out of education for a year you are not treated as a normal taxpayer.

Personal allowances – that is the amount you can earn before paying tax – are reviewed in the budget each year in April. To find out the current tax-free personal allowance rate call the Inland Revenue helpline or go to: **www.hmrc.gov.uk/nic**

Minimum wages, maximum hours

In the UK, workers aged 16 and 17 should get a 'development rate' of £3.72 an hour; 18-to 21-year-old workers should receive £5.03 an hour; and workers aged 22 and over should get £6.31 per hour.

To check on how the National Minimum Wage applies to you, go to the Department for Business, Enterprise and Regulatory Reform (formerly called the DTI) website: **www.gov.uk/national-minimum-wage**

Alternatively, phone the National Minimum Wage Helpline on 0845 6000 678.

If you think you are not being paid the national minimum wage you can call this helpline number: 0800 917 2368.

All complaints about underpayment of the National Minimum Wage are treated in the strictest confidence.

The UK also has a law on working hours to comply with European Union legislation. This says that (with some exemptions for specific professions) no employee should be expected to work more than 48 hours a week. Good employers do give you time off in lieu if you occasionally have to work more than this. Others take no notice, piling a 60-hour-a-week workload on you. This is against the law and, unless you like working a 12-hour day, they must stop.

Please see the directory pages starting on page 359 for information on companies and organisations offering opportunities to work in the UK on your gap-year.

Volunteering in the UK

Volunteering in the UK

Volunteering doesn't have to be done in a developing country, amongst the poorest on the planet, to bring a sense of satisfaction. There are many deserving cases right on your doorstep. You might also find that, if you do voluntary work close to home, it will make you more involved in your own community.

What's more, the global recession has prompted a greater need for volunteers, as charities have had to cut back on paid staff in the wake of reduced donations.

Equally some, like the British Red Cross, have also reported a huge increase in the numbers of potential volunteers – in some cases up to four times as many per month as they'd normally expect. Arguably this reflects the numbers of graduates coming out of university unable to find work as well as high numbers of reported redundancies.

The National Union of Students believe volunteering at home is well worth considering (although they add a few words of warning):

"If you decide to volunteer, consider doing so in your local community where your support can make a huge difference to your own community and comes with the added bonus of giving you experience of working in an environment similar to the one that you're more likely to be eventually working in.

"Be careful to ensure that any job you take for experience will give the opportunities you are looking for. There's no point in spending a year filing invoices if your ambition is to work as a museum curator.

"There is also an unfortunate trend towards unpaid 'internships' with the term applied to anything from a flexible, well-structured placement that can nonetheless be difficult to access for those without other sources of funding to long, menial, and ultimately fruitless jobs that would barely be worth your time if they were paid.

"Some employers are unscrupulous about using internships to bypass minimum wage legislation. If you have any doubts about whether you should be paid for your work, contact Citizens' Advice."

Benefits of UK volunteering

You can:

- Do some things you couldn't do abroad. Good examples are counselling, befriending and fundraising, all of which need at least some local knowledge.
- Have more flexibility: you can do a variety of things rather than opting for one programme or project.
- Combine volunteering with a study course or part-time job.
- Get to know more about your own community.
- Get experience before committing to a project abroad.
- Develop career options – a now well-accepted route into radio for example is to do a volunteer stint on hospital radio.

British Red Cross

If you choose to spend at least some of your gap doing something for the benefit of others here in the UK, you'll get the same satisfying sense of achievement as volunteers who have been on programmes elsewhere.

To get the most out of volunteering during your gap-year, you must consider what you would like to achieve. Try asking yourself about your interests, skills and experience to define what type of volunteering role you are looking for.

Volunteering England (**www.volunteering.org.uk**) is a volunteer development agency committed to supporting, enabling and celebrating volunteering in all its diversity. Their work links research, policy innovation, good practice and grant making in the involvement of volunteers.

Here's what they told us: "There are literally thousands of exiting gap-year projects going on in exotic locations all around the globe; but if you are serious about building skills and improving your employability, a job specific placement in the UK may be more useful.

"If you would like a career in the media, three months at a local hospital radio station may not sound as exciting as counting bottle-nosed dolphins in Costa Rica but it is a lot more relevant to prospective employers.

"If you are considering a competitive career such as law or media, bear in mind internships can be difficult to get, but even a day's work shadowing or working more hours at your part-time job can help demonstrate those all-important employability skills such as team working and motivation. If you are interested in law, see if you can help out at your local citizen's advice bureau. If you would like to be a doctor, see if you can help out at your local hospital. They often need volunteers to run the hospital shop and to befriend patients and it will also give you a good idea of what working in a hospital will be like.

"Volunteering in the UK has other benefits too: it is usually cheaper and it can provide a tangible benefit to your local community. For example student volunteers contribute over £42million to the economy each year through their activities (*National Student Volunteering Survey*) and many people go on to find jobs as a direct result of their volunteering.

"Research has also proved that those who do voluntary work, or are helped by volunteers, adopt healthier lifestyles, can cope better with their own ill-health, have greater confidence and self-esteem, have an improved diet and even have a higher level of physical activity."

To find out more about volunteering you can visit Volunteering England's website **www.volunteering.org.uk**, where you can find your nearest volunteer centre.

www.do-it.org.uk or **vinspired.com/opportunities/marketplace** also list volunteering opportunities online.

Wherever you are, volunteering is an opportunity to learn about other people and about yourself.

If you're just starting out on a career path and are unsure what you want to do, volunteering can be an opportunity to gain relevant work experience. If you know, for example, that you want a career in retail, a stint with Oxfam will teach you a surprising amount. Many charity shops recognise this and offer training. Careers in the charity sector are also extremely popular and can be quite hard to get into, so a period of voluntary work will demonstrate your commitment and willingness to learn.

Volunteering for a while can also be useful for those who are maybe thinking of a career change or development. For example you could use your skills to develop a charity's website, or perhaps you have experience of marketing or campaigning.

While you're volunteering your services you can also use the time to find out more about the organisation's work, whom to talk to about training or qualifications and about work opportunities within the organisation.

British Red Cross

What can you do?

Before contacting organisations it is a good idea to think about what you would like to do in terms of the activity and type of organisation you would like to work for. There's good advice on this at: **www.volunteering.org.uk/IWantToVolunteer**

The UK has its share of threatened environments and species, homeless people and the economically disadvantaged, and those with physical disabilities or mental health problems. In some ways, therefore, the choices for projects to join are no different in the UK from the ones you'd be making if you were planning to join a project abroad.

Cash-strapped hospitals are always in need of volunteers – Great Ormond Street Children's Hospital in London is a good example. They look after seriously

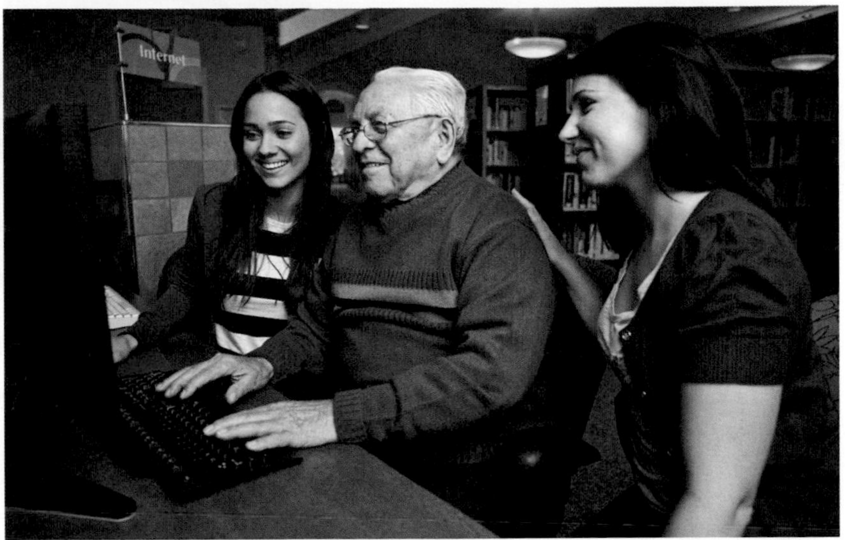

ill children and need volunteers to play with the children and make their stay less frightening. It also runs a hospital radio station – Radio Lollipop – in the evenings and on Sundays, for which it needs volunteers.

Or you could help with a youth sports team, get involved in a street art project, or with a holiday camp for deprived inner-city youngsters – there are many options and there are any number of inner-city organisations working to improve relations between, and provide/identify opportunities for, people from different ethnic groups, faiths and cultures.

Remember, though, that any volunteer work you do that puts you directly in contact with young people and other vulnerable groups, such as people with mental health problems, or care of the elderly, is likely to mean you'll need a CRB (Criminal Records Bureau) check for both their protection and yours. In some cases, you'll have to pay for this yourself.

Where to start?

Your own home town will have its share of charity shops on the high street, and they're always in need of volunteers. But you could also try local churches or sports groups. Check your local paper for stories on campaigns, special conservation days and other stories about good causes close to home that you might be able to support.

CSV (Community Service Volunteers) is the UK's leading volunteering and learning charity. Every year, they involve 150,000 volunteers in high-quality opportunities that enrich lives and tackle real need, helping transform the lives of people across the UK.

A gap-year with CSV lasts between six months and a year and does not cost a penny. Volunteers live away from home and are provided with accommodation and subsistence which includes food and day to day expenses.

Volunteers are aged between 18 and 35 and can start throughout the year. Volunteers are given the opportunity to take part in exciting projects including supporting adults or children with physical disabilities, learning disabilities or mental

my gap-year
Hannah Lockwood

I was taking a gap-year after leaving school and before starting uni. I wanted to 'do' something with my year; I wanted to do something which I knew would help and improve someone's life. I also wanted to gain some life experience and some life skills. That is why I applied to CSV. I hadn't heard about it before, I just found the website when I was looking up volunteering, but it just sounded exactly what I wanted to do. It was easy to apply and I received a lot of information about the organisation and when I got an interview I also received lots of information about where to go *etc.* Everyone I met was really nice and helpful and after the interview I really felt that they would find me a placement that would suit me.

I was so excited when I found out where and what my placement was, especially because I had TONS of information about it: what I would be doing, where it would be, where I would be living and what sort of people I would be helping. I was placed at Orchard Manor, a residential centre in Hertfordshire supporting young adults with physical and learning disabilities and additional support needs. The centre supports the residents in their transition between school and adult life and helps to develop skills to enable them to live as independently as possible later on.

Even though I was really looking forward to it and everyone I met was really welcoming and friendly, I still found my first couple of weeks quite difficult. It was the first time I had lived away from home so I was missing my family and for the first time I had to be totally independent. I ate a lot of tins of beans in my first month! I also found it difficult to deal with the young disabled people I was working with. Their disabilities were so severe that I had no idea how to communicate with them, how to help them without hurting them, how they could get any enjoyment out of life, basically I just didn't know what to do. I had some training which helped with the practical aspects such as personal care and moving and handling, but it still took me a while to feel confident with what I was doing. However it was the staff that really made me feel comfortable. There would always be someone who could supervise me until I felt confident and there was always someone I could ask if I had a question or a problem. I think time was also a big factor. Just spending time with the residents and getting to know them made all the difference. When I started I couldn't see past their disabilities, even though I knew that I should be able to and that made me feel guilty. But I very quickly got to know them and their personalities. It was hard work, but I feel that made it easier for me to get stuck in and get to know people – residents and staff – and just to feel comfortable with what I was doing.

I loved volunteering in Orchard Manor and since leaving I have missed it a lot. I miss the people I volunteered with and I miss the residents. I am so pleased that I decided to take a gap-year and that I decided to apply to CSV, it was one of the best decisions I have ever made. It has given me so many life skills and has changed how I view the world. I have made friends for life and it is a year that I will never forget!

health issues, befriending homeless people, mentoring young people and many others across the UK.

For volunteer information about gap-year volunteering with CSV call 0800 374 991 or apply online at www.csv.org.uk/gapyear.

What qualities does a good volunteer need?

The Samaritans is one organisation that's reported an upsurge in calls to its confidential helpline as a result of the recession – and if you've been in the position of losing your job, and are maybe thinking of volunteering to help others, it would be a good idea to think hard about whether you're able to offer what's needed.

Here's what the Samaritans have to say:

"Samaritans volunteers need to be able to listen. They are not professional counsellors. They can also:

- question gently, tactfully – without intruding;
- encourage people to tell their own story in their own time and space;
- refrain from offering advice and instead offer confidential emotional support; and
- always try to see the other point of view, regardless of their own religious or political beliefs."

Go to this section on the Samaritans website: **www.samaritans.org/volunteer-us**

You can find out more here on the training and support you will be given before you are taken on.

ChildLine too has good advice for volunteers on its website and sees them as the essential basis of ChildLine's service. They need volunteers to speak to children

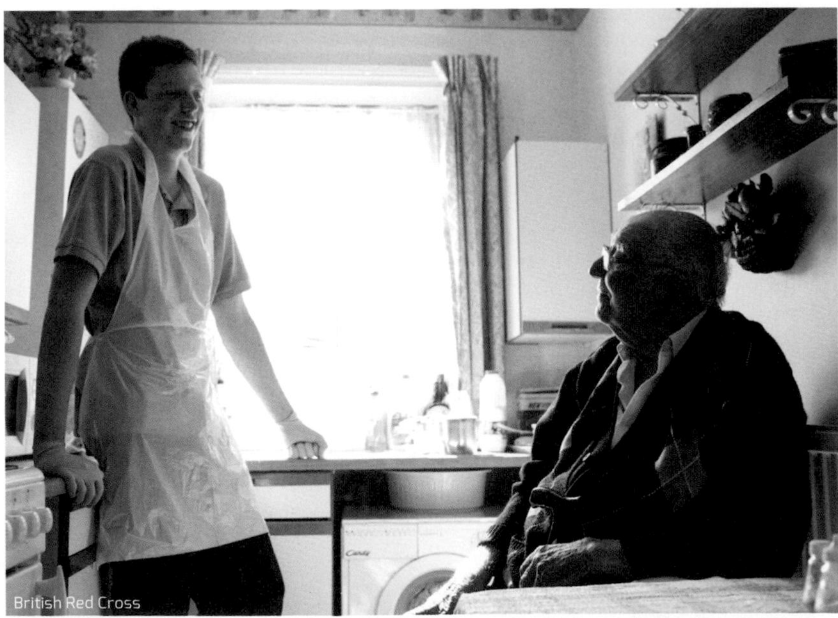

British Red Cross

British Red Cross

and young people on their helpline, to work with them in schools, and to support fundraising, administration and management.

The charity provides full training and support, and has centres in London, Nottingham, Glasgow, Aberdeen, Manchester, Swansea, Rhyl, Leeds, Belfast, Exeter and Birmingham. Follow this link for more information:
www.nspcc.org.uk/get-involved/volunteer-your-time/childline-volunteering/childline-helpline_wda85308.html

There's a need for volunteers to help with disadvantaged people of all ages and if you're older, and considering volunteering, your work skills could come in handy. Many charities may need professional advice from time to time. If you have expertise in accountancy, administration, construction and maintenance, the law, psychiatry or treasury you might be able to help.

Helping refugees

The International Red Cross has a long history of helping traumatised and displaced people around the world, from being the first port of call in an emergency to monitoring the treatment of political prisoners, it is often trusted as the only impartial authority allowed access to detainees.

The British Red Cross has a specific scheme dedicated to helping refugees adjust to life in the UK. Trained volunteers provide much needed support to thousands of people every year, helping them to access local services and adjust to life in a new country. The Red Cross's services provide practical/emotional help to vulnerable asylum seekers and refugees. This includes offering orientation services to help refugees adapt to life in the UK, providing emergency support for large-scale arrivals, providing emergency provisions for those in crisis and offering peer-befriending support to young refugees.

You can volunteer to help out in charity shops or with fundraising. To find out more about volunteering with the Red Cross go to: **www.redcross.org.uk**

Conservation

Perhaps you're more interested in conservation work? The British Trust for Conservation Volunteers is a good place to start. It offers short (and longer) training courses that are informal and designed to be fun – including practical skills such as building a dry stone wall, creating a pond or a wildlife garden. It also has a number of options for volunteer schemes you can join: **www.tcv.org.uk/volunteering**

Animals

Volunteer jobs with animal welfare organisations can vary from helping with kennel duties, assisting with fundraising events, carrying out wildlife surveys, to working on specific projects.

Animal Jobs Direct has information on paid work with animals but it also has a section for volunteers.

The web address below gives direct links to animal welfare and rescue charities that offer a variety of different and interesting volunteering opportunities –there are an amazing range of voluntary jobs available. Remember, many animal charities exist on limited funds and therefore voluntary workers are much needed and appreciated.

To find out more, visit: **www.animal-job.co.uk/animal-volunteer-work-uk.html**

Help with expenses

While giving your time for free is part of the definition of volunteering, financial help is often available and organisations shouldn't leave you out of pocket. Many charities will reimburse your expenses such as travel tickets and lunch costs.

For some long term volunteering placements, different rules apply and as well as having your basic expenses covered, you may be given a 'subsistence allowance' to cover living costs like heat, light, laundry and food. You may also be given free accommodation – for example if you are volunteering for several months in a care home.

If you are interested in volunteering with an organisation, ask whether they cover volunteer expenses and find out what they will reimburse.

In the directory we list the contact details of a number of charities and organisations that are grateful for volunteers. If you can't find anything that interests you there, then there are a number of organisations that place people with other charities or that have a wide national network of their own – an internet search should give you a good list.

The following websites provide useful links and information about volunteering:
www.do-it.org.uk
www.ncvo-vol.org.uk
timebank.org.uk
vois.org.uk (specifically working with young people)

Please see the directory pages starting on page 365 for information on companies and organisations offering volunteering opportunities in the UK.

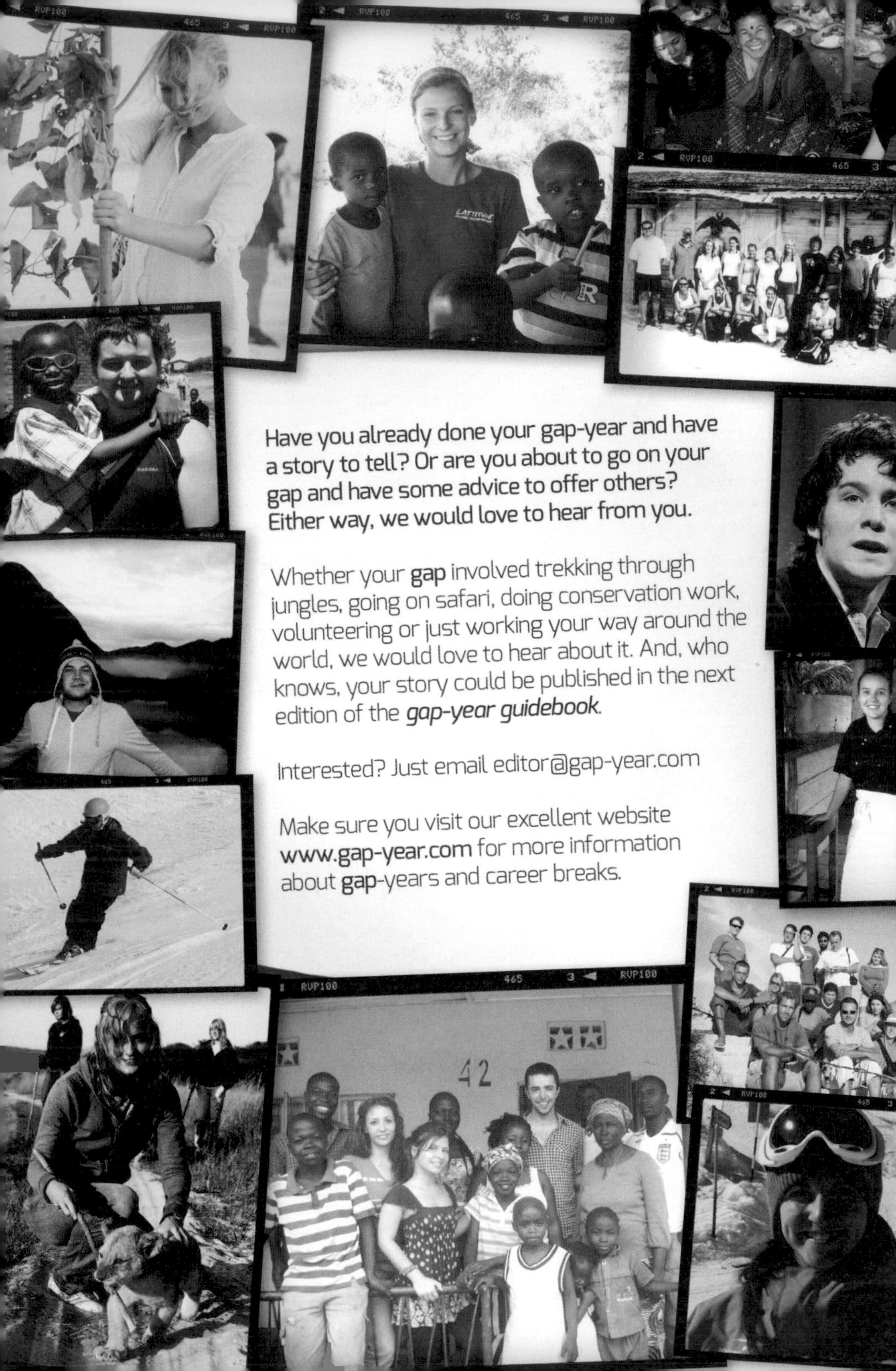
Have you already done your gap-year and have a story to tell? Or are you about to go on your gap and have some advice to offer others? Either way, we would love to hear from you.
Whether your gap involved trekking through jungles, going on safari, doing conservation work, volunteering or just working your way around the world, we would love to hear about it. And, who knows, your story could be published in the next edition of the gap-year guidebook.
Interested? Just email editor@gap-year.com
Make sure you visit our excellent website www.gap-year.com for more information about gap-years and career breaks.

Learning in the UK

Learning in the UK

You don't have to spend your gap-year travelling the globe if that doesn't appeal to you. The point about taking a gap is to try out new experiences that leave you feeling refreshed and stimulated, to learn something new and possibly come up with some new ideas about where you want your life to head next.

So if you're frustrated that hardly anything you were taught at school seems relevant to your life, why not use your gap-year to learn new skills that you choose yourself? You can make them as useful as you want.

There are plenty of evening classes available at local colleges, though usually only in term time, and, if you're thinking of training that doesn't involve university or are looking for ways to expand your skill set as part of a change of career direction, check out the Learning and Skills Council, which exists to promote lifelong learning, with the aim of young people and adults having skills to match the best in the world. There's lots of information on what's available, including financial help, on: **www.lsc.gov.uk.**

A gap is also a good opportunity to explore interests that may, up to now, have been hobbies; here are some suggestions:

Archaeology

Do relics from the past fascinate you? Would you love to find one? You could get yourself on an actual archaeological dig. One good place to start is with your local county council's archaeology department, which may know of local digs you could join. Nowadays, whenever a major building development is going through the planning application process, permission to build often includes a condition allowing for archaeological surveys to be done before any work can begin; so another source of information could be the planning departments of local district councils.

Art

If you're seriously interested in painting, sculpting or other artistic subjects, but don't know if you want to carry it through to a full degree, there is the useful option of a one-year art foundation course. These are available from a wide variety of art colleges.

A foundation course at art college doesn't count towards an art degree, in the sense that you can then skip the first year of your three-year degree course, but it can help you find out whether you are interested in becoming a practising artist, maybe an illustrator, an animator, a graphic designer, or are more interested in things like art history, or perhaps working in a gallery or a museum or in a field like interior design.

If you do want to go on to the three-year art school degree, competition for undergraduate places is based on the volume and standard of work in a candidate's

entry portfolio. Having a portfolio from your foundation course puts you at a natural advantage. Course providers also advise against specialising in one discipline, say sculpture, before covering the more wide-ranging syllabus of a foundation course.

Cookery

A cookery course is a great way of learning a fundamental skill that can change your life, whether it leads to professional cooking jobs in your time off allowing you to pay your way while travelling, or simply sets you up with skills to cook for yourself and friends throughout university and beyond.

With a just a few tips and tricks, sharp knife skills and plenty of ingredient know-how, learning basic cooking skills can transform the way you eat, shop and cook.

Offering four, six or 10-week courses in which students learn through demonstration and practical sessions, certificate cookery courses generally comprise a thorough understanding of basic cooking skills and techniques, a certificate in health and hygiene, as well as a basic grounding in pairing food with wine.

Cookery certainly appears to be a fast-rising sector of the gap-year market, and we asked our friends at the Cookery School at Little Portland Street – who offer intensive six-week courses as well as beginner courses – to explain just why:

"Cookery programmes are ideal for gap-year students: not only do they provide you with life skills and learning that lasts but they set you up to work at home or abroad during a time that students take out to grow and develop, make decisions on their career paths and explore new places," they told us.

Leiths School of Food and Wine

"We teach simple principles and culinary skills required to make confident and knowledgeable general cooks and are currently seeing a real trend for people wanting to learn the basics. Our absolute beginners courses are full of keen cooks wanting to master everything from soups and stews, roasting, desserts to salads and dressings."

Our friends at Cookery at the Grange told us: "Our students are more motivated than ever these days – results-driven and aware of the value of doing something purposeful. They know that employers like to see constructive use of time off. Some students are organised and book early before leaving school, others come to us once their results are out, or later in their gap-years when they find time between projects. Whilst others have thought about doing our course for years, and take longer to get around to it! Quite a few people are now taking gap-years at different stages, in life not just after school."

Leiths School of Food and Wine has been offering catering courses since 1975, and each year their Essential Certificate gives school and university graduates the opportunity to learn from skilled teaching staff in a professional but fun working environment.

Once graduating with a certificate, Leiths List, an agency which places qualified cooks in part-time, full-time and one-off job placements, helps you find work.

Working as a cook in ski resorts, on yachts in the Caribbean or in villas in Tuscany or the south of France not only allows you to see the world, but also pays you while you see it.

Cookery schools tell us that the majority of those who want to work after doing a cookery course do find cooking work. Here's the Cookery School again:

"We hope to produce cooks that will go on to confidently cater at home, take seasonal chalet and yacht work and go into professional kitchens. We have also seen

cookeryschool

at little portland street

Cookery School at Little Portland Street,
15B Little Portland Street,
London W1W 8BW
T: +44 (0) 20 7631 4590
E: info@cookeryschool.co.uk
W: www.cookeryschool.co.uk

Fast Track Training at Cookery School - central London

This gem of a school in central London has something to offer all food lovers: classes and courses for beginners and experienced cooks, as well as specialist topics. The school's approach to food is simple, modern and imaginative.

Ideal for Gap Year students, we offer a Cook's Certificate in Food & Wine: A six-week intensive, 'fast track' course which is a good starting point for anyone wanting to confidently, cater at home, take seasonal chalet work, work up great meals at university or go into a professional kitchen.

Our Certificate embodies principles and culinary skills required to make confident and knowledgeable general cooks. We intend to pass on skills that once would have been acquired through mothers and grandmothers that form the bedrock of cooking and engender a passion for food. The mantra at Cookery School is learning that lasts - you cannot unlearn how to chop an onion and crush a clove of garlic.

From requisite learning of knife skills through to techniques associated with breads, pastries, sauces, cakes *etc*, students will be taught other necessary practices such as weights and measures, healthy eating, sustainable sourcing and menu writing. They will also gain Health and Safety certification, complete a day of First Aid, as well as a WSET regulated wine course.

With a high ratio of pupils to chefs there are just twelve places available and at the end of the course pupils will have the opportunity to take up a week's work placement in a professional kitchen.

Alongside Cookery School's **Rosalind Rathouse**, **Lucy French** and **John Fernandez**, specialist classes will be taught by patisserie chef **Ghalid Assyb**, award-winning baker **Dan Lepard**, Indian author and teacher **Kumud Shah** and Japanese sushi specialist **Kimiko Barber**.

Cookery at the Grange

students go on to take further training in specific areas, such as patisserie, after discovering a love for a topic they had not previously considered."

What's involved in being a chalet cook depends on what a ski company or employer wants. Usually the day starts with a cooked breakfast for the ski party, then possibly a packed lunch, tea and cake when hungry skiers get back, possibly canapés later, and a three or four-course supper. The food does need more than the usual amount of carbohydrates.

Ski companies expect high standards and may ask for sample menus when you apply for chalet cooking jobs. Sometimes the menus are decided in advance and the shopping done locally by someone else; sometimes the cook has to do the shopping.

Perhaps surprisingly, ski companies and agencies rarely ask about language skills – the cooks seem to manage without.

Here's a list of highly recommended cookery schools for you to check out:

www.ashburtoncookeryschool.co.uk
www.cookeryschool.co.uk
www.cookeryatthegrange.co.uk
www.leiths.com
www.tantemarie.co.uk

Drama

The Year Out Drama Company, based at Stratford-upon-Avon, offers an intensive, practical drama course with a theatre company feel. The company, which has strong support from the Royal Shakespeare Company, has a 25-year record of specialist teaching and directing in professionally-equipped spaces.

Deborah Moody, director of Year Out Drama, told us that the course includes:

- Individual help for students wishing to gain entry to the top drama schools and university places with UCAS and audition support.

Year Out Drama

- Insight and guidance from ex-students attending a wide range of HE courses and drama schools.
- Encouragement to develop students' own extracurricular work: directing, writing, singing, music.
- The opportunity to take part in a show at the Edinburgh Fringe Festival.

This course is self-financing and the fee includes all tuition and also tickets and travel for many theatre trips throughout the year. See **www.yearoutdrama.co.uk**

There are also plenty of amateur dramatic and operatic societies in small towns across the UK. If you've always had a hankering to tread the boards, they're a great way to find out more about all the elements of putting on a production. You may be able to volunteer at your local theatre and gain valuable experience that way. Ring them up or check out their website to see if they have a bank of volunteers.

Then there are short courses and summer schools. This site lists a wide range of programmes available over the summer holidays: **www.summer-schools.info**

Driving

There may be a lot of pressure to minimise car use in an effort to reduce carbon emissions and tackle global warming, but there are still plenty of good reasons for learning to drive.

First, unless you're intending to live in an inner city indefinitely, you may need a driver's licence to get a job; secondly, it will give you independence and you won't have to rely on everyone else to give you lifts everywhere. Even though you might not be able to afford the insurance right now, let alone an actual car, your gap-year is an ideal time to take driving lessons.

The test comes in two parts, theory and practical: and you need to pass the theory test before you apply for the practical one. However, you can start learning practical driving before you take the theory part, but to do that you need a provisional driving licence. You need to complete a driving licence application form and a photocard application form D1 – available from most post offices. Send the forms, the fee

cookery at the Grange has been running the outstanding four week, residential Essential Cookery Courses since 1981. Fantastic local ingredients from the Somerset countryside near Bath, are used to learn to cook really good food, for fun, for a gap year or for a career.
"The Grange is the most beautiful place I've ever been, and I've just had the best month of my life"
Lucy Capel, 18. Student from Sydney, May 2012
www.cookeryatthegrange.co.uk

and original documentation confirming your identity such as your passport or birth certificate (make sure you keep a photocopy) and a passport-sized colour photograph to the DVLA.

You also need to check that you are insured for damage to yourself, other cars or other people, and if you are practising in the family car, your parents will have to add cover for you on their insurance.

The DSA (Driving Standards Authority) is responsible for driving tests. However, to avoid duplication, all information on learning to drive, including fees, advice on preparing for the test and booking one has been moved to the Government services website: **www.gov.uk/browse/driving/learning-to-drive**

Theory

The theory test is in two parts: a multiple-choice part and a hazard perception section. You have to pass both. If you pass one and fail the other, you have to do both again.

The multiple-choice is a touch-screen test where you have to get at least 43 out of 50 questions right. You don't have to answer the questions in turn and the computer shows how much time you have left. You can have 15 minutes' practice before you start the test properly. If you have special needs you can get extra time for the test – ask for this when you book it.

In the hazard test, you are shown 14 video clips filmed from a car, each containing one or more developing hazards. You have to indicate as soon as you see a hazard developing, which may necessitate the driver taking some action, such as changing speed or direction. The sooner a response is made the higher the score. Test results and feedback information are given within half an hour of finishing. The fee for the standard theory test is currently £31.

Your driving school, instructor or local test centre should have an application form, although you can book your test over the phone (0300 200 1122) or online at: **www.gov.uk/book-a-driving-theory-test**

Practical test

You have two years to pass the practical test once you have passed the theory part. The practical test for a car will cost £62, unless you choose to take it in the evening or on Saturday, in which case the cost will increase to £75. It's more expensive for a motorbike and the test is now in two modules – module 1 is £10 for both evenings and weekends, module 2 is £70 for weekday and £82 for weekend and evening tests. You can book the practical test in the same way as the theory test. The bad news is that the tests are tough and it's quite common to fail twice or more before a pass. The practical test requires candidates to drive on faster roads than before – you'll need to negotiate a dual carriageway as well as a suburban road. You'll fail if you commit more than 15 driving faults. Once you pass your practical test, you can exchange your provisional licence for a full licence.

Instructors

Of course some unqualified instructors (including parents) are experienced and competent, as are many small driving schools – but some checking out is a good idea if a driving school is not a well-known name. You can make sure that it is registered with the Driving Standards Agency and that the instructor is qualified. AA and BSM charges can be used as a benchmark if you're trying other schools. There's information about choosing an instructor and what qualifications they must have if they're charging you here: **www.gov.uk/find-driving-schools-and-lessons**

TANTE MARIE

Culinary Academy

Gordon Ramsay's Tante Marie Culinary Academy, Woodham House,
Carlton Road, Woking GU21 4HF
T: +44 (0) 1483 726957
E: info@tantemarie.co.uk W: www.tantemarie.co.uk

Co-owned by Gordon Ramsay, Tante Marie Culinary Academy is the UK's oldest independent cookery school and is now the only school in the world able to award both our internationally acclaimed Cordon Bleu Diploma, and the CTH Level 4 Diploma in Professional Culinary Arts - one of the world's highest rated practical cookery qualifications, worth 96 points on the Qualifications Credit Framework.

This means that students attending the Diploma course during their gap year, may earn valuable credit towards future training.

In addition to our Diploma course, we run a 4 week Essential Skills course and our 10-week Cordon Bleu Certificate course. Both of these courses are popular with gap year students and offer excellent employment prospects with skiing and yachting agencies and other gap year employers.

At Tante Marie, we don't just teach you how to cook a week's worth of menu's to get you through your ski season, or to give you a selection of recipes you can follow. We focus on teaching you the skills and knowledge so that you can create your own dishes and menus, run your own kitchen in a profitable and organised manner, and fully understand the complex and intricate art of cooking.

Our courses are designed to be fun and offer a set of skills that will remain with you for life. On our Gap Year courses you will earn a Level 2 Award in Food Safety in Catering and also learn about menu planning and budgeting, ensuring the best possible preparation for working while at uni or during a year out. The options are endless! Come and take up the challenge!

Met Film School

Film

For those wanting to forge a career in the filmmaking industry it can be difficult to navigate the world of film school and to decide whether it is the right option for you.

To gain access to the industry it is important to have as much practical experience on your CV as possible. There are many options available, from working as a runner and camera trainee to gaining experience in post-production houses and internships in feature film production companies.

You can also spend your gap-year making your own films and learning from industry professionals to develop the skills needed for a career in filmmaking.

Met Film School, who are based at Ealing Studios in London, told us:

"We're part of the Met Film group consisting of the school, Met Film Production and Met Film Post. Unlike any other film school we are completely integrated within the film industry. Met Film Production develops and produces a number of feature films each year and Met Film Post is a leading post-production business, specialising in end-to-end sound and picture post.

"On most of our courses, students write, produce, direct and edit their own short films – benefiting from hands-on experience via numerous shooting and directing exercises, tailored coaching through one-to-one and group sessions with our tutors and access to state-of-the-art digital technology.

"It's worth remembering that it only takes one piece of work to kick-start your career and every time you get behind a camera you have a chance to make that film."

LEITHS

SCHOOL OF FOOD AND WINE

Leiths School of Food and Wine, 16-20 Wendell Road, Shepherd's Bush, London W12 9RT
T: +44 (0) 20 8749 6400
E: info@leiths.com W: www.leiths.com

Leiths School of Food and Wine is a leading London cookery school for both professional and enthusiastic home cooks. Whether you want to learn how to cook for your own pleasure, take on part-time cookery jobs during your gap year or university holidays, or want a career in the food industry, Leiths have a course to suit you.

* Leiths four-week Essential Certificate, starting in August, teaches a range of cookery skills which can be used to gain employment in chalets, holiday homes or one-off catering jobs.

* Leiths ten-week Foundation Certificate starting in late September is an in-depth cookery course designed to build your cookery skills and confidence. Graduates can use their certificate to work for catering companies, private cooking and holiday cooking.

* If you are passionate about food, Leiths three-term Diploma is a full-time course from September to July. Designed for those looking for a career in food, it is highly respected in the food industry and can lead to a range of exciting careers including restaurants, catering, farmers' markets, pop-up restaurants, food styling, writing and recipe development.

All Leiths professional courses are exam-based certificate courses and include health and safety, food hygiene, budgeting, healthy eating and menu planning. Once qualified, Leiths List, our agency for cooks, can help you find a suitable job.

Leiths also run informal one day to one week classes, running throughout the year for the keen cook.

"The Leiths Essential Certificate qualification has ensured that I can cook meals for not just myself but my whole house. Leiths has also taught me to cook healthy food, whilst sticking to a reasonable budget. During the holidays there are always jobs available."
Diana Cheal, graduated 2007

Contact Leiths for a prospectus on +44 (0) 20 8749 6400 or visit www.leiths.com. For any queries please email info@leiths.com.

Language courses

Even if the job you are applying for doesn't require them, employers are often impressed by language skills. With the growth of global business, most companies like to think of themselves as having international potential at the very least.

If you didn't enjoy language classes at school, that shouldn't necessarily put you off. College courses and evening classes are totally different – or at least they should be. If in doubt, ask to speak to the tutor, or to someone who has already been on the course, before you sign up.

And even if you don't aspire to learn enough to be able to use your linguistic skills in a job, you could still take conversation classes so you can speak a bit of the language when you go abroad on your holidays. It is amazing what a sense of achievement and self-confidence you can get when you manage to communicate the simplest things to a local in their own language: such as ordering a meal or buying stamps for your postcards home.

The best way to improve your language skills is to practice speaking; preferably to a native speaker in their own country. But if you don't have the time or the money to go abroad yet, don't worry. There are plenty of places in the UK to learn a wide variety of languages, from Spanish to Somali. We've listed some language institutions in the directory, but also find out what language courses your local college offers, and what evening classes there are locally.

Music

Perhaps you always wanted to learn the saxophone, but never quite got round to it? Now would be an ideal time to start. If you're interested, your best bet is to find a good private tutor. Word of mouth is the best recommendation, but some teachers advertise in local papers, and you could also try an online search engine like **www.musicteachers.co.uk**

If you already play an instrument, you could broaden your experience by going on a residential course or summer school. These are available for many different ability levels, although they tend to be quite pricey. There's no central info source on the net, as there is for drama courses, but we searched the internet for residential summer music schools and found loads of individual schools offering courses, so there are bound to be some near you. See the directory for more information.

my gap-year Rowena McCrae

After Rowena McCrae completed the Essential Cookery Course at The Grange she worked as a chalet girl in Courchevel, before studying sociology at Newcastle University. She financed her student life by cooking all over the country during her holidays, in lodges and holiday homes. And after university couldn't resist a second ski season back in Courchevel, because the first had been such fun! Since then she has worked in the ski travel industry selling holidays, worked as an estate agent - both residential and commercial - and went on to set up and run her own PR company.

Her experience and knowledge of cooking has led her to set up her own cooking agency Macaroon (www.macaroon.com). She is passionate about her plans for this and aims to develop a reputation for successfully placing cooks in just the sort of places where she herself enjoyed working, here and abroad. She is still firm friends with all those she met at The Grange and continues to love cooking.

For more information about Cookery at The Grange, visit:
www.cookeryatthegrange.co.uk

Online learning

There are plenty of online language learning courses for those who are welded semi-permanently to their computers.

You can now get very comprehensive language courses on CD-ROM, which include booklets or pages that can be printed off. The better ones use voice recognition as well, so you can practise your pronunciation. These can also be found in bookstores.

The internet itself is also a good source of language material. There are many courses, some with free access, some that need a very healthy credit card. If all you want is a basic start, then take a look at: **www.bbc.co.uk/languages**

This site offers you the choice of beginner's French, German, Italian, Mandarin, Portuguese, Greek, Spanish, Japanese, Urdu and some other languages, complete with vocabulary lists to download, all for free.

As well as courses, there are translation services, vocabulary lists and topical forums – just do a web search and see how many sites come up. Many are free but some are extremely expensive so check before you sign up.

Practice makes perfect

When you need to practise, find out if there are any native speakers living in your town – you could arrange your own language and cultural evenings.

Terrestrial TV stations run some language learning programmes, usually late at night. If you have satellite or cable TV you can also watch foreign shows though this can be a bit frustrating if you're a beginner. It's best to record the programmes so you can replay any bits that you didn't understand the first time round.

Once you get a bit more advanced then you can try tuning your radio into foreign speech-based shows from the relevant countries. This is also a good way to keep up-to-date with current affairs in your chosen country, as well as keeping up your listening and understanding skills. Subjects are wide-ranging, and there's something to interest everyone.

Most self-teach language tapes have been well received by teachers and reviewers, but can be a bit expensive for the average gap-year student. So, you might be glad to hear that, if you have iTunes, you can download language podcasts from the store. Most of these are free and you have the option of subscribing so that new podcasts are automatically downloaded next time you log on.

Photography

There are lots of photography courses available, from landscape photography to studio work. Don't kid yourself that a photography course is going to get you a job and earn you pots of money, but there's nothing to stop you enjoying photography as a hobby or sideline.

If you do want to find out more about professional photography you could try contacting local studios and asking about the possibility of spending some time with them as a studio assistant. Another option is to contact your local paper and ask if you can shadow a photographer, so you can get a feel for how they work and perhaps start building a portfolio of your own.

Sport

After all that studying maybe all you want to do is get out there and do something. The same applies if you've been stuck in an office at a computer for most of your working life. If you're the energetic type and hate the thought of spending your gap-year stuck behind a desk, why not get active and do some sport? There are sports courses for all types at all levels, from scuba diving for beginners to advanced ski instructor qualification courses. Of course if you manage to get an instructor's qualification you may be able to use it to get a job (see **Chapter 8 – Sport**).

TEFL

Teaching English as a Foreign Language qualifications are always useful for earning money wherever you travel abroad. The important thing to check is that the qualification you will be gaining is recognised by employers. Most courses should also lead on to help with finding employment. There's more on TEFL courses in **Chapter 5 – Working abroad**.

X-rated

If you hated sport at school, try giving it another chance during your gap-year – you may be surprised how much you like it. There are plenty of unusual sports to try.

For a real adrenalin rush, go for one of the extreme sports like sky boarding, basically a combination of skydiving and snowboarding – you throw yourself out of a plane wearing a parachute and perform acrobatic stunts on a board.

Or, if you like company when you're battling against the elements, then you could get involved in adventure racing: teams race each other across rugged terrain without using anything with a motor, *eg* skiing, hiking, sea kayaking. Team members have to stay together throughout the race. Raid Gauloises (five person teams, two weeks, five stages, half the teams don't finish!) and Eco-Challenge (ten days, 600km, several stages and an environmental project) are the two most well-known adventure race events.

The annual X Games feature a wide range of extreme sports and take place during one week in summer (including aggressive in-line skating) and another week in winter (including mountain bike racing on snow). Check out their website (**xgames.espn.go.com**) for the full details.

If you want to get wet, then try diving, kayaking, sailing, surfing, water polo, windsurfing, or white-water rafting.

And if those don't appeal then there's always abseiling, baseball, basketball, bungee jumping, cave diving, cricket, fencing, football, golf, gymnastics, hang gliding, hockey, horse riding, ice hockey, ice skating, jet skiing, motor racing, mountain biking, mountain boarding, parachuting, polo, rock climbing, rowing, rugby, running, skateboarding, skating, ski jumping, skiing, skydiving, sky surfing, snowmobiling, snowboarding, squash, stock car racing, tennis or trampolining! If the sport you are interested in isn't listed in our directory then try contacting the relevant national association (*eg* the LTA for tennis) and asking them for a list of course providers.

Please see the directory pages starting on page 373 for information on companies and organisations offering learning opportunities in the UK.

Further study

12 Further study

Please note: The information contained in this chapter is for guidance only. We would strongly advise you to talk to your school or college examination officer, chosen university or exam board for up-to-the-minute advice and information.

Retakes

There are several reasons why you might find yourself considering retakes: maybe because your grades are too low to meet a conditional offer (and the university won't negotiate with you to admit you on lower grades), or because illness interfered with exams.

But beware, getting better grades second time round doesn't guarantee you a university place – often universities will demand even higher grades if it's taken you two bites at the cherry (unless of course you've got a really good excuse, like illness).

Grade appeals

The now almost habitual media comment about the devaluation of A level marks has left many people wondering just how much we can trust exam results. If you really think you've been done down by a tired exam marker, a misleading or misprinted question or some other factor, you can appeal against your result.

You appeal first to the examination board that set the exam, and if you don't think the adjudication is just, you can go on to appeal to the **Examinations Procedures Review Service (EPRS) at Ofqual**. But be warned: this process takes a long time and there's no guarantee the appeal will go your way.

Retake timing

Now that modular A levels are firmly entrenched, you may be able to retake the modules you did badly while you are still at school, instead of having to retake them in your year out.

However, you need to check with both your exam board and chosen university before you make any plans.

Every exam board has its own timetable for retakes (see p387 for contact details) and universities also vary considerably in their regulations on retakes.

You need to make sure your chosen university course doesn't set higher entry grades for exams taken at a second sitting.

In some cases you may find that when you retake a certain exam you have to change exam board – this can be a problem in some subjects (*eg* languages with set texts) and you may therefore have to resit your A levels a whole year after the original exams, which can seriously disrupt your gap-year. Check with your exam board as early as you can.

Tutorial colleges like to keep students working on A levels for a full year. That keeps the college full and tutors paid. But many agree that the best thing is to get resits over before you forget the work you've already done. So the best timing, if you are academically confident and want to enjoy your gap-year, is to go to a tutorial college in September and resit the whole exam or the relevant modules in January – if sittings are available then.

Languages

If you have only language AS levels, A2 levels or A levels to retake, there are several options:

- Take an extra course or stay in the country of the relevant language and return to revise for a summer resit, choosing the same exam board (courses abroad, however, are not usually geared to A level texts).
- Check with tutorial colleges how much of your syllabus module or modules (the chosen literature texts are crucial) overlap with those of other exam boards. This may give you the chance to switch exam boards and do a quick retake in January.
- Cram for as long as necessary at a specialist language college. Some British tutorial colleges and language course organisers have links with teaching centres in other countries so it's worth checking this out before signing on.

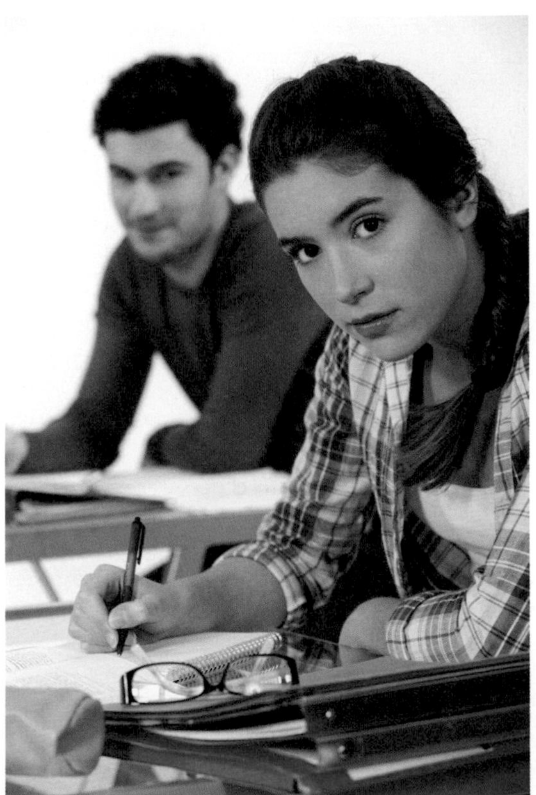

Retake results

Those who sit A level retakes in January, and get the grades needed for a chosen place, will not have to wait until August for that place to be confirmed.

Examining boards will feed the result directly into UCAS so you will know your place has been clinched. A technicality, but comforting for gap-year students who want to travel.

And don't forget that if you have a firm choice conditional offer and you make the grades asked for, the university can't back out. It has an obligation to admit you.

Applying to university

At the time of writing, the latest UCAS figures show that the total number of applicants to university and college places has risen in 2013 (up 3.1% on 2012 figures as of 30 June 2013). The total number of applicants as at 30 June 2012 was 637,456 compared to 618,247 on the same date in 2012, although that's still short of the 2011 figure of 669,956. The drop from 2011 to 2012 was largely blamed on the rise in tuition fees.

For some, the decision to take a year off is made well in advance. Often students make the decision to defer their entry into higher education with specific projects in mind. Some choose not to apply at all until after their A level results.

Others find themselves taking a gap-year at much shorter notice once they receive their grades. If UCAS applicants have not met the conditions of the offers they are holding then a gap-year can allow them to reassess their plans.

Equally, one option for those who have done better than expected is to use the time to aim for something they had originally considered beyond them.

Application process

UCAS (the Universities and Colleges Admissions Service) handles applications to all UK universities (except the Open University) as well as to most other institutions that offer full-time undergraduate higher education courses. This includes applications for Oxford, Cambridge and for degrees in medicine, dentistry and veterinary science/medicine, although they have to be in earlier than for other universities and colleges and for other subjects.

You can follow UCAS on Twitter at **twitter.com/ucas_online** and ask a question or see what others are asking on Facebook at **www.facebook.com/ucasonline**. You can also watch videos of UCAS advisers answering frequently asked questions on YouTube at **www.youtube.com/ucasonline**

There are many video guides to help you with all stages of the UCAS application process, including: How to choose your courses, Attending events, and How to apply. These can all be viewed at **www.ucas.tv** or in the relevant section of **www.ucas.com**

UCAS
PO Box 28
Cheltenham, GL52 3LZ

Tel: +44 (0) 871 468 0468

Email: enquiries@ucas.co.uk

Sending an email to this address will get you an automated response with general information and guidance on UCAS procedures.

If you have hearing difficulties, you can call the Text Relay service on 18001 0871 468 0 468 from within the UK or on 0044 151 494 1260 (text phone) from outside the UK. You will need to ask the operator to dial 0871 468 0468. There is no extra charge for this service. Calls are charged at normal rates.

UCAS offers a distribution service to companies who wish to send promotional material to students. UCAS handles the distribution itself and does not pass on your personal details, which remain confidential. If you prefer not to receive this kind of material however, you can opt out when completing your UCAS application.

You can apply for five different courses at any UCAS institutions, except for medicine, dentistry and veterinary science/medicine courses for each of which you can make just four choices. Note that some art and design courses use the deadline of 24 March for the receipt of applications at UCAS while others use 15 January – be sure to check the UCAS search tool at **http://search.ucas.com** for which deadline applies to each of your chosen courses. You can hold on to no more than two of the offers you get: one 'firm (first choice) offer' and one 'insurance (second choice) offer'. So you may have to be cautious about the courses you pitch for.

Online application

UCAS has a secure, web-based application system called Apply. Each school, college, careers agency or British Council office that has registered with UCAS to use Apply appoints a coordinator who manages the way it is used. For students, registering to the new system takes a few minutes and costs nothing. Once a student has registered, they are given a username and are asked to choose a password that they will need to use each time they want to access their application. Applicants can use this system anywhere that has access to the web. The service works in tandem with the online search tool at **http://search.ucas.com**. Check out the UCAS website for more information at: **www.ucas.com**

Students who are not at a school or college also make their applications using the online Apply system. Independent applicants can either ask their referee to enter their reference online or contact their old school or college and ask whether they will supply a reference online. In either case they send the completed application together with payment to UCAS themselves.

Please remember you do not have to apply for all your choices at the same time. You can add further choices up to 30 June as long as you have not used up all your choices and have not yet replied to any offers and places are still available.

A level results

A level results come out in mid-August. Depending on your grades one of the following will happen:

- Firm (first) choice university confirms offer of a place. (If your grades meet and exceed your offer conditions, you may research alternatives for up to five days while retaining your firm offer, a process known as Adjustment)
- Insurance (second choice) university confirms offer of a place.
- Clearing.
- Retakes.

Before you make any decisions make sure you know all the angles. Retakes may be the only way for you to get to university, but most universities will demand even higher results the second time around. The advice from Glasgow University is: "We expect slightly higher requirements if you don't get good enough grades in one A level attempt."

The UCAS Tariff

The UCAS Tariff was first used for those applying to enter higher education (HE) in 2002. Since its introduction it has expanded to cover additional qualifications. It is a points-based system that establishes agreed equivalences between different types of qualifications. It provides admissions tutors with a way of comparing applicants with different types and volumes of achievement. Over three quarters of universities and colleges now use the Tariff, but some admissions tutors still choose to make offers in terms of grades. For more information about the Tariff, visit **www.ucas.com/how-it-all-works/explore-your-options/entry-requirements/ucas-tariff**

In July 2010, UCAS announced plans to review the Tariff. For information about the Qualifications Information Review, visit **www.ucas.com/about-us/our-work-sector/ucas-consultations**

Key dates

This is what will happen if you apply for a university course starting in autumn 2014 or for deferred entry in 2015, so if you are thinking of taking a gap-year you'll need to know that:

- The main deadline for applications for all universities (except all courses at Oxford and Cambridge, medicine, dentistry, veterinary medicine or veterinary science courses at all universities and certain art and design programmes) is 15 January. See list of dates below.
- There is a 'commitment to clear, transparent admissions policies' and the UCAS search tool at **http://search.ucas.com** provides the entry requirements for individual courses. This information is often included on universities' own websites as well.
- A service called Extra has been designed for applicants who have used all five of their choices, but who do not have a place. Extra allows them to make additional choices through UCAS, one at a time. The service runs from the end of February until early July, so you don't have to wait until Clearing to find a place. If you are eligible for Extra, UCAS will tell you how to apply to a university or college with vacancies, using the Track service on its website.

- 'Invisibility of choices' means that universities and colleges cannot see which other universities or colleges an applicant has applied to until that applicant has replied to an offer or has no live choices.

The autumn term is when Year 13 students usually begin to apply for university and college places through the UCAS system (though some super-organised schools and students start preparations in the summer of Year 12).

The information you need for applying to university or college is online at **www.ucas.com** where an up-to-date list of courses is always available.

Here are some key dates:

- University open days are organised from spring each year.
- UCAS has three main application deadlines. The first is 15 October for all applications to Oxford and Cambridge universities and applications for medicine, dentistry and veterinary medicine/science course at all universities. The deadline for all other courses except some art and design courses is 15 January. The third deadline is 24 March, which applies to all art and design courses not using the 15 January deadline.
- Universities and colleges do not guarantee to consider applications they receive after 15 January, and some popular courses may not have vacancies after that date. Please check with individual universities and colleges if you are not sure. You are advised to apply as early as possible.
- Not all courses start in September or October – some start between January and May. Check the start dates for the courses you are interested in on the 'Course information' screen in the UCAS search tool. For courses that start between January and May, you may need to apply before the three application deadlines above, as the universities and colleges will need time to consider your application. Contact the university or college direct for advice about when they need your application. Although some will be happy to receive applications right up to the start of the course, be prepared to send your application early.
- Applications for 2014 entry that include any courses at Oxford or Cambridge or medicine, dentistry, or veterinary science/medicine courses, D100, D101 and D102 at any university must be at UCAS by 15 October 2013.
- When your application is processed UCAS sends you a welcome letter stating your choices and your Personal ID. If there seems to be a mistake, call UCAS immediately, quoting your Personal ID.

Applicants receive decisions via UCAS (unconditional offer, conditional offer or unsuccessful application). If the university or college want you to attend an interview or audition, or submit a portfolio or other additional material, they will contact you directly or send you an invitation via UCAS Track (the online system that allows you to follow the progress of your application on www.ucas.com). You should reply to offers by the deadline given when you receive all your university decisions from UCAS.

Remember:

Scottish Qualifications Authority (SQA) results will be published in early August 2013

- AS and A level results will be published on 14 August 2014.
- UCAS Track automatically notifies all eligible applicants about Clearing – all those who have: missed their grades and have been turned down; not received offers earlier in the year; declined all offers made to them; applied after the final closing date (see above); or not found a place using Extra.

- A list of vacancies for degrees, HNDs and other undergraduate courses is published on the UCAS search tool at **http://search.ucas.com** as soon as results have been processed by UCAS. This online vacancy service is updated several times a day. Vacancy listings are also published in the national media.
- The last date to submit UCAS applications for courses starting in 2014 is 20 September.

Track

The Track facility on the UCAS website enables those who have applied not only to check the progress of their application, but also to reply to offers online, to cancel choices from which they no longer wish to hear and even to change their email and postal address. It is an invaluable tool for managing an application, but particularly useful to those who apply during a gap-year and are overseas when important decisions are being made.

Deferred entry, rescheduled entry, or post A level application?

There are three ways to handle university entrance if you want to take a gap-year. The safest is usually to apply for deferred entry, but not all courses accept deferred entry candidates. Our advice is to talk to the admissions office before making a decision about taking a gap-year.

1. Deferred entry

- Check first with the appropriate department of the university you want to go to that they are happy to take students after a gap-year. If it's a popular course, preference may go to the current year applications.
- On your UCAS application there is a 'Start date' field in the 'Choices' section. For each choice click on the 'see list' button to the right of the 'Start date' field and choose a deferred entry start date or current entry start date. Talk to your teachers first and follow instructions in the Apply online help text.
- If you are planning to take a gap-year, you will need to explain why in your personal statement on the UCAS application. You need to convince the university that a year off will make you a better applicant, so give an outline of what you plan to do and why.
- Send your completed application to UCAS, like any other student applying for entry without taking a gap-year. Those who do so well before the appropriate deadline, however, may be among the first to start receiving decisions (via UCAS). You will get a call for selection interview(s) (directly from the university or college or through UCAS), an unsuccessful decision, an offer which is conditional on getting specific exam grades or Tariff points score, or an unconditional offer.
- Up until 30 June, UCAS will continue to forward applications to universities 'for consideration at their discretion'. Applications received after 30 June go straight into Clearing.

Note: Some academics are not happy with deferred entry because it means it might be nearly two years before you start your higher education. During that time a course may have changed, or you may have changed. So your application may be looked on unfavourably without your knowing why. Most departments at many universities are in favour of a gap-year but they are not all in favour of deferred entry. If they interview you in November 2013 for a place in October 2015 it will be 23 months before they see you again. Check it out with the university department first.

2. Deferring entry after you have applied

If you apply for a place in the coming university year and, after A level results, decide to defer, you can negotiate direct with the university or college at which you are holding a place. If they agree to defer your place they will inform UCAS, who will confirm this to you by updating your application in Track.

Note: Some admissions tutors say that to give up a place on a popular course is risky, because the university will not be happy after you have messed them about. Others say that if a course has over-recruited, your deferral will be welcome. Tread carefully.

3. Post A level applications

If you take A levels in June 2014, you can still apply through UCAS after the results come out in August. You will go straight into Clearing. If you do not send in a UCAS application before the end of the 2014 entry cycle (20 September 2014), you should apply – between early September 2013 and the appropriate deadlines for your universities or courses – for entry in the following year. Universities and colleges will not accept those who do not apply through UCAS.

Faculty check: all subjects

If you want to take a gap-year, remember (before you apply) to contact the appropriate department or faculty at the university you would like to go to, and find out if they approve of a gap-year or not. Prepare a good case for it before you phone. It is advisable to do this even if you are an absolutely outstanding candidate, because on some courses a year off is considered a definite disadvantage. This is usually the case where a degree course is very long or requires a large amount of remembered technical knowledge at the start.

Art and design

Applying through UCAS to your chosen college of art and design might involve applying to courses using either of two deadline dates, 15 January or 24 March. Check the date for each of the courses you are interested in on the UCAS search tool.

Medicine, dentistry and veterinary science/medicine

If you hope to pursue a career in medicine, dentistry or veterinary science/medicine, you can use no more than four (of your possible five) choices in any one of those three subject areas.

Don't forget that UCAS must receive ALL applications for these courses by 15 October.

Foundation degrees

Foundation degrees are the equivalent of the first two years of an honours degree, may be studied full or part-time, and consist of academic study integrated with relevant work-based learning undertaken with an employer. They may be studied as a stand-alone qualification or, upon completion, you may progress to the final year of an honours degree.

Financing your studies

How you obtain finance for your study depends on where you live (your family home), because there are significant differences between the systems in England, Scotland, Wales and Northern Ireland. The government-funded student finance systems are Student Finance England, the Student Awards Agency for Scotland (SAAS), Student Finance Wales and Student Finance Northern Ireland.

Course fees information is available on the UCAS search tool – any questions about fees should be directed to the universities and colleges themselves.

The most up-to-date information on financial support for students is available from the following organisations' websites:

Student Finance England – **www.direct.gov.uk/studentfinance**
Student Finance Wales – **www.studentfinancewales.co.uk**
Student Finance Northern Ireland – **www.studentfinanceni.co.uk**
Student Awards Agency for Scotland – **ww.saas.gov.uk**

Scholarships and sponsorship

The National Scholarship Programme (NSP) started in September 2012. It gives financial help to students studying in higher education in England. The scheme is designed to help students whose family income is £25,000 or less. NSP awards are in addition to any other loans or grants students might apply for. More information is available on the HEFCE website at: **www.hefce.ac.uk/whatwedo/wp/currentworktowidenparticipation/nsp.**

Every university is an Independent institution with its own rules and most have their own special bursaries and scholarships for academic excellence, which they award on their own criteria.

In addition, there are still many organisations that offer sponsorship to students to study for a degree. This is sometimes on condition that they join the sponsoring company or institution for a period when they graduate. The Army is one example from the public sector, information is available on: **www.armyjobs.mod.uk/education/grants/Pages/default.aspx**

If you're looking for sponsorship, The Year in Industry improves your chances and removes the need to write endless letters. Go to: **www.yini.org.uk**

Business colleges

Office work is based on information technology, so being trained in this field is a great start to earning quick cash. Office temping is a very common job that pays reasonably well and there is usually plenty of it around.

Office skills are pretty basic to many careers and, in an increasingly global market, could lead to chances to work abroad – so you can even combine travel or living in another culture with work.

Skills for work

What are the skills that you need in order to get that vital job? Don't forget that you only have a limited time, so you don't want to be training for too long as that will cut down on your earning time and therefore enjoyment time. This is why many people choose to go into trades such as bartending or retail, where the company tends to provide the training, though this might not prove to be nearly as lucrative as office work.

If you've done a computer-based course during sixth form, then that could well prove to be enough. If you can type at around 40-45 words per minute, or you're comfortable designing websites, then you stand a good chance of landing a fairly well-paid job.

Qualifications – who needs them?

Qualifications are needed when you can't otherwise prove that you're capable of whatever the job involves. For example, if you're not French and have never lived in France, then you'll have to have a qualification showing that you can *speak* French, if that's what the job involves. In office work the agency that you use will put you through some tests first, before putting your name forward to the employer.

More important than any paper qualification, is that your typing speed and accuracy are strong enough to take you through the tests agencies will ask you to undertake. Practice is vital in building up your speeds but you shouldn't despair if you don't reach that magic 45 words per minute, there are other options available to help you build up your speeds while you are working.

Many offices, especially the smaller ones, will offer a trial, for around three days, just to make sure that you have what it takes.

No excuses

Training for information technology has dramatically changed recently. Skills that used to take a full year can now take as little as one month. The prices have dropped too.

Evening courses at a local FE college can be under £100 and public libraries also run courses on the internet. IT is already very firmly in schools' curricula so most of you should already have the skills to cope within the office. If not, then get going and get trained.

Which college?

There are lots of different things to look at when choosing a college. Convenience (location, hours) is very important, along with price. However, you don't want to compromise the quality of the qualification you will receive because of practical concerns.

A good idea might be to check with an agency about the value of a qualification from particular colleges. Or check with the actual college on the employment record of their past students.

Finding the right course

Of course you want to start earning as soon as possible, so is it worth spending a longer time studying for a qualification that you don't really need?

How do you know which course is best for you? Can you compare different word processing courses against each other; surely word processing is just word processing? Also, you don't want to pay to learn something that you already know how to do. To help with this little dilemma the City & Guilds, which awards over a million certificates a year, defines the levels of its qualifications (which continue up to Level 7).

Level 1: Introductory awards for those new to the area covering routine tasks or basic knowledge and understanding.

Level 2: Qualifications for those with some knowledge of, and ability in, the areas that acknowledge individual responsibility.

Level 3: Qualifications that recognise complex work involving supervisory ability.

If you think that you already know Level 2, for example, then it's worth your while going straight on to Level 3.

How much should you pay?

The most important thing here is to get value for money. Of course the better the course the more expensive it's likely to be, but what things can you check for to make sure that you're not being conned? Be aware of the VAT and any other hidden costs that there might be. To test the value of the course compare the total hours of tuition to the price, check out each course and just be sure that what you are going to do will be of benefit, before parting with any money.

In the directory pages (starting on p387) you'll find a list of colleges, from all over the country, that run intensive business skills courses. It is only an indicator of what's available, not a guarantee of quality.

We're happy to hear from (and report about) any training centres that offer short courses in office skills.

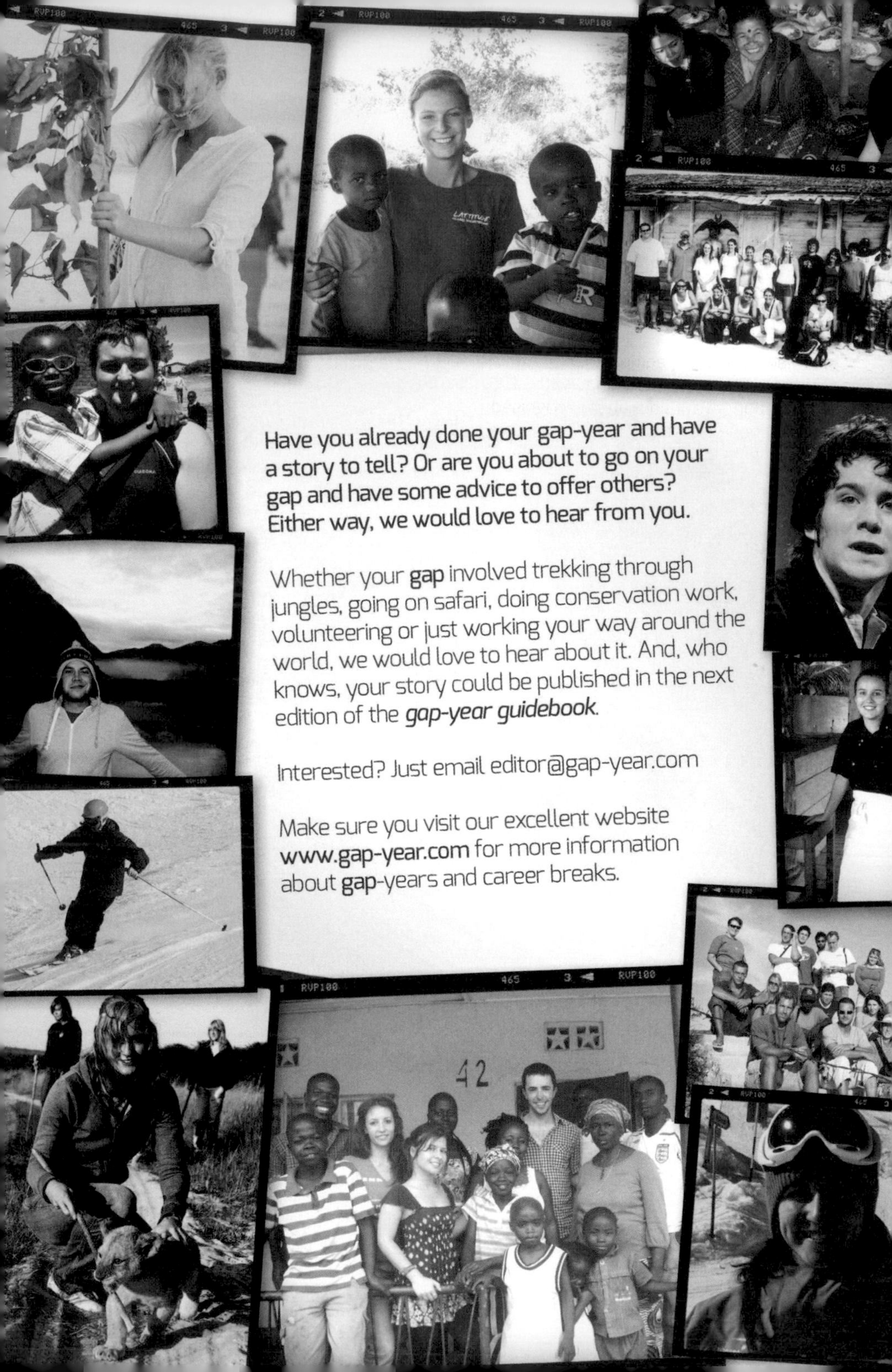

Have you already done your gap-year and have a story to tell? Or are you about to go on your gap and have some advice to offer others? Either way, we would love to hear from you.

Whether your **gap** involved trekking through jungles, going on safari, doing conservation work, volunteering or just working your way around the world, we would love to hear about it. And, who knows, your story could be published in the next edition of the ***gap-year guidebook***.

Interested? Just email editor@gap-year.com

Make sure you visit our excellent website **www.gap-year.com** for more information about **gap**-years and career breaks.

Being Safe

Adventure Expeditions
UK
info@adventure-expeditions.net
+44 (0) 1305 813107
www.adventure-expeditions.net
Outdoor First Aid training with ITC Certification - a nationally recognised qualification that fulfils training requirements for insurance purposes and those stipulated by training bodies.

Adventure First Aid
UK
info@adventurefirstaid.co.uk
+44 (0) 844 357 1426
www.adventurefirstaid.co.uk
Travel first aid and crisis management courses, delivered by experienced professional trainers.

British Red Cross
UK
information@redcross.org.uk
+44 (0) 844 871 1111
www.redcross.org.uk
The Red Cross (Charity No. 220949) offers first aid courses around the UK lasting from one to four days depending on your experience and the level you want to achieve.

Free European Health Insurance Card
UK
0191 218 1999
www.nhs.uk
The European Health Insurance Card (EHIC) enables access to state-provided healthcare in all European Economic Area countries at a reduced cost or sometimes free of charge.

Healthy Travel
UK
enquiries@healthy-travel.co.uk
www.travelwithcare.com
Healthy Travel stock a range of health products and travel products suitable for all types of outdoor activities, from a walk in the country to trekking in the jungle.

InterHealth Worldwide
UK
info@interhealth.org.uk
+44 (0)20 7902 9000
www.interhealth.org.uk
InterHealth provide clinics and travel health advice, eg on immunisations.

Intrepid Expeditions
UK
nigel@intrepid-expeditions.co.uk
+44 (0) 800 043 2509
www.intrepid-expeditions.co.uk
Runs many different survival courses, including a first aid course, ranging from two to 14 days.

Lifesavers (The Royal Life Saving Society)
UK
info@rlss.org.uk
+44 (0) 1789 773 994
www.lifesavers.org.uk
Contact them for information about qualifications in life saving, lifeguarding and lifesupport.

MASTA
UK
enquiries@masta.org
020 7291 9333
MASTA healthcare provide travel clinics across the UK offering professional advice to travellers about their specific travel health needs including anti-malarials, vaccinations and disease prevention.

Objective Travel Safety Ltd
UK
office@objectiveteam.com
+44 (0) 1788 899 029
www.objectivegapyear.com
A fun one-day safety course or personalised safety courses for travellers, designed to teach them how to think safe and prepare for challenges they may face.

Pacsafe
China
+852 2575 0921
www.pacsafe.com
Offers a range of travel security products.

RYA
UK
admin@rya.org.uk
023 8060 4100
The RYA is the national body for all forms of boating and offers courses specialising in the technique of sea survival at training centres across the UK.

Safe Gap Year
UK
Info@safegapyear.co.uk
0845 602 55 95
www.safegapyear.co.uk
Safe Gap Year is a training and consultancy company specialising in Independent Travel Safety and Cultural Awareness.

St John Ambulance
UK
+44 (0)8700 104950
www.sja.org.uk
The St John Ambulance Association runs first aid courses throughout the year around the country. Courses last a day and are suitable for all levels of experience.

Taurus Insurance Services
Gibraltar
office@taurus.gi
http://taurus.gi
Gap year and working holiday travel insurance.

TravelPharm
UK
info@travelpharm.com
+44 (0)115 951 2092
www.travelpharm.com
Provides travellers with a range of medication and equipment at very competitive prices to make your journey both healthier and safer!

Ultimate Gap Year
UK
info@ultimategapyear.co.uk
www.ultimategapyear.co.uk
Personalised safety training suitable for anyone embarking on a gap-year. Training held at homes throughout south-east England.

Communication

0044 Ltd
UK
+44 (0) 1926 332153
www.0044.co.uk
Their global SIM card could save you money on international calls.

Abroadband
Austria
+43 6888 4000 40
www.abroadband.com
Abroadband provide mobile internet access for travellers in over 50 countries by providing sim cards which can be used with unlocked smartphones, unlocked mobile broadband modems or laptops with integrated modems.

Aether Mobile Ltd
UK
customersupport@aether-mobile.com
www.aether-mobile.com
Get your SIM now and cut your mobile phone calls by up to 90% when abroad and get free incoming texts and calls in all countries.

Cyber Cafés
UK
info@cybercafe.com
www.cybercafes.com
Useful website enabling travellers to locate more than 4000 internet cafes in 141 countries.

ekit
UK
shout@ekit.com
0800 028 2402/0800 376 2370
www.ekit.com
ekit is a global provider of integrated communications, mobile, VOIP and Internet services, designed to keep travelers in touch.

EuroCallingCards.com
UK
contactus@eurocallingcards.com
+44 (0) 208 099 5899
www.eurocallingcards.com
Leading online supplier of international phone cards.

Go Sim
UK
0800 376 2370
www.gosim.com
Supplier of pre-paid international mobile SIM cards for travellers wishing to make phone calls abroad.

Internet Outpost
Australia
info@internet-outpost.com
+61 7 4051 3966
www.internet-outpost.com
Provide internet outpost retail stores throughout Australia, New Zealand and Indonesia. Some of the facilities you have access to are: CD Burning, Printing, Microsoft Word, Microsoft Excel, Faxing, Scanning, Photocopying and more.

My UK Mail
UK
contact@my-uk-mail.co.uk
0845 838 1815
www.my-uk-mail.co.uk
UK based company providing a mail holding and forwarding service to international destinations including permaneant and temporary addresses.

NobelCom
Bermuda
help@NobelCom.co.uk
0800 652 1979
www.nobelcom.co.uk
Supplier of pre-paid phone cards for international long distance calling that can be tailored to travellers needs.

O²
UK
0800 230 0202
www.o2.co.uk
Provider of international broadband dongles enabling travellers to connect to the internet by simply plugging their broadband dongle into their laptop.

Orange
UK
0800 079 0409
www.orange.co.uk
Provider of international broadband dongles enabling travellers to connect to the internet by simply plugging their broadband dongle into their laptop.

PocketComms Ltd
UK
sales@pocketcomms.co.uk
+44 (0)1635 799484
www.pocketcomms.co.uk
A manual pocket sized universal language system in pictorial form to help travellers communicate through language barriers.

Talkmobile
UK
0870 071 5888
www.talkmobile.co.uk
Talkmobile provides monthly or pay as you go international mobile SIM cards for travellers wishing to make phone calls abroad.

Virgin Broadband
UK
0845 650 4500
www.virginmedia.com
Provider of international broadband dongles enabling travellers to connect to the internet by simply plugging their broadband dongle into their laptop.

Planning the route

Gap Advice
UK
info@gapadvice.org
07973 548316
www.gapadvice.org
Independent gap year travel advice, information, help and ideas on projects and placements.

Gap Year Directory
UK
www.gapyeardirectory.co.uk
Gap Year Directory is dedicated to helping you plan your time out... whatever you choose to do.

iGapyear
UK
info@igapyear.com
+44 (0)845 643 9338
www.igapyear.com
iGapyear.com helps you do your prep work and make sure you arrange your perfect gap year. Choose from jobs, courses, placements and trips.

What to take

Ardern Healthcare Ltd
UK
info@ardernhealthcare.com
01584 781777
www.ardernhealthcare.com
Ardern Healthcare Ltd specialise in offering travellers a suitable insect repellent, in the form of sprays, wipes and creams, whatever their age or destination.

Blacks
UK
customercare@blacks.co.uk
0844 257 2078
www.blacks.co.uk
Blacks has 90 UK stores and provides a wide range of outdoor equipment and clothing from leading brands including The North Face, Berghaus and Craghoppers.

Brunton Outdoor
USA
support@bruntongroup.com
+44 (0) 2392528711
www.bruntonoutdoor.com
Compact personal power device, from the brunton freedom range, which recharges devices like MP3 players, smart phones, digital cameras and more via car or sun ray.

Cotswold Outdoor Ltd

UK
customer.services@cotswoldoutdoor.com
+44 (0) 844 557 7755
www.cotswoldoutdoor.com
Cotswold Outdoor Limited have stores across the UK and provide camping equipment, clothes, maps, climbing gear and footwear from brands such as Osprey, Scarpa and Solomon.

Craigdon Mountain Sports

UK
sales@craigdon.com
+44 (0)1467 629394
www.craigdonmountainsports.com
Craigdon Mountain Sports is Scotland's premier independent outdoor retailer and has 4 retail stores which stock a wide range of clothing and equipment.

Field and Trek

UK
www.fieldandtrek.com
Field & Trek has stores all over the UK and supplies outdoor equipment and performance clothing ranges from brands such as Berghaus, The North Face, Mountain Equipment, Merrell, and Lowe Alpine.

Gap Year Travel Store

UK
info@gapyeartravelstore.com
0845 652 5508
www.gapyeartravelstore.com
Online store selling quality travel kit and equipment to backpackers and independent travellers.

Go Outdoors

UK
enquiries@gooutdoors.co.uk
+44 (0)844 387 6800
www.gooutdoors.co.uk
Go Outdoors operates from 41 retail stores across the UK and offers a wide choice of outdoor accessories and equipment from brands such as Hi Gear, Ragatta, North Ridge and Outwell.

Lifesaver Systems

UK
info@lifesaversystems.com
0808 1782799/+44 (0) 1206 580999
www.lifesaversystems.com
All-in-one filtration system, in a bottle, which will turn the foulest water into safe drinking water without the use of chemicals, allowing for much lighter packing.

Millets

UK
customercare@millets.co.uk
0844 257 2079
www.millets.co.uk
Millets, with over 150 stores, is one of the UK's largest travel and outdoor retailer. Brands include Berghaus, Eurohike, Merrell, North Face and Peter Storm.

Nikwax Ltd

UK
info@nikwax.com
+44 (0)1892 786400
www.nikwax.com
To clean and waterproof all your gear, extend its life and maintain high performance with low environmental impact - Nikwax it!

Nomad Travel & Outdoor

UK
orders@nomadtravel.co.uk
+44 (0) 845 260 0044
www.nomadtravel.co.uk
As well as the usual stock of clothing, equipment, books and maps their 8 travel stores also hold medical supplies.

off

UK
info@outdoor-spirit.co.uk
+44.1387 252891
www.outdoor-spirit.co.uk
Online shop offering a rangre of out door clothing, including Dr Martens shoes and boots.

Outdoor Megastore
UK
admin@outdoormegastore.co.uk
0151 944 2202
www.outdoormegastore.co.uk
Online store for all your outdoor equipment.

Simply Hike
UK
info@simplyhike.co.uk
0844 567 7070
www.simplyhike.co.uk
Simply Hike - dor camping gear, outdoor clothing and accessories.

Snow and Rock
UK
manager.direct@snowandrock.com
01483 445335
www.snowandrock.com
Snow & Ice have stores across the UK offering a wide choice of outdoor clothing and equipment including Arc'teryx, Merrell, The North Face and Salomon.

Steri Pen
USA
support@steripen.com
+1 207 374 5800
www.steripen.com
Steripen is a portable, fast and easy way to ensure water is safe to drink through harnessing the power of ultraviolet light.

The Instant Mosquito Net Company Ltd
UK
steven.spedding@mosinet.co.uk
www.mosinet.co.uk
Fully portable, self supporting mosquito net. Lightweight, easy to use and folds into its own carry bag.

Travelbagsize.com
UK
info@travelbagsize.com
www.travelbagsize.com
Travel size toiletries, cosmetics, fragrance and accessories.

Vango
UK
info@vango.co.uk
01475 744122
www.vango.co.uk
Evergrowing range of tents, sleeping bags, rucsacks and outdoor accessories.

Yeomans Outdoors
UK
+44 (0)1246 571270
www.yeomansoutdoors.co.uk
With over 90 stores across the UK, Yeomans Outdoors stocks a wide range of tents, camping equipment and outdoor clothing from brands such as Vango, Trekmates, Easycamp and Karrimor.

Finance

Credit Cards

Advanced Payment Solutions Ltd
UK
0871 277 5599
www.mycashplus.co.uk
Produce the Cashplus Card, a pre-paid card which ensures you do not go overdrawn, incure interest or fall prey to credit card fraud.

CashCase (Visa Prepaid Card)
UK
info@cashcase.co.uk
0800 756 7723
www.cashcase.co.uk
CashCase is a reloadable prepaid card that enables you to access your money wherever you are. Convenient, secure and always ready for your next trip, it's the one card that should be in every traveller's wallet.

EZ Pay Ltd
UK
customersupport@escape-prepaid-card.com
0844 871 5444
www.ezpayltd.co.uk
With the 'Escape Travel Money Prepaid MasterCard' you can withdraw cash from over 1.5 million ATMs worldwide, usually without having to pay a fee.

my Travel Cash
UK
0845 867 6496
www.mytravelcash.com
my Travel money offer the pre-paid multi currency card which allows travellers to withdraw cash in any currency without ATM fees.

Virgin Money
UK
info@virginmoney.com
0845 089 6278
http://uk.virginmoney.com
Offers a 'Pre-paid Travel Money Card' enabling travellers to budget more easiliy and spend abroad with greater security.

Insurance

ACE European Group Ltd
UK
ace.traveluk@acegroup.com
0800 028 2396
www.aceinsure.com/backpacker
Offers gap year/backpacker/student traveller insurance to anyone aged 14-44 and traveller plus insurance for those aged 45-55 years.

American Express
UK
0800 028 7573
www.americanexpress.com
Provide cover 18-49 year olds wishing to take a gap year, sabbatical, or career break up to 24 months.

Best Backpackers Insurance
UK
+44 (0) 8450 264 264
www.bestbackpackersinsurance.co.uk
Best Backpackers Insurance is designed for anyone aged 18-39 and is ideal for gap year travellers, backpackers and anyone taking an extended holiday abroad.

Blue Insurances Ltd
UK
info@multitrip.com
0844 871 6181
www.multitrip.com/backpacker-travel-insurance.asp
Multitrip.com is a domain name of Blue Insurances, offering competitive prices to anyone less than 45 years of age on back-packer insurance for trips up to 12 months in length .

Boots UK Limited
UK
+44 (0) 845 125 3810
www.bootstravelinsurance.com
The Boots UK Limited website has an area dedicated to gap-year insurance and offers policies to 18-34 year olds for 3-12 months.

BUPA Travel Services
UK
0800 030 4687
www.bupa.co.uk/travel
BUPA Explorer Travel Insurance offers three levels of cover to travellers aged 18-45 for up to an 18 month insurance period.

Columbus Direct
UK
admin@columbusdirect.com
0845 888 8893
www.columbusdirect.com
Columbus Direct offer backpacker insurance for anywhere in the world for 2-12 months. Also offer sports and activities cover.

Direct Travel Insurance
UK
info@direct-travel.co.uk
+44 (0) 845 605 2700
www.direct-travel.co.uk
Direct Travel Insurance provide basic or comprehensive insurance cover to 18-36 years olds for 3-12 months.

Dogtag Ltd
UK
enquiries@dogtag.co.uk
+44 (0) 8700 364824
www.dogtag.co.uk
Dogtag Ltd offer insurance cover for 'action minded' travellers aged 18-55 for up to 18 months.

DU Insure
UK
travel@duinsure.com
+44 (0) 800 393 908
www.duinsure.com
Save up to 60% on High Street prices plus a further 10% discount if you book online. Comprehensive travel insurance for the adventurous traveller. Working holidays covered plus over 80 adventurous sports or activities. Medical emergency and money back guarantee.
For further information see page 76

Endsleigh Insurance Services Ltd
UK
+44 (0) 800 028 3571
www.endsleigh.co.uk
Endsleigh has tailored gap-year cover to suit travellers for up to 12 months, with over 100 sports and activities covered as standard.

Essential Travel Ltd
UK
customerservices@essentialtravel.co.uk
0845 803 5434
www.essentialtravel.co.uk
Special backpacker travel insurance for anyone aged betwen 19-45 years old.

Insure and Go
UK
+44 (0) 844 888 2787
www.insureandgo.com
Insure and Go provide backpacker travel insurance for up to 18 months. Free cover for many sports and activities.

Mind The Gap Year

UK

+44 (0) 845 180 0059

www.mindthegapyear.com

Mind The Gap Year offers a low cost economy package or the fully inclusive standard package back packer insurance cover.

Navigator Travel Insurance Services Ltd

UK

sales@navigatortravel.co.uk

+44 (0) 161 973 6435

www.navigatortravel.co.uk

Navigator Travel Insurance Services Ltd offer specialist policies for long-stay overseas trips with an emphasis on covering adventure sports. These policies also cover casual working.

Post Office Travel Insurance

UK

0800 294 2292

www.postoffice.co.uk/travel

Provides cover to 18-35 year olds wishing to take a career or study break.

Round the World Insurance

UK

info@roundtheworldinsurance.co.uk

+44 (0)1273 320 580

www.roundtheworldinsurance.co.uk

Round the World Insurance provide specialist travel insurance designed for people on round-the-world or multi-stop trips.

Sainsbury's Travel Insurance

UK

0800 316 1453

www.sainsburysbank.co.uk/insuring/ins_extendedtrip_trv_skip.shtml

Sainsbury's Extended Trip Travel Insurance have a policy tailored to those between 16 and 45, providing cover for up to 12 months.

Snowcard Insurance Services Limited

UK

enquiries@snowcard.co.uk

0844 826 2699

www.snowcard.co.uk

An all-round activities insurance covering winter, general mountain and water sports as well as the standard travel risks. The unique 'Snowcard' gives 24 hour access to Assistance International.

Taurus Insurance Services

Gibraltar

office@taurus.gi

http://taurus.gi

Worldwide travel insurance.

Travel Insurance Direct

UK

info@travel-insurance.net

0800 652 9944

www.travel-insurance.net

The Discovery policy is designed for anyone travelling on a budget, backpacking or travelling light. Whilst being a low cost option it still maintains excellent levels of medical insurance, including vital medical emergency repatriation cover.

Travelinsurance.co.uk

UK

Information@travelinsurance.co.uk

0844 888 2757

www.travelinsurance.co.uk

Provides cover for up to 18 months travelling. Cover can be arranged for medical expenses, personal accident to repayment of student loan.

True Traveller Insurance

UK

sales@truetraveller.com

0800 840 8098

www.adventuretravelinsurance.co.uk

True Traveller Insurance offers Single Trip cover for durations from 1 day to 1 year, Backpacker Travel Insurance for travellers going from 1 month to 1 year, and Annual Multi-Trip Insurance.

World Nomads Ltd

UK

+44 (0) 1543 432 872

www.worldnomads.com

World Nomads Ltd offer an insurance package specifically targeted at independent travellers under the age of 60 for up to 18 months.

Worldtrekker Travel Insurance

UK

info@preferential.co.uk

0843 208 1928

www.preferential.co.uk/worldtrekker

World Trekker Travel Insurance offers four levels of cover from Standard to Ultra to UK resident travellers up to the age of 45 years.

Career breaks and older gappers

Career Breaks

Africa in Focus
UK
info@africa-in-focus.com
01803 770 956
www.africa-in-focus.com
A travel agency which offers overland travel tours throughout East and Southern Africa with more comfort and innovative facilities.

African Conservation Experience
UK
info@conservationafrica.net
+44 (0) 1454 269182
www.conservationafrica.net
African Conservation Experience offer volunteering opportunities at wildlife conservation projects in southern Africa. You can count on our full support and more than 10 years experience. See our main advert in Conservation.

Experience Travel
UK
info@experiencetravelgroup.com
020 3468 3029
www.experiencetravelgroup.com
Travel agent specialists which can arrange tailor made travel to Vietnam, Thailand, Cambodia, Sri Lanka, The Maldives and Laos.

Globalteer
UK
0117 2309998
www.globalteer.org
Globalteer is a registered UK charity offering career breakers affordable, sustainable volunteer placements within community and conservation projects overseas.

Inspire
UK
info@inspirevolunteer.co.uk
0800 032 3350
www.inspirevolunteer.co.uk
Inspire offers meaningful volunteer opportunities in Africa, Asia, South America & Europe. Share skills and change lives on teaching, childcare, conservation & business programmes overseas.

Inspired Breaks
UK
info@inspiredbreaks.co.uk
01892 701881
www.inspiredbreaks.co.uk
Company specialising in career breaks and volunteer work for the over 30s, hundreds of programmes in over 20 countries from two weeks to 12 months.

JET - Japan Exchange and Teaching Programme UK
UK
ukjet@ld.mofa.go.jp
+44 (0)20 7465 6668
www.jet-uk.org
The JET Programme, the official Japanese government scheme, sends UK graduates to promote international understanding and to improve foreign language teaching in schools for a minimum of 12 months.

Nonstop Adventure
UK
info@nonstopadventure.com
+44 (0)1225 632 165
www.nonstopadventure.com
Nonstop Adventure provide action sport instructor courses and improvement camps around the world. Their courses are ideal for a gap year, career break or career change.

PoD

UK
info@podvolunteer.org
01242 250 901
www.podvolunteer.org

PoD (Personal Overseas Development) is a leading non-profit organisation arranging ethical and inspiring volunteering opportunities around the world.

Projects Abroad Pro

UK
info@projects-abroad-pro.org
01903 708300
www.projects-abroad-pro.org

Projects Abroad Pro is an arm of Projects Abroad, designed to encourage professionals on a career break and retired seniors to take part in voluntary work in a developing country.

Raleigh International

UK
info@raleighinternational.org
+44 (0) 20 7183 1286
www.raleighinternational.org

Develop new skills, meet people from all backgrounds and make a difference on sustainable community and environmental projects around the world.

For further information see page 86

Sunvil Traveller

UK
020 8758 4774
www.sunvil.co.uk/traveller

A travel agency which can arrange long stay travel across Latin America.

The AfriCat Foundation

Namibia
africat@mweb.com.na
+264 (0)67 304566
www.africat.org

P.A.W.S offer career breakers volunteer project work, in association with the world renowned AfriCat Foundation, aimed at restoring the Okonjima's reserve back into a game reserve.

The Book Bus

UK
info@thebookbus.org
+44 (0) 1822 616 191
www.thebookbus.org

The Book Bus provides a mobile service and actively promotes literacy to underpriviledged communities in Zambia and Ecuador.

For further information see page 90

Undiscovered Destinations Ltd

UK
info@undiscovered-destinations.com
0191 296 2674
www.undiscovered-destinations.com

An adventure travel agency dedicated to providing truly authentic experiences, through small group tours or tailormade trips, to some of the worldís most exciting regions.

VentureCo Worldwide

UK
+44 (0) 1822 616 191
www.ventureco-worldwide.com

VentureCo provides the ideal combination for career break travellers who want to explore off the beaten track, learn about the host country and give something back to the communities they stay with.

Visitoz

UK
will@vistoz.org
07966 528 644
www.visitoz.org

Visitoz provides training and guarantees work for young people between the ages of 18 and 30 in agriculture, hospitality, child care and teaching all over Australia.

For further information see page 92

Accommodation

An Óige - Irish Youth Hostel Association
Ireland
info@anoige.ie
+353 01 830 4555
www.anoige.ie
The Irish YHA consists of more than 20 hostels throughout Ireland. They have a range of hostels, from large city centre buildings to small hostels in rural settings. Online booking available.

Gap Year Backpacker Hostel
Singapore
info@gapyearhostel.com
+65 6297 1055
http://gapyearhostel.com
A new design hostel inspired, managed and designed by backpackers.

Hostelbookers.com
UK
support@hostelbookers.com
+44 (0) 207 406 1800
www.hostelbookers.com
Youth hostels and cheap accommodation in over 3500 destinations worldwide, with no booking fees.

For further information see page 120

Hostelling International
UK
info@hihostels.com
+44 (0) 1707 324170
www.hihostels.com
Research, plan and book your trip online with Hostelling International. HI hostels are a great way to travel the world safely - explore new cultures and meet friends.

Hostelling International - Canada
Canada
info@hihostels.ca
+1 613 237 7884
www.hihostels.ca
Contact details for the Canadian branch of this worldwide hostel service.

Hostelling International - Iceland
Iceland
info@hostel.is
+354 575 6700
www.hostel.is
Hostelling International Iceland has 36 hostels all around the country, offering comfortable, budget accommodation which is open to all ages.

Hostelling International - USA
USA
+1 240 650 2100
www.hiusa.org
Hostelling International USA has a network of hostels throughout the United States that are inexpensive, safe and clean.

Hostelworld.com
USA
customerservice@hostelworld.com
+353 1 524 5800
www.hostelworld.com
Online booking site which operates a network of over 27,000 hostels in more than 180 countries. Provides confirmed reservations at a selection of youth hostels, independent hostels and international hostels.

Scottish Youth Hostel Association

UK
info@syha.org.uk
01786 891400
www.syha.org.uk

There are over 70 SYHA hostels throughout Scotland. You can book online but you must be a member - you can join at the time of booking. Registered Charity No. SC013138.

Swiss Youth Hostels

Switzerland
contact@youthhostel.ch
+41 (0) 44 360 1414
www.youthhostel.ch

They have 52 hostels, ranging from traditional Swiss chalets, to modern buildings, large historic houses and even one or two castles.

VIP Backpackers

Australia
info@vipbackpackers.com
+61 (0) 2 9211 0766
www.vipbackpackers.com

VIP Backpackers is the largest independent backpacker accommodation network in the world, with over 1,200 hostels across 80+ countries, and counting.

Youth Hostel Association New Zealand

New Zealand
+64 (0)3 379 9970
www.yha.co.nz

Budget accommodation in New Zealand. Hostels open to all ages. Book online before you go.

Youth Hostels Association of India

India
contact@yhaindia.org
+91 (011) 2611 0250
www.yhaindia.org

Youth Hostel Association in India, with hostels which can be booked online through their website.

Car Hire

Auto Europe

UK
customerservice@auto-europe.co.uk
0800 358 1229
www.auto-europe.co.uk

Auto Europe can provide travellers with a vast selection of vehicles for hire in over 8,000 locations around the world.

AVIS

UK
0844 581 0147
www.avis.co.uk

AVIS worldwide can provide travellers with car hire from 4,000 locations in 114 countries.

Budget International

UK
0844 444 0002
www.budgetinternational.com

Budget International can provide travellers with car hire from 3,400 locations in 128 countries.

Europcar UK Ltd

UK
reservationsuk@europcar.com
0371 384 1087
www.europcar.co.uk

Europcar and its alliance partner Enterprise can provide travellers with car hire from more than 13,000 locations in about 150 countries.

Hertz
USA
0843 309 3099
www.hertz.co.uk
Hertz Global Holdings is an American car rental company providing a wide range of options for car hire around the world.

International Motorhome Hire
UK
enquiry@rv-network.com
01780 482 565
www.international-motorhome-hire.com
International Motor Home are an agency that organises the hire of motor homes, on behalf of travellers, throughout the world.

Motorhome International
USA
info@motorhome-international.com
+1 847 531 1454
www.motorhome-international.com
Motorhome International provide RV Rentals and Motorhome Hire in the USA, Canada, Europe, New Zealand Australia & South Africa.

Spaceships
New Zealand
info@spaceshipsrentals.co.nz
+64 9 526 2130
www.spaceshipsrentals.co.nz
Company offering campervan rentals in New Zealand and Australia.

Travellers Auto Barn
Australia
info@travellers-autobarn.com.au
+61 2 9360 1500 (outside Australia) 1800 674 374 (within Australia)
www.travellers-autobarn.com.au
No cheaper way to travel around Australia than in any of our campervans or stationwagons - we have offices all around Australia and all our rentals come with unlimited KM, free insurance, special discounts.

Travel Companies

African Conservation Experience
UK
info@conservationafrica.net
+44 (0) 1454 269182
www.conservationafrica.net
African Conservation Experience offer volunteering opportunities at wildlife conservation projects in southern Africa. You can count on our full support and more than 10 years experience. See our main advert in Conservation

Gapwork.com
UK
info@gapwork.com
0113 266 0880
www.gapwork.com
Gapwork is an independent information provider specialising in gap years, gap year jobs, gap year vacancies, activities and voluntary work either in the UK or abroad.

Goa Way
UK
sales@goaway.co.uk
+44 (0) 20 7258 7800
www.goaway.co.uk
Goaway specialises in organising travel to Goa and Kerala. You can book flights, hostels or even package tours.

Greyhound Lines Inc

USA
ifsr@greyhound.com
www.greyhound.com
The most famous and largest bus company in America. Book online and join the millions of others who travel across America on the 'old grey dog'.

Journey Latin America

UK
flights@journeylatinamerica.co.uk
+44 (0) 20 8747 3108
www.journeylatinamerica.co.uk
Journey Latin America is the UK's major specialist in travel to Central and South America. Learn a new skill with their 'Learn to ... ' holidays.

Oasis Overland

UK
info@oasisoverland.co.uk
+44 (0) 1963 363400
www.oasisoverland.co.uk
Oasis Overland provide exciting and affordable adventure travel experiences, where you'll work as part of a team with like-minded travellers as you explore different cultures and regions.

For further information see page 112

Rainforest Expeditions

Peru
sales@rainforest.com.pe
+51 9935 12265
www.perunature.com
Rainforest Expedition is a Peruvian Ecotourism company. Since 1989 our guests and lodges, have added value to standing tropical rain forest turning it into a competitive alternative to unsustainable economic uses.

Smaller Earth UK

UK
uk@smallerearth.com
+(44) 0151 702 6808
www.smallerearth.co.uk
Smaller Earth is a gap year consultant working with you to create a customized program for your gap year.

STA Travel

UK
0333 321 0099
www.statravel.co.uk
This company has branches or agents worldwide and a Help Desk telephone service, which provides essential backup for travellers on the move.

Travel Talk

Turkmenistan
info@traveltalktours.com
+44 (0) 20 7183 0910
www.traveltalkeurope.com
Turkish travel agency specializing in the Mediterranean and fun, adventure tours.

Travelbag Ltd

UK
+44 (0) 871 703 4698
www.travelbag.co.uk
Book flights, hotel, holidays and even find insurance on their website.

TrekAmerica

UK
+44 (0) 208 682 8920
www.trekamerica.co.uk
With year round departures and over 50 unique itineraries from 3 to 64 days in length TrekAmerica tours are the ideal way to explore North America.

USIT
Ireland
info@usit.ie
+353 (0)1602 1906
www.usit.ie
Irish travel agents offering cheap flights from Dublin, Cork and Shannon specifically aimed at students.

Wildlife Worldwide
UK
sales@wildlifeworldwide.com
0845 130 6982
www.wildlifeworldwide.com
Wildlife Worldwide has been organising tailor-made wildlife tours since 1992. We provide tailor-made Indian & African safari holidays, whale watching holidays, wildlife cruising and Antarctic & Arctic voyages.

Getting about

Cheap Flights
UK
www.cheapflights.co.uk
This useful website does not sell tickets but can point you in the right direction to get the best deal.

EasyJet Plc
UK
www.easyjet.com
Offers cheap flights to European destinations with further reductions if you book over the internet.

ebookers.com
UK
www.ebookers.com
Cheap flights can be booked through their website.

Florence by Bike
Italy
info@florencebybike.it
+39 055 488992
www.florencebybike.it
Scooter, motorbike and bike rental company in Florence. Also sells clothing and accessories as well as bike parts.

International Rail
UK
sales@internationalrail.com
+44 (0)871 231 0790
www.internationalrail.com
InterRail Pass provides unlimited travel on the sophisticated European Rail network. The pass is very flexible allowing you to choose either one country or all 30 countries.

Kiwi Experience
New Zealand
+64 9 336 4286
www.kiwiexperience.com
Extensive bus network covering the whole of New Zealand. Passes valid for 12 months.

Rail Europe Ltd
UK
08448 484 064
www.raileurope.co.uk
Specializes in selling tickets and passes for travel throughout Europe by train. Available to buy online or via their call centre.

Ryanair
UK
www.ryanair.com
Low cost airline to European destinations.

Stray Ltd

New Zealand
enquiries@straytravel.co.nz
www.straytravel.com
Stray is New Zealand's fastest growing backpacker bus network - designed for travellers who want to get off the beaten track.

Thomas Cook

UK
www.thomascook.com
General travel agent with high street branches offering flights and late deals.

Travellers Contact Point

Australia
+61 2 9211 7900
www.travellers.com.au
A specialist travel agency for independent and working holiday travellers. We have shops in Australia, New Zealand and the UK.

Tours

Acacia Adventure Holidays

UK
info@acacia-africa.com
+44 (0) 20 7706 4700
www.acacia-africa.com
Acacia offers exciting and affordable overland tours and small group safaris across Africa. Enjoy game viewing, desert adventures, beach breaks, dive courses or trekking!

Adventure Tours Australia

Australia
admin@adventuretours.com.au
+61 (0)3 8102 7800
www.adventuretours.com.au
Adventure Tours Australia is an award winning company specialising in small group nature-based tours for the active traveller.

Adventure Tours NZ

New Zealand
reservations@adventuretoursnz.co.nz
+64 9 526 2149
www.adventuretours.com.au
Adventure Tours NZ offer specialised small group nature-based tours for the active traveller on a budget. Go off the beaten track, see unique scenery and wildlife.

Adventure Travellers Club P Ltd

Nepal
info@nepaltravellers.com
www.nepaltravellers.com
Offers trekking and adventure tours in Nepal, Tibet, Bhutan and Indian regions. Includes peak climbing, jungle safaris, river rafting and much more.

Afreco Tours Ltd

UK
info@afrecotours.com
+44 (0) 845 812 8222
www.afrecotours.com
Afreco Tours specialises in African safari ranger training and wildlife adventures - from seven days to one year.

Africa Travel Co

South Africa
cpt@africatravelco.com
+27 21 3851530
www.africatravelco.com
Specialists in trips around Africa ranging from three to 56 days.

African Horizons

Zambia
safariplans@gmail.com
+877 256 1074
www.africanhorizons.com
Provides quality African travel not only to the savvy globetrotters among us but also to those who have never experienced the thrill of an African safari or wildlife tour.

Alaska Heritage Tours
USA
info@AlaskaHeritageTours.com
+1 907 777 2805
www.alaskaheritagetours.com
At Alaska Heritage Tours we strive to give you the best of Alaska, the way you want it - with pre-packaged Alaska vacations and itineraries. Explore Alaska's top destinations.

Alpine Exploratory
UK
info@alpineexploratory.com
+44 (0) 1729 823197
www.alpineexploratory.com
Alpine Exploratory specialises in self-guided walking and trekking tours in Europe. Full programme of guided tours also offered, as well as bespoke holidays.

Andean Trails
UK
info@andeantrails.co.uk
+44 (0) 131 467 7086
www.andeantrails.co.uk
Andean Trails is an owner run specialist adventure travel company organising small group tours to Peru, Bolivia, Ecuador, Cuba, Guyana and Patagonia.

Argentina Travel Plan
UK
info@argentinatravelplan.co.uk
+44 (0)1273 322 380
www.argentinatravelplan.co.uk
Sail amongst icebergs in Patagonia, go on Andes outback drives to sunny Salta and relax in the rainforest at Iguazu Falls. We'll help you build your very own Argentina and Chile adventure with our organised tours for independent travellers.

Australia Travel Plan
UK
www.australiatravelplan.co.uk
Australia Travel Plan is a small specialist internet based tour operator, offering a unique way of travelling around Australia.

Backpacker Travel Auctions
Australia
info@safaripete.com
www.safaripete.com
Safari Pete can offer you directions to the best deals on tours around Australia and New Zealand.

Bicycling Empowerment Network
South Africa
andrew@benbikes.org.za
+27 21 788 4174
www.benbikes.org.za
BEN, a non-profit organisation, promotes the use and sale of refurbished bicycles. They conduct Bicycle Township Tours empowering local people and winning International Responsible Tourism Awards.

Black Feather - The Wilderness Adventure Company
Canada
info@blackfeather.com
+1 705 746 1372
www.blackfeather.com
Company offering canoeing and kayaking trips and expeditions to remote artic locations. Offer women only trips and will do a customized trip for groups of four or more.

Borneo Anchor Travel & Tours/ Sabah Divers
Malaysia
sabahdivers2u@yahoo.com
+60 88 256 483
www.borneoanchortours.com
They offer various wildlife, nature and adventure packages all over Sabah, Malaysian Borneo.

Brazil Travel Plan

UK
info@braziltravelplan.co.uk
+44 (0)1273 322 381
www.braziltravelplan.co.uk

From Copacabana to Bahia Turtle beach. Catch your breath at Devil's throat, discover caimans in the Amazon jungle, explore the Pantanal wetlands and hike on foot through Diamond Canyon. Build your own trip with our organised tours for independent travellers.

BridgeClimb Sydney

Australia
admin@bridgeclimb.com
+61 (0) 2 8274 7777
www.bridgeclimb.com

BridgeClimb provides the ultimate experience of Sydney, with guided climbs to the top of the world famous Sydney Harbour Bridge. Climbers can choose between The Express Climb, The Bridge Climb or The Discovery Climb.

Cambodia Travel Plan

UK
info@cambodiatravelplan.co.uk
+44 (0)1273 322 042
www.cambodiatravelplan.co.uk

Cambodian hill tribes and totem poles. Watch sunrise at Angkor Wat and relax in a Rabbit Island beach retreat. We'll help you build your very own Cambodia adventure with our organised tours for independent travellers.

Cape York Motorcycle Adventures

Australia
adventures@capeyorkmotorcycles.com.au
+61 (07) 4059 0220
www.capeyorkmotorcycles.com.au

Motorcycle tours in north Queensland from one to eight days duration. Private charter also available. They have their own motorbikes and a support vehicle that accompanies the longer excursions.

China Travel Plan

UK
info@chinatravelplan.co.uk
+44 (0)1273 322 048
www.chinatravelplan.co.uk

Bamboo sailing through karst mountains. Discover Tiger Leaping Gorge. Try an ice mountain horseback trek and stay at home with the Tibetans. We'll help you build your very own China adventure with our organised trips for independent travellers.

Cordillera Blanca Trek

Peru
info@cordillerablancatrek.com
+51 (0) 43 427 635
www.cordillerablancatrek.com

Offers treks in Machu Picchu, a volcanco tour and more.

Cuba Travel Plan

UK
info@cubatravelplan.co.uk
+44 (0)1273 322 059
www.cubatravelplan.co.uk

Explore the mountains of the Sierra Maestra and rolling tobacco fields. Try a Baracoa coast and jungle drive to Cuba's coral beaches. We'll help you build your very own Cuba adventure with our organised tours for independent travellers.

Do Something Different

UK
contact-us@dosomethingdifferent.com
+44 (0)208 090 3890
www.dosomethingdifferent.com

Want to dog sled in the Rockies? Take a Hong Kong Island or helicopter tour? Or climb Auckland Harbour Bridge?

Dolphin Encounter
New Zealand
info@dolphin.co.nz
+64 3 319 6777
www.dolphinencounter.co.nz
Swim or watch dolphins in Kaikoura. You do need to book in advance as there is a limit to how many swimmers are allowed per trip.

Dorset Expeditionary Society/ Leading Edge Expeditions
UK
dorsetexp@gmail.com
+44 (0) 1305 777277
www.dorsetexp.org.uk
Dorset Expeditionary Society promotes adventurous expeditions to remote parts of the world. Open to all. May qualify for two sections of the Duke of Edinburgh's Gold Award.

Dragoman
UK
info@dragoman.co.uk
+44 (0)1728 861133
www.dragoman.com
Overlanding is stil the most authentic and accessible way of discovering new countries, their people and culture. Join us in Africa, America and Asia.

For further information see page 111

Eco Trails Kerala
India
mail@ecotourskerala.com
+91 48125 24447
www.ecotourskerala.com
This tour company provides budget holiday tour packages in the Kumarakom and Alleppey Backwater areas.

Egypt Travel Plan
UK
info@egypttravelplan.co.uk
+44 (0)1273 322 058
www.egypttravelplan.co.uk
Wander through the Valley of the Kings, float down the Nile on a felucca and wake up in the White Desert. Build your own Egypt adventure with our organised tours for independent travellers.

Equitours - Worldwide Horseback Riding Adventures
USA
+1 307 455 3363
www.ridingtours.com
With over 30 years experience, Equitours offer tested and tried horseback tours on six continents. Rides from three to eight days (or longer) for riders of all experience.

Explore Worldwide Ltd
UK
res@explore.co.uk
0845 291 4541
www.explore.co.uk
Company organising special tours in small groups. Types of worldwide tours available are walking holidays, dog-sledding, wildlife and railway tours amongst others.

Fair Dinkum Bike Tours
Australia
dave@fairdinkumbiketours.com.au
+61 0()7 4053 6999
www.fairdinkumbiketours.com.au
Offer a range of tours using local guides to cater for all levels.

Flying Kiwi
New Zealand
info@flyingkiwi.com
+64 3 547 0171
www.flyingkiwi.com
Flying Kiwi bus tours around New Zealand offer a unique and fun experience. Camping or cabin options are available in exciting locations and usually meals are included.

Fräulein Maria's Bicycle Tours
Austria
biketour@aon.at
+43 650 3426297
www.mariasbicycletours.com
Maria's Bicycle tours take you to the main attractions from the film The Sound Of Music! The tour lasts three hours with stop points along the way and operates between May and September.

G Adventures
Canada
travel@gadventures.com
+1 416 260 0999
www.gadventures.com
G Adventures offers one of the widest selection of affordable small-group tours, safaris and expeditions across the world.

Go Differently Ltd
UK
info@godifferently.com
+44 (0) 1273 732236
www.godifferently.com
Company offering small-group, short-term volunteering and tailor-made holidays based on the appreciation and respect of the local environment and people.

Grayline Tours of Hong Kong
China
sales@grayline.com.hk
+852 2368 7111
www.grayline.com.hk
Special sightseeing day tours around Hong Kong and Macau.

Haka Tours
New Zealand
info@hakatours.com
+64 3 980 4252
www.hakatours.com
Haka Tours represents the ultimate in New Zealand adventure holidays, from small group adventures to New Zealand snow tours exploring the impressive Southern Alps and the active volcanoes of the North.

High & Wild
UK
adventures@highandwild.co.uk
+44 (0)845 0047801
www.highandwild.co.uk
High and Wild plan some of the most unusual and exciting adventures to destinations worldwide.

High Places Ltd
UK
holidays@highplaces.co.uk
+44 (0)845 257 75
www.highplaces.co.uk
Independent specialist trekking company organising tours to 22 countries.

Highland Experience Tours
UK
info@highlandexperience.com
+44 (0)131 226 1414
www.highlandexperience.com
Travel company offering one day and private tours around Scotland, such as a two day highland tour, a whisky tasting tour, or a tour of Scotland personalised to your own requirements.

In the Saddle Ltd

UK
rides@inthesaddle.com
+44 01299 272 997
www.inthesaddle.com

Specializes in horse riding holidays all over the world, catering for all levels of experience. From ranches in the Rocky Mountain states of Montana and Wyoming, to expeditions in remote and unexplored parts of the world.

India Travel Plan

UK
info@indiatravelplan.co.uk
+44 (0)1273 322 044
www.indiatravelplan.co.uk

Camels and castles in Rajasthan. Kerala backwaters and sandy beaches. Cycle through the spice hills and try a Himalayan homestay trek. Weíll help you build your very own India adventure with our organised trips for independent travellers.

Indonesia Travel Plan

UK
info@indonesiatravelplan.co.uk
+44 (0)1273 322 052
www.indonesiatravelplan.co.uk

Footsteps across the rumbling volcano. Sleep in beach bungalows in Bali paradise and cycle through the rice paddies. We'll help you build your very own Indonesia adventure with our organised tours for independent travellers.

Inside Japan Tours

UK
info@insidejapantours.com
+44 (0)117 370 9751
www.insidejapantours.com

Specialist company offering tours of Japan, including small group tours and individual, self-guiding tours. You can also book a Japan Rail Pass online here.

Intrepid Travel

UK
islington@intrepidtravel.com
0800 781 1660
www.intrepidtravel.com

For travellers with a yearning to get off the beaten track, Intrepid opens up a whole new world of adventure travel.

Jungle Surfing Canopy Tours

Australia
info@junglesurfing.com.au
+61 7 4098 0043
www.junglesurfing.com.au

Night walks in a tropical rainforest or jungle surf through the Daintree Rainforest.

Kande Horse Trails

Malawi
info@kandehorse.com
+265 (0) 8500416
www.kandehorse.com

Experience the Malawi bush on horseback. All ages and riding abilities catered for.

Kenya Travel Plan

UK
info@kenyatravelplan.co.uk
+44 (0)1273 322 053
www.kenyatravelplan.co.uk

Meet the Masai and climb Mt Kenya. Sleep in tented lodges in lion territory private camps beneath Serengeti stars. We'll help you build your very own Kenya & Tanzania adventure with our organised tours for independent travellers.

Killary Adventure Company

Ireland
adventure@killary.com
00 353 (0) 95 43411
www.killaryadventure.com
We specialise in adventure activities that range from bungee jumping to kayaking on Irelands only fjord and much more in between. Whether you are a soft adventurer or after the extreme adrenaline thrill we have something for you.

KT Adventure

Vietnam
info@vivutravel.com
+84 4 36740486
www.vivutravel.com
KT Adventure, part of Vivu Travel, offer specialised tours in Vietnam, from adventure tours to motorbiking.

Kudu Expeditions Ltd

UK
info@kuduexpeditions.com
+44(0)1929427744
www.kuduexpeditions.com
Explore the world by motorcycle. Amazing trips, from three week multi-country tours to four month trans-continental expeditions, designed to challenge and inspire you.

Laos Travel Plan

UK
info@laostravelplan.co.uk
+44 (0)1273 322 043
www.laostravelplan.co.uk
Explore waterfalls and rainforests of the Boloven plateau. Trek the Namtha mountain trail. See the dolphins of Lovina and islands of the Mekong. We'll help you build your very own Laos adventure with our organised tours for independent travellers.

Live Travel

UK
phil.haines@live-travel.com
+44 (0) 208 894 6104
www.live-travel.com
Personalised travel plans offered as well as group tours.

M. Trek and Tour

Morocco
info@moroccotrek.co.uk
00212 524330597
www.mtrekandtour.com
Trekking trips, tailormade tours, group holidays and specialised activity weeks in Morocco.

Malaysia Travel Plan

UK
info@malaysiatravelplan.co.uk
+44 (0)1273 322 054
www.malaysiatravelplan.co.uk
Rainforest monkey business in Borneo. Laze around on Langkawi and take a mangrove jungle trek. Island hopping along the tropical east coast. We'll help you build your very own Malaysia adventure with our organised trips for independent travellers.

Melbourne Street Art Tour

Australia
booking@melbournestreettours.com
+61 (03) 9328 5556
www.melbournestreettours.com
Melbourne Street Art Tours, led by one of Melbourne's elite street art stars, gives you an overview of the Melbourne underground street art scene.

Morocco Travel Plan
UK
info@moroccotravelplan.co.uk
+44 (0)1273 322 056
www.moroccotravelplan.co.uk
Follow the Berber trail through Atlas mountain villages, sleep in Sahara desert tents and traditional riads, explore imperial cities, munch couscous in the souqs, and take it easy on the beaches of Agadir. We'll help you build your own Morocco adventure with our organised tours for independent travellers.

Mountain Kingdoms Ltd
UK
info@mountainkingdoms.com
+44 (0)1453 844400
www.mountainkingdoms.com
Himalayan Kingdoms is the UK's foremost quality trekking company, running treks and tours to the great mountain ranges of the world.

Nepal Travel Plan
UK
info@nepaltravelplan.co.uk
+44 (0)1273 322 045
www.nepaltravelplan.co.uk
Footsteps across the rumbling volcano. Sleep in beach bungalows in Bali paradise and cycle through the rice paddies. We'll help you build your very own Indonesia adventure with our organised tours for independent travellers.

Olympic Bike Travel
Greece
info@olympicbike.com
+30 283 1072 383
www.olympicbike.com
A variety of bike tours available for all ages. From a ride down the highest mountain in Greece, to bike and hiking tours.

On The Go Tours
UK
info@onthegotours.com
+44 (0) 207 371 1113
www.onthegotours.com
Special tours such as solar eclipse tours and railways of the Raj can be arranged.

Oyster Trekking
UK
trek@oystertrekking.com
www.oystertrekking.com
Take the trek of a lifetime in the stunning Himalayas, with full Oyster support and a fair price. Adventurous treks include Everest Base Camp, The Langtang, Ghale Gaun and Annapurna Base Camp.

Oyster Worldwide Limited
UK
info@oysterworldwide.com
+44 (0) 1892 770 771
www.oysterworldwide.com
Take the trek of a lifetime in the stunning Himalayas, with full Oyster support and a fair price. Adventurous treks include Everest Base Camp, The Langtang, Ghale Gaun and Annapurna Base Camp.

Palmar Voyages
Ecuador
gerencia@palmarvoyages.com
+593 9 480 2268
www.palmarvoyages.com
Tailor-made programmes for tours in Ecuador, Peru, South America, the Andes and the Galapagos Islands.

Pathfinders Africa
Zimbabwe
info@pathfindersafrica.com
+263 4 870 573
www.pathfindersafrica.com
Pathfinders Africa is an African-based expedition company that operates from Zimbabwe. Developed to meet the needs of the adventurous traveller, Pathfinders' over-riding philosophy is of friendliness and individuality.

Peregrine Adventures Ltd

UK

travel@peregrineadventures.co.uk

+44 0844 736 0170

www.peregrineadventures.com

Peregrine offer small group adventure tours worldwide. They offer a vast range of tours from polar expeditions to trekking the Himalayas.

Peru Travel Plan

UK

info@perutravelplan.co.uk

+44 (0)1273 322 057

www.perutravelplan.co.uk

Trek through the snow-capped Andes, go island hopping on Lake Titicaca, try an Amazon jungle lodge adventure and follow the Inca trail to epic Machu Picchu. Build your own Peru adventure with our organised tours for independent travellers.

Pura Aventura

UK

info@pura-aventura.com

01273 961928 / +44 1273 961 921

www.pura-aventura.com

Various beautiful tailor-made tours in exotic locations. Career break to fulfil a long held dream or a special diversion on your gap-year perhaps?

Pure Australia Travel Guide

UK

info@pure-australia.co.uk

www.pure-australia.co.uk

Pure Australia - everything you need to know before travelling or working in Australia.

Rickshaw Travel

UK

info@rickshawtravel.co.uk

+44 (0) 1273 322 399

www.rickshawtravel.co.uk

Rickshaw Travel is a UK based ABTA/ ATOL bonded travel operator, that uses locally owned accommodation with an authentic feel that is a cut above the usual backpacker haunts.

Ride With Us

UK

sales@ridewithustours.co.uk

(+44) 0870 850 4136

www.ridewithustours.co.uk

Organised motorcycle holidays around western and eastern Europe that offer something for everyone regardless of their touring experience.

Saddle Skedaddle

UK

info@skedaddle.co.uk

+44 (0)191 265 1110

www.skedaddle.co.uk

Some say there is no better way to see a country, its culture, its wildlife and its people, than by bike! This company offers off-road, road or leisure cycling.

Safari Par Excellence

UK

+44 (0) 1548 830 059

www.zambezi.co.uk

Safari company with a 'no fuss or frills' ethos. They cover Zimbabwe, Zambia, Botswana, Namibia and other countries in Africa.

Scenic Air

Namibia

windhoek@scenic-air.com

www.scenic-air.com

Scenic Air caters for individual travellers, families as well as groups. They offer flights to all of the popular tourist destinations in Namibia.

Selective Asia

UK
contact@selectiveasia.com
+44 (0) 1273 670001
www.selectiveasia.com
Selective Asia offers a range of unique, privately guided tours and adventure holidays in Cambodia, Laos, Vietnam and Thailand.

Specialtours Ltd

UK
info@specialtours.co.uk
+44 (0) 20 7386 4690
www.specialtours.co.uk
International art and cultural tours. Access wonderful private houses, art collections and gardens. Most tours are accompanied by an expert lecturer.

Suntrek

UK
0800 781 1660
www.intrepidsuntrek.com
Adventure tours arranged in the USA, Mexico, Alaska, Canada, Central and South America and Australia.

Sunvil

UK
+44 (0) 20 8568 4499
www.sunvil.co.uk
A range of active holidays/trips available including sailing holidays around the world.

Thailand Travel Plan

UK
info@thailandtravelplan.co.uk
+44 (0)1273 322 040
www.thailandtravelplan.co.uk
Khao Yai jungle trails. Island hopping to hidden paradise. Sleep in the Thai countryside and floating huts along the River Kwai. Weíll help you build your very own Thailand adventure with our organised trips for independent travellers.

The adventure company

UK
0808 115 5881
www.adventurecompany.co.uk
Offers inspirational holidays and trips worldwide that venture off the well trodden tourist trails.

The Bundu Safari Company

UK
0800 781 1660
www.intrepidbundu.com
The Bundu Safari Company has teamed up with Intrepid Travel to offer exciting safari adventures.

The Dragon Trip Pte Ltd

UK
info@thedragontrip.com
+44 (0)207 936 4884
thedragontrip.com
The Dragon Trip is a provider of affordable holidays in China in the form of backpacking trips.

For further information see page 104

The Imaginative Traveller

UK
online@imtrav.net
0845 287 2908
www.imaginative-traveller.com
Individual, escape and volunteering tours available.

For further information see page 111

The Oriental Caravan

UK
info@theorientalcaravan.com
+44 (0)1424 883 570
www.theorientalcaravan.com
The Oriental Caravan is a truly independent adventure tour operator specialising in escorted small group travel in the Far East.

The Russia Experience

UK

expert@trans-siberian.co.uk

0845 521 2910

www.trans-siberian.co.uk

The Trans-Siberian is a working train covering 9,000 km, 10 time zones, 16 rivers and some 80 towns and cities. A once in a lifetime experience.

The Unique Travel Company

UK

info@theuniquetravel.co.uk

01264 889 644

www.theuniquetravel.co.uk

We provide a personal, affordable Sri Lankan experience that gives you a truly unique experience knowing that you are also putting money back into the island to help it grow and prosper - we feel this is what responsible tourism is about.

Timberline Adventures

USA

timber@earthnet.net

+1 800 417 2453

www.timbertours.com

Hiking and cycling tours in the USA.

Top Deck

UK

info@topdecktravel.co.uk

0845 257 5212

www.topdeck.travel

Providing unforgettable travel experiences for 18 to 30 somethings. Extended trips, festivals, ski and sailing in Europe, holidays in Egypt, Morocco, Jordan and Israel, safaris in Africa, adventures in Australia and New Zealand.

For further information see page 106

Tour Bus

Australia

questions@tourbus.com.au

www.tourbus.com.au

If you are looking for Tour Bus options within Australia or around the world you will likely find some great resources here.

Tourism Queensland

UK

44 20 7367 0981

www.experiencequeensland.com

Explore the many beautiful destinations Queensland has to offer.

Travel Nation

UK

+44 (0)1273 320580

www.travelnation.co.uk

Independent specialist travel company providing expert advice and the best deals on round-the-world trips, multi-stop itineraries, overland/adventure tours and Trans-Siberian rail journeys.

Travellers Connected.com

UK

info@travellersconnected.com

www.travellersconnected.com

A totally free community site for gap-year travellers. Register and contact travellers around the world for to-the-minute advice on the best places to go and best things to do.

Tribes Travel

UK

enquiries@tribes.co.uk

+44 (0)1473 890499

www.tribes.co.uk

A Fair Trade Travel company with lots of exciting tours for you to choose from, such as budget priced walking safaris to the more expensive once in a lifetime trips.

Tucan Travel

UK
0800 804 8435
www.tucantravel.com
Budget Expeditions offer a wide range of tours at low prices.

Vietnam Travel Plan

UK
info@vietnamtravelplan.co.uk
+44 (0)1273 322 041
www.vietnamtravelplan.co.uk
Anchors away in Halong Bay. Meet the hilltribes of Sapa and drift along the Mekong to tropical Phu Quoc Island. We'll help you build your very own Vietnam adventure with our organised trips for independent travellers.

Vodkatrain

UK
+44 (0) 20 8877 7650
www.vodkatrain.com
Experience the Trans-Mongolian railway and the Silk Road, travelling with local people, sampling local food and travel at local prices.

Walks Worldwide

UK
sales@walksworldwide.com
0845 301 4737
www.walksworldwide.com
Walks Worldwide is a leading independent specialist for trekking and walking holidays, offering a wide choice of walking holidays to all the world's great trekking and walking destinations, many of which are unique to Walks Worldwide.

World Expeditions

UK
enquiries@worldexpeditions.co.uk
+44 (0)20 8545 9030
www.worldexpeditions.com
Adventure travel company offering ground breaking itineraries on every continent. They offer exciting all inclusive adventures and challenges worldwide.

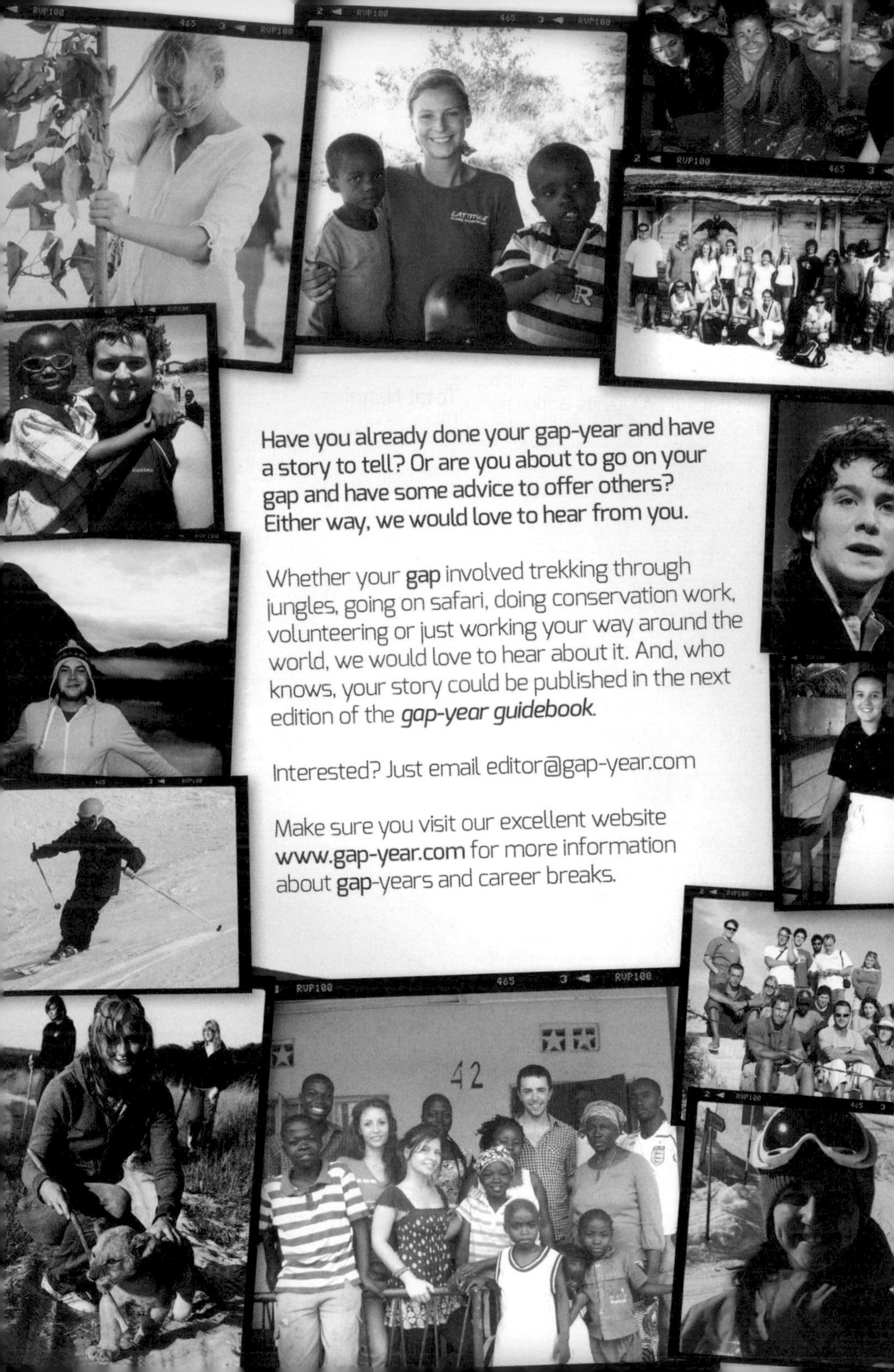
Have you already done your gap-year and have a story to tell? Or are you about to go on your gap and have some advice to offer others? Either way, we would love to hear from you.
Whether your gap involved trekking through jungles, going on safari, doing conservation work, volunteering or just working your way around the world, we would love to hear about it. And, who knows, your story could be published in the next edition of the gap-year guidebook.
Interested? Just email editor@gap-year.com
Make sure you visit our excellent website www.gap-year.com for more information about gap-years and career breaks.

Working abroad

Au Pairing

Au Pair Ecosse
UK
ruth@aupairecosse.com
+44 (0) 1786 474573
www.aupairecosse.com
Au Pair Ecosse places au pairs with families in Scotland and sends British au pairs to families in Europe and America using established, reputable agent partners.

Au Pair in America (APIA)
UK
info@aupairamerica.co.uk
+44 (0) 20 7581 7322
www.aupairamerica.co.uk
Agency which specifically matches au pairs and nannies with families in America.

Childcare International
UK
office@childint.co.uk
+44 (0) 20 8906 3116
www.childint.co.uk
Childcare International, together with their partner agencies abroad, arrange au pair placements across Europe, Australia, New Zealand, Canada and the US.

Gap 360
UK
info@gap360.com
01892 527392
www.gap360.com
Gap 360 is an exciting travel company offering an amazing range of affordable gap year adventures.
For further information see page 130

Planet Au Pair
Spain
info@planetaupair.com
+34 96 320 6491
www.planetaupair.com
Company placing au pairs throughout Europe and the USA.

Total Nannies
UK
+44 (0)207 0601213
www.totalnannies.com
This company places nannies and au pairs worldwide.

Internships

African Conservation Experience
UK
info@conservationafrica.net
+44 (0) 1454 269182
www.conservationafrica.net
African Conservation Experience offer volunteering opportunities at wildlife conservation projects in southern Africa. You can count on our full support and more than 10 years experience. See our main advert in Conservation

AgriVenture
UK
clare@agriventure.com; judy@agriventure.com
+44 (0)1664 560044
www.agriventure.com
Spend your gap year getting fantastic work experience in South Pacific/North America/Japan/Europe. Work in agriculture or horticulture. Get paid for the work you do whilst living and working with one of our fully approved hosting enterprises.

Gap 360
UK
info@gap360.com
01892 527392
www.gap360.com
Gap 360 is an exciting travel company offering an amazing range of affordable gap year adventures.

For further information see page 130

Global Choices
UK
+44 (0) 20 8533 2777
www.globalchoices.co.uk
Offers internships and working holidays in USA, Australia, Canada, UK, Ireland, Brazil, Argentina, Spain, Greece and Italy.

Graduate Gap Year
UK
enquiries@graduategapyear.com
www.graduategapyear.com
Graduate Gap Year offers unrivaled opportunities to gain substantial work experience, through a placement overseas - in Africa, China, India and South-East Asia.

InterExchange
USA
info@interexchange.org
+1 212 924 0446
www.interexchange.org
InterExchange offers J-1 & H-2B visa programs throughout the US. Options include au pair, internship, seasonal work and travel and summer camp positions.

International Exchange Programme UK (IEPUK)
UK
ws@iepuk.com
+44(0)1572 823 934
www.iepuk.com
Based in the United Kingdom IEPUK is offering a wide range of international exchange programmes and educational packages to support study and work experience abroad.

IST Plus
UK
+44 (0) 20 7788 1877
www.istplus.com
Internships in the USA, Australia, New Zealand. Summer work in the USA. Summer camp in the USA. Gap-year work in Australia, New Zealand. Volunteer in Thailand. Teach in Thailand, China (for graduates).

Lucasfilm
USA
https://jobs.lucasfilm.com/
As you can imagine, internships with Lucasfilm are few and far between. They are also quickly filled. See their website for further details.

Mountbatten Institute
UK
info-uk@mountbatten.org
+44 (0) 845 370 3535
www.mountbatten.org
Grab a whole year's worth of paid work experience through the Mountbatten Programme and enhance your CV.

The New England Wild Flower Society & Garden in the Woods
USA
information@newenglandwild.org
+1 508 877 7630
www.newfs.org
The oldest plant conservation organization in the USA and a leader in regional plant conservation programmes and native plant studies. They have volunteering and internship opportunities.

Twin Work & Volunteer
UK
+44 (0)20 8297 3278
www.workandvolunteer.com
Work and volunteer programmes listed. Also offers a travel insurance package.

Visitoz

UK
will@vistoz.org
07966 528 644
www.visitoz.org

Visitoz provides training and guarantees work for young people between the ages of 18 and 30 in agriculture, hospitality, child care and teaching all over Australia.

For further information see page 144

Work the World Ltd

UK
info@worktheworld.co.uk
+44 (0) 1273 573 863
www.worktheworld.co.uk

Organises healthcare and community development projects that provide maximum benefit to both the participants and the overseas communities they support.

Seasonal work

Acorn Venture Ltd

UK
jobs@acornadventure.co.uk
+44 (0) 121 504 2066
www.jobs-acorn.co.uk

Acorn Adventure runs adventure holiday camps from April until September based in eight centres in France, Italy, and the UK - their main customers are school/youth groups and families.

AmeriCamp

UK
info@americamp.co.uk
+44 (0) 161 4083570
www.americamp.co.uk

We offer people around the world the chance to work in the USA at a summer camp and become an AmeriCamper. We pay at least $1500 and you make memories that last a lifetime! Join the AmeriCamp Revolution!

Beaumont Château Ltd

UK
holidays@chateau-beaumont.co.uk
+44 (0) 844 8000 124
www.chateau-beaumont.co.uk

Chateau Beaumont is a small friendly language and activity centre based in the Normandy region of France.

BUNAC

UK
info@bunacusa.org
+44 (0)20 7870 9570
www.bunac.org

Overseas work and travel programmes for people aged 18 and above. A BUNAC working holiday gives you the freedom and flexibility of spending an extended period of time living and working in another country.

Camp America

UK
enquiries@campamerica.co.uk
+44 (0) 20 7581 7373
www.campamerica.co.uk

Camp America sends over 7,500 people to work on summer camps in the USA every year with up to 4 weeks independent travel after camp!

Camp Leaders In America

UK
uk@campleaders.com
+44 (0) 151 708 6808
www.campleaders.com

Activity leaders, camp counselors and support staff needed in their summer camps. See website for further details.

Canvas Holidays

UK
+44 (0) 1383 629012
www.canvasholidaysrecruitment.com

We have paid positions at over 100 campsites across Europe. We require a minimum of eight weeks commitment for July and August.

Castaway Resorts

Thailand
+66 (0)831 387 472 / +66 (0)811 707 605
www.castaway-resorts.com
Castaway Resorts invite enthusiastic active young people on a gap year to join our friendly teams at one of our tropical beach resorts in Thailand.

CCUSA

UK
info@ccusa.co.uk
+44 (0) 20 8874 6325
www.ccusa.com
Work in summer camps in beautiful locations in America. You don't need any experience or qualifications but you do need to be at least 18 years old. Also available, a range of worldwide programs including winter seasons in Canada.

Gap 360

UK
info@gap360.com
01892 527392
www.gap360.com
Gap 360 is an exciting travel company offering an amazing range of affordable gap year adventures.
For further information see page 130

Go Workabout

Australia
info@goworkabout.com
+61 (0) 8 6420 5000
www.goworkabout.com
Arranges work in Australia for working holiday makers before they travel.

Immigration New Zealand

UK
09069 100 100 (premium rate number)
www.immigration.govt.nz/branch/londonbranchhome
New Zealand government website offering details on working holidays for visitors to the country.

Leiths List, Agency for Cooks

UK
info@leithslist.com
+44 (0) 1225 722983
www.leithslist.com
Find short term cookery jobs such as chalet and holiday home work. Once qualified (see cookery section), you can earn money in your gap year or university holidays.
For further information see page 140

Mark Warner Ltd

UK
newbookings@markwarner.co.uk
0844 273 7332
www.markwarner.co.uk
Leading independent tour operator with opportunities all year round in ski and beach resorts. Variety of hotel positions and fully inclusive benefits package on offer.

Natives.co.uk

UK
info@natives.co.uk
+44 (0)1772 639604
www.natives.co.uk
Seasonal recruitment website for ski or summer resorts.

Neilson Holidays

UK
sales@neilson.com
0844 879 8155 / 8817
www.neilson.co.uk
This company offers a selection of worldwide sporting holidays.

Oyster Worldwide Limited

UK
info@oysterworldwide.com
+44 (0) 1892 770 771
www.oysterworldwide.com

Oyster is the specialist gap-year provider offering paid work projects abroad. Whether you're a ski nut or budding jackaroo, you'll get excellent, personal support throughout.

For further information see page 128

Season Workers

UK
info@seasonworkers.com
0845 6439338
www.seasonworkers.com

A free resource featuring information on destinations and itineraries, as well as a searchable database of paid and voluntary opportunities.

The Travel Visa Company Ltd

UK
info@thetravelvisacompany.co.uk
+44 (0) 1270 250 590
www.thetravelvisacompany.co.uk

The Travel Visa Company Ltd specialises in obtaining all types of visas for destinations right across the world including Australia, USA, India, Russia, China and Sri Lanka.

Unschool Adventures

USA
office@unschooladventures.com
+1 541 728 3227
www.unschooladventures.com

International trips and US-based educational programmes for self-directed young adults, ages 14-21.

Visas Australia Ltd

UK
sales@visas-australia.com
+44 (0)1270 250 590
www.visas-australia.com

Visas Australia Ltd specialises in processing and issuing all types of visas, particularly suited to gap-year travellers. Their service is approved by both the Australian Tourist Board and Australian High Commission.

Visitoz

UK
will@vistoz.org
07966 528 644
www.visitoz.org

Visitoz provides training and guarantees work for young people between the ages of 18 and 30 in agriculture, hospitality, child care and teaching all over Australia.

For further information see page 144

Xtreme Gap

Netherlands
info@xtremegapyear.co.uk
+44 (0)20 32867065
www.xtremegapyear.co.uk

Gap company offering extreme sporting adventures.

TEFL

Adventure Alternative

UK
office@adventurealternative.com
+44 (0) 28 708 31258
www.adventurealternative.com

Teaching and volunteering in needy schools and orphanages in Kenya and in schools in Kathmandu (includes Himalayan trek).

CAPS - Home to Home

Spain
caps@hometohome.es
+34 93 864 88 86
www.hometohome.es

CAPS is a programme designed for young people who would like to spend a year in Spain helping in a School as Conversation Teaching Assistant.

For further information see page 138

Link Ethiopia

UK
chris@linkethiopia.org
+44 (0)20 8045 4558
www.linkethiopia.org

Experience Ethiopia and teach basic English to small groups on a very inexpensive three-month placement with us. Registered Charity No. 1112390.

Oyster Worldwide Limited

UK
info@oysterworldwide.com
+44 (0) 1892 770 771
www.oysterworldwide.com

Highly motivated University Graduate? We can find you a job teaching in China and help you organise your TEFL. Spend 12 months in China and earn at least £600 per month (this goes a long way in China!).

For further information see page 128

Syndicat Mixte Montaigu-Rocheservière

France
anglais@sm-montaigu-rocheserviere.fr
+33 (0) 2 51 46 45 45
www.gapyear-france.com

Receives local government funding to teach English in primary schools, offering five posts annually - and it also employs a sixth person to work as a language assistant in a local college and lycÈe.

The Language House

France
info@teflanguagehouse.com
www.teflanguagehouse.com

TEFL/TESOL programme available. Also courses in French, Arabic, Spanish or Italian. Small classes.

Volunteering abroad

Conservation

African Conservation Trust
South Africa
talk@projectafrica.com
+27 (0)33 342 2844
www.projectafrica.com
The mission of ACT is to provide a means for conservation projects to become self funding through active participation by the public.

All Out Africa
Swaziland
info@alloutafrica.com
+268 2416 2260
www.alloutafrica.com
They run cutting edge wildlife conservation and social development projects in some of Africa's most amazing locations.

Amanzi Travel
UK
info@amanzitravel.co.uk
+44 (0) 117 253 0888
www.amanzitravel.co.uk
Amanzi Travel - Leading UK Specialist in Volunteer Travel throughout Africa.

Azafady
UK
info@azafady.org
+ 44 (0) 20 8960 6629
www.madagascar.co.uk
Pioneer Madagascar is a 2-10 week volunteer scheme that offers first-hand experience of frontline development and conservation work in beautiful and remote areas.

Biosphere Expeditions
UK
uk@biosphere-expeditions.org
0870-4460801
www.biosphere-expeditions.org
Biosphere Expeditions is an international non-profit wildlife volunteer organisation, founded in 1999, that runs conservation expeditions for environmental volunteers all across the globe.

Blue Ventures
UK
info@blueventures.org
+44 (0)20 7697 8598
www.blueventures.org
Blue Ventures runs award-winning marine research projects for conservation, education and sustainable development. Volunteers participate in diving and terrestrial activities in partnership with local communities.

For further information see page 164

Camps International Limited
UK
info@campsinternational.com
+44 (0) 844 800 1127
www.campsinternational.com
Gap-year volunteer holidays available. Spend time in community and wildlife camps and still have the time and opportunity to trek mountains and dive in the ocean.

Concordia International Volunteers

UK
info@concordiavolunteers.org.uk
+44 (0) 1273 422 218
www.concordiavolunteers.org.uk
Concordia offers the opportunity to join international teams of volunteers working on short-term projects in 60 countries in Europe, North America, Latin-America, Africa and Asia.

Conservation Volunteers Australia

Australia
info@conservationvolunteers.com.au
+61 (0) 3 5330 2600
www.conservationvolunteers.com.au
Conservation Volunteers Australia offers projects across Australia, including tree planting, wildlife surveys, track building, year-round. Contribution for meals, accommodation and travel applies.

Conservation Volunteers New Zealand

Australia
info@conservationvolunteers.com.au
+61 (0) 3 5330 2600
www.conservationvolunteers.com.au
Conservation Volunteers New Zealand offers projects year-round, including habitat restoration, tree planting, track building. Contribution for meals, accommodation and travel applies.

Coral Cay Conservation

UK
+44 (0) 20 7620 1411
www.coralcay.org
Volunteer with award-winning specialists in coral reef and rainforest conservation expeditions. Scuba dive or trek in tropical climes and work with local communities to aid long-term conservation efforts.

Discover Nepal

Nepal
stt@mos.com.np
+977 1 4413690
www.discovernepal.org.np
The aim of Discover Nepal is to provide opportunities for the involvement in the development process, and to practically contribute towards the socio-economic development of the country.

Dyer Island Cruises

South Africa
bookings@whalewatchsa.com
+27 (0)82 801 8014
www.whalewatchsa.com
Offer shark cage diving, boat based whale watching and also volunteer work.

Earthwatch Institute

UK
info@earthwatch.org.uk
+44 (0) 1865 318 838
www.earthwatch.org.uk
Work alongside leading scientists around the world and help solve pressing environmental problems. With expeditions on over 25 research projects to choose from, conduct hands-on conservation research in stunning locations whilst having an experience of a lifetime.

Earthwise Valley

New Zealand
info@earthwisevalley.org
+64 9 355 0333
www.earthwisevalley.org
Join the Rainforest Sanctuary as a residential volunteer and experience New Zealand, while making a real difference to our natural world.

Ecoteer
UK
contact@ecoteer.com
+44 (0)1752 426285
www.ecoteer.com
Community-based placements in countries around the world and most are free! Volunteer with us and make everlasting friends across the whole world!

Ecoteer (Malaysia)
Malaysia
explore@ecoteer.com
+6 012 217 3208 (Malaysia)
www.ecoteerresponsibletravel.com
With Ecoteer Responsible Travel you will help communities and wildlife at our various projects across Asia.

Edge of Africa
South Africa
info@edgeofafrica.com
+27 (0) 443820122
www.edgeofafrica.com
Edge of Africa offer volunteer programmes to suit your personality, preference and budget. Give the edge and volunteer in Africa.

Entabeni Nature Guide Training School
South Africa
sarah@natureguidetraining.co.za
+27 15 453 0645
www.natureguidetraining.co.za
Situated on a private game reserve three hours drive from Johannesburg, Entabeni offer a series of programmes in nature guiding and other tailor-made courses.

Essential Croatia
UK
info@essentialcroatia.com
www.essentialcroatia.com
Join the Griffon Vulture and nature protection programme. Volunteer opportunities available year round on the beautiful and upspoilt island of Cres-Croatia.

Fauna Forever Tambopata
Peru
www.faunaforever.org
Volunteer researchers needed for wildlife project in the Peruvian Amazon. Fauna Forever Tambopata is a wildlife monitoring project based in the Amazon rainforest of Tambopata in south-eastern Peru.

FirstStep.me
South Africa
contact@firststep.me
www.firststep.me
FirstStep.me is an information and reference based online magazine.

Forest Animal Rescue
USA
info@forestanimalrescue.org
+1 352 625 7377
forestanimalrescue.org
A non-profit-making exotic animal sanctuary located in Florida. Its all-volunteer staff provides long-term care for confiscated, abused, neglected or unwanted exotic animals to prevent them from being destroyed.

Friends of Conservation
UK
focinfo@aol.com
+44 (0) 20 7348 3408
www.foc-uk.com
There are some opportunities to volunteer on overseas projects such as the Namibian based Cheetah Conservation Fund. Volunteers are also needed in the UK and at their head office in London. Registered Charity No. 328176.

Frontier
UK
info@frontier.ac.uk
+44 (0) 20 7613 2422
www.frontier.ac.uk
With 250 projects around the world Frontier offers volunteers the chance to get involved in an array of activities from wildlife and marine conservation to trekking and biodiversity research, teaching and community development.

Galapagos Conservation Trust
UK
gct@gct.org
+44 (0) 207 399 7440
www.savegalapagos.org
The Galapagos Conservation Trust has two aims: to raise funds to support the expanding conservation work and to raise awareness of the current issues the islands face. Registered Charity No. 1043470.

Gapforce
UK
info@gapforce.org
+44 (0)20 7384 3028
www.gapforce.org
Gapforce has established itself as a leading provider for enjoyable gap adventures worldwide including volunteering. It is the parent company of Trekforce and Greenforce.

Global Action Nepal
UK
info@gannepal.org.np
+44 (0) 7941 044063
www.gannepal.org.np
Global Action Nepal projects are always closely in harness with grass roots level needs, focusing on community-led, participatory development. Registered Charity No. 1090773.

Global Action Plan
UK
all@globalactionplan.org.uk
020 7420 4444
www.globalactionplan.org.uk
An environmental behavioural change charity helping businesses, schools and communities reduce their impact on the environment.

Global Vision International (GVI)
UK
+44 (0) 1727 250 250
www.gvi.co.uk
With unparalled in-country support, GVI volunteers benefit from exceptional training and a Careers Abroad job placement scheme.

Global Volunteer Network
New Zealand
info@volunteer.org.nz
+64 0800 032 5035
www.globalvolunteernetwork.org
Volunteer through the Global Volunteer Network to support communities in need around the world. Volunteer placements include schools, refugee camps, wildlife sanctuaries and nature reserves.

Greenforce
UK
info@greenforce.org
+44 (0) 20 7384 3028
www.greenforce.org
Greenforce is a not-for-profit organisation offering voluntary and paid work overseas. With ten years experience and a range of opportunities, Greenforce will have a programe to suit you.

InvAID

UK
info@invasionjobs.com
01612121051
www.invasiontravel.com/invaid

We offer people around the world the opportunity to volunteer in countries such as Brazil, The Maldives and Thailand. Not only do you get the Invasion experience, but you get to make a real difference in people's lives whilst being based in some of the most rewarding locations in the world.

Junglemantra

UK
contact@junglemantra.com
+919910481207
www.junglemantra.com

Wildlife resort in the Bandhavgarh National Park, offering tiger sighting opportunities.

Kaya Responsible Travel

UK
info@kayavolunteer.com
+44 (0)161 870 6212
www.kayavolunteer.com

Kaya offer over 200 volunteer projects worldwide working with local communities and conservation initiatives from 2 weeks to 12 months. Placements are tailored to specific needs and skills of students, career breakersí, retirees, families or groups.

For further information see page 160

On African Soil

South Africa
julia@onafricansoil.com
+27 78 820 3353
www.onafricansoil.com

Become an On African Soil Volunteer and take part in wildlife conservation and social upliftment projects.

Orangutan Foundation

UK
+44 (0) 20 7724 2912
www.orangutan.org.uk

Participate in hands on conservation fieldwork that really makes a difference and see orangutans in their natural habitat.

Outreach International

UK
info@outreachinternational.co.uk
+44 (0) 1458 274957
www.outreachinternational.co.uk

Outreach International places committed volunteers in carefully selected projects on the Pacific coast of Mexico, Sri Lanka, Kenya, Cambodia, Nepal, Costa Rica, Ecuador and the Galapagos Islands.

Oyster Worldwide Limited

UK
info@oysterworldwide.com
+44 (0) 1892 770 771
www.oysterworldwide.com

Oyster is the specialist gap-year provider offering genuine opportunities with endangered or abused animals. Vets, zoologists and animal lovers all welcome. Excellent, personal support throughout.

For further information see page 154

ProWorld (Real Projects...Real Experience)

UK
info@proworldvolunteers.org
+44 (0) 18 6559 6289
www.proworldvolunteers.org

Projects offered: conservation, health care, education, human rights, journalism, and business projects. Programmes start every month of the year.

Real Gap Experience

UK
info@realgap.co.uk
+44 (0)1273 647220
www.realgap.co.uk

Real Gap offers a wide and diverse range of programmes. These include: volunteering, conservation, adventure travel and expeditions, sports, teaching English, round the world, paid working holidays and learning.

ReefDoctor Org Ltd

UK
volunteer@reefdoctor.org
+44 (0) 7866 250 740
www.reefdoctor.org

Become a volunteer ReefDoctor and contribute to marine research, education, conservation and sustainable community development alongside our team of local and international scientists.

Rempart

France
contact@rempart.com
+33 (0)1 42 71 96 55
www.rempart.com

Rempart, a union of conservation associations organises short voluntary work in France. The projects are all based around restoration and maintenance of historic sites and buildings.

Samara Wildlife Volunteer Programme

South Africa
lodge@samara.co.za
+2749 892 3275 / 891 0880
www.samara.co.za/volunteer.htm

Join ongoing wildlife and research management programmes at a private game reserve that is a hub of conservation and animal reintroduction projects.

Shumba Experience

UK
info@shumbaexperience.co.uk
+44 (0)845 257 3205
www.shumbaexperience.co.uk

Join our exciting wildlife and marine conservation projects in Africa. Youíll be volunteering on game reserves to help conserve lions, elephants, leopards and rhinos.

Starfish Ventures Ltd

UK
+44 (0)20 8133 5191
www.starfishvolunteers.com

Starfish has a volunteer placement for you, whatever your skills, they can be put to good use in our various projects in Thailand.

Sumatran Orangutan Society

UK
+44 (0) 1865 403 341
www.orangutans-sos.org

SOS is looking for committed, energetic volunteers to support our small team. The roles will involve fundraising, campaigning, and raising awareness about orangutans and the work we do in Sumatra.

Sunrise Volunteer Programmes

UK
info@sunrint.com
+44 (0) 121 5722795
http://en.sunrint.com

Specialist for volunteer projects in China, offering volunteer opportunities in social, environment, education, medical, journalism and community areas around China.

The British Exploring Society (BSES Expeditions)

UK
info@britishexploring.org
+44 (0)20 7591 3141
www.britishexploring.org

BSES Expeditions organises challenging scientific expeditions to remote, wild environments. Study climate change whilst mountaineering or kayaking in the Arctic, measure biodiversity in the Amazon or investigate human interaction with the environment in the Himalayas.

The Great Projects

UK
info@thegreatprojects.com
+44 (0) 845 371 3070
www.thegreatprojects.com

Volunteer on one of our Great Projects for a chance to meet new people, work with and help some of the most endangered animals on the planet.

The Leap Overseas Ltd

UK
info@theleap.co.uk
+44 (0) 1672 519922
www.theleap.co.uk

Team or solo placements in Africa, Asia or South America. Volunteer to get stuck into our unique mix of eco-tourism, community and conservation projects. Connect with local people.

TrekFORCE

UK
info@trekforce.org.uk
+44 (0) 207 384 3028
www.trekforce.org.uk

TrekFORCE offers expeditions in Bornea, Central America, Nepal and Papua New Guinea. Learn survival skills, jungle training and work on conservation and community projects. Expedition leadership training also available.

Tropical Adventures Foundation

Costa Rica
info@tropicaladventures.com
+506 8868-0296
www.tropicaladventures.com

Provides volunteer tour packages for individuals, families and groups interested in exploring the culture, language and natural beauty of Costa Rica.

Turtle Conservation Project

Sri Lanka
www.tcpsrilanka.org

Gap year students can come and work for TCP for 3 or 6 months. Help with marine turtle research, guide tourists at the turtle nesting beach, rescue turtles, develop educational literature and much more.

UNA Exchange

UK
info@unaexchange.org
+44 (0) 29 2022 3088
www.unaexchange.org

Registered charity that supports people to take part in international volunteer projects in over 50 countries across the world. Each project is organised by one of our international partner organisations, based in the country of the project. Projects cover a large range of themes including; social, environmental, construction and cultural projects.

Vivisto Ltd

UK
info@vivisto.co.uk
+44 (0) 845 603 5719
www.vivisto.co.uk

You can make a difference volunteering on conservation and community programmes in South Africa.

Volunteer Latin America
UK
info@volunteerlatinamerica.com
+44 (0)20 7193 9163
www.volunteerlatinamerica.com
Volunteer abroad for free or at low-cost in Central and South America via the greenest volunteer advisor on the planet.

Volunteers Making a Difference - vMaD
Cambodia
info@madcambodia.org
+855 63 69 087 96
www.volunteer-cambodia.org
A non profit organization offering international volunteer work opportunities abroad in Siem Reap, Cambodia. vMaD placements are all in rural areas, so youíll get to see the real Cambodia and experience the local culture.

Voluntour South Africa
South Africa
info@voluntoursouthafrica.com
+27 (0)82 416 6066
www.voluntoursouthafrica.com
VSA offers you a chance to make a lasting difference to the lives of others. If you have a sense of adventure and feel the urge to experience new cultures and make a difference then VSA is the right place for you

Wilderness Awareness School
USA
+1 425 788 1301
www.wildernessawareness.org
The school, a not for profit environmental organisation, offers courses for adults in tracking, wilderness survival skills and a stewardship programme.

Wildlife PACT
India
wildlifepact@gmail.com
+91 99 10 586006
www.wildlifepact.org
A wildlife protection and conservation trust, mostly working in and around Bandhavgrah Tiger Reserve.

Worldwide Experience
UK
+44 (0) 1483 860 560
www.worldwideexperience.com
Worldwide Experience specialises in volunteer gap-year placements in conservation, marine and community projects throughout Africa.
For further information see page 168

WWOOF (World Wide Opportunities on Organic Farms)
UK
www.wwoof.org.uk
Join WWOOF and participate in meaningful work that reconnects with nature, share the lives of people who have taken practical steps towards alternative, sustainable lifestyles.

Humanitarian

2Way Development
UK
volunteer@2waydevelopment.com
+44 (0) 20 7148 6110
www.2waydevelopment.com
2Way offer a support service to people looking for volunteering experiences worldwide.

Action Aid

UK

supportercare@actionaid.org

+44 (0)1460 238000

www.actionaid.org.uk/experiences

Take part in ActionAid's First Hand Experience and change lives, including your own. ActionAid is offering volunteering opportunities in South Africa and Nepal, working alongside local people to build homes and centres to benefit whole communities for the better.

Africa & Asia Venture

UK

av@aventure.co.uk

+44 (0)1380 729009

www.aventure.co.uk

Established in 1993 AV specialises in community, sports coaching and teaching volunteer projects in Africa, Asia and Latin America. We offer group based projects from 3 weeks to 5 months, including designated travel time.

African Impact

South Africa

info@africanimpact.com

+27 (0)86 618 3370

www.africanimpact.com

African Impact is a volunteer travel organisation providing meaningful interactive volunteer programs throughout Africa for a positive and measurable impact on local communities and conservation efforts.

Alliance Abroad Group

USA

+1 (512) 904 1136

www.allianceabroad.com

Alliance Abroad is a non-profit organisation that provides international teaching, work and volunteer placements. Our services include guaranteed placement and 24/7 personal assistance.

Asociacion Nuevos Horizontes

Guatemala

honoris@intelnet.net.gt

+502 7761 6140

www.ahnh.org

The shelter is a home for families who have survived situations of domestic violence. Volunteers are needed to help with the children at the daycare centre.

ATD Fourth World

UK

atd@atd-uk.org

+44 (0) 20 7703 3231

www.atd-uk.org

ATD Fourth World is an international voluntary organisation working in partnership with people living in poverty worldwide.

Be the Change Worldwide

UK

info@bethechangeworldwide.com

+44 (0)208 144 2423

http://bethechangeworldwide.com

Be the Change Worldwide specialises in Gap Year experiences, placing volunteers from all over the world into key developmental projects in under-resourced schools within underprivileged communities.

BERUDA

Cameroon

berudepservices@gmail.com

+237 7760 1407

www.berudep.org

BERUDA's vision is 'to eradicate poverty and raise the living standards of the rural population of Cameroonís North West province'. They rely on volunteers to help them achieve this.

BMS World Mission

UK

+44 (0) 1235 517700

www.bmsworldmission.org

BMS World Mission is a Christian organisation which sends people in teams and as individuals or families to 34 countries worldwide.

Brathay Exploration Group

UK

+44 (0) 15394 33942

www.brathayexploration.org.uk

Brathay provides ëchallenging experiences for young peopleí. It runs a range of expeditions from one to five weeks long which vary each year.

Bruce Organisation

Peru

info@bruceorg.org

http://bruceperu.org

Our mission is to help as many of the poorest children in the third world as we can to receive as good an education as their circumstances permit.

Cameroon Association for the Protection and Education of the Child (CAPEC)

Cameroon

info@capecam.org

+237 22 03 01 63

www.capecam.org

Volunteer to teach children in Cameroon. See website for vacancies and details of programmes available.

Camphill Communities

UK

www.camphill.net

There are more than 100 Camphill communities in over 20 countries in Europe, North America, southern Africa and India where those with special needs are offered the support they need to develop their potential.

Challenges Worldwide

UK

info@challengesworldwide.com

+44 (0)131 225 9549

www.challengesworldwide.com

Volunteers with professional skills and experience needed to work on their many projects.

Changing Worlds

UK

info@changingworlds.co.uk

+44 (0)1883 340960

www.changingworlds.co.uk

We offer placements in: Argentina, Australia, China, Dubai, Ghana, Honduras, India, Kenya, Madagascar, New Zealand, Romania, South Africa, Thailand and Uganda. So, if you like the idea of travel, meeting people and don't mind working hard, then this is for you!

Cicerones de Buenos Aires AsociaciÛn Civil

Argentina

contacto@cicerones.org.ar

+54 11 5258 0909

www.cicerones.org.ar

Volunteering in Argentina: Cicerones in Buenos Aires works in a friendly atmosphere ensuring contact with local people, experiencing the city the way it should be!

City Year

USA

+1 617 927 2500

www.cityyear.org

City Year unites young people of all backgrounds for a demanding year of community service and leadership development throughout the US. This organisation recruits from US only.

Cosmic Volunteers

USA
info@cosmicvolunteers.org
+1 215 609 4196
www.cosmicvolunteers.org

American non-profit organisation offering volunteer and internship programmes in China, Ecuador, Ghana, Guatemala, India, Kenya, Nepal, Peru, the Philippines, and Vietnam.

Cross-Cultural Solutions

UK
www.crossculturalsolutions.org

Cross-Cultural Solutions operates volunteer programmes in 12 countries in partnership with sustainable community initiatives. CCS brings people together to work side-by-side with members of the local community while sharing perspectives and cultural understanding.

Cultural Canvas Thailand

USA
info@culturalcanvas.com
www.culturalcanvas.com

Cultural Canvas Thailand offers unique and meaningful volunteer experiences in Chiang Mai, Thailand. Placements are available in the following areas: hill tribe education, women's empowerment and Burmese refugee education and assistance.

Development in Action

UK
info@developmentinaction.org
+44 (0)7813 395957
www.developmentinaction.org

Development in Action is a youth and volunteer led development education charity, whose main aim is to engage young people in global issues and promote global citizenship.

Discover Adventure Ltd.

UK
01722 718444
www.discoveradventure.com

Discover Adventure Fundraising Challenges are trips that are designed to be challenging, to push your limits. They are not holidays! They involve preparation in terms of fundraising and improving fitness.

Ecuador Volunteer

Ecuador
+593 2 255 7749
www.ecuadorvolunteer.org

Ecuador Volunteer Foundation, is a non-profit organization that offers volunteer work opportunities abroad.

EIL (Experiment for International Living)

UK
info@eiluk.org
+44 (0) 168 456 2577
www.eiluk.org

Offers a diverse range of programmes in the UK and worldwide, including volunteering, individual homestays and group learning.

Gap Medics

UK
info@gapmedics.com
+44 (0)191 230 8080
www.gapmedics.co.uk

Gap Medics organise medical and nursing placements and projects in Africa and Asia.

Gap Year South Africa

UK
info@gapyearsouthafrica.com
+44 (0) 208 144 2423
www.gapyearsouthafrica.com

Specialises in sports coaching, teaching, health awareness projects in South Africa. Our project duration is between three weeks and three months.

Glencree Centre for Peace and Reconciliation

Ireland
info@glencree.ie
+353 (0) 1 282 9711
www.glencree.ie

Glencree welcomes international volunteers who provide practical help in exchange for a unique experience of working with those building peace in Ireland, Britain and beyond.

Global Media Projects

UK
info@globalmediaprojects.co.uk
+44 (0) 191 222 0404
www.globalmediaprojects.co.uk

Offers print/online and broadcast media projects in China, India, Ghana, Mexico, Romania and Tanzania.

Global Volunteer Projects

UK
info@globalvolunteerprojects.org
0191 222 0404
www.globalvolunteerprojects.org

With Global Volunteer Projects you can teach conversational English in schools, help in orphanages or work with animals on conservation projects.

For further information see page 172

Global Volunteers

USA
email@globalvolunteers.org
(800) 487 1074
www.globalvolunteers.org

Join a team of short-term volunteers contributing to long-term, comprehensive community projects on a volunteer vacation abroad or a USA volunteer program.

Great Aves

UK
+44 (0) 1832 275038
www.greataves.org

Great Aves is a Gap Year Charity that runs volunteer projects in South America. Volunteers work on the Arajuno Road Project teaching English or working on community based conservation and development projects.

Habitat for Humanity Great Britain

UK
supporterservices@habitatforhumanity.org.uk
+44 (0) 1295 264240
www.habitatforhumanity.org.uk

Habitat for Humanity aims to eliminate poverty housing and homelessness. Volunteers travel to their chosen country to spend 8-16 days living and working alongside the local community.

i volunteer

India
dehli@ivolunteer.in
+91 11 65672160
www.ivolunteer.in

Volunteering opportunites are shown on their website. You could end up working in an orphanage, on a helpline, on relief effort or in a school.

ICYE UK (Inter Cultural Youth Exchange)

UK
info@icye.org.uk
+44 (0) 20 7681 0983
www.icye.org.uk

Sends people aged between 18 and 30 to work in voluntary projects overseas in including counselling centres, human rights NGOs, farms, orphanages and schools for the disabled. Registered Charity No. 1081907.

i-to-i Volunteering

UK
enquiries@i-to-itravel.com
+44 (0)1273 647 210
www.i-to-i.com

At i-to-i, we work in partnership with locally run projects in over 20 countries offering you the chance to make a difference on your next trip in a safe, supported, and sustainable manner.

IVS (International Voluntary Service)

UK
info@ivsgb.org
+44 (0) 131 243 2745
http://ivsgb.org/info/

IVS brings volunteers together from many different countries, cultures and backgrounds to live and work on projects of benefit to local communities.

Josephite Community Aid

Australia
help@jcaid.com
+61 (0) 2 9838 8802
www.jcaid.com

Australian organisation committed to helping poor and underprivileged with the aid of volunteers.

Karen Hilltribes Trust

UK
+44 (0) 1904 612 829
www.karenhilltribes.org.uk

The Karen Hilltribes Trust (Registered Charity No. 1093548) sends volunteers to teach English in Thailand. You will live with a Karen Hilltribe family and your placement can be between 2 and 5 months teaching 5 days a week.

Kaya Responsible Travel

UK
info@kayavolunteer.com
+44 (0)161 870 6212
www.kayavolunteer.com

Kaya offer over 200 volunteer projects worldwide working with local communities and conservation initiatives from 2 weeks to 12 months. Placements are tailored to specific needs and skills of students, career breakersí, retirees, families or groups.

For further information see page 160

Khaya Volunteer

South Africa
info@khayavolunteer.com
+27 (0) 41 369 0898
www.khayavolunteer.com

Khaya Volunteer offers affordable and unique volunteering projects and programs in South Africa, Tanzania, Uganda and more.

Kings World Trust for Children

UK
annemarie@kingschildren.org
+44 (0)1428 653504
www.kingschildren.org

The Kings World Trust for Children aims to provide a caring home, an education and skills training for orphaned and homeless children and young people in south India.

L'Arche UK

UK
info@larche.org.uk
+44 (0) 800 917 1337
www.larche.org.uk

LíArche is an international movement where people with and without learning difficulties share life together. There are Communities in 34 countries. Volunteers are involved in all aspects of community life, are trained and supported, have free board and accommodation, a modest income and other benefits.

Lattitude Global Volunteering

UK
volunteer@lattitude.org.uk
+44 (0) 118 959 4914
www.lattitude.org.uk

Lattitude Global Volunteering is a youth development and volunteering charity that send young people to a huge range of challenging and rewarding placements worldwide.

For further information see page 156

Madventurer

UK
volunteer@madventurer.com
+44 (0)191 645 2014
www.madventurer.com

Offer group community projects in towns and villages in Ghana, Kenya, Uganda, Tanzania, South Africa, Fiji and Thailand.

Otra Cosa Network

UK
info@otracosa.org
00 44 1926 730029
www.otracosa.org

Based in Huanchaco, northern Peru, Otra Cosa Network offers a wide variety of affordable and satisfying volunteering opportunities to well-motivated volunteers from around the world.

Outreach International

UK
info@outreachinternational.co.uk
+44 (0) 1458 274957
www.outreachinternational.co.uk

Outreach International places committed volunteers in carefully selected projects on the Pacific coast of Mexico, Sri Lanka, Cambodia, Nepal, Costa Rica, Ecuador and the Galapagos Islands.

Oyster Worldwide Limited

UK
info@oysterworldwide.com
+44 (0) 1892 770 771
www.oysterworldwide.com

Oyster is the specialist gap-year provider with teaching and childcare projects around the world. We offer a personal approach with experienced managers supporting you throughout your trip.

For further information see page 174

PBI UK (Peace Brigades International)

UK
+44 (0)20 7281 5370
www.peacebrigades.org.uk

PBI provides protection, support and recognition to local human rights defenders who work in areas of repression.

Pepper

UK
hello@pepperexperience.com
+44 (0)20 3514 5390
www.pepperexperience.com

Pepper is a unique gap-year and adventure travel company offering tailor-made experiences, as well as custom trips, in South Africa.

Peru's Challenge

Peru
volunteer@peruschallenge.com
+51 84 272 508
www.peruschallenge.com

Join a volunteer and travel programme and assist the work of charity organisation, Peru's Challenge, in rural communities in Peru.

Project Trust
UK
info@projecttrust.org.uk
+44 (0) 1879 230 444
www.projecttrust.org.uk
Project Trust (charity no. SC025668) offers long term structured volunteering placements for school leavers (between ages of 17-19) in over twenty countries in Africa, Asia and Central and South America. Projects, lasting 8 or 12 months, include teaching, social care, journalism and outward bound.

Projects Abroad
UK
info@projects-abroad.co.uk
+44 (0) 1903 708300
www.projects-abroad.co.uk
Overseas placements. Teach English, gain invaluable experience in Medicine, Conservation, Journalism, Business, Care and Community, Sports, Law and Human Rights, Veterinary and more.

For further information see page 158

Quest Overseas
UK
info@questoverseas.com
+44 (0) 1273 777 206
www.questoverseas.com
Quest Overseas specializes in gap-year adventures into the very heart and soul of South America and Africa. We offer volunteers the chance to understand life far removed from home.

Raleigh International
UK
info@raleighinternational.org
+44 (0) 20 7183 1286
www.raleighinternational.org
Develop new skills, meet people from all backgrounds and make a difference on sustainable community and environmental projects around the world.

For further information see page 162

Restless Development
UK
info@restlessdevelopment.org
+44 (0)20 7976 8070
www.restlessdevelopment.org
Restless Development run Health Education and Community Resource Programmes in South Asia and Africa. Volunteers are asked to fundraise a donation to the charity.

ROKPA UK
UK
charity@ROKPAuk.org
01387 373232
www.rokpauk.org
ROKPA - meaning 'help' in Tibetan - is an international charity, helping communities in need in Tibetan areas of China, Nepal, Zimbabwe, South Africa, Europe and the UK.

Serenje Orphans School Home
Switzerland
contactzoa@yahoo.com
www.zoaonline.org
Our Zambian orphanage offers a rewarding and safe experience in rural Zambia for committed volunteers.

Skillshare International UK
UK
info@skillshare.org
0116 242 4146
www.skillshare.org
Skillshare International recruits professionals from different sectors to share their skills, experience and knowledge with local partner organisations in Africa and Asia as volunteers.

SL Volunteers
UK
info@slvolunteers.com
020 7096 1718
www.slvolunteers.com
Projects include clinical psychology and occupational therapy work experience placements at hospitals and centres for people with special needs.

Smile Society
India
www.smilengo.org
SMILE Society invite international volunteers and students to join us in our welfare projects, international work camps, summer camps, internship programmes and volunteer projects in India.

Spirit of Adventure Trust
New Zealand
info@spiritofadventure.org.nz
+64 (0) 9 373 2060
www.spiritofadventure.org.nz
Become part of the volunteer crew on one of the Trust's youth development voyages around New Zealand each year.

Tanzed
UK
tanzeduk@yahoo.co.uk
www.tanzed.org.uk
Working alongside Tanzanian nursery teachers as a classroom assistant you will be living in a rural village with plenty of opportunity to contribute to the community using your energy and enthusiasm.

Task Brasil Trust
UK
www.taskbrasil.org.uk
Charity helping impoverished children in Brazil. Volunteers always needed. Registered Charity No. 1030929.

The Book Bus
UK
info@thebookbus.org
+44 (0) 1822 616 191
www.thebookbus.org
The Book Bus provides a mobile service and actively promotes literacy to underpriviledged communities in Zambia, India, Malawi and Ecuador.

For further information see page 150

The Bridge Camphill Community
Ireland
thebridge@camphill.ie
+353 (0)45 481 597
www.camphill.ie
Registered charity (CHY5861) in County Kildare working with adults after they leave the sister community of Camphill Dunshane. Check out their website for volunteering opportunities.

The Castle Rock Institute
USA
info@castle-rock.org
828-862-3759
www.castle-rock.org
The Castle Rock Institute is an educational organization devoted to balancing academic study of the Humanities and outdoor adventure.

The Dragon Trip Pte Ltd
UK
info@thedragontrip.com
+44 (0)207 936 4884
thedragontrip.com
The Dragon Volunteer Trips offer the chance to learn Mandarian, change children's lives and travel in breathtaking scenery.

For further information see page 166

The Humanity Exchange

USA
admin@thehumanityexchange.org
+1 778 300 2466
www.thehumanityexchange.org

The Humanity Exchange provides grassroots Volunteer Abroad programs in communities across Ghana, Cameroon, Benin, Columbia and Mexico, and unique opportunities to volunteer and Learn French in Africa.

For further information see page 176

The Worldwrite Volunteer Centre

UK
world.write@btconnect.com
+44 (0) 20 8985 5435
www.worldwrite.org.uk

Join WORLDwrite's campaign for young volunteers who feel strongly about global inequality, want to make an impact and use film to do it. Registered charity No. 1060869.

The Year Out Group

UK
info@yearoutgroup.org
www.yearoutgroup.org

The Year Out Group is an association of the UK's leading Year Out organisations, promoting the concepts and benefits of well-structured year out programmes and helping young people and their advisers in selecting suitable and worthwhile projects.

Think Pacific

UK
info@thinkpacific.com
0113 253 8684
www.thinkpacific.com

Think Pacific offer you the chance to make a difference to the communities and places you visit, guiding you on a meaningful adventure through the glorious islands of Fiji.

Travellers Worldwide

UK
info@travellersworldwide.com
+44 (0) 1903 502595
www.travellersworldwide.com

Travellers is a leading international provider of voluntary placements and work experience internships overseas.

UBELONG

USA
programs@ubelong.org
+1 202 250 3706
www.ubelong.org

A social venture that empowers people to make a difference in communities around the world by offering them affordable and flexible opportunities to volunteer abroad.

Unipal

UK
info@unipal.org.uk
www.unipal.org.uk

Unipal (A Universities' Trust for Educational Exchange with Palestinians) seeks to facilitate a two-way process of education; providing English-language teaching in Palestinian refugee camps in the West Bank, Gaza and Lebanon and introducing British students to a knowledge and understanding of the situation and daily lives of refugees.

VAP (Volunteer Action for Peace)

UK
action@vap.org.uk
+44 (0) 844 2090 927
www.vap.org.uk

Organises international voluntary work projects in the UK each summer and recruits volunteers to take part in affordable placements abroad that range between two weeks and 12 months.

VESL Ltd (Volunteer for Educational Support and Learning)
UK
enquiries@vesl.org
www.vesl.org
Volunteering opportunities from 4 weeks to 12 months in Thailand, India and Sri Lanka.

Volunteer for Africa
UK
info@volunteer4africa.org
www.volunteer4africa.org
Non-profit organisation that helps volunteers and responsible travellers truly make a difference. Search the site for volunteer work or organisations needing supplies in the area you plan to visit.

Volunteer Maldives PVT Ltd
Republic of Maldives
info@volunteermaldives.com
+960330 0605
www.volunteermaldives.com
Volunteer Maldives is committed to making a real and tangible difference to these warm and friendly communities. When you travel with us you can rest assured that the work you do will directly benefit the islanders that have been identified by these local communities and the NGO's we work with.

For further information see page 178

Volunteer Vacations
UK
info@volunteervacations.co.uk
01483 331551
www.volunteervacations.co.uk
Voluntary sports coaching, teaching and orphange work abroad helping disadvantaged children.

Volunteer Work Thailand
UK
info@volunteerworkthailand.org
www.volunteerworkthailand.org
Non-profit organisation that helps people find volunteer work in Thailand including many opportunities to volunteer for free.

Volunteers for International Partnership
USA
info@partnershipvolunteers.org
+1-802-246-1154
www.partnershipvolunteers.org
VIP offers volunteer opportunities for individuals or groups to do international community service in health, social services, environment and education.

VRI
UK
enquiries@vri-online.org.uk
+44 (0) 20 8864 4740
www.vri-online.org.uk
VRI is a small UK registered charity (No. 285872) supporting sustainable development projects in rural India, and offering opportunities to stay in one.

WaterAid
UK
+44 (0) 20 7793 4594
www.wateraid.org
WaterAid is an international charity enabling the world's poorest people access to safe water and sanitation. You can volunteer to help them in the UK.

Whipalong Volunteer Program
South Africa
info@whipalong.co.za
+27 (0) 83 626 6324
www.whipalong.co.za
Volunteer horse rehabilitation programmes in South Africa.

Willing Workers in South Africa (WWISA)

South Africa
+27 (0)44 534 8958
www.wwisa.co.za
The core aim of WWISA is to help bring desperately needed community development services to poorly provisioned and frequently overlooked historically disadvantaged rural townships.

WLS International Ltd

UK
info@gapyearinasia.com
+44 203 384 7024
www.gapyearinasia.com
WLS International is one of the leading volunteer organizations with programs in Cambodia, China, Nepal, India, Indonesia, Sri Lanka, Thailand and Vietnam.

Work & Volunteer Abroad (WAVA)

UK
0800 80 483 80
www.workandvolunteer.com
Experience the world on one of WAVA's Gap Year programmes. Choose from a range of volunteer and work Gap Year travel projects around the world, and let WAVA help you See more & Do more around the world.

WorldTeach

USA
info@worldteach.org
(857) 259-6646
www.worldteach.org
WorldTeach partners with governments and other organizations in developing countries to provide volunteer teachers to meet local needs and promote responsible global citizenship.

WorldWide Volunteering for Young People

UK
+44 (0) 1935 825588
www.wwv.org.uk
Registered charity (No. 1038253), set up to help people of all ages to find their ideal volunteering project either in the UK or in any country in the world.

Medical

Global Medical Projects

UK
info@globalmedicalprojects.co.uk
+44 (0)191 222 0404
www.globalmedicalprojects.co.uk
Offers medical projects in Cambodia, India, Romania, Ghana, Tanzania, Mexico and China.

Kaya Responsible Travel

UK
info@kayavolunteer.com
+44 (0)161 870 6212
www.kayavolunteer.com
Kaya offer over 200 volunteer projects worldwide working with local communities and conservation initiatives from 2 weeks to 12 months. Placements are tailored to specific needs and skills of students, career breakers, retirees, families or groups .

For further information see page 160

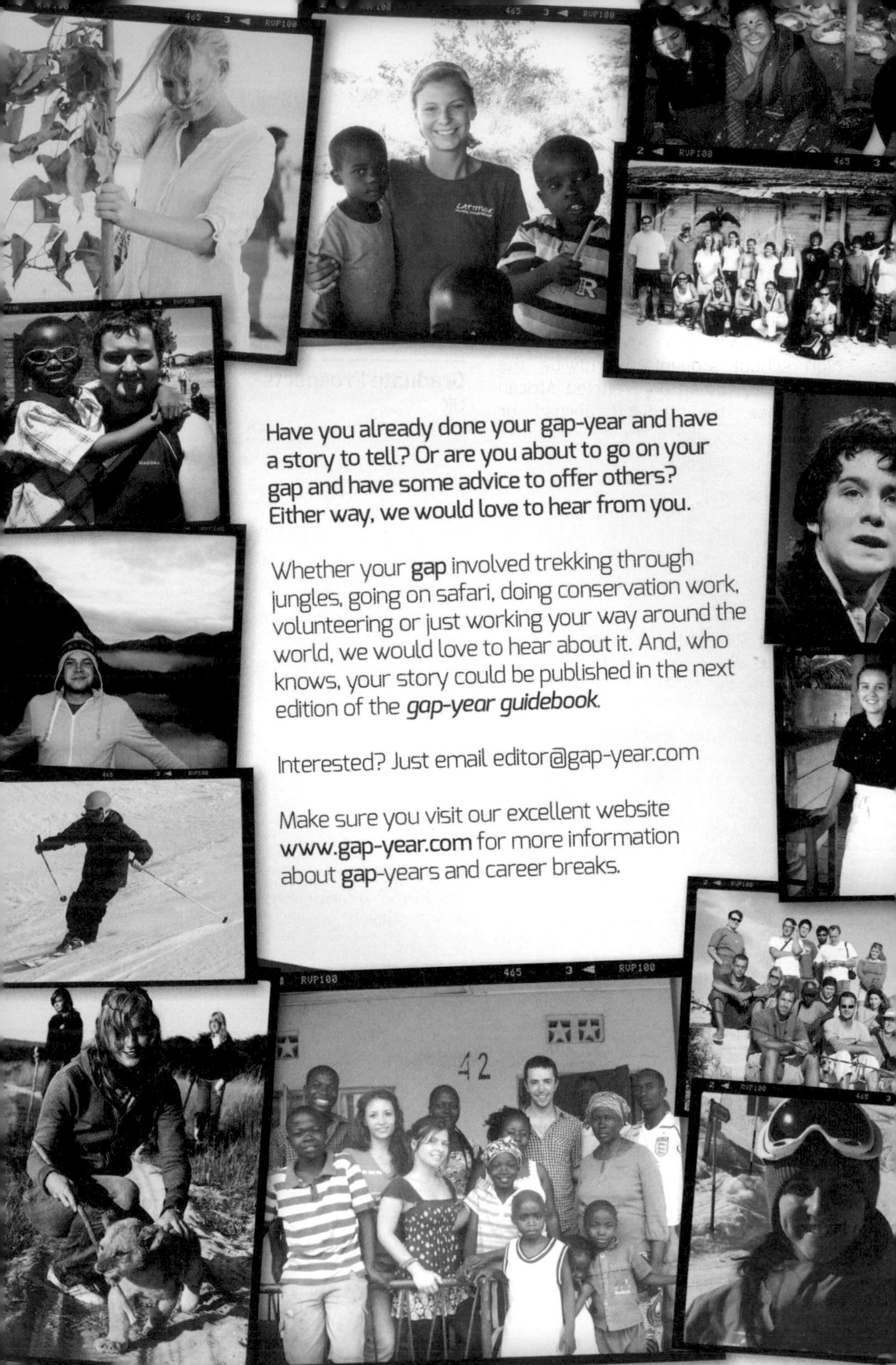
Have you already done your gap-year and have a story to tell? Or are you about to go on your gap and have some advice to offer others? Either way, we would love to hear from you.
Whether your gap involved trekking through jungles, going on safari, doing conservation work, volunteering or just working your way around the world, we would love to hear about it. And, who knows, your story could be published in the next edition of the gap-year guidebook.
Interested? Just email editor@gap-year.com
Make sure you visit our excellent website www.gap-year.com for more information about gap-years and career breaks.
42

Learning abroad

Academic year abroad

African Leadership Academy
South Africa
www.africanleadershipacademy.org
African Leadership Academy offers high school students worldwide the opportunity for an unparalleled African experience, by studying abroad or spending a gap-year with them.

Aidan College
Switzerland
info@aidan.ch
+41 (0)24 485 11 23
www.aidan-college-switzerland.ch
Aidan College provides a unique environment where you can combine a wide range of challenging pursuits, both intellectual and physical, to make the most of your gap year.

Class Afloat
Canada
info@classafloat.com
+1 902 634 1895
www.classafloat.com
Sail on a tall ship to exotic ports around the world and earn university credits. Also offers Duke of Edinburgh's Award Scheme.

Council on International Educational Exchange (CIEE)
USA
contact@ciee.org
1-207-553-4000
www.ciee.org
CIEE offer a wide range of international study programs such as study abroad programs for US students, gap-year abroad programs and seasonal work in the USA for international students.

Diablo Valley College
USA
+1 925 685 1230
www.dvc.edu
Diablo Valley College offers a varity of programmes to international students.

Graduate Prospects
UK
enquiries@prospects.ac.uk
+44 (0) 161 277 5200
www.prospects.ac.uk
Prospects - the UK's official graduate careers website.

IE University
Spain
university@ie.edu
+34 921 412 410
www.ie.edu/university
IE University is an international university which takes a humanistic approach to higher education: a university of entrepreneurs whose education and research model integrates knowledge and enables students to specialize flexibly.
For further information see page 200

Institute of International Education
USA
iiedirectories@eircom.net
www.iiepassport.org
Search for international education opportunities by country, city, subject and many other criteria.

John Cabot University
Italy
admissions@johncabot.edu
+39 06 681 9121
www.johncabot.edu
John Cabot University - and American university in the heart of Rome.
For further information see page 202

Leiden University
Netherlands
+31 (0) 71 527 2727
www.leiden.edu
Leiden University is one of Europe's foremost research universities. This prominent position gives our graduates a leading edge in applying for academic posts and for functions outside academia.

Minds Abroad
China
info@mindsabroad.com
+86 (871) 532 5089
www.mindsabroad.com
Minds Abroad is a US-based organization that conducts study abroad programs in China and India for both individual students and also customized faculty-led groups from college and universities across the US and Europe.

Office of International Education, Iceland
Iceland
ask@hi.is
+354 525 4311
www.ask.hi.is
Find information on all the higher education institutions in Iceland, as well as practical things to do before arriving, visas, admissions, residence permits, etc.

Queenstown Resort College
New Zealand
+64 3 409 0500
www.queenstownresortcollege.com
Offers a diverse range of world class courses and programmes including diplomas, internships, a range of English language courses, leadership development programmes, and short courses for visitors.

Scuola Leonardo da Vinci
Italy
scuolaleonardo@scuolaleonardo.com
www.scuolaleonardo.com
One of Italy's largest provider of in-country Italian courses in Italy, for students who wish to experience living and studying in Italy.

The English-Speaking Union
UK
jacqueline.finch@esu.org
+44 (0)20 7529 1561
www.esu.org
The English-Speaking Union organises educational exchanges in high schools (mostly boarding) in the US and Canada, awarding up to 30 scholarships a year to gap-year students.

The US-UK Fulbright Commission
UK
advising@fulbright.co.uk
0845 894 9524
www.fulbright.co.uk
The US-UK Fulbright Commission promotes peace and cultural understanding through educational exchange.

University of New South Wales
Australia
summerdownunder@unsw.edu.au
www.summerdownunder.unsw.edu.au
UNSW's Summer Down Under program gives students the opportunity to sample courses and experience university life alongside local and international UNSW students during the Australian summer.

Where There Be Dragons
USA
info@wheretherebedragons.com
+1 303 413 0822
www.wheretherebedragons.com
Runs semester, gap-year and college-accredited programmes in the Andes, China, Himalayas and more.

Art

Aegean Center for the Fine Arts
Greece
studyart@aegeancenter.org
+30 22840 23 287
www.aegeancenter.org
The Aegean Center offers small group and individualized study in the visual arts, creative writing and music. Facilities are located in two stunning locations: the Aegean islands of Greece and Italy's Tuscany.

ARTIS - Art Research Tours
USA
david@artis.info.
1-000-232-6893
www.artis-tours.org
ARTIS (Art Research Tours and International Studios) provide high quality international art and cultural study abroad programmes at affordable prices, located in beautiful art capitals throughout the world.

Atelier Montmiral
France
bmnewth@gmail.com
+44 (0)1843 853240
www.ateliermontmiral.com
Atelier Montmiral offer painting and printmaking courses in south-west France. Courses offered are seven or ten days in length and can accommodate all levels of ability.

Hellenic International Studies in the Arts (HISA)
Greece
hisa@paros-island.com
+30 6948516797
www.hisa-studyabroad.com
HISA endorses the gap-year concept and encourages students to immerse themselves in the culture, historical and classical landscape of Paros, Greece.

SACI Florence
Italy
info@saci-florence.edu
(39) 055-289948
www.saci-florence.org
A non-profit educational institution for students seeking fully accredited studio art, design, and liberal arts instruction.

SAI - Study Abroad Italy
USA
mail@saiprograms.com
+1 (707) 824 8965
www.studyabroadflorence.com
In conjunction with Florence University SAI offer the chance for international students to live in the heart of this bustling Renaissance city while experiencing modern Florentine life.

Studio Escalier
USA
info@studioescalier.com
www.studioescalier.com
Admission to their three month intensive courses in painting and drawing is by advance application only. Anyone is welcome to apply who has a dedicated interest in working from the human figure.

The British Institute of Florence
Italy
+39 (0) 55 2677 81
www.britishinstitute.it
Located in the historic centre of Florence within minutes of the main galleries, museums and churches, the British Institute offers courses in history of art, Italian language and life drawing.

The Marchutz School
France
+33 442 966 013
www.marchutz-school.org
Offers artists a unique opportunity to live, learn and grow in the incomparable Provencal setting of Aix-en-Provence, France.

Culture

Alderleaf Wilderness College
USA
+1 360 793 8709
www.wildernesscollege.com
A centre for traditional ecological knowledge offering innovative wilderness survival, animal tracking and nature courses in the Pacific Northwest of the United States.

American Institute for Foreign Study (AIFS)
USA
info@aifs.com
(203) 399 5000
www.aifs.com
One of the oldest, largest and most respected cultural exchange organizations in the world. Their programmes include college study abroad, au pair placement, camp counselors and staff.

Art History Abroad (AHA)
UK
info@arthistoryabroad.com
+44 (0)1379 871 800
www.arthistoryabroad.com
Travel through stylish Italy with a group of people just like you. Study beautiful art and architecture with brilliant tutors. Have fun and make friends for life.
For further information see page 188

Cultural Experiences Abroad (CEA)
USA
info@gowithcea.com
+1 800 266 4441
www.gowithcea.com
CEA sends thousands of students on study abroad programmes at multiple universities in 15 countries including Argentina, China, Costa Rica, Czech Republic, England, France, Germany, Ireland, Italy, South Africa and Spain.

Eastern Institute of Technology
New Zealand
info@eit.ac.nz
+64 6 974 8000
www.eit.ac.nz
Te Manga M,ori - EIT in Hawke's Bay offers the opportunity to study the Maori language and culture from beginners through to advanced level.

El Casal
Spain
john@elcasalbarcelona.com
+34 93 217 90 38
www.elcasalbarcelona.com
Based in Barcelona, El Casal offers the chance to soak in Catalan culture through a programme specifically for gappers who want to learn Spanish.

Istituto di Lingua e Cultura Italiana Michelangelo
Italy
+39 055 240 975
www.michelangelo-edu.it
The Michelangelo Institute offers cultural courses on art history, Italian language, literature, commerce and commercial correspondence, and ëLíltalia oggií.

John Hall Venice
UK
info@johnhallvenice.com
+44 (0)20 8871 4747
www.johnhallvenice.com
Courses based in Venice, London, Florence and Rome with a sensational combination of lectures, visits and classes in art, music, world cinema, Italian, cookery and photography.
For further information see page 190

Knowledge Exchange Institute (KEI)
USA
info@keiabroad.org
1 212 931 9953
www.keiabroad.org
Study abroad and intern abroad programmes designed to meet your academic, professional and personal interests.

Lexia Study Abroad
USA
info@lexiaintl.org
+1 800 775 3942
www.lexiaintl.org
Cultural study programmes that encourage students to connect with their community while pursuing academic research. Participate in the daily life and work of a community in countries worldwide.

Petersburg Studies
UK
alexandra.chaldecott@gmail.com
+44 (0) 7762 947 656
www.petersburgstudies.com
Offer a winter course designed to make St Petersburg accessible; its history, architecture, museums, music, literature and contemporary life are explored in the company of lecturers, guides and local contacts.

Road2Argentina
Argentina
info@road2argentina.com
+54 11 4826 0820
www.road2argentina.com
Study abroad in Argentina and learn all about the country and its culture.

SIT Study Abroad
USA
studyabroad@sit.edu
+1 888 272 7881
www.sit.edu/studyabroad/
Offers undergraduate study abroad programmes in Africa, Asia and the Pacific, Europe, Latin America and the Middle East.

Design & Fashion

Blanche Macdonald Centre
Canada
info@blanchemacdonald.com
+1 604 685 0347
www.blanchemacdonald.com
Courses available in make up, nail techniques, spa therapy and fashion.

Domus Academy
Italy
info@domusacademy.it
www.domusacademy.com
In 2009 Domus Academy joined the Laureate International Universities Network, an international high-level education network for art and design. The Academy offers 10 masters courses, attended by students from all over the world.

Florence Institute of Design International
Italy
registrar@florence-institute.com
+39 055 23 02 481
www.florence-institute.com
The Florence Institute is an international design school specialising in design courses for students from around the world, with all classes taught in English.

Istituto di Moda Burgo
Italy
imb@imb.it
(+39) 02783753
www.imb.it
International fashion design school Istituto di Moda Burgo offers high-quality courses in fashion design, fashion stylist and pattern making.

Metallo Nobile
Italy
school@metallo-nobile.com
+39 055 2396966
www.metallo-nobile.com
Courses in jewellery making and jewellry design, located in the heart of Florence.

NABA - Nuova Accademia de Belle Arti
Italy
+39 02 973721
www.design-summer-courses.com
NABA summer courses are divided into three levels: introduction, workshop and advanced. They have courses in design, fashion, graphic design and visual arts.

Polimoda Institute of Fashion Design and Marketing
Italy
info@polimoda.com
+39 055 275061
www.polimoda.com
Based in Florence, Polimoda Fashion School offers a variety of summer courses for those interested in all aspects of fashion.

RMIT Training
Australia
enquiries@rmit.edu.acu
+61 (0) 3 9925 8111
www.shortcourses.rmit.edu.au
Has a Career Discovery Short Course in fashion. An intensive programme which includes lectures by experienced industry professionals alongside studio workshops.

Film, Theatre & Drama

Actors College of Theatre and Television
Australia
info@actt.edu.au
+61 (0) 2 9213 4500
www.actt.edu.au
ACTT is Australia 's leading independent college for the performing arts and the only acting school in Sydney offering an extensive range of accredited acting courses and technical production courses for overseas students.

Ariège Arts
France
attenburrow@wanadoo.fr
+33 (0)5 61 65 44 36
www.ariegearts.com
AriËge Arts offer the chance to make documentary films in the French Pyrenees. Students learn the techniques of narrative in film and experience tuition by broadcast professionals.

EICAR - The International Film & Television School Paris
France
inquiries@eicar.fr
(+33) 01 49 98 11 11
www.eicar-international.com
Offers short summer workshops taught in English during July and September in the following areas: filmmaking, script writing, editing, HD Video and sound.

European Film College
Denmark
info@europeanfilmcollege.com
0045 86 34 00 55
www.europeanfilmcollege.com
Offering students a unique experience, an international learning environment offering young filmmakers and actors an intense eight-month course.

Flashpoint Academy
USA
info@tfa.edu
+1 312 332 0707
www.tfa.edu
This is a two-year, direct-to-industry college focusing exclusively on the following disciplines: film/broadcast, recording arts, visual effects and animation and game development.

Full Sail University
USA
+1 407 679 6333
www.fullsail.edu
If you're after a career in music, film, video games, design, animation, entertainment business, or internet marketing, Full Sail is the right place for you.

Hollywood Film & Acting Academy
USA
www.hwfaa.com
The traditional film school alternative, offering shorter more intense programme in feature films, movie making and acting.

Met Film School
UK
info@metfilmschool.co.uk
+44 (0)20 8832 1933
www.metfilmschool.co.uk
Practical courses for aspiring filmmakers. Short courses and one year intensive course available.

For further information see page 192

NYFA (New York Film Academy)
USA
film@nyfa.edu
+1 212 674 4300
www.nyfa.com
The New York Film Academy runs programmes all year round in New York City and at Universal Studios in Hollywood.

PCFE Film School
Czech Republic
info@filmstudies.cz
+420 257 534 013
www.filmstudies.cz
Offers workshops, semester and year programmes in filmmaking including directing, screenwriting, cinematography, editing and film history and theory.

The Acting Center
USA
+1 (323) 962-2100
www.theactingcenterla.com
No audition is necessary but an interview is required. Classes are available in evenings during the week and on weekends.

The Los Angeles Film School
USA
323 860 0789
www.lafilm.com
Has degree programmes in filmmaking, game production and animation. International students must acquire a student visa before studying in the United States.

TVI Actors Studio - Los Angeles
USA
+1 818 784 6500
www.tvistudios.com
Offers acting classes, workshops, and seminars for aspiring and professional actors.

Vancouver Film School
Canada
+1 604 685 5808
www.vfs.com
Centre for both training and higher learning in all areas related to media and entertainment production.

Music

Backbeat Tours
USA
tours@backbeattours.com
+1 901-272-BEAT (2328)
www.backbeattours.com
Offer 'rockin' rides' through Memphis music history on a vintage 1950s bus. The three hour Hound Dog Tour follows in the footsteps of the King of Rock 'n' Roll, Elvis.

Brooks Institute
USA
(805) 585-8000
www.brooks.edu
This school offers training in filmmaking, graphic design and photojournalism. The courses are designed for anyone who aspires to a career in photography, filmmaking, visual journalism, or graphic design.

Country Music Travel
USA
mail@countrymusictravel.com
www.countrymusictravel.com
Country music-themed vacations and escorted tours, from trips to Dollywood entertainment park, to music cities tours in Nashville and Memphis.

Jazz Summer School
UK
+44 (0) 208 989 8129
www.jazzsummerschool.com
Jazz Summer School offering places at the French jazz summer school in the South of France or The Cuban music school in Havana.

Scoil Acla - Irish Music Summer School
Ireland
info@scoilacla.com
+353 98 20400
www.scoilacla.com
Summer school established to teach Irish Piping (Irish War Pipes), tin whistle, accordian, banjo, flute and harp.

Songwriter Girl Camps
USA
info@songwritergirl.com
+1 615 323 2915
www.songwritergirl.com
They offer weekend songwriting camps for girls and women of all ages and ability!

SummerKeys
USA
+1-973-316-6220
www.summerkeys.com
Music vacations for adults in Lubec, Maine. Open to all 'musical people' regardless of ability with workshops and private tuition in a variety of instruments.

SummerSongs Inc.
USA
register@summersongs.com
+1 845 594 1867
www.summersongs.com
A not-for-profit corporation dedicated to the art and craft of songwriting.

Taller Flamenco
Spain
info@tallerflamenco.com
(+34) 954 56 42 34
www.tallerflamenco.com
Courses include flamenco dance, flamenco guitar, singing and percussion.

United DJ Mixing School

Australia
admin@djsunited.com.au
+61 (03) 9639 9990
www.djsunited.com.au

Offer an introductory course over two weekends, which gives the basics of DJ-ing and a longer comprehensive course that runs over twelve weeks.

World Rhythms Arts Program (WRAP)

USA
www.drum2dance.com

Classes develop your working knowledge of instruments, rhythms, dances, songs, styles, methods and applications.

Photography

c4 Images & Safaris

South Africa
shem@c4images-safaris.co.za
+27 (0) 12 993 1946
www.c4images-safaris.co.za

Offers short photography workshops and wildlife safaris in South Africa with emphasis on helping you to improve your photography skills.

Europa Photogenica

USA
FraPhoto@aol.com
www.europaphotogenica.com

This company provides carefully planned, high quality, small group photo tours designed for photographers of all levels who wish to improve their photographic skills using Europe as their classroom.

Joseph Van Os Photo Safaris

USA
info@photosafaris.com
(206) 463-5383
www.photosafaris.com

Joseph Van Os Photo Safaris guide you to some of the world's finest wild and scenic locations with the main purpose of making great photographs.

London Photo Tours & Workshops

UK
+44 (0)7738 942 099
www.londonphototours.co.uk

Offers short courses and photography workshops. Also specialises in small group photo travel.

Nigel Turner Photographic Workshop

USA
npturner@cox.net
+1 702 7695110
www.nigelturnerphotography.com

Offers wo-week workshops on photographic technique. Your chance to capture some of the most breathtaking scenery the American West has to offer.

Photo Holidays France

UK
aw@andrewwhittuck.co.uk
www.photoholidaysfrance.co.uk/index.html

A private photography school in the south of France offering one to one photography tuition specialising in landscape and portrait photography.

Photographers on Safari

UK
info@photographersonsafari.com
(+44) 01664 474040
http://www.photographersonsafari.com/index.htm

Offers a variety of exciting workshops in the UK and photography Safaris overseas, ideal for the wildlife lover.

Steve Outram Crete Photo Tours & Workshops
Greece
steveoutram@gmail.com
+30 28210 32201
www.steveoutram.com
Professional photographer Steve Outram uses his local knowledge of Zanzibar, Lesvos and western Crete to show you how to make the most of photographic opportunities and develop your skill as a photographer.

Languages

Chinese

Bridging the Gap China
China
enquiries@bridgingthegapchina.co.uk
+86 777 562 8765
www.bridgingthegapchina.co.uk
Courses combine Mandarin Chinese learning with sightseeing and cultural activities in the Yunnan province, China.

Hong Kong Institute of Languages
China
info@hklanguages.com
+852 2877 6160
www.hklanguages.com
Courses available in Mandarin and Cantonese. Good central location on Hong Kong Island.

Hong Kong Language Learning Centre
China
hkllc@netvigator.com
+852 2572 6488
www.hkllc.com
Language school in Hong Kong which specialises in Cantonese and Mandarin conversation and Chinese reading and writing for expatriates, locals and overseas Chinese.

The Dragon Trip Pte Ltd
UK
info@thedragontrip.com
+44 (0)207 936 4884
thedragontrip.com
The Dragon Volunteer Trips offer the chance to learn Mandarian, change children's lives and travel in breathtaking scenery.

For further information see page 166

WorldLink Education US Office
USA
www.worldlinkedu.com
WorldLink Education's Chinese language programme immerses you in Mandarin Chinese through class instruction, after-class tutoring, language exchanges with native speakers and a range of optional extra activities.

French

Accent Français
France
contact@accentfrancais.com
+33 (0) 467 58 12 68
www.accentfrancais.com
This school runs intensive French courses in Montpellier particularly for non-French speakers. They last between one week and several months.

Alliance Française de Londres
UK
info@alliancefrancaise.org.uk
+44 (0) 20 7723 6439
www.alliancefrancaise.org.uk
Alliance FranÁaise is a non-profit-making organisation whose goal is to teach French and bring cultures together (group classes and bespoke tuition available).

BWS Germanlingua

Germany
info@bws-germanlingua.de
+49 (0) 89 599 892 00
www.bws-germanlingua.de
BWS Germanlingua is based in Munich and Berlin; all staff are experienced teachers, and classes have a maximum of 12 students.

CESA Languages Abroad

UK
info@cesalanguages.com
+44 (0) 1209 211 800
www.cesalanguages.com
Perfect your language skills, experience the culture first-hand and have an amazing gap-year with CESA.

CMEF, Centre Mèditerranèen d'Etudes Françaises

France
centremed@monte-carlo.mc
+33 (0)4 93 78 21 59
www.centremed.monte-carlo.mc
Located in the South of France between Nice and Monaco - Monte Carlo. An international language school with a long tradition on French language courses.

En Famille Overseas

UK
info@enfamilleoverseas.co.uk
+44 (0)1273 588636
www.enfamilleoverseas.co.uk
En Famille organises tailor-made homestays in France, Spain and Italy, for individuals and groups. Travellers stay in a host family and learn the language, as well as joining in the life of the family.

France Langue (BLS)

France
bordeaux@france-langue.fr
+33 (0)5 56 06 99 83
www.france-langue.com
Based in Bordeaux and Biarritz, BLS offer a wide range of French courses to suit your exact requirements.

Institut Français

UK
box.office@institutfrancais.org.uk
+44 (0)20 7871 3515
www.institut-francais.org.uk
The Institut FranÁais is the official French Government centre of language and culture in London.

Institut Savoisien d'Etudes Françaises pour Etrangers

France
isefe@univ-savioe.fr
+33 (0) 4 79 75 84 14
www.isefe.univ-savoie.fr
An institute which specialises in teaching French as a foreign language to adults from non-Francophone countries.

Live Languages Abroad

UK
info@livelanguagesabroad.co.uk
+44 (0)7581 052300
www.livelanguagesabroad.com
At Live Languages Abroad we believe that the best way to learn a language is to live the language abroad. With our experience of providing language courses abroad, we will be able to provide you with the best course, accommodation and location.

For further information see page 194

Lyon Bleu International

France
learnfrenchinlyon@lyon-bleu.fr
+33 (0) 437 480 026
www.lyon-bleu.fr
Lyon Bleu International, in Lyon, is dedicated to teaching the French language and culture.

TASIS, The American School in Switzerland

Switzerland
admissions@tasis.ch
+41 91 960 5151
www.tasis.ch

Each year, the TASIS schools and summer programmes attracts students from around the world who share in a caring, family-style international community.

Vis-à-Vis

UK
+44 (0) 20 8786 8021
www.visavis.org

French courses offered in France. Various accommodation options are available, and there is the usual range of course length, level and intensity.

German

German Academic Exchange Service (DAAD)

UK
info@daad.org.uk
+44 (0) 20 7831 9511
www.daad.org.uk

The German Academic Exchange Service is the German National Agency for the support of international academic cooperation.

Goethe Institut

UK
info@london.goethe.org
+44 (0) 20 7596 4000
www.goethe.de/enindex.htm

The Goethe Institut is probably the best-known international German language school network.

Live Languages Abroad

UK
info@livelanguagesabroad.co.uk
+44 (0)7581 052300
www.livelanguagesabroad.com

At Live Languages Abroad we believe that the best way to learn a language is to live the language abroad. With our experience of providing language courses abroad, we will be able to provide you with the best course, accommodation and location.

For further information see page 194

Greek

International Center for Hellenic and Mediterranean Studies

Greece
programs@dikemes.edu.gr
+30 210 7560-749
www.cyathens.org

College Year in Athens offers unparalleled learning opportunities for English-speaking students seeking a programme of study in Greece.

Live Languages Abroad

UK
info@livelanguagesabroad.co.uk
+44 (0)7581 052300
www.livelanguagesabroad.com

At Live Languages Abroad we believe that the best way to learn a language is to live the language abroad. With our experience of providing language courses abroad, we will be able to provide you with the best course, accommodation and location.

For further information see page 194

Italian

Accademia del Giglio
Italy
info@adg.it
+39 055 23 02 467
www.adg.it
This quiet, small school takes about 30 students, taught in small classes. As well as Italian language courses, they offer classes in drawing and painting.

Accademia Italiana
Italy
study@accademiaitaliana.com
+39 055 284 616
www.accademiaitaliana.com
An international design, art and language school, the Accademia Italiana puts on summer language courses as well as full-year and longer academic and Masters courses.

Centro Machiavelli
Italy
school@centromachiavelli.it
+39 (0) 55 2396 966
www.centromachiavelli.it
Small language school in the Santo Spirito district of Florence. Set up to teach Italian to foreigners.

Europass
Italy
europass@europass.it
0039 055 2345802
www.europass.it
Europass has offered individual and varied Italian language courses in the heart of Florence since 1992.

Il Sillabo
Italy
info@sillabo.it
+39 333 9379126
www.sillabo.it
Il Sillabo, a small, family-run school, in San Giovanni Valdarno.

Istituto Europeo
Italy
info@istitutoeuropeo.it
+39 05523 81071
www.istitutoeuropeo.it
The Italian Language Music Art School in Florence. Enjoy yourself learning a beautiful language: come study Italian, music, art with us.

Live Languages Abroad
UK
info@livelanguagesabroad.co.uk
+44 (0)7581 052300
www.livelanguagesabroad.com
At Live Languages Abroad we believe that the best way to learn a language is to live the language abroad. With our experience of providing language courses abroad, we will be able to provide you with the best course, accommodation and location.
For further information see page 194

Lorenzo de' Medici
Italy
info@lorenzodemedici.it
+39 055 287 203
www.ldminstitute.com
Lorenzo de' Medici offers a combination of language and cultural courses.

Japanese

Kichijoji Language School
Japan
+81 (0) 422 47 7390
www.klschool.com
Language school in Tokyo which has been teaching non-native speakers the Japanese language and about Japanese culture since 1983.

The Yamasa Institute
Japan
info@yamasa.org
+81 (0) 564 55 8111
www.yamasa.org
The Yamasa Institute is an independent teaching and research centre under the governance of the Hattori Foundation. It is APJLE accredited.

Multi-languages

Caledonia Languages Abroad
UK
info@caledonialanguages.co.uk
+44 (0) 131 621 7721
www.caledonialanguages.co.uk
Short courses in French, Italian, German, Russian, Spanish and Portuguese in Europe and Latin America, for all levels, start all year round, most for a minimum of two weeks.

CERAN Lingua International
Belgium
customer@ceran.com
+32 (0) 87 79 11 22
www.ceran.com
CERAN runs weekly intensive residential language programmes in Dutch, French, German and Spanish.

EF International Language Schools
UK
+44 (0)207 341 8500
www.ef.com
EF International Language Schools offer you a range of programmes; perfect for perfecting an ëAí Level language, for a great Gap Year, for gaining internship experience in a foreign country.

ESL - Language Travel
UK
info@esl.co.uk
+44 (0) 20 7451 0943
www.esl.co.uk
ESL Language Travel offers immersion language courses abroad in over 20 languages in more than 300 inspirational destinations. The start dates and durations of our courses are very flexible allowing you to easily fit language learning abroad into your Gap Year.

For further information see page 184

Eurolingua Institute
UK
www.eurolingua.com
Eurolingua is a network of institutes teaching 12 languages in 37 countries. Group programmes give 15 hours of tuition a week, according to your level.

Inlingua International
Switzerland
www.inlingua.com
Inlingua International runs language colleges throughout Europe.

Language Courses Abroad
UK
info@languagesabroad.co.uk
+44 (0) 1509 211612
www.languagesabroad.co.uk
Languages courses available in French, German, Greek, Italian, Portuguese, Russian, Spanish and others.

Learn Languages Abroad
Ireland
info@languages.ie
+353 (0)1451 1674
www.learn-languages-abroad.co.uk
Learn Languages Abroad will help you find the course best suited to your needs.

Live Languages Abroad
UK
info@livelanguagesabroad.co.uk
+44 (0)7581 052300
www.livelanguagesabroad.com
At Live Languages Abroad we believe that the best way to learn a language is to live the language abroad. With our experience of providing language courses abroad, we will be able to provide you with the best course, accommodation and location.
For further information see page 194

Modern Language Studies Abroad (MLSA)
USA
info@mlsa.com
(815) 464-1800
www.mlsa.com
Offers language study abroad programmes in the following countries: Spain, Italy, France and Costa Rica.

OISE Oxford
UK
www.oise.com
Have their own unique teaching philosophy which leads students to gain confidence, fluency and accuracy when speaking another language taught by a native-speaker.

Portuguese

CIAL Centro de Linguas
Portugal
portuguese@cial.pt
+351 217 940 448
www.cial.pt
With schools in Lisbon and Faro, CIAL organises courses in Portuguese for foreign students.

Live Languages Abroad
UK
info@livelanguagesabroad.co.uk
+44 (0)7581 052300
www.livelanguagesabroad.com
At Live Languages Abroad we believe that the best way to learn a language is to live the language abroad. With our experience of providing language courses abroad, we will be able to provide you with the best course, accommodation and location.
For further information see page 194

Russian

Live Languages Abroad
UK
info@livelanguagesabroad.co.uk
+44 (0)7581 052300
www.livelanguagesabroad.com
At Live Languages Abroad we believe that the best way to learn a language is to live the language abroad. With our experience of providing language courses abroad, we will be able to provide you with the best course, accommodation and location.
For further information see page 194

Obninsk Humanities Centre
Russian Federation
lara.bushell@btinternet.com
+44 (0) 208 858 0614 (UK number)
www.dubravushka.ru
Learn Russian in Russia, with qualified English-speaking Russian teachers and students, at Dubravushka, Russiaís leading independent boarding school.

The Russian Language Centre
UK
info@russiancentre.co.uk
+44 (0) 20 7831 5330
www.russiancentre.co.uk
The Russian Language Centre in London offers a range of courses for groups and individuals: intensive, accelerated and private.

Spanish

Academia Hispánica Córdoba
Spain
info@academiahispanica.com
+34 957 488 002
www.academiahispanica.com
Small-group language tuition to suit all levels.

AIL Madrid Spanish Language School
Spain
+34 91 725 6350
www.ailmadrid.com/gap-year/home
They offer flexible gap-year programmes tailored to your needs. Learn Spanish in Madrid.

Amigos Spanish School
Peru
amigos@spanishcusco.com
+51 (84) 24 22 92
www.spanishcusco.com
Non-profit Spanish school. With every hour of your Spanish classes, you pay for the basic care of a group of underprivileged children at their foundation.

Apple Languages
UK
info@applelanguages.com
+44 (0) 1509 211 612
www.applelanguages.com
Offers Spanish courses throughout Spain and central and south America lasting from a week to nine months.

Bridge Year, Spanish Programs
Chile
info@bridgeyear.com
+44 (0) 20 7096 0369
www.bridgeyear.com/general
Study Spanish in Chile and Argentina! There are plenty of activities and excursions plus the homestay could be the most rewarding part of the experience.

CAPS - Home to Home
Spain
caps@hometohome.es
+34 93 864 88 86
www.hometohome.es
CAPS is a programme designed for young people who would like to spend a year in Spain helping in a School as Conversation Teaching Assistant.
For further information see page 138

CESA Languages Abroad
UK
info@cesalanguages.com
+44 (0) 1209 211 800
www.cesalanguages.com
Perfect your language skills, experience the culture first-hand and have an amazing gap-year with CESA.

Comunicacion Language School
Spain
info@comunicacionee.com
+34 950 33 34 15
www.comunicacionee.com
Come and enjoy professional Spanish classes, a great beach and lots of outdoor and cultural activities in Almerìa province, Spain. Stay in an apartment, a hostel or with a Spanish host family.

Don Quijote
UK
+44 (0)20 8786 8081
www.donquijote.org
Don Quijote is a leading network of schools teaching Spanish in Spain and Latin America.

Enforex
Spain
info@enforex.es
+34 91 594 3776
www.enforex.com
Learn to speak Spanish in Spain or Latin America. Over 30 centres all in Spanish speaking countries. Summer camps also available.

Expanish

Argentina
contact@expanish.com
+54 11 5252 3040
www.expanish.com
Learn Spanish in Buenos Aires located in the city centre, home to some of the oldest historical sites in the city.

International House Madrid

Spain
info@ihmadrid.com
+34 913 197 224
www.ihspanishinmadrid.com
Learning Spanish in Madrid allows you to bask in the culture of the Spanish people, converse first hand with Spanish native speakers, and enjoy the full beauty of this beautiful vibrant city.

Live Languages Abroad

UK
info@livelanguagesabroad.co.uk
+44 (0)7581 052300
www.livelanguagesabroad.com
At Live Languages Abroad we believe that the best way to learn a language is to live the language abroad. With our experience of providing language courses abroad, we will be able to provide you with the best course, accommodation and location.

For further information see page 194

Mente Argentina

Argentina
info@menteargentina.com
+44 (0)20 3286 3438
www.menteargentina.com
Visit Argentina and learn Spainish in a unique and different way.

Pichilemu Institute of Language Studies

Chile
info@studyspanishchile.com
+56 (72) 842488/449
www.studyspanishchile.com
Offers group, private, and certified courses. Students can surf and experience rural Chile.

Simón Bolivar Spanish School

Ecuador
info@simon-bolivar.com
+593 (2) 2234 708
www.simon-bolivar.com
One of the biggest Spanish schools in Ecuador. Spanish lessons are offered at the main building in Quito, the Pacific coast and the Amazon jungle.

Universidad de Navarra - ILCE

Spain
ilce@unav.es
+34 948 425 600
www.unav.es/ilce/english/
A wide range of programmes are offered for people who wish to travel to Spain to learn about the culture and the language.

TEFL

Cactus TEFL

UK
+44 (0)1273 725200
www.cactustefl.com
Cactus TEFL is an independent advice and admissions service working with over 125 TEFL course providers in 35 different countries.

Shane Global Language Centres

UK
marketing@shaneglobal.com
+44 (0) 20 7499 8533 (option 1)
www.shaneglobal.com

If you donít yet have your TEFL qualification, Saxoncourt runs full time four-week courses in London and Oxford, leading to either the Trinity TESOL diploma or the Cambridge CELTA qualification.

Sport

Air

Mokai Gravity Canyon
New Zealand
+64 6 388 9109
www.gravitycanyon.co.nz
Mokai Gravity Canyon boasts three world-class adventure activities: our extreme flying fox; our mighty 80-metre bungy; or feel the thrill of a 50-metre freefall on our bridge swing.

New Zealand Skydiving School
New Zealand
bookings@skydivingnz.com
+64 (03)3029 143
www.skydivingnz.com
New Zealand's longest established skydiving school with more programmes, facilities and experience than any other in the country.

Nimbus Paragliding
New Zealand
contact@nimbusparagliding.co.nz
64 03 326 7373
www.nimbusparagliding.co.nz
Paragliding courses and paragliding equipment sales in Christchurch, New Zealand.

Nzone
New Zealand
skydive@nzone.biz
+64 3 442 5867
www.nzone.biz
Experience the ultimate adrenaline rush of tandem parachuting while on vacation in New Zealand. Or train to be a Sport Skydiver yourself with an Accelerated Freefall Course, no prior training needed.

Paul's Xtreme Skydiving
Australia
info@australiaskydive.com.au
+61 2 6684 1323
www.australiaskydive.com.au
Challenge yourself to the thrill of a lifetime with an Xtreme Skydive with Paul's.

Skydive Arizona
USA
jump@skydiveaz.com
+1-520 466-3753
skydiveaz.com
Located halfway between Phoenix and Tucson is the largest skydiving resort in the world! The clear desert weather allows over 340 flying days a year.

Skydive Cairns
Australia
info@australiaskydive.com
+61 (02) 6684 1323
www.skydivecairns.com.au
Based in Cairns, North Queensland, this company specializes in tandem skydiving for both the novice and the professional skydiver.

Skydive Las Vegas
USA
+1 702 759-3483
www.skydivelasvegas.com
Skydive over the quiet and peaceful views of Hoover Dam, Lake Mead, the Colorado River, the Las Vegas Strip and the entire Las Vegas Valley. Tandem skydiving is the easiest, fastest, cheapest and safest way to make your first skydive.

Skydive Switzerland GmbH

Switzerland
+41 (0) 33 821 0011
www.skydiveswitzerland.com
Learn how to skydive in Switzerland. Tandem jumps, fun and glacier jumps also available.

Taupo Bungy

New Zealand
0800 888408
www.taupobungy.co.nz
Located in the Waikato River Valley, Taupo Bungy is considered one of the worldís most spectacular bungy sites. Featuring the worldís first cantilever platform and New Zealandís first ësplash camí.

Earth

Awol Adventures

New Zealand
info@awoladventures.co.nz
+(+64 9) 834 0501
www.awoladventures.co.nz
Join us in the Waitakere Rainforest for an amazing Auckland Adventure in the rainforest and beach adventure zone of Piha. We offer canyoning and abseiling experiences, as well as boogie boarding and cater for any level of ability.

Bucks and Spurs

USA
csonny@getgoin.net
+1 417-683-2381
www.bucksandspurs.com
Horseback riding vacations in Missouri. Round up cattle, see a horse whisperer use his natural horsemanship, and enjoy the ride at this Missouri Dude Ranch.

Gravity Assisted Mountain Biking

Bolivia
gravityoffice@gravitybolivia.com
+591 2 231 3849
www.gravitybolivia.com
Downhill mountain biking in Bolivia, also cross-country.

Jagged Globe

UK
+44 (0) 845 345 8848
www.jagged-globe.co.uk
Jagged Globe provides mountaineering expeditions and treks. They also offer courses which are based in Wales, Scotland and the Alps for both the beginner and those wishing to improve their skills.

Megalong Australian Heritage Centre

Australia
admin@megalongcc.com.au
+61 (02) 4787 8188
www.megalongcc.com.au
Horse riding in the Blue Mountains of New South Wales. Jackaroo and Jillaroo courses available.

Mountaineering Council of Ireland

Ireland
info@mountaineering.ie
+353 1 625 1115
www.mountaineering.ie
They have lists of mountaineering clubs in Ireland, useful information and can give advice on insurance.

Quest Japan

Japan
info@questjapan.co.jp
+81 (0)3 6902 2551
www.hikejapan.com
Guided walking holidays and tailor-made tours for individuals and small groups, from the island of Yakushima south of Kyushu, to the Kii mountain range in Central Japan, and the island of Hokkaido.

Qufu Shaolin Kung Fu School China

China
shaolinskungfu@gmail.com
+86 151 537 30991
www.shaolinskungfu.com
Shaolin Temple in Shandong, China, where you can learn Kung Fu and Mandarin Chinese.

Rock'n Ropes

New Zealand
info@rocknropes.co.nz
+64 7 374 8111
www.rocknropes.co.nz
A Rock'n Ropes course is 'as exciting as skydiving or bungee jumping'. Check out their website for full details.

Rua Reidh Lighthouse

UK
info@ruareidh.co.uk
+44 (0) 1445 771 263
www.ruareidh.co.uk
Courses in basic rock climbing available - one or two days also one to one teaching.

Sporting Opportunities

UK
info@sportingopportunities.com
+44 (0)208 123 8702
www.sportingopportunities.com
Sports coaching projects and sports tours for gap years, career breaks and volunteer travel.

White Peak Expeditions

UK
mail@whitepeakexpeditions.co.uk
www.whitepeakexpeditions.co.uk
Specialists in trekking and climbing for small groups in Nepal, Tibet, Kazakhstan/Kyrgyzstan, Ecuador and Peru. Climbs are suitable for the less experienced climber and are generally combined with trekking expeditions.

Snow

Alltracks Limited

UK
info@alltracksacademy.com
+44 (0) 1794 388034
www.alltracksacademy.com
This company runs high performance ski and snowboard instructor courses at Whistler in Canada. Ideal for a constructive and fun gap-year.

Altitude Futures - Gap Course Verbier

Switzerland
info@altitude-futures.com
+44 7539 071166
www.altitude-futures.com
Altitude Futures run official BASI and CSIA ski and snowboard instructor courses in Verbier, Whistler and Tignes. See www.altitude-futures.com for more details.

For further information see page 216

Basecamp Ski and Snowboard

UK
+44 (0) 20 8789 9055
www.basecampgroup.com
Basecamp is the no. 1 choice for anyone looking to take their skiing and snowboarding to the next level as part of a gap year or career break.

BASI (British Association of Snowsport Instructors)

UK
08448 044 099
www.basigap.com
Fast track your snowsport career and become a qualified ski or snowboard instructor in 10 weeks with approved BASIGap.

Cardrona Alpine Resort

New Zealand
info@cardrona.com
+64 3 443 7341
www.cardrona.com
Ski resort in New Zealand with ski school attached.

Harris Mountains Heli-Ski

New Zealand
hmh@heliski.co.nz
+64 3 442 6722
www.heliski.co.nz
If you are a strong intermediate skier or ski-boarder, then try this for that extra thrill!

ICE Snowsports Ltd

UK
info@icesi.org
+44 (0) 870 760 7360
www.icesi.org
With ICE you can attend official BASI courses in Val d'Isere, including a range of ski instructor courses and snowboard instructor courses.

Interski

UK
enquiries@interskisnowsportschool.co.uk
01623 456 333
www.interskisnowsportschool.co.uk
Interski Gap Year Instructor Training Courses run in the resorts of Aosta/Pila and Courmayeur. The only fully-inclusive gap course on the market with guaranteed employment for all successful students.

Non-Stop Ski

UK
info@nonstopsnow.com
+44 (0)1225 632 165
www.nonstopsnow.com
Offering a variety of ski and snowboard instructor courses in western Canada, New Zealand and France. An ideal gap-year, career break or chance to fast track into the ski industry.

OnTheMountain Pro Snowsports Instructor Training in Switzerland

Switzerland
gap@onthemountainpro.co.uk
+44 (0)27 288 3131
www.onthemountainpro.co.uk
Provides exceptional training and loads of fun, after training stay and enjoy the slopes until the end of the season at no extra cost.

Outdoor Interlaken AG

Switzerland
mail@outdoor-interlaken.ch
+41 (0) 33 826 77 19
www.outdoor-interlaken.ch
Ski/Snowboard school for complete beginners and for those who wish to brush up their skills. Have local guides who know the best trails, snow and shortest lift lines.

Oyster Worldwide Limited

UK
info@oysterworldwide.com
+44 (0) 1892 770 771
www.oysterworldwide.com
Guaranteed paid work in one of 3 famous ski resorts in Canada: The Rockies; Tremblant or Whistler. Intermediate skiers can become instructors in world-renowned Whistler with our included Level 1 course and qualification.

For further information see page 218

SITCo Ski and Snowboard Training New Zealand

New Zealand
ski@sitco.co.nz
+64 21 341 214
www.sitco.co.nz
SITCo has been training keen skiers and snowboarders since 2002. Come to Queenstown NZ to start living the dream. Accommodation, lift pass, training, qualifications, and a Heli-ski, plus much more are all included.

For further information see page 214

Ski Instructor Academy
Austria
info@ski-instructor-academy.com
+44 7528 131 567
www.ski-instructor-academy.com
Skiing lessons leading to ski instructor exams.

Ski le Gap
Canada
info@skilegap.com
+1 819 429 6599
www.skilegap.com
Offers ski and snowboard instructor training courses based in the popular Canadian resort of Tremblant.

Ski-Exp-Air
Canada
info@ski-exp-air.com
+1 418 520 6669
www.ski-exp-air.com
Ski-exp-air is a Canadian ski and snowboard school offering quality, professional instruction in a fun atmosphere.

SnowSkool
UK
team@snowskool.co.uk
+44 (0)1962 713342
www.snowskool.co.uk
Ski and Snowboard instructor courses in Canada, New Zealand, France and the USA. SnowSkool offers four, five, nine and eleven week programmes earning internationally recognised qualifications.

Whistler Summer Snowboard Camps
Canada
info@whistlersnowboardcamps.com
+1 604 902 9227
www.whistlersnowboardcamps.com
Summer camp for snowboarders who want to improve their skills.

Yamnuska Mountain Adventures
Canada
info@yamnuska.com
+1 403 678 4164
http://yamnuska.com
Located in Canmore, Alberta at the Banff National Park gates, Yamnuska are a premier provider of mountaineering, ice climbing, rock climbing, backcountry skiing, avalanche training and trekking experiences in the Canadian Rockies.

Various

Adventure Ireland
Ireland
info@adventure-ireland.com
+1 973 610 5125
www.adventure-ireland.com
Live and work in Ireland. Learn to surf, climb, kayak. Classes on Irish culture, history, language and literature.

Bear Creek Outdoor Centre
Canada
info@bearcreekoutdoor.com
+1 888 453 5099
www.bearcreekoutdoor.com
Offers courses in canoeing skills and also swiftwater rescue courses and wilderness first aid.

Camp Challenge Pte Ltd
Singapore
enquiries@camp-challenge.com
+65 6257 4427
www.camp-challenge.com
At Camp-Challenge, we believe that every youth is a cell of this global community. We provide the platform for this growth through our programmes.

Canyon Voyages Adventure Co
USA
+1 435 259 6007
www.canyonvoyages.com
River rafting, kayaking, canoeing, hiking, horseback, mountain bike and 4x4 trips available in the canyons of Utah.

Class VI River Runners
USA
info@class-vi.com
+1 888 383 9985
www.class-vi.com
Organised sporting trips for students and also family and corporate groups.

Mendip Snow Sport
UK
info@mendip.me
01934 852335
www.mendipsnowsport.co.uk
Centre is on the edge of the Mendip hills, where you can ski, snowboard, mountain board, as well as pursue archery, rifle shooting, power kiting, 4x4 driving, quad biking, rock climbing, abseiling and more.

Peak Leaders
UK
info@peakleaders.com
+44 (0) 1337 860 079
www.peakleaders.com
Make the most of your once in a lifetime experience in some of the worldís leading resorts whilst gaining internationally recognised instructor qualifications, plus plenty of CV enhancing extras.

Raging Thunder
Australia
info@ragingthunder.com.au
+61 (0)7 4030 7990
www.ragingthunder.com.au
Selection of day tours, once in a lifetime experiences available, such as Great Barrier Reef excursions, sea kayaking, ballooning and white water rafting.

Rapid Sensations Rafting
New Zealand
+64 7 374 8117, 0800 35 34 35
www.rapids.co.nz
White water rafting, kayaking and mountain biking on offer. They also have a kayaking school.

River Deep Mountain High
UK
+44 (0) 15395 28666
www.riverdeepmountainhigh.co.uk
Outdoor activities and activity Holidays in the Lake District. Where you can try canoeing, kayaking, gorge walks, abseiling, climbing, sailing, walking, trail-cycling or mountain biking.

River Rats Rafting
New Zealand
+64 7 345 6543
www.riverrats.co.nz
River Rats are located in Rototua, New Zealand and are specialists in rafting. They also offer a gondola ride up Mount Ngongotaha other activities.

Rogue Wilderness Adventures
USA
webmaster@wildrogue.com
+1 (541) 479 9554
www.wildrogue.com
Hiking, fishing and rafting trips are designed to give you a thrilling, relaxing and fun experience. Based in Rogue River Canyon.

Sport Lived Ltd
UK
0844 858 9103
www.sportlived.co.uk
Sporting gap-year company which arranges for young people to play sport overseas.

Wilderness Aware Rafting
USA
+1 719 395 2112
www.inaraft.com
Extreme tours, also downhill mountain biking, horseback riding and 4X4 tours in Arkansas and Colorado.

Water

Adventure Bound
USA
info@adventureboundusa.com
+1 970 245 5428
www.adventureboundusa.com
Whitewater rafting in Colorado and Utah. Also kayaking on the Colorado and Green Rivers.

Adventure Under Sail Ltd
UK
enquiries@adventureundersail.com
+44 (0)1305 858274
www.adventureundersail.com
TS Pelican of London is a unique square rigger that sails thousands of miles each year with a voyage crew of young people and the young at heart!

All Outdoors California Whitewater Rafting
USA
rivers@aorafting.com
+1 925 932 8993
www.aorafting.com
California River Rafting trips for the beginner, intermediate and experienced rafter.

Allaboard Sailing Academy
Spain
info@sailing.gi
+350 200 50202
www.sailing.gi
Tailor-made sailing courses available in Gibraltar.

Alpin Raft
Switzerland
info@alpinraft.com
+41 (0) 33 823 41 00
www.alpinraft.com
Located in Interlaken in the Swiss Alps, Alpin Raft offers fantastic fun and adventures - join us for some thrilling and scenic rafting, canyoning or bungy-jumping!

Aquatic Explorers
Australia
+61 2 9523 1518
www.aquaticexplorers.com.au
Aquatic Explorers is an SSI (Scuba Schools International) Facility offering new divers, as well as local and international scuba divers the best scuba diving training at Cronulla Beach in Sydney, Australia.

Barque Picton Castle
Canada
info@picton-castle.com
+1 (902) 634 9984
www.picton-castle.com
Explore Europe, Africa and the Caribbean as crew on a three-masted tall ship. No experience needed. Join Barque Picton Castle. Come aboard, come alive!

Bermuda Sub-Aqua Club
Bermuda
chairman@bsac.bm
+ 1 441 291 5640
sites.google.com/a/bsac.bm/bermuda-sub-aqua-club/
The Bermuda Sub-Aqua Club is a branch of the British Sub-Aqua Club and offers members a varied programme of club-organised dives; a safe, structured, proven training programme.

Cairns Dive Centre

Australia
info@cairnsdive.com.au
+61 7 40 510 294
www.cairnsdive.com.au
CDC offers daily day or live aboard snorkel and dive trips to the Outer Great Barrier Reef. We also offer SSI learn-to-dive courses from beginners through to instructor level.

Catalina Ocean Rafting

USA
catalinatours@gmail.com
+1 310 510 0211
www.catalinaoceanrafting.com
Half day and full day excursions around Catalina. Snorkelling trips also available.

Cave Diving Florida

USA
richard@superiordivetraining.com
+1 386 965 5832
www.superiordivetraining.com
Superior Dive Training is dedicated to providing the highest quality technical diving instruction available, offering a wide range of technical diving courses and instructor programs.

Challenge Rafting

New Zealand
challenge@raft.co.nz
+64 3 442 7318
www.raft.co.nz
Challenge Rafting offers exciting half-day whitewater rafting trips on the Shotover and Kawarau Rivers.

Dart River Safaris

New Zealand
info@dartriverjetsafaris.co.nz
+64 3 442 9992
www.dartriver.co.nz
Jet boat up the Dart River and kayak back or take the bus back. In between explore the ancient forest. The Dart River Valley featured in the Lord of the Rings films.

Deep Sea Divers Den

Australia
info@diversden.com.au
+61-7-4046 7333
www.diversden.com.au
Your guide to the finest Great Barrier Reef scuba diving and snorkelling off Cairns Tropical Queensland, Australia.

Dive Kaikoura

New Zealand
divekaikoura@xtra.co.nz
+64 03 319 6622
www.divekaikoura.co.nz
Professional instructors and small groups make Dive Kaikoura the ideal place to start your diving journey or advance your diving qualification.

Dive Pro Africa

Kenya
scubaexperiences@diveproafrica.com
+254 (0)716 430 725
diveproafrica.com
Dive Pro Africa organize professional scuba diving training packages, dive training courses and dive career internships where you can go all the way to instructor in just a few short months.

For further information see page 210

Dvorak Expeditions

USA
+1 719 539 6851
www.dvorakexpeditions.com
White water rafting, kayaking and fly fishing trips offered in Colorado, Utah, New Mexico, Idaho, Texas and Mexico.

Elite Sailing

UK
sue@elitesailing.co.uk
01634 890512
www.elitesailing.co.uk
Sailing school and RYA Training Centre based at Chatham, Kent. Suitable for absolute beginner to professional skippers and crew.

Gap Year Diver Ltd

UK
+44 (0)1608 738 419
www.gapyeardiver.com
Diver training and a wide range of activities and excursions included which make the entire experience more exciting and enjoyable.

Island Divers

Thailand
+66 (0)898732205
www.islanddiverspp.com
Looking for a new adventure? Then join our friendly and highly qualified staff for dive courses and dive trips for all levels, from beginner to professional.

Island Star Excursions

USA
info@islandstarexcursions.com
+1 808 661 7238
www.hawaiioceanrafting.com
Whale watching, rafting, sailing and speed boating all off the coast of Hawaii. Small groups only.

Kiwi River Safaris

New Zealand
rafting@krs.co.nz
+64 7 386 0352
www.krs.co.nz
White water rafting, scenic rafting and kayaking trips in Taupo.

Ocean Rafting

Australia
crew@oceanrafting.com.au
+61 7 4946 6848
www.oceanrafting.com
Ocean rafting around the coast of Queensland and the Whitsunday Islands which includes exploring Whitehaven Beach.

OzSail

Australia
bookings@ozsail.com.au
+61 7 4946 6877
http://ozsail.com.au
OzSail presents an extensive range of sailing and diving holidays from which to choose.

Penrith Whitewater Stadium

Australia
+61 2 4730 4333
www.penrithwhitewater.com.au
Introduction packages and courses in whitewater rafting offered and whitewater kayaking.

Plas Menai

UK
info@plasmenai.co.uk
+44 (0) 1248 670964
www.plasmenai.co.uk
Plas Menai, the National Watersports Centre in North Wales, offers RYA training courses in dinghy sailing, windsurfing, powerboating and cruising throughout the year and also run kayaking courses and sea kayak expeditions.

Pocono Whitewater

USA
info@poconowhitewater.com
+1 570 325 3655
www.poconowhitewater.com
Trail biking, paintball skirmish, kayaking and whitewater rafting available in the LeHigh River Gorge.

River Expeditions

USA
+1 800 463 9873
www.raftinginfo.com
Rafting in West Virginia on the New and Gauley Rivers.

Sabah Divers
Malaysia
sabahdivers2u@yahoo.com
+6088256483
www.sabahdivers.com
Sabah Divers operate one of the leading scuba diving education & training centres in South East Asia, running a full-service dive shop and offer scuba diving courses as well as recreational dives.

Scuba Junkie
Malaysia
info@scuba-junkie.com
+60 89 785372
www.scuba-junkie.com
Scuba Junkie is a fully licensed and insured PADI operation offering courses for beginners to advanced in the Celebes Sea.

South Sea Nomads
Indonesia
info@southseanomads.com
+6282145804522
www.southseanomads.com
A floating backpackers' hostel. Our aim is to provide dive and exploration safaris to locations that will appeal to anyone with a love of the sea and a sense of adventure.

Sunsail
UK
+44 (0)844 2732 454
www.sunsail.com
Sunsail offers the full range of RYA yacht courses as well as their own teaching programmes. Their instructors are RYA qualified.

Surfaris
Australia
surf@surfaris.com
1800 00SURF
www.surfaris.com
Surfaris - licensed to a greater range of surf breaks than any other operator in Australia. Located on the east coast of NSW, half-way between Sydney and Byron Bay in the coastal surfing village of Crescent Head.

Surfing Queensland
Australia
info@surfingqueensland.com
+61 07 552 011 65
www.surfingqueensland.com.au
Surfing Queensland has a surf school system with over 20 licensed surf schools operating on beaches from Coolangatta to Yeppoon.

Tall Ships Youth Trust
UK
info@tallships.org
02392 832055
http://tallships.org
The Tall Ships Youth Trust is dedicated to the personal development of young people through the crewing of ocean going sail training vessels. It is the UK's oldest and largest sail training charity for young people aged 12-25.

Taupo Kayaking Adventures
New Zealand
info@tka.co.nz
027 480 1231
www.tka.co.nz
Specialising in kayaking trips around the crystal clear water of Lake Taupo, under the shadow of an active volcano, and metres away from Maori rock carvings.

Ticket To Ride

UK
info@ttride.co.uk
+44 (0) 20 8788 8668
www.ttride.co.uk

Ticket to Ride develop all of our worldwide surfing adventures around the combination of doing something for yourself, something for others, travelling the world and having something to show for it all at the end.

Torquay Wind & Surf Centre

UK
info@kitesurfingtorquay.co.uk
+44 (0)1803 212411
www.kitesurfingtorquay.co.uk

Courses available in kitesurfing, kitebuggying and stand up paddle surfing.

Wavehunters UK

UK
mail@wavehunters.co.uk
+44 (0)1208 880617
www.wavehunters.co.uk

Wavehuntyers excel in providing people of all ages personal attention and specifically tailored surf lessons from experienced committed and professional surf coaches.

Sport Instructors

Britannia Sailing East Coast

UK
enquiry@britanniasailingschool.co.uk
+44 (0) 1473 787019
www.britanniasailingschool.co.uk

Based at Shotley Marina near Ipswich, Britannia Sailing is a well-established company with first-class facilities offering all aspects of sailing instruction and yacht charter.

Coaches across Continents

USA
brian@coachesacrosscontinents.org
http://coachesacrosscontinents.org

The worldís only development organization with a proven track record in using soccer as a vehicle for social change in developing communities, mobilizing volunteers, financial resources, and equipment to work with local teachers and community leaders in disadvantaged communities on three continents

Flying Fish UK Ltd

UK
mail@flyingfishonline.com
+44 (0)1983 280641
www.flyingfishonline.com

Flying Fish trains and recruits over 1000 people each year to work worldwide as yacht skippers and as sailing, diving, surfing, windsurfing, ski and snowboard instructors.

International Academy

UK
info@international-academy.com
+44 (0)2380 206 977
www.international-academy.com

Become a ski or snowboard Instructor on a gap-year or career break course. Experience world class resorts and gain recognised CSIA, CASI, NZSIA or SBINZ instructor qualifications.

Oyster Worldwide Limited

UK
info@oysterworldwide.com
+44 (0) 1892 770 771
www.oysterworldwide.com

Spend 5 months in Whistler, Canada. Take part in our 4 week CSIA Level 1 Training Course and then work as a Kids Instructor for the rest of the winter season. Excellent Oyster support throughout.

For further information see page 218

8 Sport

PJ Scuba

Thailand
pjscuba@gmail.com
+66 (0) 382 322 19
www.pjscuba.com
Offers the chance to study scuba diving to instructor level (PADI) and then teach in Thailand.

Ski Academy Switzerland

UK
info@skiacademyswitzerland.com
+44(0)113 3141510
www.skiacademyswitzerland.com
Provider of quality ski instructor programmes for gap-year students and for those on a career break or just fancy a challenge!

skivo2 Instructor Training

UK
dave.beattie@skivo2.co.uk
+44 (0)1635 278847
www.skivo2.co.uk
For those wanting to become Ski Instructors, an opportunity to train with the highest qualified coaches in the worldís largest ski area! Courchevel Trois VallÈes.

The Instructor Training Co

New Zealand
info@sitco.co.nz
+64 (0)21 341 214
www.sitco.co.nz
The Instructor Training Co offers you the opportunity to train for your ski instructor qualification in New Zealand. Five, eight and ten week courses available.

Working in the UK

Festivals

Brighton Festival
UK
info@brightonfestival.org
+44 (0) 1273 700747
www.brightonfestival.org
A handful of volunteer posts are open during the festival in May, working in the education and press office departments.

Cheltenham Festivals
UK
0844 880 8094
www.cheltenhamfestivals.com
This company runs festivals throughout the year, including jazz, science, music, folk, fringe and literary events.

Edinburgh Festival Fringe
UK
admin@edfringe.com
+44 (0) 131 226 0026
www.edfringe.com
Big and long-established late summer festival that has managed to stay cutting-edge.

Harrogate International Festival
UK
info@harrogate-festival.org.uk
+44 (0) 1423 562 303
www.harrogate-festival.org.uk
Harrogate International Festival hosts a number of arts festivals, and offers internships and short-term work experience placements during festivals.

Hay Festival
UK
admin@hayfestival.com
+44 (0) 1497 822 620
www.hayfestival.com/wales/jobs.aspx
One of the most famous literary festivals in the UK. Most departments take on extra workers for festival fortnight, including stewards, extra staff for the box-office and the bookshop and three interns.

Holloway Arts Festival
UK
info@therowanartsproject.com
020 7700 2062
www.therowanartsproject.com
Volunteering opportunities include being a steward for a day. Check out their website for further details.

Ilkley Literature Festival
UK
info@ilkleyliteraturefestival.org.uk
+44 (0) 1943 601 210
www.ilkleyliteraturefestival.org.uk
If you want to become a volunteer at the Ilkley Literature Festival fill in their online form. Jobs include stewarding and helping with mailouts.

Lichfield Festival
UK
info@lichfieldfestival.org
+44 (0) 1543 306 270
www.lichfieldfestival.org
Volunteers required backstage, to assist with stage management and to help with the education programmes. Contact Richard Bateman, volunteer coordinator, for more details.

Mananan International Festival of Music and the Arts

UK

information@erinartscentre.com

+44 (0) 1624 835 858

www.erinartscentre.com/get_involved/volunteer.html

Volunteers needed for stewarding duties, programme selling, transportation of artists, administration, catering, bar duties, technical support and manning galleries and shops.

Norfolk and Norwich Festival Ltd

UK

info@nnfestival.org.uk

+44 (0) 1603 877 750

www.nnfestival.org.uk

Volunteers needed from January to May to help out with administration, marketing and even event production.

Portsmouth Festivities

UK

info@portsmouthfestivities.co.uk

+44 (0)23 9268 1390

www.portsmouthfestivities.co.uk

Volunteers required to help out with the many varied festivities in Portsmouth.

Salisbury International Arts Festival

UK

info@salisburyfestival.co.uk

+44 (0) 1722 332 241

www.salisburyfestival.co.uk

Volunteering opportunities include stage manager, helping out with crowd management and leaflet distribution. Registered charity No. 276940.

Winchester Hat Fair

UK

info@hatfair.co.uk

+44 (0)1962 844600

www.hatfair.co.uk

This vibrant and entertaining festival takes over the centre of Winchester each year during the first weekend in July. Volunteers are needed to help out before and during the festival.

Youth Music Theatre

UK

+44 (0) 844 415 4858

www.youthmusictheatreuk.org

Internships are available in their London office for recent arts graduates or for professionals looking to change career direction. Also need UK-wide volunteers for one to two days per week.

Graduate opportunities & work experience

3M United Kingdom Plc

UK

www.3m.com

Industrial placement opportunities available, also graduate opportunities. See their website for more details.

Absolute Radio

UK

www.absoluteradio.co.uk/about

They have work experience places for over 18-year-olds currently studying media related courses. Send CV and covering letter.

Accenture

UK

ukgraduates@accenture.com

+44 (0) 500 100 189

www.accenture.com/ukschemes

Apply for graduate placements with Accenture, a global management consulting, technology services and outsourcing company.

Arcadia Group plc
UK
0844 243 0000
www.arcadiagroup.co.uk
They have placement postions in their finance and HR departments, suitable for those undertaking a year's placement as part of their degree. See their website for more details.

BBC Recruitment
UK
www.bbc.co.uk/careers
Work experience placements available across the UK in all areas. These are unpaid placements that can last up to four weeks. Competition is fierce so you need to apply at least a year in advance.

Cancer Research UK
UK
volunteering@cancer.org.uk
www.cancerresearchuk.org
Internships of 12 week duration for people who wish to gain valuable work experience in fundraising, as well as marketing, campaigning and communications. Registered Charity No. 1089464.

Civil Service Recruitment
UK
www.civilservice.gov.uk/recruitment
There are a number of specific schemes open to new and experienced graduates looking for a career change. If youíre successful, you could be posted to a number of government departments.

Deloitte
UK
www.deloitte.co.uk/careersevenings
Whether you're interested in a graduate role, an internship or a work placement, our exclusive careers evenings will tell you everything you need to know.

EMI Group plc
UK
ukrecruitment@emimusic.com
www.emimusic.com/about/careers/uk
See website for details about a career or work experience with one of the largest record companies in the world.

Engineering Development Trust (EDT)
UK
info@etrust.org.uk
01707 871520
www.etrust.org.uk
The EDT is the largest provider of STEM (science, technology, engineering and mathematics) enrichment activities for UK youth.

Foreign & Commonwealth Office
UK
+44 (0) 20 7008 1500
www.fco.gov.uk
See their website for more about careers and opportunities in the Diplomatic Service.

GlaxoSmithKline UK
UK
+44 (0) 20 8047 5000
www.gsk.com/careers/uk-students-graduates.htm
Industrial placements available.

HSBC Holdings plc
UK
+44 (0) 20 7991 8888
www.hsbc.com/1/2/student-careers
HSBC has a worldwide graduate and internship programme. See their website for further details.

IBM
UK
ibmstudent@uk.ibm.com
+44 (0) 870 542 6426
www-05.ibm.com/employment/uk/
IBM run a number of Student Schemes for 'very talented individuals' in all aspects of their business.

IMI plc
UK
info@imiplc.com
+44 (0)121 717 3700
www.imiplc.com
IMI operates a global graduate development programme and offers vacation work from June to September to penultimate year engineering (mechanical, electrical or manufacturing) students leading to possible sponsorship through the final year at university.

Kraft Foods
UK
www.kraftfoodscompany.com
Each year Kraft Foods offer plenty of graduate and internship opportunities across Europe.

L'OrÈal (UK) Ltd
UK
www.loreal.co.uk
LíOrÈal have over 2000 internships worldwide. Apply online.

Marks & Spencer Plc
UK
+44 (0) 20 7935 4422
http://corporate.marksandspencer.com/mscareers/opportunities/graduates
The M&S Graduate scheme offers many different opportunities in Retail Management, Head Office and HR.

Penguin Group UK
UK
jobs@penguin.co.uk
www.penguin.co.uk
Penguin offers business internships which last for eight weeks, journalism internships at the Financial Times which last for twelve weeks, the Pearson Diversity Summer Internship Programme as well as two-week work experience placements throughout the year.

RAF
UK
+44 (0) 845 605 5555
www.raf.mod.uk/careers/
Work experience places are available in RAF bases all over the UK. As each base runs its own work experience programme you need to check the RAF website to find one near you.

S & N Genealogy
UK
manager@genealogysupplies.com
+44 (0) 1722 717007
www.sandn.net/vacancies.htm
Gap-year students required to do office work such as document scanning.

Santander UK
UK
www.santanderukgraduates.com
If you are a graduate interested in working with Santander UK, submit an application for consideration when a position arises.

The Random House Group Ltd
UK
+44 (0)20 7840 8400
www.careersatrandom.co.uk/rhc_workexperience.asp
Work experience opportunities are available in editorial, publicity and marketing. Complete their online form to apply.

UNHCR

UK

gbrloea@unhcr.org

+44 (0) 20 7759 8090

www.unhcr.org.uk/interns/index.html

The UNHCR have six month internships which give the participant the opportunity to gain valuable experience working with refugees.

Wii Select

UK

enquires@wiiselect.co.uk

0207 801 2490

events.wiiselect.co.uk

Looking to earn some money to pay for your gap-year? Wii Select is a hospitality recruitment company that supply temporary staff to events and hospitality industry.

Seasonal

Brightsparks Recruitment

UK

recruitment@brightsparksUK.com

+44 (0)20 3627 9710

www.brightsparkslife.com

Immediate vacancies in bar, waiting and hospitality work in the UK.

Facilities Management Catering

UK

resourcing.fmc@aeltc.com

+44 (0) 20 8971 2465

www.fmccatering.co.uk

If you would like to work at the most prestigious sporting event of the year then log onto our website now and click on the work opportunities page to apply online.

Hot Recruit

UK

sales@hotrecruit.com

+44 0845 468 0568

www.hotrecruit.com

Search for temporary work, paid or unpaid, charity and fundraising jobs and seasonal holiday jobs abroad.

PGL

UK

enquiries@pgl.co.uk

0844 3710 101

www.pgl.co.uk/gapyear

As the UK's market-leading provider of residential activity holidays and educational courses for children, PGL have an immense variety of Gap Year Jobs to offer for your Gap Year: and we pay you!

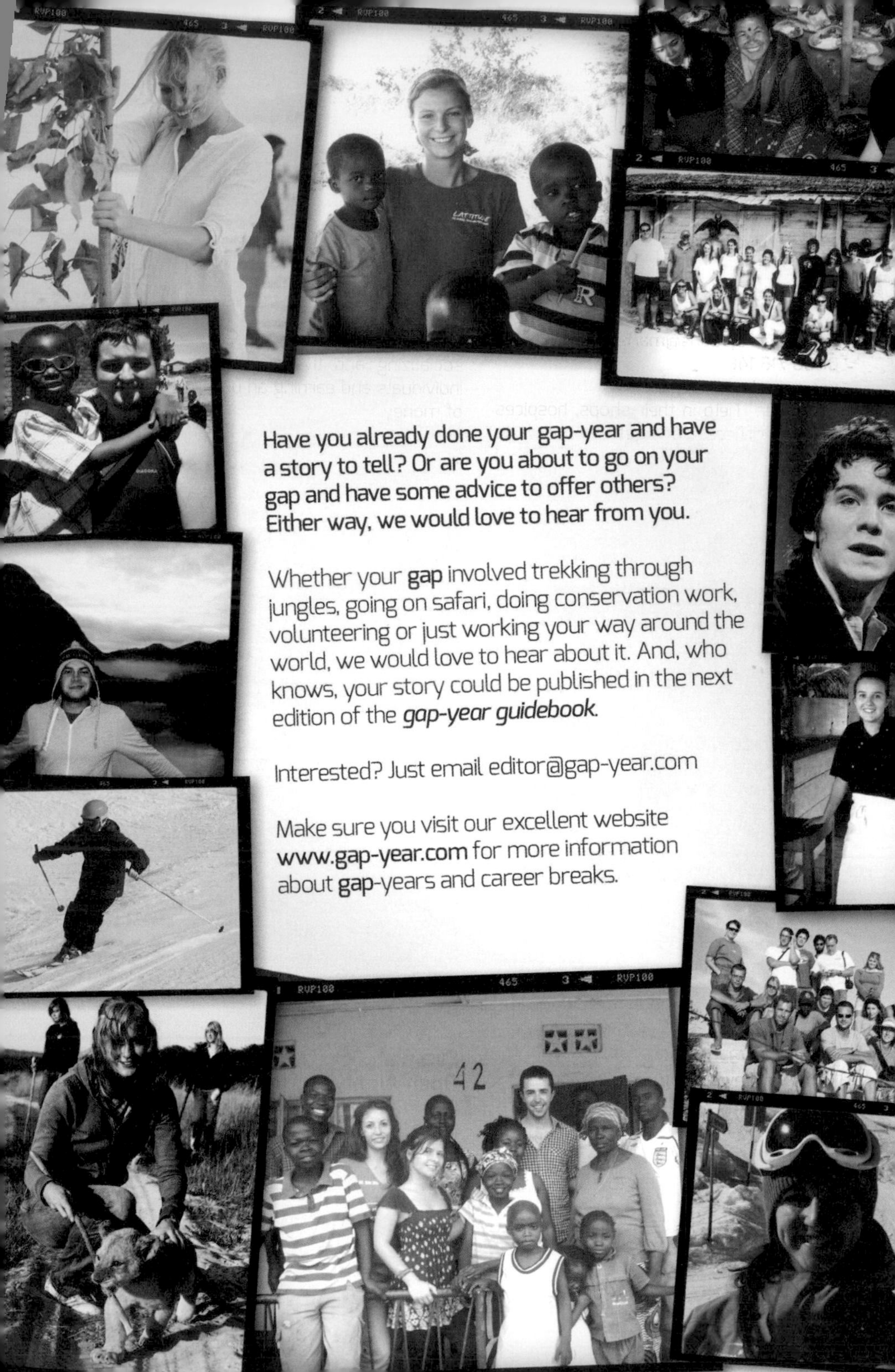
Have you already done your gap-year and have a story to tell? Or are you about to go on your gap and have some advice to offer others? Either way, we would love to hear from you.
Whether your gap involved trekking through jungles, going on safari, doing conservation work, volunteering or just working your way around the world, we would love to hear about it. And, who knows, your story could be published in the next edition of the gap-year guidebook.
Interested? Just email editor@gap-year.com
Make sure you visit our excellent website www.gap-year.com for more information about gap-years and career breaks.
42

Fundraising

Marie Curie Cancer Care (Head Office)

UK
supporter.relations@mariecurie.org.uk
0800 716 146
www.mariecurie.org.uk
Volunteer. Help in their shops, hospices and/or offices, or get involved in fundraising for Marie Curie (Registered Charity No. 207994).

Scope

UK
supportercare@scope.org.uk
+44 (0)20 7619 7100
www.scope.org.uk
Cerebral palsy charity (No. 208231) which needs your help in raising funds.

SOS Rhino

Malaysia
info@sosrhino.org
+60 88 388 405
www.sosrhino.org
SOS Rhino needs donations to help them in their work to save the Borneo rhinoceros. Why not choose them as your charity fundraising beneficiary?

War on Want

UK
support@waronwant.org
+44 (0)20 7324 5040
www.waronwant.org
Fundraise for War on Want. Registered Charity No. 208724.

Wesser UK

UK
recruitment@wesser.co.uk
01462 704 860
www.wesser.co.uk
Wesser offers you the chance to fundraise for St John Ambulance, work outside, socializing and living with like-minded individuals and earning an uncapped sum of money.

Volunteering

Action Centres UK

UK
isabelharlow@actioncentres.co.uk
+44 (0)1604 499 699
www.go-gap.com
Go-Gap provides international volunteers with the opportunity to gain valuable service-work experience in a safe and comfortable Christian environment.

Amnesty International

UK
sct@amnesty.org.uk
+44 (0) 20 7033 1777
www.amnesty.org.uk/volunteer.asp
Amnesty International (registered charity No: 1051681) have a selection of volunteering vacancies throughout their UK offices. Volunteer roles are advertised on their website. Speculative applications are not accepted.

Beamish, The North of England Open Air Museum

UK
info@friendsofbeamish.co.uk
+44 (0) 191 370 1104
friendsofbeamish.co.uk/volunteers.html
Beamish Museum is a unique place. They rely on volunteers to help them in their work: from taking visitor surveys to working on their many restoration projects.

Beanstalk

UK

+44 (0)20 7729 4087

www.beanstalkcharity.org.uk

Volunteer Reading Help is a national charity, helping children who struggle with their reading to develop a love of reading and learning.

Blue Cross

UK

info@bluecross.org.uk

+44 (0) 300 777 1897

www.bluecross.org.uk

The Blue Cross is Britain's pet charity (No. 224392), providing practical support, information and advice for pet and horse owners. For information on volunteering visit their website.

Born Free Foundation

UK

info@bornfree.org.uk

+44 (0)1403 240 170

www.bornfree.org.uk

The Born Free Foundation has grown into a global force for wildlife. Volunteer with their major international projects devoted to animal welfare, conservation and education. They also list other possible overseas volunteering vacancies.

Cats Protection League

UK

helpline@cats.org.uk

+44 (0) 8707 708 649

www.cats.org.uk

Volunteering opportunities available in a wide variety of roles, please see our website for more details. Registered charity No. 203644.

Central Scotland Forest Trust

UK

simon.rennie@csft.org.uk

+44 (0)1501 824770

www.csft.org.uk

CSFT organises volunteers to help with ecological improvements in Central Scotland. Work includes fence repairing and path building. Reg Charity SC015341

Centre for Alternative Technology

UK

vacancy@cat.org.uk

+44 (0) 1654 705 950

www.cat.org.uk

CAT has volunteer placements. Reg Charity 265239

Challenge Team UK

UK

info@challengeteamuk.org

(+44) 01323 721047

www.challengeteamuk.org

The Challenge Team UK is a group of young volunteers who educate teenagers about healthy sexuality.

Change Agents UK

UK

contact@changeagents.org.uk

01572 723419

www.changeagents.org.uk

CHANGE AGENTS UK are creating a force for a sustainable future; working with young people, graduates, businesses and communities motivated by sustainability to create change.

Children with Cancer

UK

info@childrenwithcancer.org.uk

+44 (0)20 7404 0808

www.childrenwithcancer.org.uk

Volunteer with us and help to save young lives. If you've got some spare time, and would like to help our charity, why not join our volunteer team.

Children's Country Holidays Fund
UK
volunteering@cchf-allaboutkids.org.uk
+44 (0) 1273 847 770
www.cchf-allaboutkids.org.uk
CCHF (registered charity number 206958) Volunteers required to help out on week long or weekend activity breaks for severely disadvantaged children.

Christian Aid Gap Year
UK
info@christian-aid.org
+44 (0)20 7620 4444
http://www.christianaid.org.uk/getinvolved/volunteer/gapyear/gap_year.aspx
Have placements between mid-August and June each year for volunteers in their offices around the UK.

CSV (Community Service Volunteers)
UK
volunteer@csv.org.uk
+44 (0) 800 374 991
www.csv.org.uk/gapyear
CSV is the largest volunteering organisation in the UK. Has full-time volunteering programme provides hundreds of free gap-year placements at social care projects throughout the UK.

Dogs Trust
UK
+44 (0)20 7837 0006
www.dogstrust.org.uk
Volunteers needed to help out in the following areas: fundraising, dog walking, dog socialising and pre-adoption home visiting. Registered Charity No. 227523.

Elizabeth Finn Care
UK
info@elizabethfinn.org.uk
+44 (0) 20 8834 9200
www.elizabethfinncare.org.uk
Charity (No. 207812) that aims to help those with limited resources who live in their own homes, or by providing accommodation for older people in their own care homes. Volunteers always needed.

Emmaus UK
UK
contact@emmaus.org.uk
+44 (0) 1223 576 103
www.emmaus.org.uk
Emmaus Communities (Registered Charity No. 1064470) offer homeless people a home and full time work refurbishing and selling furniture and other donated goods. They list various volunteer opportunities on their website.

English Heritage
UK
volunteer.enquiries@english-heritage.org.uk
+44 (0)870 333 1181
www.english-heritage.org.uk
English Heritage are looking for people who are aged 18 and over to assist with workshops, tours and other activities associated with learning and school visits.

Friends of The Earth
UK
+44 (0) 20 7490 1555
www.foe.co.uk
Friends of The Earth welcomes volunteers at their head office in London, or at any of their regional offices. Registered Charity No. 281681

Global Adventure Challenges Ltd
UK
enquiries@globaladventurechallenges.com
+44 (0) 1244 676 454
www.globaladventurechallenges.com
Raise money for your chosen charity whilst having the adventure of a lifetime. Many adventures to choose from are listed on their website.

Greenpeace
UK
recruitment.uk@greenpeace.org
+44 (0) 20 7865 8100
www.greenpeace.org.uk
Greenpeace need volunteers either as an active supporter or in their London office to help out with their administration.

Groundwork Oldham & Rochdale
UK
+44 (0) 161 624 1444
www.northwest.groundwork.org.uk
Whether youíre looking to gain work experience, fulfil your passion in environmental issues or simply want to give a few hours a week to a cause that benefits your community Groundwork can help you to do something special.

Hearing Dogs for Deaf People
UK
volunteer@hearingdogs.org.uk
+44 (0)1844 348 100
www.hearingdogs.org.uk
Become a volunteer with Hearing Dogs for Deaf People (Registered charity No.293358). Contribute to the life changing work of this Charity by visiting their website and clicking on 'Get involved'.

ILA (Independent Living Alternatives)
UK
paservices@ilanet.co.uk
+44 (0) 20 8906 9265
www.ilanet.co.uk
Aims to enable people who need personal assistance, to be able to live independently in the community and take full control of their lives.

Latin Link
UK
+44 (0)118 957 7100
www.stepteams.org
Latin Link sends teams and individuals to work in mission with Latin American and Spanish Christians for between three weeks and four months. Registered Charity No. 1020826.

Macmillan Cancer Support (UK Office - Volunteering)
UK
recruitment@macmillan.org.uk
+44 (0) 20 7840 7840
www.macmillan.org.uk
Share your skills to improve the lives of people affected by cancer. Assist our fundraising activities or support us in our offices and gain new experience whilst having fun. Registered Charity No. 261017.

Mind
UK
contact@mind.org.uk
+44 (0) 20 8519 2122
www.mind.org.uk
Mind (Registered Charity No. 424348) would like to hear from you if you would like to take part in a fundraising event, or have an idea for fundraising for the charity.

Museum of London

UK
recruitment@museumoflondon.org.uk
+44 (0) 20 7814 5792
www.museumoflondon.org.uk
Volunteer at the Museum of London. See their website for further details.

NSPCC

UK
recruitmentenquiry@nspcc.org.uk
+44 (0)20 7825 2500
www.nspcc.org.uk
Volunteers needed to help with fundraising, office work, manning the switchboard at Childline or even helping on a specific project. (Reg. Charity No. 216401)

PDSA

UK
0800 854 194
www.pdsa.org.uk
A wide range of volunteering opportunities offered. Use the contact form on their website to find out about opportunities in the UK and Ireland. Registered Charity No. 208217.

Plan UK

UK
+44 (0) 20 7608 1311
www.plan-uk.org
Plan UK works with children and their communities in the worldís poorest countries aiming to vastly improve their quality of life. Volunteer opportunities and internships available.

Rainforest Concern

UK
info@rainforestconcern.org
+44 (0)1225 481 151
www.rainforestconcern.org
Sends volunteers to Ecuador, Costa Rica and Panama to work with important conservation programmes.

RNLI

UK
+44 (0) 845 045 6999
www.rnli.org.uk
Volunteer lifeguards required. Registered Charity No. 209603.

Rock UK

UK
job.enquiry@rockuk.org
+44 (0) 844 8000 222
www.rockuk.org
At Frontier Centre, Rock UK has a volunteer programme taking on overseas volunteers. Placements are for nine months from 2012, volunteers must be at least 18 years old and are typically up to 28 years old.

Royal Botanic Gardens

UK
info@kew.org
+44 (0) 20 8332 5655
www.kew.org/about-kew/volunteers
Volunteers can help out at the Royal Botanic Gardens in four different areas: school & family, discovery, information and horticultural volunteers.

RSPB (Royal Society for the Protection of Birds)

UK
volunteers@rspb.org.uk
+44 (0) 1767 680 551
www.rspb.org.uk/volunteering/residential
Want a career in conservation? Check out the volunteering pages on the RSPBs website for advice, volunteering opportunities and case studies (Registered Charity No. 207076)

RSPCA

UK
0300 1234 555
www.rspca.org.uk/volunteer
The RSPCA (registered charity no. 219099) are always looking for volunteers. Check out their website for vacancies in a home near you.

Samaritans

UK
volunteering@samaritans.org
+44 (0)8705 62 72 82
www.samaritans.org
The Samaritans (Registered Charity No. 219432) depend entirely on volunteers. They are there 24/7 for anyone who needs help. Can you spare the time to help them?

Sense

UK
info@sense.org.uk
+44 (0) 845 127 0060
www.sense.org.uk
Volunteers always required by Sense (Registered Charity No. 289868) in a variety of areas. See their website for further details of how you can help.

SHAD

UK
volunteering@shad.org.uk
+44 (0) 20 8675 6095
www.shad.org.uk
Personal Assistants are needed to enable physically disabled adults to live independently in their own homes.

Shelter

UK
info@shelter.org.uk
+44 (0) 844 515 2000
www.shelter.org.uk
Volunteering opportunities available throughout the UK. Registered Charity No. 263710.

TCV The Conservation Volunteers

UK
information@tcv.org.uk
+44 (0) 1302 388 883
www.tcv.org.uk
The Conservation Volunteers have been reclaiming green places since 1959.

The National Trust

UK
enquiries@nationaltrust.org.uk
0844 800 1895
www.nationaltrust.org.uk/get-involved/volunteer
Learn new skills whilst helping to conserve the UK's heritage. Volunteering opportunities can be found on their website. Registered Charity No. 205846.

The National Trust for Scotland

UK
+44 (0) 844 493 2100
www.nts.org.uk/Volunteering
The National Trust for Scotland is a conservation charity that protects and promotes Scotland's natural and cultural heritage. Contact them to find out about volunteering opportunities.

The Prince's Trust

UK
webinfops@princes-trust.org.uk
+44 (0)20 7543 1234
www.princes-trust.org.uk
Volunteer with the Prince's Trust (Registered Charity No. 1079675) and help young people achieve something with their lives. Opportunities in fundraising, personal mentoring, volunteer co-ordinator and training.

The Simon Community

UK
info@simoncommunity.org.uk
+44 (0) 20 7485 6639
www.simoncommunity.org.uk
The Simon Community is a partnership of homeless people and volunteers living and working with Londonís homeless. They need full-time residential volunteers all year round. Registered Charity No. 283938.

The Waterway Recovery Group
UK
iwa@waterways.org.uk
01494 783453
www.waterways.org.uk
WRG has helped restore many derelict waterways throughout Britain. Thanks to the hard work of the volunteers many canals have been reopened.

The Wildlife Trusts
UK
enquiry@wildlifetrusts.org
+44 (0) 1636 6777 11
www.wildlifetrusts.org
The Wildlife Trusts (Registered Charity No. 207238) always need volunteers. Check out their website or contact your local office for information about vacancies in your area.

UNICEF UK
UK
+44 (0) 844 801 2414
www.unicef.org.uk
UNICEF UK regularly recruit voluntary interns to support teams within the UK. These internships usually last between two and six months and are based at offices in London or Billericay.

vInspired
UK
info@vinspired.com
+44 (0) 800 089 9000
www.vinspired.com
vInspired connects 14-25 year olds with volunteering opportunities.

Vitalise
UK
volunteer@vitalise.org.uk
+44 (0) 845 330 0148
www.vitalise.org.uk
Vitalise is a national charity providing short breaks and other services for people with physical disabilities, visually impaired people, and carers. They offer inspirational opportunities for volunteers through one of the largest, most diverse volunteer programmes in the UK.

Whizz-Kidz
UK
volunteers@whizz-kidz.org.uk
+44 (0)20 7233 6600
www.whizz-kidz.org.uk
Whizz-Kidz is looking for volunteers to join their national Volunteer Network, you just need to be 16 or older. If you have an open mind, tons of enthusiasm and a positive attitude there are opportunities to suit you!

Wild Futures' Monkey Sanctuary
UK
volunteer@wildfutures.org
0844 272 1271
www.wildfutures.org
Residential volunteering opportunities available, offering an ideal opportunity to learn more about primates and their conservation and welfare whilst also helping with the day-to-day running of a busy sanctuary.

Youth Hostel Association
UK
volunteers@yha.org.uk
0800 0191 700
www.yha.org.uk/volunteering
If you've got some free time and would like to support YHA, there are many volunteering activities you can get involved with.

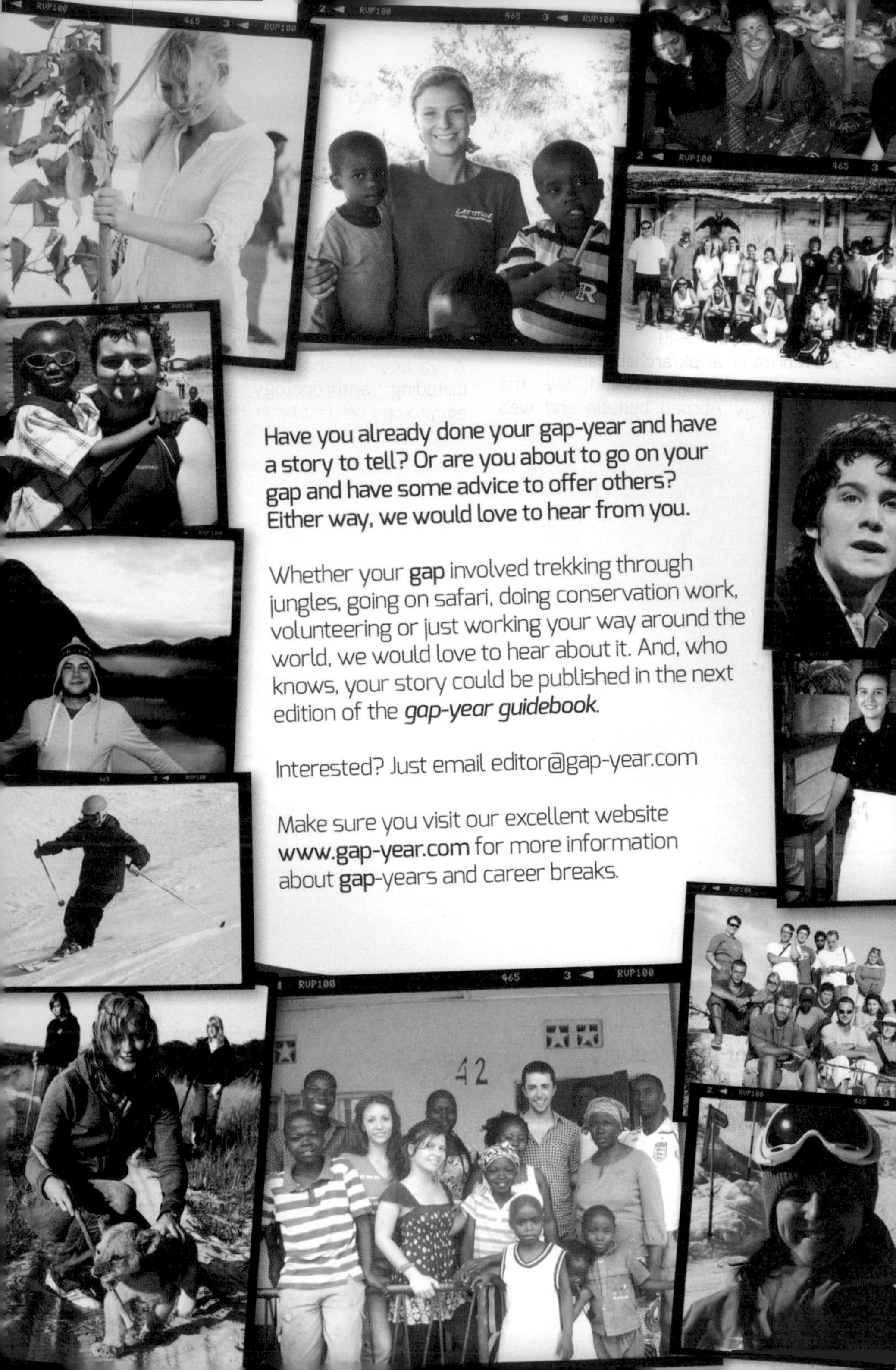

Have you already done your gap-year and have a story to tell? Or are you about to go on your gap and have some advice to offer others? Either way, we would love to hear from you.

Whether your **gap** involved trekking through jungles, going on safari, doing conservation work, volunteering or just working your way around the world, we would love to hear about it. And, who knows, your story could be published in the next edition of the ***gap-year guidebook***.

Interested? Just email editor@gap-year.com

Make sure you visit our excellent website **www.gap-year.com** for more information about **gap**-years and career breaks.

Archaeology

Archaeology Abroad
UK
arch.abroad@ucl.ac.uk
+44 (0) 20 8537 0849
www.britarch.ac.uk/archabroad
For info on digs abroad try the Archaeology Abroad bulletin and web pages.

Council for British Archaeology
UK
info@britarch.ac.uk
+44 (0) 1904 671 417
www.britarch.ac.uk
CBA's magazine, British Archaeology, contains information about events and courses as well as digs. Reg Charity 287815.

School of Archaeology & Ancient History
UK
arch-anchist@le.ac.uk
+44 (0) 116 252 2611
www.le.ac.uk/archaeology/dl/dl_intro.html
Offers a series of modules in archaeology which can be studied purely for interest, or as part of a programme towards a Certificate in Archaeology.

University College London - Institute of Archaeology
UK
ioa-ugadmissions@ucl.ac.uk
+44 (0) 207 679 7495
www.ucl.ac.uk/archaeology/
UCL offers a range of short courses in archaeology many of which are open to members of the public.

University of Bristol - Department of Archaeology & Anthropology
UK
sart-ugadmin@bristol.ac.uk
+44 (0)117 954 6050
www.bristol.ac.uk/archanth
A variety of short courses offered, including: anthropology, archaeology, egyptology, history, Latin, Minoan, Roman and techniques. They also have a one week intensive 'get started in archaeology' course.

Art

Cardiff School of Art and Design
UK
csad@cardiffmet.ac.uk
+44 (0) 29 2041 6154
www.cardiff-school-of-art-and-design.org
They run a ten week summer school programme designed to introduce you to the variety of art and design.

Heatherley School of Art
UK
info@heatherleys.org
+44 (0) 20 7351 4190
www.heatherleys.org
Offers various summer courses in art as well as part-time and full-time courses.

The Prince's Drawing School
UK
admin@princesdrawingschool.org
+44 (0) 20 7613 8568
www.princesdrawingschool.org
The Prince's Drawing School is an educational charity (No. 1101538) dedicated to teaching drawing from observation. Daytime, evening and summer school courses are run for artists and the general public.

University College London - Slade School of Fine Art

UK

slade.enquiries@ucl.ac.uk

+44 (0) 20 7679 2313

www.ucl.ac.uk/slade

The Slade Summer School for Fine Art runs each summer.

University of the Arts - Central Saint Martins College of Art and Design

UK

info@csm.arts.ac.uk

+44 (0)20 7514 7000

www.csm.arts.ac.uk

Short courses available in fashion, photography, graphic design, textiles and more.

University of the Arts - Wimbledon College of Art

UK

info@wimbledon.arts.ac.uk

+44 (0) 20 7514 9641

www.wimbledon.arts.ac.uk

They have a series of short courses in fashion, etching, filmmaking, sewing and more.

University of the Arts Camberwell

UK

info@camberwell.arts.ac.uk

+44 (0) 20 7514 6302

www.camberwell.arts.ac.uk

Offers various short courses in art and art related subjects.

University of the Arts London - Chelsea

UK

info@chelsea.arts.ac.uk

+44 (0) 20 7514 7751

www.chelsea.arts.ac.uk

Short courses available in interior design, drawing, painting and life drawing.

Cookery

Ashburton Cookery School

UK

info@ashburtoncookeryschool.co.uk

+44 (0) 1364 652784

www.ashburtoncookeryschool.co.uk

Cookery courses available from one to five days.

For further information see page 244

Belle Isle School of Cookery

UK

info@belle-isle.com

+44 (028) 95810546

www.irishcookeryschool.com

Essential Cooking is an intensive four week course designed for people who are interested in learning the key skills for a gap-year job in cooking

CookAbility

UK

venetia@cookability.com

+44 (0) 1823 461394

www.residentialcookery.com

CookAbilty caters for all types of gap-year students. Whether you have set your sights on a chalet cooking season, self-catering at university or a new life skill, then this is the place to become inspired in the culinary arts.

Cookery at The Grange

UK

info@cookeryatthegrange.co.uk

+44 (0) 137 383 6579

www.cookeryatthegrange.co.uk

Cookery at the Grange has been running the outstanding four week, residential Essential Cookery Courses since 1981. Fantastic local ingredients from the Somerset countryside near Bath, are used to learn to cook really good food, for fun, for a gap year or for a career.

For further information see page 250

Cookery School at Little Portland Street

UK
info@cookeryschool.co.uk
+44 (0) 20 7631 4590
www.cookeryschool.co.uk

Cookery School at Little Portland Street has something to offer all food lovers: check out the huge array of classes on offer on our website.

For further information see page 246

Cutting Edge Food & Wine School

UK
+44 (0) 07747 654680

Based in a 16th century farmhouse you will be taught in small groups by Cutting Edge London Chef, who has an excellent reputation.

Edinburgh New Town Cookery School

UK
info@entcs.co.uk
+44 (0)131 226 4314
www.entcs.co.uk

1, 3 and 6 month courses designed for gap year students who want to work in ski chalets, luxury live aboard yachts or shooting lodges.

Edinburgh School of Food and Wine

UK
info@esfw.com
+44 (0) 131 333 5001
www.esfw.com

Courses of interest to gappers are the four week Intensive Certificate Course which is geared towards chalet work, and the one week Survival Course which is ideally suited to those leaving home for the first time.

Food of Course

UK
info@foodofcourse.co.uk
+44 (0) 1749 860116
www.foodofcourse.co.uk

A four-week residential course providing all essential skills to cook in a ski chalet, on a yacht or in holiday homes worldwide.

Gordon Ramsay's Tante Marie Culinary Academy

UK
info@tantemarie.co.uk
+44 (0) 1483 726957
www.tantemarie.co.uk

Tante Marie Culinary Academy is the UK's oldest independent cookery school and is now the only school in the world able to award both the internationally acclaimed Cordon Bleu Diploma and the CTH Level 4 Diploma in Professional Culinary Arts.

For further information see page 252

Le Cordon Bleu

UK
london@cordonbleu.edu
+44 (0) 20 7400 3900
www.lcblondon.com

Le Cordon Bleu has courses ranging from their famous diplomas in ëCuisine and P,tisserieí to shorter courses in techniques, seasonal cooking, essentials and healthy eating.

Leiths School of Food and Wine

UK
info@leiths.com
+44 (0) 20 8749 6400
www.leiths.com

Learn how to cook and earn money from it on your gap year. Leiths certificate cookery courses will give you the confidence and skill to achieve this.

For further information see page 254

Orchards Cookery
UK
+44 (0) 1789 490 259
www.orchardscookery.co.uk
Specialises in training and recruiting chalet cooks. Courses are one or two weeks long, residential and great fun with 24 students trained in three separate kitchens.

The Avenue Cookery School
UK
info@theavenuecookeryschool.com
+44 (0) 208 788 3025
www.theavenuecookeryschool.com
Offer one and two week courses aimed specifically at gap-year students, chalet assistants and undergraduates.

The Bertinet Kitchen
UK
info@thebertinetkitchen.com
+44 (0) 1225 445531
www.thebertinetkitchen.com
They run a beginners' course for those who have no clue what a kitchen is actually for.

The Cook Academy (Hampshire)
UK
kate@cookacademy.co.uk
07825 393856
www.cookacademy.co.uk
The Cook Academy offers cookery tuition and experiences for all ages, abilities and occasions.

The Cordon Vert School
UK
enquiries@cordonvert.co.uk
+44 (0)161 925 2015
www.cordonvert.co.uk
Cookery school run by the Vegetarian Society (Charity No. 259358). One and two day courses available.

The Foodworks Cookery School
UK
admin@foodworkscookeryschool.co.uk
01242 870538
www.foodworkscookeryschool.co.uk
A purpose-built cookery school in Gloucestershire that offers courses that range from beginners to experienced chefs.

The Gables School of Cookery
UK
info@thegablesschoolofcookery.co.uk
+44 (0) 1454 260 444
www.thegablesschoolofcookery.co.uk
Achieve your dreams through a professional four week cookery course where you can learn the skills required to work your gap-year in a ski resort or on a yacht.

Webbe's Cookery School
UK
+44 (0) 1797 222226
www.webbesrestaurants.co.uk
Respected five-day, complete, hands-on, intensive, cutting edge foundation cooking certificate course for healthy eating and cooking for friends on a budget at university and beyond.

Drama and film

Met Film School
UK
info@metfilmschool.co.uk
+44 (0)20 8832 1933
www.metfilmschool.co.uk
Practical courses for aspiring filmmakers. Short courses and one year intensive course available.

RADA (Royal Academy of Dramatic Art)
UK
enquiries@rada.ac.uk
+44 (0) 20 7636 7076
www.rada.org
This legendary drama college runs a variety of summer school courses.

The Central School of Speech and Drama

UK
enquiries@cssd.ac.uk
+44 (0) 20 7722 8183
www.cssd.ac.uk

Central offers short courses in acting, singing, stand-up comedy, puppetry, cabaret and burlesque, and directing.

The Oxford School of Drama

UK
info@oxforddrama.ac.uk
+44 (0) 1993 812883
www.oxforddrama.ac.uk

The Oxford School of Drama runs a six-month Foundation Course, including acting, voice, movement, music and stage fighting. Registered Charity No. 1072770.

Year Out Drama

UK
yearoutdrama@stratford.ac.uk
+44 (0) 1789 266 245
www.yearoutdrama.co.uk

Full-time practical drama course with a unique Company feel; work with theatre professionals to develop a wide range of skills; perform in a variety of productions; write and direct your own work; benefit from close contact with the RSC.

For further information see page 248

Driving

AA (Automobile Association)

UK
+44 (0) 161 495 8945
www.theaa.co.uk

The AA website has lots of useful information on driving in the UK and abroad, including stuff about breakdown, insurance and travel planning. You can find hotels, good places to stop whilst driving and you're even able to find out about up-to-date traffic news.

Driving Standards Agency

UK
customer.services@dsa.gsi.gov.uk
0300 200 1122
www.dft.gov.uk/dsa

Information on theory and practical driving tests, fees and other relevant information.

DVLA (Driver and Vehicle Licencing Agency)

UK
www.dvla.gov.uk

UK government agency responsible for driving licences and vehicle registration.

RAC Motoring Services

UK
+44 (0)1922 437000
www.rac.co.uk

The RAC website has lots of useful information on driving in the UK and abroad, with breakdown, insurance and other services.

Fashion & Design

Leicester College - St Margaret's

UK
info@leicestercollege.ac.uk
+44 (0) 116 224 2240
www.leicestercollege.ac.uk

Has part-time courses in footwear, fabrics and pattern cutting.

Newcastle College

UK
enquiries@ncl-coll.ac.uk
+44 (0) 191 200 4000
www.ncl-coll.ac.uk

Short courses available in fashion illustration, bridalwear design, textile dyeing and printing, pattern cutting and embroidery.

The Fashion Retail Academy

UK
info@fra.ac.uk
+44 (0) 20 7307 2345
www.fashionretailacademy.ac.uk

Short courses available in visual merchandising, styling, PR, buying and range planning there are also tailor-made courses for those wishing to run their own retail business.

The Session School

UK
info@thesessionschool.com
+44 (0)20 7998 7353
www.thesessionschool.com

Independent make-up school for professional make-up courses, workshops and masterclasses for all levels and abilities, with tuition by make-up experts.

University of the Arts - London College of Fashion

UK
shortcourses@fashion.arts.ac.uk
+44 (0) 20 7514 7566
www.fashion.arts.ac.uk

Short courses available in pattern cutting, principles of styling techniques, film and TV make up, childrenswear and maternitywear, retro fashion design and how to recycle your second hand clothes.

University of Westminster - School of Media, Arts & Design

UK
+44 (0)20 7911 5000
www.westminster.ac.uk/about-us/schools/media

Westminster offers a range of short courses in fashion, including fashion design, textile printing, and pattern cutting.

Land studies

Berkshire College of Agriculture

UK
enquiries@bca.ac.uk
+44 (0) 1628 824 444
www.bca.ac.uk

Short courses in wildlife care, animal behaviour, lambing management, poultry breeding, BHS stages 1 & 2, BHS teaching test, pasture management, horticulture, garden design, hedge laying, wildlife gardening, hurdle making, machinery management, tractor management and more ...

Bishop Burton College

UK
+44 (0)1964 553 000
www.bishopburton.ac.uk

Short courses available in tractor driving, pest control, tree felling, sheep shearing, animal husbandry and more...

Capel Manor College

UK
enquiries@capel.ac.uk
+44 (0) 8456 122 122
www.capel.ac.uk

They have short courses in lorinery, flower arranging, CAD in garden design, practical gardening, aboriculture, botanical illustration, leathercraft and more ...

Chichester College

UK
+44 (0) 1243 786321
www.chichester.ac.uk

Short courses available in animal care, farming, bushcraft, coppicing, hedgerow planting and managment, watercourse management, moorland management and more ...

Plumpton College

UK
+44 (0) 1273 890 454
www.plumpton.ac.uk
Courses available in animal care, welding, tractor driving, machinery, wine trade, aboriculture, chainsaw, bushcraft, pond management, wildlife, woodcraft and more...

Rodbaston College

UK
rodenquiries@rodbaston.ac.uk
+44 (0)1785 712209
www.southstaffs.ac.uk
Short courses available in keeping chickens, tractor driving, animal care, hurdle fencing, machinery, pest control and chainsaws.

Royal Agricultural College

UK
+44 (0) 1285 652531
www.rac.ac.uk
Have a two day residential taster course in April which gives an insight into the career options in land-based industries.

Sparsholt College

UK
enquiry@sparsholt.ac.uk
+44 (0) 1962 776441
www.sparsholt.ac.uk
Have part-time courses in forklift operation, tractor driving, health & safety, horticulture, floristy, landscaping and more.

The Open College of Equine Studies

UK
info@equinestudies.co.uk
+44 (0)1284 811 401
www.equinestudies.co.uk
Have a series of short courses available in horse training, estate management, business etc.

Warwickshire College - Moreton Morrell

UK
info@warkscol.ac.uk
0300 45 600 47
www.warkscol.ac.uk
Have taster days in land-based studies. Also have an Equine Centre and the first purpose built School of Farriery in the UK.

Languages

Berlitz - London

UK
+44 (0) 20 7611 9640
www.berlitz.co.uk
International language school. Intense courses in Chinese French, German, Italian, Japanese, Portuguese, Russian and Spanish available. Other schools in the UK can be found in Birmingham, Brighton, Bristol, Edinburgh, Manchester and Oxford.

Canning House

UK
enquiries@canninghouse.org
+44 (0)20 7811 5600
www.canninghouse.org
Canning House runs evening courses in Brazilian Portuguese, as well as a wide range of events on Latin America, Spain and Portugal.

International House London

UK
info@ihworld.com
+44 (0) 207 394 6580
www.ihworld.com
Worldwide network of language schools offering courses in Arabic, Chinese, French, German, Italian, Japanese and Spanish.

Italian Cultural Institute in London

UK
icilondon@esteri.it
+44 (0) 20 7235 1461
www.icilondon.esteri.it/IIC_Londra
The Italian Cultural Institute has a wide programme of Italian language courses as well as a mass of information about Italy and its culture.

Languages @ Lunchtime

UK
student.recruitment@glasgow.ac.uk
+44 (0) 141 330 6521
www.gla.ac.uk/schools/mlc/languagecentre
Small informal classes run at Glasgow University for two hours per week over 18 weeks.

Rosetta Stone (UK) Ltd

UK
cs@rosettastone.co.uk
0800 005 1220
www.rosettastone.co.uk
Learn languages with Rosetta Stone's interactive CD-ROM software plus online features.

The Japan Foundation - London Language Centre

UK
info.language@jpf.org.uk
+44 (0) 20 7436 6698
www.jpf.org.uk/language
The Japan Foundation London Language Centre provides courses in Japanese. Also has regular newsletter and resource library.

Music

BIMM - Brighton Institute of Modern Music

UK
info@bimm.co.uk
+44 (0) 844 2 646 666
www.bimm.co.uk
Various part-time courses available, also summer schools, for bass, drums, guitar, vocals, songwriting and live sound/tour management.

Dartington International Summer School

UK
summerschool@dartington.org
+44 (0) 1803 847 080
www.dartington.org/summer-school
Dartington International Summer School (Registered Charity No. 279756) is both a festival and a music school. Teaching and performing takes place all day, every day.

Lake District Summer Music

UK
info@ldsm.org.uk
+44 (0) 845 6 44 25 05
www.ldsm.org.uk
The Lake District Summer Music School is an ensemble-based course for string players and pianists intending to pursue careers as professional musicians. Registered Charity no 516350.

London Music School

UK
info@londonmusicschool.com
+44(0)208 986 7885
www.tlms.co.uk
The London Music School offers a Diploma in Music Technology, open to anyone with musical ability aged 17 or over. The course explores professional recording and you get to use a 24-track studio.

London School of Sound
UK
info@londonschoolofsound.co.uk
+44 (0) 20 7720 6183
www.londonschoolofsound.co.uk
Based in the recording studio previously owned by Pink Floyd, we offer part and full-time courses of between five weeks and two years in music production, sound engineering and DJ skills.

Music Worldwide Drum Camp
UK
gary@musicworldwide.org
+44 (0) 1603 462907
www.musicworldwide.org
Drum Camp is an annual worldwide percussion event in Norfolk specialising in world rhythms and drum and dance programs. Offers an amazing variety of classes over four days, in music, singing and dance.

NLMS Music Summer School
UK
c.gomme@btinternet.com
www.nlmsmusic-summerschool.co.uk
Each year over 100 enthusiastic adult amateur musicians get together for a week of enjoyment.

North London Piano School
UK
+44 (0) 20 8958 5206
www.learn-music.com/nlps2
The North London Piano School offers a residential Summer Course.

The British Kodály Academy
UK
enquiries@britishkodalyacademy.org
+44 (0) 208 651 3728
www.britishkodalyacademy.org
They run various music courses for teachers and young children but also have courses for those wishing to improve their skills.

The DJ Academy Organisation
UK
andyking221@btinternet.com
07980 915424
www.djacademy.org.uk
Offer an eight-week part time DJ course (in various cities in the UK), private tuition, one day superskills course, the ultimate mobile DJ course and the superclub experience.

The Recording Workshop
UK
recordingworks@btconnect.com
+44 (0) 20 896 88 222
www.recordwk.dircon.co.uk
The Recording Workshop offer part time and full time courses on all aspects of music production, sound engineering and music technology.

UK Songwriting Festival
UK
+44 (0) 1225 876 133
www.uksongwritingfestival.com
Five-day event held at Bath Spa University every August. The Songwriting Workshop includes daily lectures on the craft of songwriting, small group sessions, live band sessions, studio sessions with a producer and an acoustic live recording on CD.

Photography

Digitalmasterclass
UK
brian@digitalmasterclass.co.uk
+44 (0) 1233 280606
www.digitalmasterclass.co.uk
Small group classes in digital photography for beginners and those wishing to improve their basic skills.

Experience Seminars
UK
info@experience-seminars.co.uk
+44 (0) 1487 772804
www.experience-seminars.co.uk
Experience Seminars hosts a range of workshops throughout the UK, which are designed to provide a fast track way of learning photography and digital imaging techniques.

London School of Photography
UK
lsp@lsptraining.co.uk
+44 (0)207 659 2085
www.lsptraining.com
Short courses available in digital photography, photojournalism, as well as travel, adventure and street photography. Small classes of up to eight people. One to one training also available.

Photo Opportunity Ltd
UK
chris@photoopportunity.co.uk
+44 (0) 20 8940 0256
www.photoopportunity.co.uk
Courses offered lasting from one to five days in length. Tailored to suit your own particular needs and classes are small.

Photofusion
UK
info@photofusion.org
+44 (0) 20 7738 5774
www.photofusion.org
This independent photography resource centre, situated in Brixton, offers digital photography courses.

Picture Weddings - Digital wedding photography workshops
UK
info@pictureweddings.co.uk
(+44) 01793 780501
www.pictureweddings.co.uk
Fast-track workshops in digital wedding photography.

The Photography School
UK
info@thephotographyschool.co.uk
+44 (0) 118 901 7272
www.thephotographyschool.co.uk
Offers intensive photography courses for beginners and professionals.

The Royal Photographic Society
UK
reception@rps.org
+44 (0) 1225 325 733
www.rps.org/workshops
Holds photography courses, from landscape photography to studio work, throughout the year.

The Trained Eye
UK
info@thetrainedeye.co.uk
+44 (0)1494 353637
www.thetrainedeye.co.uk
Offer creative courses in wedding and portrait photography, for amateurs or advanced photographers to improve their skills.

Sport

BASP UK Ltd
UK
skipatrol@basp.org.uk
+44 (0) 1855 811 443
www.basp.org.uk
BASP offers First Aid and Safety Training courses designed specifically for the outdoor user, suitable for all NGB Awards.

Big Squid Scuba Diving Training and Travel
UK
info@bigsquid.co.uk
+44 (0) 20 7627 0700
www.bigsquid.co.uk
Big Squid offers a variety of dive courses using the PADI and TDI systems of diver education.

British Hang Gliding & Paragliding Association Ltd

UK
office@bhpa.co.uk
+44 (0)116 289 4316
www.bhpa.co.uk
The BHPA oversees the standards of instructor training and runs coaching course for pilots. They also list all approved schools in the field of paragliding, hang gliding and parascending.

British Mountaineering Council

UK
office@thebmc.co.uk
+44 (0) 161 445 6111
www.thebmc.co.uk
BMC travel insurance covers a range of activities and is designed by experts to be free from unreasonable exclusions or restrictions, for peace of mind wherever you travel.

British Offshore Sailing School - BOSS

UK
+44 (0) 23 8045 7733
www.boss-sail.co.uk
BOSS offers complete RYA shore-based and practical training courses, also women only courses, from Hamble Point Marina.

British Sub Aqua Club

UK
info@bsac.com
+44 (0) 151 350 6200
www.bsac.com
Why not discover scuba diving or snorkelling during your gap-year?

CricketCoachMaster Academy

UK
info@ccmacademy.co.uk
+44 (0) 7815 081744
www.ccmacademy.co.uk
The CCM Academy has a coaching programme to further develop players with the recognised potential to play at county and international level.

Curling in Kent

UK
info@curlinginkent.co.uk
+44 (0)1892 826 004
www.fentonsrink.co.uk
Come to Fenton's Rink and try your hand at this exciting Olympic sport. New season begins 1st October.

Fly Sussex Paragliding

UK
info@sussexhgpg.co.uk
+44 (0) 1273 858 170
www.flysussex.com
Learn to paraglide or hang glide over the beautiful Sussex countryside.

Flybubble Paragliding

UK
+44 (0) 1273 812 442
www.flybubble.co.uk
A paragliding school registered with the British Hang Gliding and Paragliding Association (BHPA).

Glasgow Ski & Snowboard Centre

UK
info@ski-glasgow.org
+44 (0) 141 427 4991
www.ski-glasgow.org
Learn to ski, improve your existing skills or learn to snowboard. Fully qualified instructors waiting to teach you.

Green Dragons

UK
fly@greendragons.co.uk
01883 652 666
www.greendragons.co.uk
Paragliding and hang gliding centre. You do not need any experience or knowledge, just the desire to fly and follow your instructor's guidance on positions for take off, time spent in the air and landing.

Jubilee Sailing Trust

UK
info@jst.org.uk
+44 (0) 23 8044 9108
www.jst.org.uk
Tall Ships Sailing Trust. Join their JST Youth Leadership@Sea Scheme, no sailing experience needed. Registered Charity No. 277810.

London Fencing Club

UK
+44 (0)7951 414409
www.londonfencingclub.co.uk
Fencing tuition available in various centres in London - beginners to advanced training available.

London Scuba Diving School

UK
info@londonscuba.com
0845 544 1312
www.londonscuba.com
The London Scuba Diving School teaches beginners in swimming pools in Battersea and Bayswater. They also offer advanced courses for the experienced diver.

Mendip Outdoor Pursuits

UK
info@mendip.me
+44 (0)1934 834 877
www.mendipoutdoorpursuits.co.uk
Lessons in abseiling, archery, bridge building, caving, climbing, bush craft, kayaking, navigation, orienteering and more available.

New Forest Activities

UK
info@earth-events.co.uk
+44 (0) 1590 612 377
www.newforestactivities.co.uk
Organises group activities such as canoeing, rope work, cycling and climbing. Also offer environmental courses in the New Forest.

North London Skydiving Centre Ltd

UK
office@ukskydiving.com
+44 (0) 871 664 0113
www.ukskydiving.com
They have different sky diving and parachuting experiences and various courses for the complete beginner.

Plas y Brenin - The National Mountain Centre

UK
info@pyb.co.uk
+44 (0) 1690 720 214
www.pyb.co.uk
For those hoping to reach dizzy heights, Plas y Brenin offers a vast range of activities and courses.

Pod Zorbing

UK
info@zorbing.co.uk
0845 430 3322
www.zorbing.co.uk
Harness zorbing in London - two person ball. Also do aqua zorbing.

Poole Harbour Watersports

UK
info@pooleharbour.co.uk
+44 (0) 1202 700503
www.pooleharbour.co.uk
Learn to windsurf and kitesurf at Poole in Dorset. Courses available for both beginners and improvers.

ProAdventure Limited

UK
sales@proadventure.co.uk
+44 (0)1978 861912
www.proadventure.co.uk
Based in Wales, ProAdventure offers different activity courses around the UK, including canoeing, kayaking, rock climbing and mountain biking.

Skydive Brid
UK
info@skydivegb.com
+44 (0)1262 228033
www.skydivebrid.co.uk
Skydiving courses for complete beginners. Free skydiving in aid of charity and jumps organised for more experienced people.

South Cambridgeshire Equestrian Centre
UK
+44 (0) 1763 263 213
www.scec.co.uk
This riding school is set in 260 acres of Cambridgeshire countryside. They offer riding tuition to the beginner and also more advanced teaching for experienced riders.

Sportscotland National Centre Cumbrae
UK
cumbraecentre@sportscotland.org.uk
+44(0) 1475 530757
www.nationalcentrecumbrae.org.uk
Sportscotland national watersport centre offer a range of courses from a fully residential three weeks Powerboat Instructor or 18 weeks Professional Yachtmaster Training, to a one day introduction to Windsurfing.

Suffolk Ski Centre
UK
info@suffolkskicentre.co.uk
+44 (0) 1473 602347
www.suffolkskicentre.co.uk
Learn to ski or snowboard in Suffolk. Courses also available for those wishing to improve their existing skills.

Sussex Polo Club
UK
info@sussexpolo.co.uk
+44 (0) 1342 714 920
www.sussexpolo.co.uk
Learn something new - learn to play polo.

The Lawn Tennis Association
UK
Info@LTA.org.uk
+44 (0) 20 8487 7000
www.lta.org.uk
You're never too young or too old to learn to play tennis and the LTA will help you.

The Talland School of Equitation
UK
secretary@talland.net
+44 (0) 1285 740155
www.talland.net
World renowned BHS and ABRS approved equestrian centre offering top class training for professional qualifications. Variety of courses including competition training on quality horses.

Tollymore Mountain Centre
UK
livetheadventure@tollymore.com
+44 (0)28 4372 2158
www.tollymore.com
Tollymore have a range of courses designed to suit your own skills and experience. Their courses include rambling, mountaineering, climbing, canoeing and first aid.

UK Parachuting
UK
jump@ukparachuting.co.uk
07769 721036
www.ukparachuting.co.uk
AFF courses available. Also tandem skydiving and Accelerated Free Fall tuition slots available every day.

UKSA (United Kingdom Sailing Academy)
UK
info@uksa.org
+44 (0)1983 294941
www.uksa.org
A wealth of options for a thrilling gap-year to suit all budgets, from extreme watersports instructor programmes to the six-week crew training course, designed to provide the yachting skills and experience for a career on luxury yachts and superyachts!

Wellington Riding
UK
info@wellington-riding.co.uk
+44 (0) 118 932 6308
www.wellington-riding.co.uk
Riding lessons available for any level - children and adults.

TEFL

CILC - Cheltenham International Language Centre
UK
cilc@glos.ac.uk
+44 (0)1242 714092
www.glos.ac.uk/CILC
Gloucestershire University offer intensive courses in TEFL leading to the Cambridge ESOL CELTA award.

ETC - The English Training Centre
UK
info@englishtc.co.uk
+44 (0) 121 449 2221
www.englishtc.co.uk
Professionally-designed TESOL courses offeredaccreditedby ACTDEC.Experienced tutors provide comprehensive feedback and helpful support. Free grammar guide and teaching resource book.

Golders Green Teacher Training Centre
UK
+44 (0) 208 905 5467
www.englishlanguagecollege.co.uk
Full-time and part-time TEFL/TESOL courses available.

ITC - Intensive TEFL Courses
UK
info@tefl.co.uk
+44 (0) 8456 445464
www.tefl.co.uk
Intensive TEFL Courses (ITC) have been running weekend TEFL (Teach English as a Foreign Language) courses throughout the UK since 1993.

LTTC - London Teacher Training College
UK
lttc@teachenglish.co.uk
+44 (0)208 133 2027
www.teachenglish.co.uk
Over the years the college has trained a vast number of teachers from around the world, and prides itself on the quality of its courses and the individual attention it provides every student who enrols.

OxfordTEFL
UK
tesol@oxfordtefl.com
+34 93 458 0111
www.oxfordtefl.com
OxfordTEFL offer a four week training course, accredited by Trinity College London, at the end of which you should get a Certificate in TEFL.

Windsor TEFL
UK
info@windsorschools.co.uk
+44 (0) 1753 858 995
www.windsorschools.co.uk
Offer their TEFL course in their centres in London and Windsor as well as in Europe. Also offer the CELTA TEFL course in various places worldwide.

Further study

A level examining boards

There are five A level examining boards: AQA (Assessment and Qualifications Alliance), Edexcel, OCR (Oxford, Cambridge & RSA), Northern Ireland (CCEA) and Wales (WJEC). There's also the IB, which has its own curriculum and syllabus, geared towards the IB Diploma. All these boards now provide their exam timetables on the internet about nine months in advance: we've provided their contact details below, along with those of other exam-related organisations.

AQA
Stag Hill House,
Guildford, Surrey GU2 7XJ
www.aqa.org.uk
Tel: 0844 209 6614
Email: mailbox@aqa.org.uk

CCEA
29 Clarendon Road, Clarendon Dock
Belfast, County Antrim BT1 3BG
Tel: +44 (0) 28 9026 1200
Fax: +44 (0) 28 9026 1234
Email: info@ccea.org.uk

Edexcel
190 High Holborn,
London WC1V 7BH
www.edexcel.org.uk
Tel: see website for contact numbers

Examinations Procedures Review Service (EPRS)
Ofqual, Spring Place,
Coventry Business Park, Herald Avenue,
Coventry CV5 6UB
Tel: 0300 303 3346
Email: rich.smalley@ofqual.gov.uk

The EPRS has replaced the Examinations Appeals Board (EAB). It deals with appeals against examination results. For details on the appeal process, visit this page: **http://ofqual.gov.uk/complaints-and-appeals/exam-results-appeals**

IB (International Baccalaureate)
IB Global Centre
Churchillplein 6, 2517 JW
The Hague, The Netherlands
www.ibo.org
Tel: +44 (0) 29 2054 7777
Fax: +44 (0) 29 2054 7778
Email: ibaem@ibo.org

The central body for the development, administration and assessment of the International Baccalaureate Diploma Programme.

OCR (Oxford Cambridge & RSA Examinations)
1 Hills Road,
Cambridge,
Cambridgeshire CB1 2EU
www.ocr.org.uk
Tel: +44 (0) 1223 553 998
Fax: +44 (0) 1223 552 627
Email: general.qualifications@ocr.org.uk

QCA (Qualifications and Curriculum Authority)
83 Piccadilly,
London W1J 8QA
www.qca.org.uk
Tel: +44 (0) 20 7509 5555
Fax: +44 (0) 20 7509 6666
Email: info@qca.org.uk

The QCA is the body that (along with the Qualifications, Curriculum and Assessment Authority for Wales: ACCAC) approves all syllabuses and monitors exams (grading standards, for example).

SQA (Scottish Qualifications Authority)
The Optima Building, 58 Robertson Street,
Glasgow, Lanarkshire G2 8DQ

www.sqa.org.uk
Tel: +44 (0) 845 279 1000
Fax: +44 (0) 845 213 5000
Email: customer@sqa.org.uk

Central body for the development, administration and assessment of Scottish qualifications, including Standard Grade, Highers, Advanced Highers, HNCs, HNDs and SVQs.

WJEC
245 Western Avenue,
Cardiff, Glamorgan CF5 2YX

www.wjec.co.uk
Tel: +44 (0) 29 2026 5000
Email: info@wjec.co.uk

WJEC's qualifications include Entry Level, GCSE and AS/A level, as well as Key Skills. They also handle the Welsh Baccalaureate and provide examinations, assessment, educational resources and support for adults who wish to learn Welsh.

Tutorial colleges accredited by BAC and CIFE

The following independent sixth form and tutorial colleges offering A level tuition (one-year, two-year, complete retakes, modular retakes or intensive coaching) were recognised by the British Accreditation Council (BAC, Tel: 0300 330 1400, **www.the-bac.org**) and/or the Council for Independent Further Education (CIFE, Tel: 020 8767 8666, **www.cife.org.uk)** as of October 2013. Of course a college can have a good reputation and achieve excellent results without accreditation.

Abacus College (Oxford)
BAC
Tel:+44 (0) 1865 240 111

Abbey College (London)
CIFE
Tel: +44 (0) 207 824 7300

Academic Summer (Taunton)
BAC
Tel: +44 (0) 208 123 8083

Ashbourne Independent Sixth Form College, (London W8)
CIFE
Tel:+44 (0) 20 7937 3858

Bales College (London W10)
CIFE
Tel:+44 (0) 20 8960 5899

Basil Paterson College (Edinburgh)
BAC
Tel:+44 (0) 131 225 3802

Bath Academy (Bath)
BAC/CIFE
Tel:+44 (0) 1225 334 577

Bosworth Independent College (Northampton)
CIFE
Tel:+44 (0) 1604 239 995

Brooke House College (Market Harborough)
CIFE
Tel:+44 (0) 1858 462 452

Cambridge Seminars
BAC
Tel:+44 (0) 1223 313 464

Cambridge Centre for Sixth Form Studies
CIFE
Tel: +44 (0) 1223 716890

Cambridge Tutors College
CIFE
Tel: +44 (0) 20 8688 5284

Carfax Tutorial Establishment (Oxford)
BAC/CIFE
Tel: +44 (0) 1865 557 317

CATS College London
BAC
Tel:+44 (0) 20 7841 1580

Chelsea Independent College
CIFE
Tel:+44 (0) 20 7610 1114

Collingham Independent Sixth-Form College
CIFE
Tel: +44 (0) 20 7244 7414

College of International Education (Oxford)
BAC
Tel:+44 (0) 1865 202238

Davies, Laing & Dick (London, W1)
CIFE
Tel:+44 (0) 20 7935 8411

Duff Miller College (London SW7)
CIFE
Tel:+44 (0) 20 7225 0577

EF International Academy UK (Oxford)
BAC
Tel:+44 (0) 1865 759660

EF International Academy UK (Torquay)
BAC
Tel: +44 (0) 1803 202 932

Interlink College of Technology and Business Studies (London, E15)
BAC
Tel: +44 (0) 208 522 7600

INTO Manchester
BAC
Tel: +44 (0) 161 279 7272

INTO University of East Anglia (Norwich)
BAC
Tel: +44 (0) 1603 592977

International College Britain
BAC
Tel:+44 (0) 131 538 1597

Lansdowne College (London W2)
CIFE
Tel:+44 (0) 20 7616 4400

MPW Birmingham
CIFE
Tel: +44 (0) 121 454 6433

MPW London
CIFE
Tel: +44 (0) 207 835 1355

Oxford Business College
BAC
Tel:+44 (0) 1865 791 908

Oxford International College
CIFE
Tel: +44 (0) 1865 203988

Oxford Tutorial College
BAC/CIFE
Tel:+44 (0) 1865 793 333

Reach Cambridge
BAC
Tel:+44 (0) 870 8031 7320

University of Aberdeen
www.abdn.ac.uk
Tel: +44 (0) 1224 272 000

University of Abertay Dundee
www.abertay.ac.uk
Tel: +44 (0) 1382 308 000

Aberystwyth University
www.aber.ac.uk
Tel: +44 (0) 1970 623 111

Anglia Ruskin University
www.anglia.ac.uk
Tel: +44 (0) 845 271 3333

Arts University College at Bournemouth
www.aucb.ac.uk
Tel: +44 (0) 1202 533 011

Aston University
www.aston.ac.uk
Tel: +44 (0) 121 204 3000

Bangor University
www.bangor.ac.uk
Tel: +44 (0) 1248 351 151

University of Bath
www.bath.ac.uk
Tel: +44 (0) 1225 388 388

Universities in the UK

Bath Spa University
www.bathspa.ac.uk
Tel: +44 (0) 1225 875 875

University of Bedfordshire
www.beds.ac.uk
Tel: +44 (0) 1234 400 400

University of Birmingham
www.birmingham.ac.uk
Tel: +44 (0) 121 414 3344

Bishop Grosseteste University College, Lincoln
www.bishopg.ac.uk
Tel: +44 (0) 1522 527347

University of Bolton
www.bolton.ac.uk
Tel: +44 (0) 1204 900 600

Bournemouth University
www.bournemouth.ac.uk
Tel: +44 (0) 1202 524 111

University of Bradford
www.bradford.ac.uk
Tel: +44 (0) 1274 232 323

University of Brighton
www.brighton.ac.uk
Tel: +44 (0) 1273 600 900

University of Bristol
www.bris.ac.uk
Tel: +44 (0) 117 928 9000

Brunel University, West London
www.brunel.ac.uk
Tel: +44 (0) 1895 274 000

University of Buckingham
www.buckingham.ac.uk
Tel: +44 (0) 1280 814 080

Bucks New University
http://bucks.ac.uk
Tel: +44 (0) 1494 522 141

University of Cambridge
www.cam.ac.uk
Tel: +44 (0) 1223 337 733

Cardiff University
www.cardiff.ac.uk
Tel: +44 (0) 29 2087 4000

Canterbury Christ Church University
www.canterbury.ac.uk
Tel: +44 (0) 1227 767 700

Birmingham City University
www.bcu.ac.uk
Tel: +44 (0) 121 331 5000

University of Central Lancashire
www.uclan.ac.uk
Tel: +44 (0) 1772 201 201

University of Chester
www.chester.ac.uk
Tel: +44 (0) 1244 511000

University of Chichester
www.chi.ac.uk
Tel: +44 (0) 1243 816000

City University, London
www.city.ac.uk
Tel: +44 (0) 20 7040 5060

Coventry University
www.coventry.ac.uk
Tel: +44 (0) 2476 88 76 88

Cranfield University
www.cranfield.ac.uk
Tel: +44 (0) 1234 750 111

University of Cumbria
www.cumbria.ac.uk
Tel: +44 (0) 1228 616234

De Montfort University
www.dmu.ac.uk
Tel: +44 (0) 116 255 1551

University of Derby
www.derby.ac.uk
Tel: +44 (0) 1332 590 500

University of Dundee
www.dundee.ac.uk
Tel: +44 (0) 1382 383 000

Durham University
www.dur.ac.uk
Tel: +44 (0) 191 334 2000

University of East Anglia
www.uea.ac.uk
Tel: +44 (0) 1603 456 161

University of East London
www.uel.ac.uk
Tel: +44 (0) 20 8223 3000

Edge Hill University
www.edgehill.ac.uk
Tel: +44 (0) 1695 575 171

The University of Edinburgh
www.ed.ac.uk
Tel: +44 (0) 131 650 1000

University of Essex
www.essex.ac.uk
Tel: +44 (0) 1206 873 333

- Writtle College
  www.writtle.ac.uk
  Tel: +44(0) 1245 424 200

University of Exeter
www.exeter.ac.uk
Tel: +44 (0) 1392 661 000

University College Falmouth
www.falmouth.ac.uk
Tel: +44 (0) 1326 211077

University of Glamorgan
www.glam.ac.uk
Tel: +44 (0) 1443 480 480

University of Glasgow
www.gla.ac.uk
Tel: +44 (0) 141 330 2000

Glasgow Caledonian University
www.gcu.ac.uk
Tel: +44 (0) 141 331 3000

University of Gloucestershire
www.glos.ac.uk
Tel: +44 (0) 844 801 0001

University of Greenwich
www.gre.ac.uk
Tel: +44 (0) 20 8331 8000

Harper Adams University College
www.harper-adams.ac.uk
Tel: +44 (0) 1952 820280

Heriot-Watt University
www.hw.ac.uk
Tel: +44 (0) 131 449 5111

University of Hertfordshire
www.herts.ac.uk
Tel: +44 (0) 1707 284 000

University of Huddersfield
www.hud.ac.uk
Tel: +44 (0) 1484 422 288

The University of Hull
www.hull.ac.uk
Tel: +44 (0) 1482 346 311

Institute for System Level Integration
www.isli.ac.uk
Tel: +44 (0) 1506 469 300

Keele University
www.keele.ac.uk
Tel: +44 (0) 1782 732 000

University of Kent
www.kent.ac.uk
Tel: +44 (0) 1227 764 000

Kingston University
www.kingston.ac.uk
Tel: +44 (0) 20 8417 9000

Lancaster University
www.lancs.ac.uk
Tel: +44 (0) 1524 65201

Leeds College of Music
www.lcm.ac.uk
Tel: +44 (0) 113 222 3400

Leeds Metropolitan University
www.leedsmet.ac.uk
Tel: +44 (0) 113 812 0000

Leeds Trinity & All Saints
www.leedstrinity.ac.uk
Tel: +44 (0) 113 283 7100

University of Leeds
www.leeds.ac.uk
Tel: +44 (0) 113 243 1751

University of Leicester
www.le.ac.uk
Tel: +44 (0) 116 252 2522

University of Lincoln
www.lincoln.ac.uk
Tel: +44 (0) 1522 882 000

University of Liverpool
www.liv.ac.uk
Tel: +44 (0) 151 794 2000

Liverpool Hope University
www.hope.ac.uk
Tel: +44 (0) 151 291 3000

Liverpool John Moores University
www.ljmu.ac.uk
Tel: +44 (0) 151 231 2121

University of London
www.lon.ac.uk
(contact colleges directly)
Tel: +44 (0) 20 7862 8000

- Barts and The London School of Medicine and Dentistry
  www.smd.qmul.ac.uk
  Tel: +44 (0) 20 7882 3377
- Birkbeck College
  www.bbk.ac.uk
  Tel: +44 (0) 20 7631 6000
- Courtauld Institute of Art
  www.courtauld.ac.uk
  Tel: +44 (0) 20 7872 0220
- Goldsmith's College
  www.gold.ac.uk
  Tel: +44 (0) 20 7919 7171
- Heythrop College
  www.heythrop.ac.uk
  Tel: +44 (0) 20 7795 6600
- Imperial College
  www.imperial.ac.uk
  Tel: +44 (0) 20 7589 5111
- Institute of Advanced Legal Studies
  http://ials.sas.ac.uk
  Tel: +44 (0) 20 7862 5800
- Institute of Education
  www.ioe.ac.uk
  Tel: +44 (0) 20 7612 6000
- Institute in Paris
  www.ulip.london.ac.uk
  Tel: +33 (0) 1 44 11 73 76
- King's College London
  www.kcl.ac.uk
  Tel: +44 (0) 20 7836 5454
- London School of Economics and Political Science
  www.lse.ac.uk
  Tel: +44 (0) 20 7405 7686
- London School of Hygiene and Tropical Medicine
  www.lshtm.ac.uk
  Tel: +44 (0) 20 7636 8636
- Queen Mary
  www.qmul.ac.uk
  Tel: +44 (0) 20 7882 5555
- Royal Academy of Music
  www.ram.ac.uk
  Tel: +44 (0) 20 7873 7373
- Royal Free and University College Medical School
  www.ucl.ac.uk/medicalschool
  Tel: +44 (0) 20 7679 2000
- Royal Holloway
  www.rhul.ac.uk
  Tel: +44 (0) 1784 434 455
- School of Advanced Study
  www.sas.ac.uk
  Tel: +44 (0) 20 7862 8659
- School of Oriental and African Studies
  www.soas.ac.uk
  Tel: +44 (0) 20 7637 2388
- School of Slavonic and East European Studies
  www.ssees.ac.uk
  Tel: +44 (0) 20 7679 8700
- St George's
  www.sgul.ac.uk
  Tel: +44 (0) 20 8672 9944
- The Royal Veterinary College
  www.rvc.ac.uk
  Tel: +44 (0) 20 7468 5000
- The School of Pharmacy
  www.ulc.ac.uk/pharmacy
  Tel: +44 (0) 20 7753 5800

- University College London
  www.ucl.ac.uk
  Tel: +44 (0) 20 7679 2000

London Metropolitan University
www.londonmet.ac.uk
Tel: +44 (0) 20 7423 0000

London South Bank University
www.lsbu.ac.uk
Tel: +44 (0) 20 7815 7815

Loughborough University
www.lboro.ac.uk
Tel: +44 (0) 1509 263 171

The University of Manchester
www.manchester.ac.uk
Tel: +44 (0) 161 306 6000

- Manchester Business School
  www.mbs.ac.uk
  Tel: +44 (0) 161 3061 320

Manchester Metropolitan University
www.mmu.ac.uk
Tel: +44 (0) 161 247 2000

Middlesex University
www.mdx.ac.uk
Tel: +44 (0) 20 8411 5000

Napier University
www.napier.ac.uk
Tel: +44 (0) 8452 606 040

Newcastle University
www.ncl.ac.uk
Tel: +44 (0) 191 222 6000

Newman College of Higher Education
www.newman.ac.uk
Tel: +44 (0) 121 476 1181

The University of Northampton
www.northampton.ac.uk
Tel: +44 (0) 1604 735500

Northumbria University
www.northumbria.ac.uk
Tel: +44 (0) 191 232 6002

The University of Nottingham
www.nottingham.ac.uk
Tel: +44 (0) 115 951 5151

Nottingham Trent University
www.ntu.ac.uk
Tel: +44 (0) 115 941 8418

The Open University
www.open.ac.uk
Tel: +44 (0) 845 300 6090

University of Oxford
www.ox.ac.uk
Tel: +44 (0) 1865 270 000

Oxford Brookes University
www.brookes.ac.uk
Tel: +44 (0) 1865 741 111

University of Plymouth
www.plymouth.ac.uk
Tel: +44 (0) 1752 600 600

University of Portsmouth
www.port.ac.uk
Tel: +44 (0) 2392 84 84 84

Queen Margaret University
www.qmu.ac.uk
Tel: +44 (0) 131 474 0000

Queen's University Belfast
www.qub.ac.uk
Tel: +44 (0) 28 9024 5133

- Stranmillis University College
  www.stran.ac.uk
  Tel: +44 (0) 28 9038 1271

University of Reading
www.reading.ac.uk
Tel: +44 (0) 1189 875 123

Roehampton University
www.roehampton.ac.uk
Tel: +44 (0) 20 8392 3000

Royal College of Art
www.rca.ac.uk
Tel: +44 (0) 20 7590 4444

Royal College of Music
www.rcm.ac.uk
Tel: +44 (0) 20 7589 3643

University of Salford
www.salford.ac.uk
Tel: +44 (0) 161 295 5000

The University of Sheffield
www.shef.ac.uk
Tel: +44 (0) 114 222 2000

Sheffield Hallam University
www.shu.ac.uk
Tel: +44 (0) 114 225 5555

University of Southampton
www.southampton.ac.uk
Tel: +44 (0) 23 8059 5000

Southampton Solent University
www.solent.ac.uk
Tel: +44 (0) 23 8031 9000

Staffordshire University
www.staffs.ac.uk
Tel: +44 (0) 1782 294 000

St Mary's University, Belfast
www.smucb.ac.uk
Tel: +44 (0) 28 9032 7678

University of Strathclyde
www.strath.ac.uk
Tel: +44 (0) 141 552 4400

University of St Andrews
www.st-andrews.ac.uk
Tel: +44 (0) 1334 476 161

University of Stirling
www.stir.ac.uk
Tel: +44 (0) 1786 473 171

University of Sunderland
www.sunderland.ac.uk
Tel: +44 (0) 191 515 2000

University of Surrey
www.surrey.ac.uk
Tel: +44 (0) 1483 300 800

University of Sussex
www.sussex.ac.uk
Tel: +44 (0) 1273 606 755

Swansea University
www.swan.ac.uk
Tel: +44 (0) 1792 205 678

University of Teesside
www.tees.ac.uk
Tel: +44 (0) 1642 218 121

Thames Valley University
www.tvu.ac.uk
Tel: +44 (0) 208 579 5000

The Liverpool Institute for Performing Arts
www.lipa.ac.uk
Tel: +44 (0) 151 330 3000

The Robert Gordon University
www.rgu.ac.uk
Tel: +44 (0) 1224 262 000

Trinity College of Music
www.trinitylaban.ac.uk
Tel: +44 (0) 20 8305 4444

University of Ulster
www.ulster.ac.uk
Tel: +44 (0) 8 700 400 700

University College for the Creative Arts
www.ucreative.ac.uk

- Canterbury
  Tel: +44 (0) 1227 817302
- Epsom
  Tel: +44 (0) 1372 728811
- Farnham
  Tel: +44 (0) 1252 722441
- Maidstone
  Tel: +44 (0) 1622 620000
- Rochester
  Tel: +44 (0) 1634 888702

University Marine Biological Station
www.gla.ac.uk/centres/marinestation
Tel: +44 (0) 1475 530 581

University of Wales
www.wales.ac.uk
(contact institutions directly)
Tel: +44 (0) 29 2037 6999

- University of Wales – Glyndwr University
  www.glyndwr.ac.uk
  Tel: +44 (0) 1978 290 666
- University of Wales – Royal Welsh College of Music and Drama
  www.rwcmd.ac.uk
  Tel: +44 (0) 29 2034 2854
- University of Wales – Swansea Metropolitan University
  www.smu.ac.uk
  Tel: +44 (0) 1792 481 000
- University of Wales Trinity St David
  www.trinity-cm.ac.uk
  Tel: +44 (0) 1267 676 767
- University of Wales, Newport
  www.newport.ac.uk
  Tel: +44 (0) 1633 430 088
- University of Wales Institute, Cardiff
  www.uwic.ac.uk
  Tel: +44 (0) 29 2041 6070
- University of Wales Trinity St David
  www.lamp.ac.uk
  Tel: +44 (0) 1570 422 351
- University of Wales, Coleg Harlech WEA
  www.harlech.ac.uk
  Tel: +44 (0) 1766 781 900
- University of Wales, Llandrillo College
  www.llandrillo.ac.uk
  Tel: +44 (0) 1492 542 315

University of Warwick
www.warwick.ac.uk
Tel: +44 (0) 2476 523 523

University of Westminster
www.westminster.ac.uk
Tel: +44 (0) 20 7911 5000

University of The Arts
www.arts.ac.uk
Tel: +44 (0) 20 7514 6000

University of the West of England, Bristol
www.uwe.ac.uk
Tel: +44 (0) 117 965 6261

University of the West of Scotland
www.uws.ac.uk
Tel: +44 (0) 141 848 3000

The University of Winchester
www.winchester.ac.uk
Tel: +44 (0) 1962 841515

University of Wolverhampton
www.wlv.ac.uk
Tel: +44 (0) 1902 321 000

University of Worcester
www.worcester.ac.uk
Tel: +44 (0) 1905 855 000

University of York
www.york.ac.uk
Tel: +44 (0) 1904 430 000

York St John University
www.yorksj.ac.uk
Tel: +44 (0) 1904 624 624

Business colleges

Aberdeen College of Further Education
enquiry@abcol.ac.uk
www.abcol.ac.uk
Tel: +44 (0) 1224 612 330

Abingdon and Witney College
enquiry@abingdon-witney.ac.uk
www.abingdon-witney.ac.uk
Tel: +44 (0) 1235 555 585

Accrington & Rossendale College
www.accross.ac.uk
Tel: +44 (0) 1254 389 933

Alton College
enquiries@altoncollege.ac.uk
www.altoncollege.ac.uk
Tel: +44 (0) 1420 592 200

Amersham & Wycombe College
www.amersham.ac.uk
Tel: +44 (0) 1494 585555

Andover College
info@andovercollege.ac.uk
www.cricklade.ac.uk
Tel: +44 (0) 1264 360 003

Aylesbury College
enquiries@aylesbury.ac.uk
www.aylesbury.ac.uk
Tel: +44 (0) 1296 588 588

Ayr College
enquiries@ayrcoll.ac.uk
www.ayrcoll.ac.uk
Tel: +44 (0) 1292 265 184

Banff & Buchan College
info@banff-buchan.ac.uk
www.banff-buchan.ac.uk
Tel: +44 (0) 1346 586 100

Barking and Dagenham College
admissions@barkingcollege.ac.uk
www.barkinganddagenhamcollege.ac.uk
Tel: +44 (0) 2080903020

Barnet College
info@barnetsouthgate.ac.uk
www.barnetsouthgate.ac.uk
Tel: +44 (0) 20 8266 4000

Barnfield College
enquiries@barnfield.ac.uk
www.barnfield.ac.uk
Tel: +44 (0) 1582 569 569

Barnsley College
info@barnsley.ac.uk
www.barnsley.ac.uk
Tel: +44 (0) 1226 216 216

Barton Peveril College
enquiries@barton.ac.uk
www.barton-peveril.ac.uk
Tel: +44 (0) 238 036 7200

Basingstoke College of Technology
information@bcot.ac.uk
www.bcot.ac.uk
Tel: +44 (0) 1256 354 141

Bedford College
info@bedford.ac.uk
www.bedford.ac.uk
Tel: +44 (0) 1234 291000

Belfast Metropolitan College
admissions@belfastmet.ac.uk
www.belfastmet.ac.uk
Tel: +44 (0) 28 9026 5000

Bexhill College
enquiries@bexhillcollege.ac.uk
www.bexhillcollege.ac.uk
Tel: +44 (0) 1424 214 545

Bexley College
enquiries@bexley.ac.uk
www.bexley.ac.uk
Tel: +44 (0) 1322 442 331

Birmingham Metropolitan College - Matthew Boulton Campus
ask@bmetc.ac.uk
www.bmetc.ac.uk
Tel: +44 (0) 121 446 4545

Bishop Auckland College
start@bacoll.ac.uk
www.bacoll.ac.uk
Tel: +44 (0) 1388 443 000

Blackburn College
studentservices@blackburn.ac.uk
www.blackburn.ac.uk
Tel: +44 (0) 1254 551 44

Blackpool & The Fylde College
info@blackpool.ac.uk
www.blackpool.ac.uk
Tel: +44 (0) 1253 504 343

Bolton Community College
info@boltoncc.ac.uk
www.boltoncollege.ac.uk
Tel: +44 (0) 1204 482 000

Borders College
enquiries@borderscollege.ac.uk
www.borderscollege.ac.uk
Tel: +44 (0) 8700 505 152

Boston College
info@boston.ac.uk
www.boston.ac.uk
Tel: +44 (0) 1205 365 701

Bournemouth & Poole College
enquiries@thecollege.co.uk
www.thecollege.co.uk
Tel: +44 (0) 1202 205 205

Bournville College
info@bournville.ac.uk
www.bournville.ac.uk
Tel: +44 (0) 1214 771300

Bracknell & Wokingham College
study@bracknell.ac.uk
www.bracknell.ac.uk
Tel: +44 (0) 845 330 3343

Bradford College
admissions@bradford.org.uk
www.bradfordcollege.ac.uk
Tel: +44 (0) 1189 644500

Bridgwater College
enquiries@bridgwater.ac.uk
www.bridgwater.ac.uk
Tel: +44 (0) 1278 455464

Brockenhurst College
enquiries@brock.ac.uk
www.brock.ac.uk
Tel: +44 (0) 1590 625 555

Bromley College of Further and Higher Education - Bromley Campus
info@bromley.ac.uk
www.bromley.ac.uk
Tel: +44 (0) 20 8295 7000

Bromley College of Further and Higher Education - Orpington Campus
info@bromley.ac.uk
www.bromley.ac.uk
Tel: +44 (0) 20 8295 7001

Brooklands College
info@brooklands.ac.uk
www.brooklands.ac.uk
Tel: +44 (0) 1932 797 797

Budmouth Technology College
akersd@budmouth.dorset.sch.uk
www.budmouth.dorset.sch.uk
Tel: +44 (0) 1305 830 500

Burnley College
student.services@burnley.ac.uk
www.burnley.ac.uk
Tel: +44 (0) 1282 733373

Burton College
enquiries@bsdc.ac.uk
www.burton-college.ac.uk
Tel: +44 (0) 1283 494 400

Bury College
information@burycollege.ac.uk
www.burycollege.ac.uk
Tel: +44 (0) 161 280 8280

Cambridge Regional College
enquiry@camre.ac.uk
www.camre.ac.uk
Tel: +44 (0) 1223 418 200

Canterbury College
courseenquiries@canterburycollege.ac.uk
www.cant-col.ac.uk
Tel: +44 (0) 1227 811 111

Cardiff and Vale College- Colcot Road Campus
info@cavc.ac.uk
www.cavc.ac.uk
01446 725000

Cardonald College
enquiries@cardonald.ac.uk
www.cardonald.ac.uk
Tel: +44 (0) 141 272 3333

Carlisle College
info@carlisle.ac.uk
www.carlisle.ac.uk
+ 44 (0) 1228 822 703

Carnegie College - Halbeath Campus
info@carnegiecollege.ac.uk
www.carnegiecollege.ac.uk
Tel: +44 (0) 844 248 0115

Castle College
learn@castlecollege.ac.uk
www.castlecollege.ac.uk
Tel: +44 (0) 845 845 0500

Central Sussex College
www.centralsussex.ac.uk
Tel: +44 (0) 845 155 0043

Chesterfield College
advice@chesterfield.ac.uk
www.chesterfield.ac.uk
Tel: +44 (0) 1246 500 500

Cirencester College
student.services@cirencester.ac.uk
www.cirencester.ac.uk
Tel: +44 (0) 1285 640994

City & Islington College
courseinfo@candi.ac.uk
www.candi.ac.uk
Tel: +44 (0) 20 7700 9200

City College Brighton & Hove
info@ccb.ac.uk
www.ccb.ac.uk
Tel: +44 (0) 1273 667 788

City College Coventry
info@staff.covcollege.ac.uk
www.covcollege.ac.uk
Tel: +44 (0) 2476 791 000

City College Norwich
information@ccn.ac.uk
www.ccn.ac.uk
Tel: +44 (0) 1603 773 311

City College Plymouth
info@cityplym.ac.uk
www.cityplym.ac.uk
Tel: +44 (0) 1752 305 300

City College Southampton
enquiries@southampton-city.ac.uk
www.southampton-city.ac.uk
Tel: +44 (0) 023 8048 4848

City Lit
infoline@citylit.ac.uk
www.citylit.ac.uk
Tel: +44 (0) 207 492 2600

City of Bath College
enquiries@citybathcoll.ac.uk
www.citybathcoll.ac.uk
Tel: +44 (0) 1225 312 191

City of Bristol College
enquiries@cityofbristol.ac.uk
www.cityofbristol.ac.uk
Tel: +44 (0) 117 312 5000

City of Sunderland College
info@citysun.ac.uk
www.citysun.ac.uk
Tel: +44 (0) 191 511 6000

City of Westminster College
customer.services@cwc.ac.uk
www.cwc.ac.uk
Tel: +44 (0) 20 7723 8826

City of Wolverhampton College
mail@wolvcoll.ac.uk
www.wolvcoll.ac.uk
Tel: +44 (0) 1902 836 000

Clydebank College
info@clydebank.ac.uk
www.clydebank.ac.uk
+44 (0)141 951 7400

Coatbridge College
mail@coatbridge.ac.uk
www.coatbridge.ac.uk
Tel: +44 (0) 1206 712000

Colchester Institute
www.colchester.ac.uk
Tel: +44 (0) 1206 518 000

Coleg Abertawe
enquiries@swancoll.ac.uk
www.swancoll.ac.uk
Tel: +44 (0) 1792 284 000

Coleg Castell Nedd/Neath Port Talbot College
admissions@nptc.ac.uk
www.nptc.ac.uk
Tel: +44 (0) 1639 648 000

Coleg Glan Hafren/Cardiff and Vale College
info@cavc.ac.uk
www.cavc.ac.uk
Tel: +44 (0) 29 20 250 250

Coleg Glannau Dyfrdwy/Deeside College
enquiries@deeside.ac.uk
www.deeside.ac.uk
Tel: +44 (0) 1244 831 531

Coleg Gorseinon/Gower College Swansea
admin@gowercollegeswansea.ac.uk
www.gowercollegeswansea.ac.uk
Tel: +44 (0) 1792 890 700

Coleg Gwent
info@coleggwent.ac.uk
www.coleggwent.ac.uk
Tel: +44 (0) 1495 333 333

Coleg Llysfasi/Llysfasi College
enquiries@deeside.ac.uk
www.deeside.ac.uk/llysfasi
Tel: +44 (0) 1978 790 263

Coleg Menai
learner.services@menai.ac.uk
www.menai.ac.uk
Tel: +44 (0) 1248 370 125

Coleg Merthyr Tudful/Merthyr Tydfil College
enquiries@merthyr.ac.uk
www.merthyr.ac.uk
Tel: +44 (0) 1685 726100

Coleg Morgannwg
college@morgannwg.ac.uk
www.morgannwg.ac.uk
Tel: +44 (0) 1685 887500

Coleg Penybont
enquiries@bridgend.ac.uk
www.bridgend.ac.uk
Tel: +44 (0) 1656 302 302

Coleg Sir G,r
admissions@colegsirgar.ac.uk
www.colegsirgar.ac.uk
Tel: +44 (0) 1554 748 000

Collyer's, The College of Richard Collyer
admin@collyers.ac.uk
www.collyers.ac.uk
Tel: +44 (0) 1403 210 822

Cornwall College
enquiries@cornwall.ac.uk
www.cornwall.ac.uk
Tel: +44 (0) 845 2232567

Craven College
www.craven-college.ac.uk
Tel: +44 (0) 1756 791 411

Croydon College
info@croydon.ac.uk
www.croydon.ac.uk
Tel: +44 (0) 208 686 5700

Cumbernauld College
info@cumbernauld.ac.uk
www.cumbernauld.ac.uk
Tel: +44 (0) 1236 731 811

Darlington College of Technology
enquire@darlington.ac.uk
www.darlington.ac.uk
Tel: +44 (0) 1325 503 050

Dearne Valley College
learn@dearne-coll.ac.uk
www.dearne-coll.ac.uk
Tel: +44 (0) 1709 513 333

Derby College
enquiries@derby-college.ac.uk
www.derby-college.ac.uk
Tel: +44 (0) 300 123 7890

Derwentside College
enquiries@derwentside.ac.uk
www.derwentside.ac.uk
Tel: +44 (0) 1207 585 900

Dudley College
www.dudleycol.ac.uk
Tel: +44 (0) 1384 363 000

Dumfries & Galloway College
info@dumgal.ac.uk
www.dumgal.ac.uk
Tel: +44 (0) 1387 734000

Dundee College
enquiry@dundeecollege.ac.uk
www.dundeecollege.ac.uk
Tel: +44 (0) 1382 834 800

Dunstable College
enquiries@dunstable.ac.uk
www.dunstable.ac.uk
Tel: +44 (0) 1582 477 776

Ealing, Hammersmith & West London College
cic@wlc.ac.uk
www.wlc.ac.uk
Tel: +44 (0) 20 8741 1688

East Berkshire College
info@eastberks.ac.uk
www.eastberks.ac.uk
Tel: +44 (0) 845 373 2500

East Riding College
info@eastridingcollege.ac.uk
www.eastridingcollege.ac.uk
Tel: +44 (0) 845 120 0037

East Surrey College
enrol@esc.ac.uk
www.esc.ac.uk
Tel: +44 (0) 1737 772611

East Tyrone College of Further & Higher Education
info@etcfhe.ac.uk
www.etcfhe.ac.uk
Tel: +44 (0) 28 8772 2323

Eastleigh College
goplaces@eastleigh.ac.uk
www.eastleigh.ac.uk
Tel: +44 (0) 23 8091 1000

Edinburgh's Telford College
mail@ed-coll.ac.uk
www.ed-coll.ac.uk
Tel: +44 (0) 131 559 4000

Epping Forest College
enquiry@efc.ac.uk
www.epping-forest.ac.uk
Tel: +44 (0) 208 508 8311

Esher College
eshercollege@esher.ac.uk
www.esher.ac.uk
Tel: +44 (0) 20 8398 0291

Exeter College
info@exe-coll.ac.uk
www.exe-coll.ac.uk
Tel: +44 (0) 845 111 6000

Fareham College
info@fareham.ac.uk
www.fareham.ac.uk
Tel: +44 (0) 1329 815 200

Farnborough College of Technology
info@farn-ct.ac.uk
www.farn-ct.ac.uk
Tel: +44 (0) 1252 407 040

Farnham College
farnham@guildford.ac.uk
www.farnham.ac.uk
Tel: +44 (0) 1252 716 988

Fermanagh College
admissions@fermanaghcoll.ac.uk
www.fermanaghcoll.ac.uk
Tel: +44 (0) 28 6632 2431

Filton College
info@filton.ac.uk
www.filton.ac.uk
Tel: +44 (0) 117 931 2121

Franklin College
college@franklin.ac.uk
www.franklin.ac.uk
Tel: +44 (0) 1472 875 000

Furness College
info@furness.ac.uk
www.furness.ac.uk
Tel: +44 (0) 1229 825 017

Gateshead College
www.gateshead.ac.uk
Tel: +44 (0) 191 4900 300

Gloucestershire College
info@gloscol.ac.uk
www.gloscol.ac.uk
Tel: +44 (0) 845 155 2020

Godalming College
college@godalming.ac.uk
www.godalming.ac.uk
Tel: +44 (0) 1483 423 526

Great Yarmouth College
info@gyc.ac.uk
www.gyc.ac.uk
Tel: +44 (0) 1493 655 261

Guildford College
info@guildford.ac.uk
www.guildford.ac.uk
Tel: +44 (0) 1483 448 500

Hackney Community College
info@hackney.ac.uk
www.hackney.ac.uk
Tel: +44 (0) 207 613 9123

Halesowen College
info@halesowen.ac.uk
www.halesowen.ac.uk
Tel: +44 (0) 121 602 7777

Harrogate College
oncourse@harrogate.ac.uk
www.harrogate.ac.uk
Tel: +44 (0) 1423 879 466

Hartlepool College of Further Education
enquiries@hartlepoolfe.ac.uk
www.hartlepoolfe.ac.uk
Tel: +44 (0) 1429 295 000

Hartpury College
enquire@hartpury.ac.uk
www.hartpury.ac.uk
Tel: +44 (0) 1452 702345

Havant College
enquiries@havant.ac.uk
www.havant.ac.uk
Tel: +44 (0) 23 9248 3856

Havering College of Further & Higher Education
information@havering-college.ac.uk
www.havering-college.ac.uk
Tel: +44 (0) 1708 455 011

Herefordshire College of Technology
enquiries@hct.ac.uk
www.hct.ac.uk
Tel: +44 (0) 800 032 1986

Highbury College
info@highbury.ac.uk
www.highbury.ac.uk
Tel: +44 (0) 23 9238 3131

Holy Cross Sixth Form College
information@holycross.ac.uk
www.holycross.ac.uk
Tel: +44 (0) 161 762 4500

Hopwood Hall College
enquiries@hopwood.ac.uk
www.hopwood.ac.uk
Tel: +44 (0) 161 643 7560

Hove College
courses@hovecollege.co.uk
www.hovecollege.co.uk
Tel: +44 (0) 1273 772577

Hull College
info@hull-college.ac.uk
www.hull-college.ac.uk
Tel: +44 (0) 1482 598744

Huntingdonshire Regional College
college@huntingdon.ac.uk
www.huntingdon.ac.uk
Tel: +44 (0) 1480 379 100

Interlink College of Technology & Business Studies
ictbs@interlinktech.co.uk
www.interlinkcollege.org.uk
Tel: +44 (0) 20 8522 7600

Inverness College
info@inverness.uhi.ac.uk
www.inverness.uhi.ac.uk
Tel: +44 (0) 1463 273 000

Isle of Man College
mail@iomcollege.ac.im
www.iomcollege.ac.im
Tel: +44 (0) 1624 648 200

Itchen Sixth Form College
info@itchen.ac.uk
www.itchen.ac.uk
Tel: +44 (0) 23 8043 5636

Jewel & Esk College
info@jec.ac.uk
www.jec.ac.uk
Tel: +44 (0) 131 344 7000

John Wheatley College
advice@jwheatley.ac.uk
www.jwheatley.ac.uk
Tel: +44 (0) 141 588 1500

Keighley College
keighley@parklane.ac.uk
www.leedscitycollege.ac.uk
Tel: +44 (0) 1535 685 000

Kendal College
enquiries@kendal.ac.uk
www.kendal.ac.uk
Tel: +44 (0) 1539 814700

Kensington & Chelsea College
enquiries@kcc.ac.uk
www.kcc.ac.uk
Tel: +44 (0) 207 573 3600

Kidderminster College
learnerservices@kidderminster.ac.uk
www.kidderminster.ac.uk
Tel: +44 (0) 1562 820 811

Kilmarnock College
enquiries@kilmarnock.ac.uk
www.kilmarnock.ac.uk
Tel: +44 (0) 1563 523 501

Kingston College
info@kingston-college.ac.uk
www.kingston-college.ac.uk
Tel: +44 (0) 208 546 2151

Kirklees College - Dewsbury Centre
info@kirkleescollege.ac.uk
www.kirkleescollege.ac.uk
Tel: +44 (0) 1924 465916

Kirklees College - Huddersfield Centre
info@kirkleescollege.ac.uk
www.kirkleescollege.ac.uk
Tel: +44 (0) 1484 437000

Knowsley Community College
info@knowsleycollege.ac.uk
www.knowsleycollege.ac.uk
Tel: +44 (0) 845 155 1055

Lakes College
info@lcwc.ac.uk
www.lcwc.ac.uk
Tel: +44 (0) 1946 839 300

Lambeth College
courses@lambethcollege.ac.uk
www.lambethcollege.ac.uk
Tel: +44 (0) 207 501 5010

Lancaster & Morecambe College
www.lmc.ac.uk
Tel: +44 (0) 800 306 306

Langside College
enquireuk@langside.ac.uk
www.langside.ac.uk
Tel: +44 (0) 141 272 3600

Leeds City College - Technology Campus
technologycampus@leedscitycollege.ac.uk
www.leedscitycollege.ac.uk
Tel: +44 (0) 113 386 1700

Leeds City College - Thomas Danby Campus
danbycampus@leedscitycollege.ac.uk
www.leedscitycollege.ac.uk
Tel: +44 (0) 800 096 2319

Leicester College
info@leicestercollege.ac.uk
www.leicestercollege.ac.uk
Tel: +44 (0) 116 224 2240

Lewisham College
info@lewisham.ac.uk
www.lewisham.ac.uk
Tel: +44 (0) 208 692 0353

Lews Castle College
Admin.OfficeLE@lews.uhi.ac.uk
www.lews.uhi.ac.uk
Tel: +44 (0) 1851 770 000

Lincoln College
enquiries@lincolncollege.ac.uk
www.lincolncollege.ac.uk
Tel: +44 (0) 1522 876 000

Liverpool Community College
www.liv-coll.ac.uk
Tel: +44 (0) 151 252 1515

Loughborough College
info@loucoll.ac.uk
www.loucoll.ac.uk
Tel: +44 (0) 845 166 2950

Lowestoft College
www.lowestoft.ac.uk
Tel: +44 (0) 1502 583 521

Ludlow College
info@ludlow-college.ac.uk
www.ludlow-college.ac.uk
Tel: +44 (0) 1584 872 846

Macclesfield College
info@macclesfield.ac.uk
www.macclesfield.ac.uk
Tel: +44 (0) 1625 410 000

Middlesbrough College
marketing@mbro.ac.uk
www.mbro.ac.uk
Tel: +44 (0) 1642 333 333

Mid-Kent College
course.enquiries@midkent.ac.uk
www.midkent.ac.uk
Tel: +44 (0) 1622 691555

Milton Keynes College
info@mkcollege.ac.uk
www.mkcollege.ac.uk
Tel: +44 (0) 1908 684 444

Moray College
www.moray.ac.uk
Tel: +44 (0) 1343 576216

Morley College
enquiries@morleycollege.ac.uk
www.morleycollege.ac.uk
Tel: +44 (0) 207 928 8501

Motherwell College
information@motherwell.ac.uk
www.motherwell.ac.uk
Tel: +44 (0) 1698 232 425

Nelson & Colne College
reception@nelson.ac.uk
www.nelson.ac.uk
Tel: +44 (0) 1282 440 200

New College Durham
help@newdur.ac.uk
www.newcollegedurham.ac.uk
Tel: +44 (0) 191 375 4000

New College Nottingham
enquiries@ncn.ac.uk
www.ncn.ac.uk
Tel: +44 (0) 115 9100 100

New College Pontefract
reception@ncpontefract.ac.uk
www.ncpontefract.ac.uk
Tel: +44 (0) 1977 702 139

New College Stamford
enquiries@stamford.ac.uk
www.stamford.ac.uk
Tel: +44 (0) 1780 484 300

New College Swindon
admissions@newcollege.ac.uk
www.newcollege.ac.uk
Tel: +44 (0) 1793 611470

Newbury College
info@newbury-college.ac.uk
www.newbury-college.ac.uk
Tel: +44 (0) 1635 845 000

Newham College of Further Education
on-line.enquiries@newham.ac.uk
www.newham.ac.uk
Tel: +44 (0) 208 257 4000

North East Surrey College of Technology (Nescot)
info@nescot.ac.uk
www.nescot.ac.uk
Tel: +44 (0) 20 8394 3038

North East Worcestershire College
info@ne-worcs.ac.uk
www.ne-worcs.ac.uk
Tel: +44 (0) 1527 570 020

North Glasgow College
infocentre@north-gla.ac.uk
www.northglasgowcollege.ac.uk
Tel: +44 (0) 141†630 5000

North Hertfordshire College
enquiries@nhc.ac.uk
www.nhc.ac.uk
Tel: +44 (0) 1462 424242

North Nottinghamshire College
contact@nnc.ac.uk
www.nnc.ac.uk
Tel: +44 (0) 1909 504 504

North Warwickshire & Hinckley College
the.college@nwhc.ac.uk
www.nwhc.ac.uk
Tel: +44 (0) 24 7624 3000

North West Kent College
course.enquiries@nwkcollege.ac.uk
www.nwkcollege.ac.uk
Tel: +44 (0) 1322 629 400

North West Regional College
info@nwrc.ac.uk
www.nwrc.ac.uk
Tel: +44 (0) 28 7127 6000

Northampton College
enquiries@northamptoncollege.ac.uk
www.northamptoncollege.ac.uk
Tel: +44 (0) 1604 734 567

Northern Regional College - Coleraine Campus
info@nrc.ac.uk
www.nrc.ac.uk
028 7035 4717

Northern Regional College - Newtownabbey Campus
info@nrc.ac.uk
www.nrc.ac.uk
Tel: +44 (0) 28 9085 5000

Northumberland College
www.northumberland.ac.uk
Tel: +44 (0) 1670 841 200

Norton Radstock College
www.nortcoll.ac.uk
Tel: +44 (0) 1761 433 161

Oaklands College
advice.centre@oaklands.ac.uk
www.oaklands.ac.uk
Tel: +44 (0) 1727 737 080

Orkney College
orkney.college@uhi.ac.uk
www.orkney.uhi.ac.uk
Tel: +44 (0) 1856 569 000

Oxford & Cherwell Valley College
enquiries@ocvc.ac.uk
www.ocvc.ac.uk
Tel: +44 (0) 1865 550 550

Oxford Media & Business School
courses@oxfordbusiness.co.uk
www.oxfordbusiness.co.uk
Tel: +44 (0) 1865 240 963

Palmer's College
enquiries@palmers.ac.uk
www.palmers.ac.uk
Tel: +44 (0) 1375 370 121

Paston Sixth Form College
findoutmore@paston.ac.uk
www.paston.ac.uk
Tel: +44 (0) 1692 402 334

Perth College
pc.enquiries@perth.uhi.ac.uk
www.perth.uhi.ac.uk
Tel: +44 (0) 1738 877 000

Peterborough Regional College
info@peterborough.ac.uk
www.peterborough.ac.uk
Tel: +44 (0) 845 872 8722

Petroc - Barnstaple Campus
postbox@petroc.ac.uk
www.petroc.ac.uk
Tel: +44 (0) 1271 345 291

Petroc - Tiverton Campus
postbox@petroc.ac.uk
www.petroc.ac.uk
Tel: +44 (0) 1884 235 200

Pitman Training
www.pitman-training.com
Tel: +44 (0) 333 200 1300

Portsmouth College
reception@portsmouth-college.ac.uk
www.portsmouth-college.ac.uk
Tel: +44 (0) 23 9266 7521

Prior Pursglove College
www.pursglove.ac.uk
Tel: +44 (0) 1287 280 800

Queen Mary's College
info@qmc.ac.uk
www.qmc.ac.uk
Tel: +44 (0) 1256 417 500

Quest Professional Training and Recruiting for Businesses
info@questprofessional.co.uk
www.questprofessional.co.uk
Tel: +44 (0) 20 7233 5957

Redcar & Cleveland College
webenquiry@cleveland.ac.uk
www.cleveland.ac.uk
Tel: +44 (0) 1642 473 132

Reid Kerr College
sservices@reidkerr.ac.uk
www.reidkerr.ac.uk
Tel: +44 (0) 141 581 2222

Richard Taunton Sixth Form College
email@richardtaunton.ac.uk
www.richardtaunton.ac.uk
Tel: +44 (0) 23 8051 1811

Riverside College
info@riversidecollege.ac.uk
info@riverside.ac.uk
Tel: +44 (0) 151 257 2800

Royal Forest of Dean
enquiries@rfdc.ac.uk
www.rfdc.ac.uk
Tel: +44 (0) 1594 833 416

Sandwell College
enquiries@sandwell.ac.uk
www.sandwell.ac.uk
Tel: +44 (0) 121 556 6000

Selby College
info@selby.ac.uk
www.selby.ac.uk
Tel: +44 (0) 1757 211 000

Shipley College
enquiries@shipley.ac.uk
www.shipley.ac.uk
Tel: +44 (0) 1274 327 222

Solihull College
enquiries@solihull.ac.uk
www.solihull.ac.uk
Tel: +44 (0) 121 678 7000

South and West Kent College (K College) - Ashford Campus
info@kcollege.ac.uk
www.kcollege.ac.uk
Tel: +44 (0) 845 207 8220

South and West Kent College (K College) - Tonbridge Campus
info@kcollege.ac.uk
www.kcollege.ac.uk
Tel: +44 (0) 845 207 8220

South Cheshire College
info@s-cheshire.ac.uk
www.s-cheshire.ac.uk
Tel: +44 (0) 1270 654 654

South Devon College
enquiries@southdevon.ac.uk
www.southdevon.ac.uk
Tel: +44 (0) 1803 540 540

South Downs College
college@southdowns.ac.uk
www.southdowns.ac.uk
Tel: +44 (0) 23 9279 7979

South East Regional College
info@serc.ac.uk
www.serc.ac.uk
Tel: +44 (0) 845 6007555

South Essex College - Basildon Campus
learning@southessex.ac.uk
www.southessex.ac.uk
Tel: +44 (0) 845 52 12345

South Essex College - Southend Campus
learning@southessex.ac.uk
www.southessex.ac.uk
Tel: +44 (0) 845 52 12345

South Lanarkshire College
admissions@slc.ac.uk
www.south-lanarkshire-college.ac.uk
Tel: +44 (0) 1355 807780

South Leicestershire College
info@slcollege.ac.uk
www.slcollege.ac.uk
Tel: +44 (0) 116 264 3535

South Nottingham College
enquiries@snc.ac.uk
www.snc.ac.uk
Tel: +44 (0) 115 914 6414

South Staffordshire College- Cannock Campus
enquiries@southstaffs.ac.uk
www.southstaffs.ac.uk
Tel: +44 (0) 1543 462 200

South Staffordshire College- Tamworth Campus
enquiries@southstaffs.ac.uk
www.southstaffs.ac.uk
Tel: +44 (0) 1827 310202

South Thames College - Merton Campus
info@south-thames.ac.uk
www.south-thames.ac.uk
Tel: +44 (0) 20 8918 7777

South Thames College - Wandsworth Campus
studentservices@south-thames.ac.uk
www.south-thames.ac.uk
Tel: +44 (0) 208 918 7777

South Tyneside College
info@stc.ac.uk
www.stc.ac.uk
Tel: +44 (0) 191 427 3500

South West College
enquiries@swc.ac.uk
www.swc.ac.uk
Tel: +44 (0) 845 603 1881

South Worcestershire College - Evesham Campus
www.sworcs.ac.uk
Tel: +44 (0) 1386 712600

Southgate College
info@barnetsouthgate.ac.uk
www.barnetsouthgate.ac.uk
Tel: +44 (0) 20 8200 8300

Southport College
info@southport-college.ac.uk
www.southport-college.ac.uk
Tel: +44 (0) 1704 500 606

Southwark College
info@southwark.ac.uk
www.southwark.ac.uk
Tel: +44 (0) 207 815 1500

St David's Catholic College
enquiries@st-davids-coll.ac.uk
www.st-davids-coll.ac.uk
Tel: +44 (0) 29 2049 8555

St Helens College
www.sthelens.ac.uk
Tel: +44 (0) 1744 733 766

St Mary's College
reception@stmarysblackburn.ac.uk
www.stmarysblackburn.ac.uk
Tel: +44 (0) 1254 580 464

St Vincent College
info@stvincent.ac.uk
www.stvincent.ac.uk
Tel: +44 (0) 239 258 8311

Stafford College
enquiries@staffordcoll.ac.uk
www.staffordcoll.ac.uk
Tel: +44 (0) 1785 223 800

Stanmore College
enquiries@stanmore.ac.uk
www.stanmore.ac.uk
Tel: +44 (0) 20 8420 7700

Stockport College
enquiries@stockport.ac.uk
www.stockport.ac.uk
Tel: +44 (0) 161 958 3100

Stockton Riverside College
www.stockton.ac.uk
Tel: +44 (0) 1642 865 400

Stoke on Trent College
info@stokecoll.ac.uk
www.stokecoll.ac.uk
Tel: +44 (0) 1782 208 208

Stourbridge College
info@stourbridge.ac.uk
www.stourbridge.ac.uk
Tel: +44 (0) 1384 344 344

Stow College
enquiries@stow.ac.uk
www.stow.ac.uk
Tel: +44 (0)844 249 8585

Stratford-upon-Avon College
college@stratford.ac.uk
www.stratford.ac.uk
Tel: +44 (0) 1789 266 245

Strode College
courseinfo@strode-college.ac.uk
www.strode-college.ac.uk
Tel: +44 (0) 1458 844 400

Stroud College
enquire@stroudcol.ac.uk
http://stroud.ac.uk
Tel: +44 (0) 1453 763 424

Suffolk New College
info@suffolk.ac.uk
www.suffolk.ac.uk
Tel: +44 (0) 1473 382200

Sussex Downs College
info@sussexdowns.ac.uk
www.sussexdowns.ac.uk
Tel: +44 (0) 1273 483 188

Swindon College
studentservices@swindon-college.ac.uk
www.swindon-college.ac.uk
Tel: +44 (0) 1793 491 591

Tameside College
info@tameside.ac.uk
www.tameside.ac.uk
Tel: +44 (0) 161 908 6789

Thanet College
enquiries@thanet.ac.uk
www.thanet.ac.uk
Tel: +44 (0) 1843 605 040

The Adam Smith College
enquiries@adamsmith.ac.uk
www.adamsmith.ac.uk
Tel: +44 (0) 1592 223535

The Blackpool Sixth Form College
enquiries@blackpoolsixth.ac.uk
www.blackpoolsixth.ac.uk
Tel: +44 (0) 1253 394 911

The City College
admissions@citycollege.ac.uk
www.citycollege.ac.uk
Tel: +44 (0) 20 7253 1133

The College at Braintree
enquiries@braintree.ac.uk
www.colchester.ac.uk/braintree
Tel: +44 (0) 1206 814000

The College of Haringey, Enfield & North East London - Enfield Centre
admissions@conel.ac.uk
www.conel.ac.uk
Tel: +44 (0) 20 8802 3111

The College of Haringey, Enfield & North East London - Tottenham Centre
admissions@conel.ac.uk
www.conel.ac.uk
Tel: +44 (0) 208 802 3111

The College of North West London
cic@cnwl.ac.uk
www.cnwl.ac.uk
Tel: +44 (0) 208 208 5050

The College of West Anglia
enquiries@col-westanglia.ac.uk
www.cwa.ac.uk
Tel: +44 (0) 1553 761 144

The College Ystrad Mynach
enquiries@ystrad-mynach.ac.uk
www.ystrad-mynach.ac.uk
Tel: +44 (0) 1443 816 888

The Henley College
info@henleycol.ac.uk
www.henleycol.ac.uk
Tel: +44 (0) 1491 579 988

The Isle of Wight College
info@iwcollege.ac.uk
www.iwcollege.ac.uk
Tel: +44 (0) 1983 526 631

The Manchester College
enquiries@themanchestercollege.ac.uk
www.themanchestercollege.ac.uk
Tel: +44 (0) 161 909 6655

The North Highland College
info@northhighland.ac.uk
www.northhighland.ac.uk
Tel: +44 (0) 1847 889 000

The Oldham College
info@oldham.ac.uk
www.oldham.ac.uk
Tel: +44 (0) 161 785 4000

The Sheffield College
course-enquiries@sheffcol.ac.uk
www.sheffcol.ac.uk
Tel: +44 (0) 114 260 2600

Thomas Rotherham College
enquiries@thomroth.ac.uk
www.thomroth.ac.uk
Tel: +44 (0) 1709 300 600

Totton College
info@totton.ac.uk
www.totton.ac.uk
Tel: +44 (0) 2380 874 874

Tower Hamlets College
advice@tower.ac.uk
www.tower.ac.uk
Tel: +44 (0) 20 7510 7777

Trafford College
enquiries@trafford.ac.uk
www.trafford.ac.uk
Tel: +44 (0) 161 886 7070

Tresham College of Further & Higher Education
info@tresham.ac.uk
www.tresham.ac.uk
Tel: +44 (0) 845 658 8990

Truro and Penwith College - Penwith Campus
enquiry@truro-penwith.ac.uk
www.truro-penwith.ac.uk
Tel: +44 (0) 1736 335000

Truro and Penwith College - Truro Campus
enquiry@truro-penwith.ac.uk
www.truro-penwith.ac.uk
Tel: +44 (0) 1872 267000

Tyne Metropolitan College
enquiries@tynemet.ac.uk
www.tynemet.ac.uk
Tel: +44 (0) 191 229 5000

University of Derby - Buxton Campus
enquiriesudb@derby.ac.uk
www.derby.ac.uk
Tel: +44 (0) 1298 28321

Uxbridge College
enquiries@uxbridgecollege.ac.uk
www.uxbridge.ac.uk
Tel: +44 (0) 1895 853 333

Wakefield College
info@wakefield.ac.uk
www.wakefield.ac.uk
Tel: +44 (0) 1924 789 789

Walsall College
info@walsallcollege.ac.uk
www.walsallcollege.ac.uk
Tel: +44 (0) 1922 657 000

Waltham Forest College
info@waltham.ac.uk
www.waltham.ac.uk
Tel: +44 (0) 208 501 8000

Warrington Collegiate
learner.services@warrington.ac.uk
www.warrington.ac.uk
Tel: +44 (0) 1925 494 494

Warwickshire College
info@warkscol.ac.uk
www.warwickshire.ac.uk
Tel: +44 (0) 845 217 7414

West Cheshire College
info@west-cheshire.ac.uk
www.west-cheshire.ac.uk
Tel: +44 (0) 1244 656100

West Lancashire College - Skelmersdale Campus
enquiries@westlancs.ac.uk
www.westlancs.ac.uk
Tel: +44(0) 1695 52300

West Lothian College
enquiries@west-lothian.ac.uk
www.west-lothian.ac.uk
Tel: +44 (0) 1506 418181

West Nottinghamshire College
www.wnc.ac.uk
Tel: +44 (0) 808 100 3626

West Thames College
info@west-thames.ac.uk
www.west-thames.ac.uk
Tel: +44 (0) 20 8326 2000

Westminster Kingsway College
courseinfo@westking.ac.uk
www.westking.ac.uk
Tel: +44 (0) 870 060 9800

Weston College
enquiries@weston.ac.uk
www.weston.ac.uk
Tel: +44 (0) 1934 411 411

Weymouth College
lgs@weymouth.ac.uk
www.weymouth.ac.uk
Tel: +44 (0) 1305 761 100

Wigan & Leigh College
enquiries@wigan-leigh.ac.uk
www.wigan-leigh.ac.uk
Tel: +44 (0) 1942 761 600

Wiltshire College - Chippenham Campus
info@wiltshire.ac.uk
www.wiltshire.ac.uk
Tel: +44 (0) 1249 464644

Wirral Metropolitan College
http://wmc.ac.uk
Tel: +44 (0) 151 551 7777

Woking College
admissions@woking.ac.uk
www.woking.ac.uk
Tel: +44 (0) 1483 761 036

Worcestershire College of Technology
college@wortech.ac.uk
www.wortech.ac.uk
Tel: +44 (0) 1905 725 555

Yale College
college@yale-wrexham.ac.uk
www.yale-wrexham.co.uk
Tel: +44 (0) 1978 311 794

Yeovil College
info@yeovil.ac.uk
www.yeovil.ac.uk
Tel: +44 (0) 1935 423 921

Yorkshire Coast College
enquiries@ycoastco.ac.uk
www.yorkshirecoastcollege.ac.uk
Tel: +44 (0) 1723 372 105

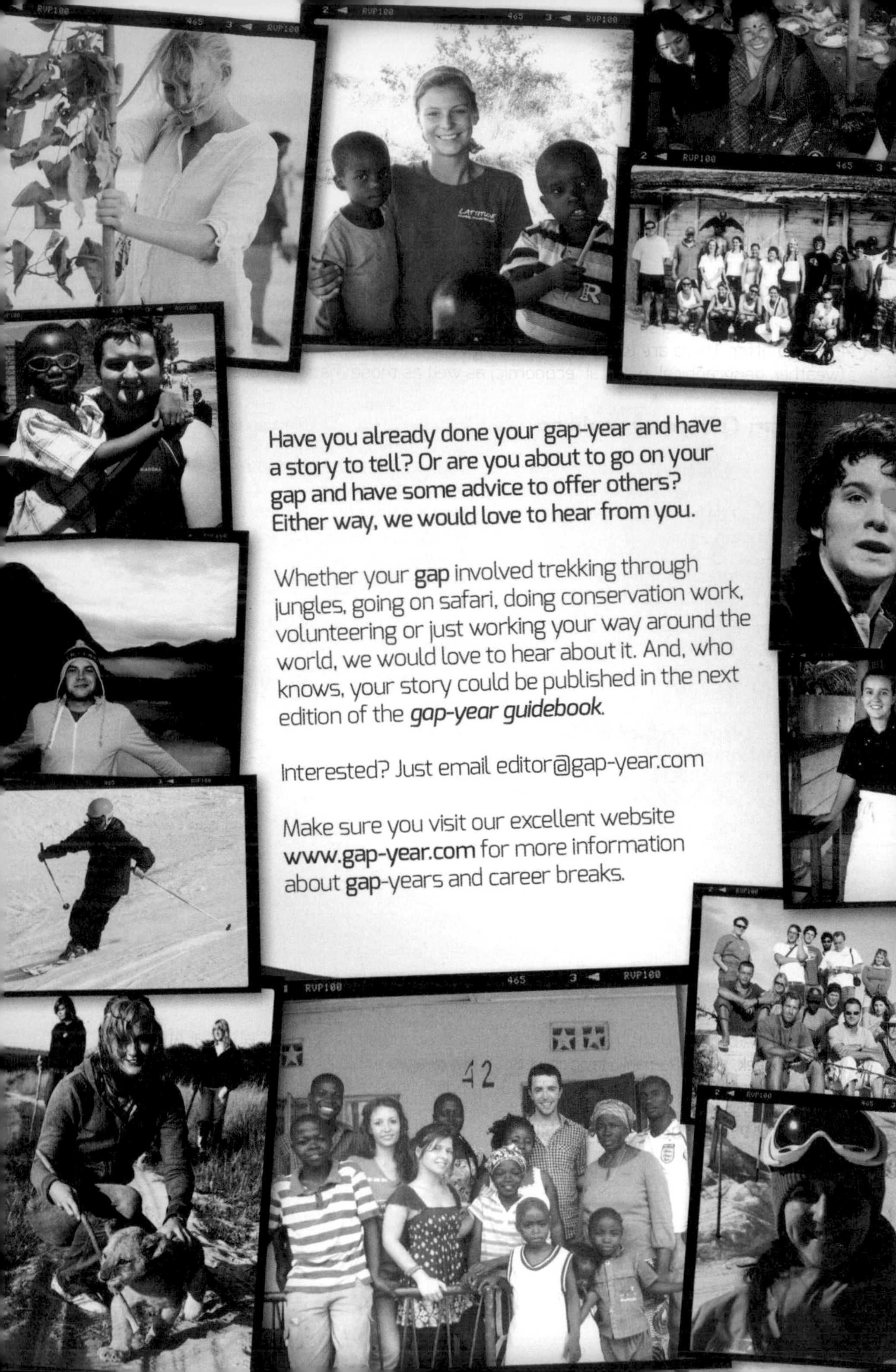
Have you already done your gap-year and have a story to tell? Or are you about to go on your gap and have some advice to offer others? Either way, we would love to hear from you.
Whether your gap involved trekking through jungles, going on safari, doing conservation work, volunteering or just working your way around the world, we would love to hear about it. And, who knows, your story could be published in the next edition of the gap-year guidebook.
Interested? Just email editor@gap-year.com
Make sure you visit our excellent website www.gap-year.com for more information about gap-years and career breaks.

Appendix

Country info

Once you have chosen where you want to go, whether one country or a dozen, do some research. It would be a shame to travel to the other side of the world and then miss what it has to offer. There are loads of websites giving interesting and useful factual advice (weather, geographical, political, economic) as well as those that are more touristy.

Foreign Office warnings

It's worth bearing in mind that economic and political situations can change rapidly in countries, so check with the Foreign and Commonwealth Office that the country is still safe to travel to before you go. There's a link to their website on: **www.gap-year.com**

It's important to look at the lists of specific areas which travellers should avoid. It's also worth noting the phone numbers of all British embassies and consulates in areas where you may be travelling, in case you need to contact them for help.

Telephone, text or email home regularly to save your family a lot of worry and British embassies a lot of wasted time. The following pages contain data for countries: make sure you check with the FCO for up-to-date information.

Afghanistan, The Islamic Republic of
Capital: Kabul
Currency: Afghani (AFN)
Religion: mainly Sunni Muslim
Languages: Farsi (Dari), Pashtu (Pashto or Pukhto)
British Embassy, Kabul: +93 (0) 700 102 000

Albania, The Republic of
Capital: Tirana
Currency: Lek (ALL)
Religion: Sunni Muslim, Albanian Orthodox, Roman Catholic
Languages: Albanian (Tosk is the official dialect), Greek, Vlach, Romani, Slavic dialects
British Embassy, Tirana: +355 4 223 4973/4/5

Algeria, The People's Democratic Republic of
Capital: Algiers
Currency: Algerian Dinar (DZD)
Religion: Sunni Muslim, Christian, Jewish
Language: Arabic (official language), French and Amazigh
British Embassy, Algiers: +213 77 00 85 000

Andorra, The Principality of
Capital: Andorra la Vella
Currency: Euro (EUR)
Religion: Roman Catholic
Language: Catalan (official), French, Spanish
British Consulate-General, Barcelona: +34 933 666 200

Angola, The Republic of
Capital: Luanda
Currency: Kwanza (AOA)
Religion: Indigenous beliefs, Roman Catholic, Christian, Muslim
Language: Portuguese (official), local African languages
British Embassy, Luanda: +244 (222) 334582

Anguilla (British Overseas Territory)
Capital: The Valley
Currency: Eastern Caribbean Dollar (XCD); US dollars accepted (USD)
Religion: Christian
Language: English
Government House, Anguilla: +1 (264) 497 2621/2

Antigua and Barbuda
Capital: Saint John's City
Currency: East Caribbean dollar (XCD)
Religion: Anglican, Moravian, Methodist and Roman Catholic
Language: English
St John's, Honorary British Consul: +1 268 561 5046

Argentina (The Argentine Republic)
Capital: Buenos Aires
Currency: Peso (ARS)
Religion: Roman Catholic, Protestant, Jewish and Muslim
Language: Spanish
British Embassy, Buenos Aires: +54 (11) 4808 2200

Armenia, The Republic of
Capital: Yerevan
Currency: Dram (AMD)
Religion: Armenian Orthodox, Christian, Yezidi
Language: Armenian, Russian, Yezidi
British Embassy, Yerevan: +374 (0) 10 264 301

Ascension Island (British Overseas Territory)
Capital: Georgetown
Currency: St Helena/Ascension Pound (SHP)
Religion: Christian
Language: English
Government House, Georgetown: +00 247 7000

Australia, The Commonwealth of
Capital: Canberra
Currency: Australian dollar (AUD)
Religion: Christian, Buddhist, Jewish, Muslim
Language: English, Aboriginal
British High Commission, Canberra: +61 (0) 2 6270 6666

Austria, The Republic of
Capital: Vienna
Currency: Euro (EUR)
Religion: Roman Catholic, Muslim and Protestant
Language: German
British Embassy, Vienna Tel: +43 (1) 716 130

Azerbaijan, The Republic of
Capital: Baku
Currency: Manat (AZN)
Religion: Muslim, Russian Orthodox, Armenian Orthodox
Language: Azeri, Russian, Armenian
British Embassy, Baku: +994 (12) 437 7878

Bahamas, The Commonwealth of The
Capital: Nassau
Currency: Bahamian Dollar (BSD)
Religion: Baptist, Anglican, Roman Catholic, Methodist, Church of God, Evangelical Protestants
Language: English, Creole (among Haitian immigrants)
refer to British High Commission, Kingston, Jamaica: +1 (876) 936 0700

Bahrain, The Kingdom of
Capital: Manama (Al Manamah)
Currency: Bahraini Dinar (BHD)
Religion: Muslim
Language: Arabic, English
British Embassy, Manama: +973 1757 4100; +973 1757 4167 (Information)

Bangladesh, The People's Republic of
Capital: Dhaka
Currency: Taka (BDT)
Religion: Muslim, Hindu, Buddhist, Christian
Language: Bangla, English, some tribal languages
British High Commission, Dhaka: +880 (2) 882 2705/6/7/8/9

Barbados
Capital: Bridgetown
Currency: Barbadian Dollar (BBD)
Religion: Protestant, Roman Catholic, Jewish, Muslim
Language: English
British High Commission, Bridgetown: +1 (246) 430 7800

Belarus, The Republic of
Capital: Minsk
Currency: Belarusian Ruble (BYR)

Religion: Eastern Orthodox Christian, Roman Catholic, Protestant, Jewish, Muslim
Language: Belarusian, Russian
British Embassy, Minsk: +375 (17) 229 8200

Belgium
Capital: Brussels
Currency: Euro (EUR)
Religion: Roman Catholic, Protestant
Language: Dutch, French, German
British Embassy, Brussels: +32 (2) 287 6211

Belize
Capital: Belmopan
Currency: Belizean Dollar (BZD)
Religion: Roman Catholic, Protestant, Muslim, Buddhist, Hindu, Bahá'í
Language: English, Creole, Spanish, indigenous languages
British High Commission, Belmopan: +501 822 2981/2717

Benin, The Republic of
Capital: Porto-Novo
Currency: CFA Franc BCEAO (XOF)
Religion: Indigenous beliefs, Christian, Muslim
Language: French, Fon, Yoruba, other African languages
Community Liaison Officer, Contonou: +229 21 30 32 65

Bermuda (British Overseas Territory)
Capital: Hamilton
Currency: Bermuda Dollar (BMD)
Religion: Christian, African Methodist Episcopalian
Language: English, Portuguese
Government House, Hamilton: +1 (441) 292 3600

Bhutan, The Kingdom of
Capital: Thimphu
Currency: Ngultrum (BTN), Indian Rupee (INR)
Religion: Buddhist, Hindu
Language: Dzongkha, various Tibetan and Nepalese dialects, English widely spoken
UK has no diplomatic representative in Bhutan. Contact British Deputy High Commission, Kolkata (Calcutta), India: +91 33 2288 5173-76

Bolivia, The Republic of
Capital: La Paz
Currency: Boliviano (BOB)
Religion: Roman Catholic, Evangelical Methodist
Language: Spanish, Quechua, Aymara and Indigenous dialects
British Embassy, La Paz: +591 (2) 243 3424

Bosnia and Herzegovina
Capital: Sarajevo
Currency: Convertible Mark (BAM)
Religion: Roman Catholic, Orthodox, Muslim
Language: Bosnian, Serbian, Croatian
British Embassy, Sarajevo: +387 33 282 200 (main); +387 33 20 4780 (Consular/Visa)

Botswana, The Republic of
Capital: Gaborone
Currency: Pula (BWP)
Religion: Christian, indigenous beliefs
Language: English, Setswana
British High Commission, Gabarone: +267 395 2841

Brazil, The Federative Republic of
Capital: Brasilia
Currency: Real (BRL)
Religion: Roman Catholic, Pentecostal, Animist
Language: Portuguese
British Embassy, Brasilia: +55 61 3329 2300

British Antartic Territory
Currency: Sterling
Language: English
refer to Foreign & Commonwealth Office, London: +44 (0) 20 7008 1500

British Virgin Islands
Capital: Road Town, Tortola
Currency: US Dollar (USD)
Religion: Christian
Language: English
Government House, Tortola: +1 284 494 2345/2370

Brunei (Darussalam)
Capital: Bandar Seri Begawan
Currency: Brunei Dollar (BND)
Religion: Muslim
Language: Malay, English, Cantonese, Mandarin, Hokkein, Hakka
British High Commission, Bandar Seri Begawan: +673 (2) 222 231;
+673 (2) 226 001 (Consular/Visa)

Bulgaria, The Republic of
Capital: Sofia
Currency: Lev (BGN)
Religion: Bulgarian Orthodox, Muslim, Roman Catholic, Jewish
Language: Bulgarian
British Embassy, Sofia: +359 (2) 933 9222

Burkina Faso
Capital: Ouagadougou
Currency: CFA Franc BCEAO (XOF)
Religion: Animist, Muslim, Christian
Language: French, indigenous languages
British Honorary Consul, Ouagadougou: +226 (50) 30 88 60

Burma (The Union of Myanmar)
Capital: Rangoon
Currency: Kyat (MMK)
Religion: Buddhist, Christian, Muslim, Animist
Language: Burmese, ethnic minority languages
British Embassy, Rangoon: +95 (1) 380 322

Burundi, The Republic of
Capital: Bujumbura
Currency: Burundi Franc (BIF)
Religion: Muslim, Roman Catholic, Animist
Language: Kirundi, French, Swahili
British Embassy, Liaison Office, Bujumbura: +257 22 246 478

Cambodia, The Kingdom of
Capital: Phnom Penh
Currency: Riel (KHR), and US Dollar (USD)
Religion: Buddhist, Muslim, Christian
Language: Khmer, Cambodian
British Embassy, Phnom Penh: +855 23 427124/48153

Cameroon, The Republic of
Capital: Yaounde
Currency: CFA Franc BEAC (XAF)
Religion: Christian, Muslim, indigenous beliefs
Language: French, English, Pidgin, numerous African dialects
British High Commission, Yaounde: +237 2222 05 45

Canada
Capital: Ottawa
Currency: Canadian Dollar (CAD)
Religion: Roman Catholic, Protestant, Muslim
Language: English, French
British High Commission, Ottawa: +1 (613) 237 1530

Cape Verde, The Republic of
Capital: Praia
Currency: Escudo (CVE)
Religion: Roman Catholic
Language: Portuguese, Crioulo
British Honorary Consulate, Sao Vincente: +238 232 3512

Cayman Islands (British Overseas Territory)
Capital: George Town (Grand Cayman)
Currency: Caymanian Dollar (KYD)
Religion: Christian
Language: English
Government House, George Town, Grand Cayman: +1 345 949 7900

Central African Republic, The
Capital: Bangui
Currency: CFA Franc BEAC (XAF)
Religion: Christian, Muslim, indigenous beliefs
Language: French, Sangho
refer to British High Commission, Yaoundé, Cameroon: +236 2161 8513

Chad, The Republic of
Capital: N'Djamena
Currency: CFA Franc BEAC (XAF)
Religion: Muslim, Christian, indigenous beliefs
Language: French, Arabic, local languages
refer to British High Commission, Yaoundé, Cameroon: +237 2222 05 45

Chile, The Republic of
Capital: Santiago de Chile
Currency: Peso (CLP)
Religion: Roman Catholic, Evangelical, Jewish, Muslim
Language: Spanish, Mapuche, Aymara, Quechua
British Embassy, Santiago: +56 (2) 370 4100

China, The People's Republic of
Capital: Beijing
Currency: Yuan Renminbi (CNY)
Religion: Officially atheist. Daoist, Buddhist, Muslim, Roman Catholic, Protestant (the 5 state-registered religions)
Language: Putonghua (Mandarin), many local Chinese dialects
British Embassy, Beijing: +86 (10) 5192 4000

Colombia, The Republic of
Capital: Bogotá
Currency: Peso (COP)
Religion: Roman Catholic, Evangelical
Language: Spanish, indigenous languages
British Embassy, Bogotá: +57 (1) 326 8300

Comoros, The Union of The
Capital: Moroni (Ngazidja)
Currency: Comoros Franc (KMF)
Religion: Muslim, Roman Catholic
Language: Comoran, French, Arabic
refer to British High Commission, Port Louis, Mauritius: +230 202 9400

Congo, The Republic of The
Capital: Brazzaville
Currency: CFA Franc BEAC (XAF)
Religion: Roman Catholic, Christian, Muslim, traditional beliefs
Language: French (official), Lingala, Kikongo, Munukutuba
refer to British Embassy, Kinshasa, Democratic Republic of Congo: +243 81 715 0761

Congo, The Democratic Republic of the
Capital: Kinshasa
Currency: Congolese Franc (CDF)
Religion: Roman Catholic, Protestant, Kimbanguist, Muslim, indigenous beliefs
Language: French (official), Lingala (trade language), Swahili, Kikongo, Tshiluba
British Embassy, Kinshasa: +243 81 715 0761

Costa Rica, The Republic of
Capital: San José
Currency: Colon (CRC)
Religion: Roman Catholic, Evangelical Protestant
Language: Spanish
British Embassy, San José: +506 2258 2025

Côte d'Ivoire, The Republic of (Ivory Coast)
Capital Yamoussoukro
Currency: CFA Franc BCEAO (XOF)
Religion: Muslim, Christian, indigenous beliefs
Language: French (official), Dioula, Baoule and other local native dialects
British Embassy, Côte d'Ivoire: +225 (22) 442 669

Croatia, The Republic of
Capital: Zagreb
Currency: Kuna (HRK)
Religion: Roman Catholic, Orthodox, Muslim
Language: Croatian
British Embassy, Zagreb: +385 (1) 6009 100

Cuba, The Republic of
Capital: Havana
Currency: Convertible Peso (CUC) or Peso (CUP)
Religion: Roman Catholic, Santeria, Protestant
Language: Spanish
British Embassy, Havana: +53 (7) 214 2200

Cyprus, The Republic of
Capital: Nicosia
Currency: Euro (EUR), Turkish Lira (in the north) (TRY)
Religion: Greek Orthodox, Muslim, Maronite, Armenian Apostolic
Language: Greek, Turkish, English
British High Commission, Nicosia: +357 22 861100

Czech Republic, The
Capital: Prague
Currency: Czech Koruna (Crown) (CZK)
Religion: Roman Catholic, Protestant, Orthodox, Atheist
Language: Czech
British Embassy, Prague: +420 257 402 111

Denmark, The Kingdom of
Capital: Copenhagen
Currency: Danish Krone (DKK)
Religion: Evangelical Lutheran, Christian, Muslim
Language: Danish, Faroese, Greenlandic (an Inuit dialect), English is the predominant second language
British Embassy, Copenhagen: +45 35 44 52 00

Djibouti, The Republic of
Capital: Djibouti
Currency: Djiboutian Franc (DJF)
Religion: Muslim, Christian
Language: French (official), Arabic (official), Somali, Afar
British Honorary Consul, Djibouti: +253 (3) 250915

Dominica, The Commonwealth of
Capital: Roseau
Currency: East Caribbean Dollar (XCD)
Religion: Roman Catholic, Protestant
Language: English (official), French patois (Creole)
British High Commission, Roseau: +767 275 7800

Dominican Republic, the
Capital: Santo Domingo
Currency: Dominican Peso (DOP)
Religion: Roman Catholic
Language: Spanish
British Embassy, Santo Domingo: +1 809 472 7111

East Timor - see Timor-Leste

Ecuador, The Republic of
Capital: Quito
Currency: US Dollar (USD)
Religion: Roman Catholic
Language: Spanish (official), Amerindian languages (especially Quechua)
British Embassy, Quito: +593 (2) 2970 800/1

Egypt, The Arab Republic of
Capital: Cairo
Currency: Egyptian Pound (EGP)
Religion: Muslim (mostly Sunni), Coptic Christian
Language: Arabic (official), English and French
British Embassy, Cairo: +20 (2) 2791 6000

El Salvador, The Republic of
Capital: San Salvador
Currency: US Dollar (USD), Colon (SVC)
Religion: Roman Catholic
Language: Spanish
British Honorary Consulate, El Salvador: +503 2236 5555

Equatorial Guinea, The Republic of
Capital: Malabo
Currency: CFA Franc BEAC (XAF)
Religion: Christian (predominantly Roman Catholic), indigenous religions
Language: Spanish (official), French (official), Fang, Bubi, Ibo
Refer to British High Commission, Abuja, Nigeria: +234 (9) 413 2010

Eritrea
Capital: Asmara
Currency: Nafka (ERN)
Religion: Christian, Muslim
Language: Tigrinya, Tigre, Arabic, English
British Embassy, Asmara: +291 1 12 01 45

Estonia, The Republic of
Capital: Tallinn
Currency: Kroon (EEK)
Religion: Lutheran, Orthodox Christian
Language: Estonian (official), Russian
British Embassy, Tallinn: +372 667 4700

Ethiopia, The Federal Democratic Republic of
Capital: Addis Ababa
Currency: Ethiopian Birr (ETB)
Religion: Orthodox Christian, Muslim, Animist, Protestant
Language: Amharic, Tigrinya, Oromigna, Guaragigna, Sidaminga, Somali, Arabic, other local dialects, English (major foreign language taught in schools)
British Embassy, Addis Ababa: +251 (11) 661 2354

Falkland Islands (British Overseas Territory)
Capital: Stanley
Currency: Falkland Island Pound (FKP)
Religion: Christian, Roman Catholic, United Reformed Church, Anglican
Language: English
Government House, Stanley: +500 282 00

Fiji (The Republic of the Fiji Islands)
Capital: Suva
Currency: Fijian Dollar (FJD)
Religion: Christian, Hindu, Muslim
Language: English (official), Hindustani, Gujarati, numerous Fijian dialects
British High Commission, Suva: +679 3229 100

Finland, The Republic of
Capital: Helsinki
Currency: Euro (EUR)
Religion: Lutheran, Orthodox
Language: Finnish (official), Swedish (official), growing Russian speaking minority and small Sami speaking community
British Embassy, Helsinki: +358 (0) 9 2286 5100/5210/5216

France (The French Republic)
Capital: Paris
Currency: Euro (EUR)
Religion: Roman Catholic, Protestant, Jewish, Muslim
Language: French
British Embassy, Paris: +33 1 44 51 31 00

Gabon (The Gabonese Republic)
Capital: Libreville
Currency: CFA Franc BEAC (XAF)
Religion: Christian, Muslim, indigenous beliefs
Language: French (official), Fang, Myene, Bateke, Bapounou/Eschira, Badjabi
British Honorary Consulate, Libreville: +241 762 200

Gambia, The Republic of
Capital: Banjul
Currency: Dalasi (GMD)
Religion: Muslim, Christian, indigenous beliefs
Language: English (official), Mandinka, Wolof, Fula, indigenous languages
British High Commission, Banjul: +220 449 5133

Georgia
Capital: Tbilisi
Currency: Lari (GEL)
Religion: Georgian Orthodox, Muslim, Russian Orthodox, Armenian Apostolic
Language: Georgian (official), Russian, Armenian, Azeri, Abkhaz
British Embassy, Tbilisi: +995 32 274 747

Germany, The Federal Republic of
Capital: Berlin
Currency: Euro (EUR)
Religion: Protestant, Roman Catholic, Muslim
Language: German
British Embassy, Berlin: +49 (30) 20457-0

Ghana, The Republic of
Capital: Accra
Currency: Cedi (GHS)
Religion: Muslim, Christian, indigenous beliefs
Language: English (official), African languages (including Akan, Mossi, Ewe, and Hausa), Fante, Ga-Adangme, 75 spoken languages
British High Commission, Accra: +233 (302) 213250

Gibraltar (British Overseas Territory)
Capital: Gibraltar
Currency: Gibraltar Pound (GIP)
Religion: Roman Catholic, Protestantism, Muslim, Hindu, Jewish
Language: English
Governor's Office, Main Street: +350 200 45 440

Greece (The Hellenic Republic)
Capital: Athens
Currency: Euro (EUR)
Religion: Greek Orthodox, Muslim
Language: Greek
British Embassy, Athens: +30 210 727 2600

Grenada
Capital: St George's
Currency: East Caribbean Dollar (XCD)
Religion: Roman Catholic, Anglican, Protestant
Language: English (official), French patois
Honorary British Consul, St George's: +473 405 8072

Guatemala
Capital: Guatemala City
Currency: Quetzal (GTQ)
Religion: Roman Catholic, Protestant, Judasim, Muslim, indigenous Mayan beliefs
Language: Spanish, there are 23 officially recognized Amerindian languages
British Embassy, Guatemala City: +502 2380 7300

Guinea, The Republic of
Capital: Conakry
Currency: Guinean Franc (GNF)
Religion: Muslim, Christian, traditional beliefs
Language: French (official), eight local languages taught in schools (Basari, Pular, Kissi, Koniagi, Kpelle, Loma, Malinke and Susu)
British Embassy, Conakry: +224 63 35 53 29

Guinea-Bissau, The Republic of
Capital: Bissau
Currency: CFA Franc BCEAO (XOF)
Religion: Muslim, Christian, indigenous beliefs
Language: Portuguese (official), Crioulo, indigenous African languages
Honorary British Consulate: +245 320 1224/1216

Guyana, The Co-operative Republic of
Capital: Georgetown
Currency: Guyanese Dollar (GYD)
Religion: Christian, Hindu, Muslim
Language: English, Amerindian dialects, Creole
British High Commission, Georgetown: +592 226 58 81

Haiti, The Republic of
Capital: Port-au-Prince
Currency: The Gourde (HTG)
Religion: Roman Catholic, Protestant, Baptist, Pentecostal, Adventist, also Voodoo
Language: French (official), Creole (official)
British Consulate, Port-au-Prince: +509 3744 6371

Holy See, Rome (Vatican City State)
Capital: Vatican City
Currency: Euro (EUR)
Religion: Roman Catholic
Language: Latin, Italian, English and French
British Embassy, Rome: +39 06 4220 4000

Honduras, The Republic of
Capital: Tegucigalpa
Currency: Lempira (HNL)
Religion: Roman Catholic, Protestant
Language: Spanish, English (business), Amerindian dialects
British Embassy, Tegucigalpa: +504 237 6577/6459

Hong Kong (The Hong Kong Special Administration of China)
Currency: Hong Kong Dollar (HKD)
Religion: Buddhist, Taoist, Christian, Muslim, Hindu, Sikhist, Jewish
Language: Chinese (Cantonese), English
British Consulate General, Hong Kong: +852 2901 3281

Hungary, The Republic of
Capital: Budapest
Currency: Forint (HUF)
Religion: Roman Catholic, Calvinist, Lutheran, Jewish, Atheist
Language: Hungarian
British Embassy, Budapest: +36 (1) 266 2888

Iceland, The Republic of
Capital: Reykjavik
Currency: Icelandic Krona (ISK)
Religion: Evangelical Lutheran, Protestant, Roman Catholic
Language: Icelandic
British Embassy, Reykjavik: +354 550 5100

India
Capital: New Delhi
Currency: Rupee (INR)
Religion: Hindu, Muslim, Christian, Sikhist
Language: Hindi (official), 18 main and regional official state languages, plus 24 further languages, 720 dialects and 23 tribal languages, English (officially an associate language, is used particularly for political, and commercial communication)
British High Commission, New Delhi: +91 (11) 2419 2100

Indonesia, The Republic of
Capital: Jakarta
Currency: Rupiah (IDR)
Religion: Muslim, Protestant, Roman Catholic, Hindu, Buddhist
Language: Bahasa Indonesia (official), over 583 languages and dialects
British Embassy, Jakarta: +62 (21) 2356 5200

Iran, The Islamic Republic of
Capital: Tehran
Currency: Rial (IRR)
Religion: Shi'a Muslim, Sunni Muslim, Zoroastrian, Jewish, Christian, Bahá'i
Language: Persian (Farsi), Azeri, Kurdish, Arabic, Luri, Baluchi

Iraq, Republic of
Capital: Baghdad
Currency: New Iraqi Dinar (IQD)
Religion: Muslim, Christian
Language: Arabic, Kurdish, Assyrian, Armenian, Turkoman
British Embassy, Bagdad: +964 7901 926 280

Ireland, Republic of
Capital: Dublin
Currency: Euro (EUR)
Religion: Roman Catholic, Church of Ireland
Language: Irish, English
British Embassy, Dublin: +353 (1) 205 3700

Israel, The State of
Capital: Tel Aviv
Currency: New Israeli Shekel (ILS)
Religion: Jewish, Muslim, Christian
Language: Hebrew, Arabic, English, Russian
British Embassy, Tel Aviv: +972 (3) 725 1222

Italy
Capital: Rome
Currency: Euro (EUR)
Religion: Roman Catholic, Jewish, Protestant, Muslim
Language: Italian (official), German, French, Slovene
British Embassy, Rome: +39 06 4220 0001

Ivory Coast - see Côte d'Ivoire

Jamaica
Capital: Kingston
Currency: Jamaican Dollar (JMD)
Religion: Anglican, Baptist and other Protestant, Roman Catholic, Rastafarian, Jewish, Seventh-Day Adventist
Language: English, Patois
British High Commission, Kingston: +1 (876) 936 0700

Japan
Capital: Tokyo
Currency: Yen (JPY)
Religion: Shinto, Buddhist, Christian
Language: Japanese
British Embassy, Tokyo: +81 (3) 5211 1100

Jordan, The Hashemite Kingdom of
Capital: Amman
Currency: Jordanian Dinar (JOD)
Religion: Sunni Muslim, Christian
Language: Arabic (official), English
British Embassy, Amman: +962 6 590 9200

Kazakhstan, The Republic of
Capital: Astana
Currency: Kazakh Tenge (KZT)
Religion: Muslim, Russian Orthodox, Protestant
Language: Kazakh, Russian
British Embassy, Astana: +7 7172 556200

Kenya, The Republic of
Capital: Nairobi
Currency: Kenyan Shilling (KES)
Religion: Protestant (including Evangelical), Roman Catholic, indigenous beliefs, Muslim
Language: English (official), Kiswahili, numerous indigenous languages
British High Commission, Nairobi: +254 (20) 284 4000

Kiribati, The Republic of
Capital: Tarawa
Currency: Australian Dollar (AUD)
Religion: Roman Catholic, Protestant (Congregational), Seventh-Day Adventist, Bahá'í, Latter-day Saints, Church of God
Language: English (official), I-Kiribati
refer to British High Commission, Suva, Fiji: +679 3229 100

Korea, The Democratic People's Republic of (North Korea)
Capital: Pyongyang
Currency: North Korean Won (KPW); foreigners are required to use Euros
Religion: Buddhist, Christian, Chondo
Language: Korean
British Embassy, Pyongyang: +850 2 381 7980 (International); 02 382 7980 (Local dialling)

Korea, The Republic of (South Korea)
Capital: Seoul
Currency: South Korean Won (KRW)
Religion: Shamanist, Buddhist, Confuciant, Chondogyo, Roman Catholic, Protestant
Language: Korean
British Embassy, Seoul: +82 (2) 3210 5500

Kosovo
Capital: Pristina
Currency: Euro (EUR)
Religion: Muslim, Serbian Orthodox, Roman Catholic
Language: Albanian, Serbian, Bosniak, Turkish
British Embassy, Pristina: +381 (38) 254 700

Kuwait, The State of
Capital: Kuwait City
Currency: Kuwaiti Dinar (KWD)
Religion: Muslim, Christian, other religions restricted
Language: Arabic (official), English (second official language)
British Embassy, Dasman: +965 2259 4320

Kyrgyzstan (The Kyrgyz Republic)
Capital: Bishkek
Currency: Som (KGS)
Religion: Muslim, Russian Orthodox, Christian minorities
Language: Kyrgyz, Russian
British Embassy, Bishkek: +996 (0) 312 69 02 32

Laos (The Lao People's Democratic Republic)
Capital: Vientiane
Currency: Kip (LAK)
Religion: Buddhist, Animist, Christian, Muslim
Language: Lao
British Embassy (resident at Bangkok): +66 (0) 2 305 8333

Latvia, The Republic of
Capital: Riga
Currency: Lat (LVL)
Religion: Lutheran, Roman Catholic, Russian Orthodox
Language: Latvian, Russian
British Embassy, Riga: +371 6777 4700

Lebanon (The Lebanese Republic)
Capital: Beirut
Currency: Lebanese Pound (LBP)
Religion: 18 registered sects including Druze, Maronite Christian, Shi'a and Sunni Muslim
Language: Arabic (official), English, French, Armenian
British Embassy, Beirut: +961 (1) 9608 00 (24 hours)

Lesotho, The Kingdom of
Capital: Maseru
Currency: Loti (LSL)
Religion: Christian, indigenous beliefs
Language: Sesotho, English
British Honorary Consulate, Maseru: +266 2231 3929

Liberia, The Republic of
Capital: Monrovia
Currency: Liberian Dollar (LRD), US Dollar (USD)
Religion: Christian, Muslim, indigenous beliefs
Language: English (official), indigenous languages
British Honorary Consulate, Monrovia: 00 231 (0) 77 530 320

Libya (The Great Socialist People's Libyan Arab Jamahiriya)
Capital: Tripoli
Currency: Dinar (LYD)
Religion: Sunni Muslim
Language: Arabic, Italian and English understood in major cities
British Embassy, Tripoli: +218 (21) 335 1084/5/6

Liechtenstein, The Principality of
Capital: Vaduz
Currency: Swiss Franc (CHF)
Religion: Roman Catholic, Protestant
Language: German (official), Alemannic dialect
refer to British Embassy, Berne, Switzerland: +41 (31) 359 7700

Lithuania, The Republic of
Capital: Vilnius
Currency: Litas (LTL)
Religion: Roman Catholic
Language: Lithuanian (official), Russian, English
British Embassy, Vilnius: +370 5 246 29 00

Luxembourg, The Grand Duchy of
Capital: Luxembourg
Currency: Euro (EUR)
Religion: Roman Catholic, Protestant, Jewish, Muslim
Language: Luxembourgish, German, French
British Embassy, Luxembourg: + 352 22 98 64

Macao (The Macao Special Administrative Region of the People's Republic of China)
Currency: Pataca (MOP)
Religion: Buddhist, Christian, Taoist
Language: Cantonese, Portuguese, English
British Honorary Consulate, Macao: +853 685 0886

Macedonia, republic of
Capital: Skopje
Currency: Macedonian Denar (MKD)
Religion: Orthodox, Muslim
Language: Macedonian, Albanian, Turkish, Serbian, Vlach, Roma
British Embassy, Skopje: +389 (2) 3299 299

Madagascar, The Republic of
Capital: Antananarivo
Currency: Ariary (MGA)
Religion: Christian, indigenous beliefs, Muslim
Language: Malagasy, French
British Consulate, Toamasina: +261 (20) 53 325 48/325 69

Malawi, The Republic of
Capital: Lilongwe
Currency: Kwacha (MWK)
Religion: Protestant, Roman Catholic, Muslim, Hindu, indigenous beliefs
Language: English (official), Chichewa (national)
British High Commission, Liongwe: +265 (1) 772 400

Malaysia, The Federation of
Capital: Kuala Lumpur
Currency: Ringgit (MYR)
Religion: Muslim, Buddhist, Taoist, Christian, Hindu, Animist
Language: Bahasa Malay (national language), Iban, English widespread, Chinese, Tamil
British High Commission, Kuala Lumpur: +60 (3) 2170 2200

Maldives, The Republic of
Capital: Malé
Currency: Rufiyaa (MVR); resort islands accept US Dollar (USD)
Religion: Sunni Muslim (other religions illegal)
Language: Dhivehi, but English widely spoken in Malé and resort islands
refer to British High Commission, Colombo, Sri Lanka: +94 (11) 539 0639

Mali, The Republic of
Capital: Bamako
Currency: CFA Franc BCEAO (XOF)
Religion: Muslim, Christian, indigenous beliefs
Language: French (official), Bambara, and numerous other African languages
British Embassy Liaison Office, Bamako: +223 2021 3412

Malta, The Republic of
Capital: Valletta
Currency: Euro (EUR)
Religion: Roman Catholic
Language: Maltese, English
British High Commission, Valletta: +356 2323 0000

Marshall Islands, Republic of the
Capital: Majuro
Currency: US Dollar (USD)
Religion: Christian (mostly Protestant)
Language: English, two major Marshallese dialects, Japanese
refer to British Embassy, Manilia: +63 (2) 858 2200

Mauritania, The Islamic Republic of
Capital: Nouakchott
Currency: Ouguiya (MRO)
Religion: Muslim
Language: Hassaniya Arabic (official), Pulaar, Soninke, Wolof, French widely used in business
British Honorary Consul, Nouakchott: +222 525 83 31

Mauritius, The Republic of
Capital: Port Louis
Currency: Mauritian Rupee (MUR)
Religion: Hindu, Christian, Muslim
Language: English, French, Creole
British Honorary Consulate, Rodrigues: +230 832 0120

Mexico (The United Mexican State)
Capital: Mexico City
Currency: Mexican Peso (MXN)
Religion: Roman Catholic, Protestant
Language: Spanish, at least 62 other regional languages
British Embassy, Mexico City: +52 (55) 1670 3200

Micronesia, The Federated States of
Capital: Palikir
Currency: US Dollar (USD)
Religion: Roman Catholic, Protestant
Language: English, Trukese, Pohnpeian, Yapese, Kosrean, Ulithian, Woleaian, Nukuoro, Kapingamarangi
refer to British Embassy, Manila: +63 (2) 858 2200

Moldova, The Republic of
Capital: Chisinau
Currency: Moldovan Leu (MDL)
Religion: Eastern Orthodox, Jewish, Baptist
Language: Moldovan, Russian (official)
British Embassy, Chisinau: +373 22 22 59 02; out of hours +373 69 10 44 42

Monaco, The Principality of
Capital: Monaco
Currency: Euro (EUR)
Religion: Roman Catholic
Language: French (official), Italian, Monegasque, English
British Honorary Consulate, Monaco: +377 93 50 99 54

Mongolia
Capital: Ulaanbaatar
Currency: Togrog (Tughrik) (MNT)
Religion: Tibetan Buddhist, Shamanist, Muslim (south-west)
Language: Khalkh Mongol, Kazakh
British Embassy, Ulaanbaatar: +976 (11) 458 133

Montenegro, Republic of
Capital: Podgorica
Currency: Euro (EUR)
Religion: Christian, Muslim
Language: Montenegrin, Serbian, Bosnian, Albanian, Croatian
British Embassy, Podgorica: +382 (20) 618 010

Montserrat (British Overseas Territory)
Capital: Plymouth (destroyed by the last volcanic eruption)
Currency: East Caribbean Dollar (XCD)
Religion: Christian
Language: English
Governor's Office, Brades: +1 (664) 491 2688/9

Morocco, The Kingdom of
Capital: Rabat
Currency: Moroccan Dirham (MAD)
Religion: Muslim, Christian, Jewish
Language: Arabic (official), Berber dialects, French (commerce, diplomacy and government)
British Embassy, Rabat: +212 (537) 63 33 33

Mozambique, The Republic of
Capital: Maputo
Currency: Metical (MZN)
Religion: Roman Catholic, Christian, Muslim, indigenous beliefs
Language: Portuguese (official), over 16 African languages and dialects
British High Commission, Maputo: +258 21 356 000

Myanmar (see Burma)

Namibia, The Republic of
Capital: Windhoek
Currency: Namibian Dollar (NAD)
Religion: Christian
Language: English (official), Afrikaans, German, and several indigenous languages
British High Commission, Windhoek: +264 (61) 274800

Nauru, The Republic of
Capital: Yaren District (unofficial)
Currency: Australian Dollar (AUD)
Religion: Protestant, Roman Catholic
Language: Nauruan (official), English (commerce and government, widely understood)
refer to British High Commission, Suva, Fiji: +679 322 9100

Nepal
Capital: Kathmandu
Currency: Nepalese Rupee (NPR)
Religion: Hindu, Buddhist, Muslim
Language: Nepali (official), Newari (mainly in Kathmandu), Tibetan languages (mainly hill areas), Indian languages (mainly Terai areas). Nepal has over 30 languages and many dialects.
British Embassy, Kathmandu: +977 (1) 441 0583/1281/4588/1590

Netherlands, The Kingdom of The
Capital: Amsterdam
Currency: Euro (EUR)
Religion: Roman Catholic, Protestant, Muslim
Language: Dutch
British Embassy, The Hague: +31 (0) 70 4270 427

New Zealand
Capital: Wellington
Currency: New Zealand Dollar (NZD)
Religion: Anglican, Presbyterian, Roman Catholic, Methodist, Baptist
Language: English, Maori
British High Commission, Wellington: +64 (4) 924 2888

Nicaragua, The Republic of
Capital: Managua
Currency: Cordoba (NIO)
Religion: Roman Catholic, Evangelical Protestant
Language: Spanish (official), English, Miskito, Creole, Mayanga, Garifuna, Rama
British Honorary Consul, Managua: +505 254 5454/3839

Niger, The Republic of
Capital: Niamey
Currency: CFA Franc BCEAO (XOF)
Religion: Muslim
Language: French (official), Arabic, local languages widely spoken
British Honorary Consul, Niamey: +227 9687 8130

Nigeria, The Federal Republic of
Capital: Abuja
Currency: Naira (NGN)
Religion: Muslim, Christian, traditional beliefs
Language: English (official), Hausa, Yoruba, Igbo
British High Commission, Abuja: +234 (9) 413 2010/2011/3885-7

Norway, The Kingdom of
Capital: Oslo
Currency: Norwegian Kroner (NOK)
Religion: Church of Norway (Evangelical Lutheran)
Language: Norwegian (bokmål and nynorsk), Sami
British Embassy, Oslo: +47 23 13 27 00

Oman, The Sultanate of
Capital: Muscat
Currency: Oman Rial (OMR)
Religion: Ibadhi Muslim, Sunni Muslim, Shi'a Muslim, Hindu, Christian
Language: Arabic (official), English, Farsi, Baluchi, Urdu
British Embassy, Muscat: +968 24 609 000; (out of hours emergencies) +968 9920 0865

Pakistan, The Islamic Republic of
Capital: Islamabad
Currency: Rupee (PKR)
Religion: Muslim, Hindu, Christian
Language: Punjabi, Sindhi, Pashtun, Urdu, Balochi, English and other local languages
British High Commission, Islamabad: +92 51 201 2000

Palau, The Republic of
Capital: Suva
Currency: United States Dollar (USD)
Religion: Christian, Hindu, Muslim
Language: English, numerous Fijian dialects, Gujarati, Fijian Hindi
refer to British Ambassador, Manila, The Philippines: +63 (2) 858 2200

Palestine (The Occupied Palestinian Territories)
Currency: New Israeli Shekel (ILS), Jordanian Dinar (JOD) (West Bank Only)
Religion: Muslim, Christian
Language: Arabic, English widely spoken
British Consulate-General, Gaza: +972 (08) 283 7724

Panama, The Republic of
Capital: Panama City
Currency: US Dollar (USD) (known locally as the Balboa (PAB))
Religion: Roman Catholic, Protestant, Jewish, Muslim
Language: Spanish (official), English
British Embassy, Panama City: +507 269 0866

Papua New Guinea, The Independent State of
Capital: Port Moresby
Currency: Kina (PGK)
Religion: Christian according to its constitution, Roman Catholic, Evangelical Lutheran, Evangelical Alliance, Pentecostal, Baptist, Anglican, Seventh Day Adventist, United Church, Buddhist, Muslim, Hindu
Language: English, Pidgin, Hiri Motu, over 820 different languages
British High Commission, Port Moresby: +675 325 1677

Paraguay, The Republic of
Capital: Asunción
Currency: Guarani (PYG)
Religion: Roman Catholic, Mennonite, Protestant, Latter-day Saints, Jewish, Russian Orthodox
Language: Spanish (official), Guaraní (official)
British Honorary Consulate, Asunción: +595 (21) 210 405

Peru, The Republic of
Capital: Lima
Currency: Nuevo Sol (PEN)
Religion: Roman Catholic
Language: Spanish (official), Quechua (official), Aymara and several minor Amazonian languages
British Embassy, Lima: +51 (1) 617 3000 (main); 3053/3054 (consular)

Philippines, The Republic of the
Capital: Metro Manila
Currency: Peso (PHP)
Religion: Roman Catholic, Protestant, Muslim
Language: Filipino (official), English (official)
British Embassy, Manila: +63 (2) 858 2200

Pitcairn, Henderson, Ducie & Oeno Islands (British Overseas Territory)
Capital: Adamstown
Currency: New Zealand Dollar (NZD)
Religion: Seventh Day Adventist
Language: English, Pitkern (a mix of English and Tahitian)
British High Commission, Auckland, New Zealand: +64 (9) 366 0186

Poland, The Republic of
Capital: Warsaw
Currency: Zloty (PLN)
Religion: Roman Catholic, Eastern Orthodox, Protestant
Language: Polish
British Embassy, Warsaw: +48 (22) 311 00 00

Portugal (The Portuguese Republic)
Capital: Lisbon
Currency: Euro (EUR)
Religion: Roman Catholic, Protestant
Language: Portuguese
British Embassy, Lisbon: +351 (21) 392 4000

Qatar, The State of
Capital: Doha
Currency: Qatari Riyal (QAR)
Religion: Muslim
Language: Arabic (official), English, Urdu
British Embassy, Doha: +974 4496 2000

Romania
Capital: Bucharest
Currency: New Leu (RON)
Religion: Orthodox, Roman Catholic, Protestant, Reformed, Greek Catholic, Unitarian
Language: Romanian (official), English, French, German
British Embassy, Bucharest: +40 (21) 201 7200

Russia Federation, The
Capital: Moscow
Currency: Ruble (RUB)
Religion: Orthodox Christian, Muslim, Jewish, Buddhist
Language: Russian, Tatar
British Embassy, Moscow: +7 (495) 956 7200

Rwanda, The Republic of
Capital: Kigali
Currency: Rwandan Franc (RWF)
Religion: Roman Catholic, Protestant, Muslim, indigenous beliefs
Language: Kinyarwanda (official), French (official), English (official), Kiswahili (used in commercial centres and by army)
British Embassy, Kigali: +250 252 556000

Saint Helena (British Overseas Territory)
Capital: Jamestown
Currency: St Helena Pound (SHP)
Religion: Christiantiy, Bahá'í
Language: English
Governor's Office, Jamestown: +290 2555

Saint Kitts & Nevis (The Federation of St Christopher & Nevis)
Capital: Basseterre
Currency: East Caribbean Dollar (XCD)
Religion: Anglican, Roman Catholic, Evangelical Protestant
Language: English
Honorary British Consul, Basseterre: +1 (869) 764 4677

Saint Lucia
Capital: Castries
Currency: East Caribbean Dollar (XCD)
Religion: Roman Catholic, Anglican, Methodist, Baptist, Jewish, Hindu, Muslim
Language: English (official), French patois (Kweyol)
British High Commission, Castries: +1 (758) 452 2484/5 (resides in Barbados)

Saint Vincent and the Grenadines
Capital: Kingstown
Currency: East Caribbean Dollar (XCD)
Religion: Anglican, Methodist, Roman Catholic, Seventh-Day Adventist, Hindu, other Protestant
Language: English
British High Consul, Kingstown: +784 457 6860

Samoa, The Independent State of
Capital: Apia
Currency: Samoan Tala (WST)
Religion: Roman Catholic, Methodist, Latter-day Saints
Language: Samoan, English
British Honorary Consulate, Apia: +685 27123

São Tomé & Príncipe, The Democratic State of
Capital: São Tomé
Currency: Dobra (STD)
Religion: Christian
Language: Portuguese, Lungwa Santomé, and other creole dialects
Refer to the British Embassy in Luanda, Angola: +244 222 334582

Saudi Arabia, The Kingdom of
Capital: Riyadh
Currency: Saudi Riyal (SAR)
Religion: Muslim (Sunni, Shia). The public practice of any other religion is forbidden
Language: Arabic, English
British Embassy, Riyadh: +966 (0) 1 488 0077

Senegal, The Republic of
Capital: Dakar
Currency: CFA Franc BCEAO (XOF)
Religion: Muslim, Christian, indigenous beliefs
Language: French (official), Wolof, Malinke, Serere, Soninke, Pular (all national)
British Embassy, Dakar: +221 33 823 7392/9971

Serbia, The Republic of
Capital: Belgrade
Currency: Serbian Dinar (RSD)
Religion: Serbian Orthodox, Muslim, Roman Catholic, Christian
Language: Serbian (majority), Romanian, Hungarian, Slovak, Croatian, Albanian (Kosovan), Ukranian, Bosniak, Montenegrin, Bulgarian, Ruthenian, Roma. Vlach, Macedonian
British Embassy, Belgrade: +381 (11) 2645 055

Seychelles, The Republic of
Capital: Victoria
Currency: Seychelles Rupee (SCR)
Religion: Roman Catholic, Anglican, Muslim, Hindu
Language: English, French, Creole (Seselwa)
British High Commission, Victoria: +248 4283 666

Sierra Leone, The Republic of
Capital: Freetown
Currency: Leone (SLL)
Religion: Muslim, Christian, indigenous beliefs
Language: English (official), Krio (English-based Creole), indigenous languages widely spoken
British High Commission, Freetown: +232 (0) 7689 25634

Singapore, The Republic of
Capital: Singapore
Currency: Singapore Dollar (SGD)
Religion: Taoist, Buddhist, Muslim, Christian, Hindu
Language: Mandarin, English, Malay, Tamil
British High Commission, Singapore: +65 6424 4200

Slovakia (The Slovak Republic)
Capital: Bratislava
Currency: Euro (EUR)
Religion: Roman Catholic, Atheist, Protestant, Orthodox
Language: Slovak (official), Hungarian
British Embassy, Bratislava: +421 (2) 5998 2000

Slovenia, The Republic of
Capital: Ljubljana
Currency: Euro (EUR)
Religion: Roman Catholic
Language: Slovene, Italian, Hungarian, English
British Embassy, Ljubljana: +386 (1) 200 3910

Solomon Islands
Capital: Honiara
Currency: Solomon Islands Dollar (SBD)
Religion: Christian, traditional beliefs
Language: English, Pidgin, 92 indigenous languages
British High Commission, Honiara: +677 21705/6

Somalia (The Somali Democratic Republic)
Capital: Mogadishu
Currency: Somali Shilling (SOS)
Religion: Sunni Muslim
Language: Somali (official), Arabic, Italian, English
British Office for Somalia, Nairobi, Kenya: +254 (20) 2844 000

South Africa, Republic of
Capital: Pretoria/Tshwane
Currency: Rand (ZAR)
Religion: Predominately Christian but all principal religions are represented
Language: 11 official languages: Afrikaans, English, Ndebele, Sepedi, Sesotho, Swati, Tsonga, Tswana, Venda, Xhosa, Zulu
British High Commission, Pretoria: +27 (12) 421 7500

South Georgia & South Sandwich Islands (British Overseas Territories)
Capital: King Edward Point
Currency: United Kingdom Pound Sterling (GBP)
Language: English
Governor's Office, Stanley, Falkland Islands: +500 282 00

Spain, The Kingdom of
Capital: Madrid
Currency: Euro (EUR)
Religion: Roman Catholic, Protestant
Language: Castilian Spanish (official), Catalan, Galician, Basque
British Embassy, Madrid: +34 (91) 714 6300

Sri Lanka, The Democratic Socialist Republic of
Capital: Colombo
Currency: Rupee (LKR)
Religion: Buddhist, Hindu, Muslim, Christian
Language: Sinhalese, Tamil, English
British High Commission, Colombo: +94 (11) 5390639

Sudan, The Republic of
Capital: Khartoum City
Currency: Sudanese pound (SDG)
Religion: Muslim, Christian, indigenous religions
Language: Arabic (official), Nubian, Ta Bedawie, dialects of Nilotic, Nilo- Hamitic, Sudanic languages, English
British Embassy, Khartoum: +249 (183) 777 105

Suriname, The Republic of
Capital: Paramaribo
Currency: Suriname Dollar (SRD)
Religion: Hindu, Muslim, Roman Catholic, Dutch Reformed, Moravian, Jewish, Bahá'í
Language: Dutch (official), English, Sranan Tongo (Creole), Hindustani, Javanese
British Honorary Consulate, Paramaribo: +597 402 558

Swaziland, The Kingdom of
Capital: Mbabane
Currency: Lilangeni (SZL)
Religion: Christian, indigenous beliefs
Language: English, Siswati
British Honorary Consulate, Mbabane: +268 551 6247

Sweden
Capital: Stockholm
Currency: Swedish Krona (SEK)
Religion: Lutheran, Roman Catholic, Orthodox, Baptist, Muslim, Jewish, Buddhist
Language: Swedish, English widely spoken
British Embassy, Stockholm: +46 (8) 671 3000

Switzerland
Capital: Berne
Currency: Swiss Franc (CHF)
Religion: Roman Catholic, Protestant, Muslim
Language: Swiss German (official), French, Italian, Rhaeto-Rumantsch
British Embassy, Berne: +41 (31) 359 7700

Syria (The Syrian Arab Republic)
Capital: Damascus
Currency: Syrian Pound (also called Lira) (SYP)
Religion: Sunni Muslim, Shi'a Muslim, Alawite, Druze, other Muslim sects, Christian, Jewish
Language: Arabic (official), Kurdish, Armenian, Aramaic, Circassian, some French, English
British Embassy, Damascus: +963 (11) 339 1513/1541 (consular)

Taiwan (Province of the People's Republic of China)
Capital: Taipei
Currency: New Taiwan Dollar (TWD)
Religion: Buddhist, Taoist, Christian
Language: Mandarin Chinese (official), Taiwanese, Hakka
British Trade & Cultural Office, Taipei: +886 (2) 8758 2088

Tajikistan, Republic of
Capital: Dushanbe
Currency: Somoni (TJS)
Religion: Sunni Muslim, Ismaili Shiite, Russian Orthodox Christian, Jewish
Language: Tajik, Russian
British Embassy, Dushanbe: +992 372 24 22 21

Tanzania, United Republic of
Capital: Dodoma (official)
Currency: Tanzania Shilling (TZS)
Religion: Christian, Muslim, indigenous beliefs
Language: Kiswahili, English
British High Commission, Dar es Salaam: +255 (022) 229 0000

Thailand, Kingdom of
Capital: Bangkok
Currency: Baht (THB)
Religion: Buddhist, Muslim, Christian, Hindu
Language: Thai, Yawi
British Embassy, Bangkok: +66 (0) 2 305 8333

Tibet – see China

Timor-Leste, Democratic Republic of
Capital: Dili
Currency: US Dollar (USD)
Religion: Roman Catholic (majority), Protestant, Muslim, Hindu, Buddhist
Language: Tetum (official), Portuguese (official), Bahasa Indonesian, English
refer to British Embassy, Jakarta: +62 (21) 2356 5200

Togo (Togolese Republic)
Capital: Lomé
Currency: CFA Franc BCEAO (XOF)
Religion: Christian, Muslim, indigenous beliefs
Language: French, Kabiye, Ewe
The British Ambassador to Togo resides in Accra, Ghana: +223 21 221665; in a genuine emergency contact the Honorary Consul in Togo: +228 2222714

Tonga, Kingdom of
Capital: Nuku'alofa
Currency: Pa'anga (TOP)
Religion: Christian
Language: Tongan, English
refer to British High Commission, Suva, Fiji: +679 322 9100

Trinidad and Tobago, Republic of
Capital: Port of Spain
Currency: Trinidad and Tobago Dollar (TTD)
Religion: Roman Catholic, Hindu, Anglican, Muslim, Presbyterian
Language: English (official), Spanish
British High Commission, Port of Spain: +1 (868) 622 2748

Tristan da Cunha (British Overseas Territory)
Capital: Edinburgh of the Seven Seas
Currency: Sterling (GBP)
Religion: Christian
Language: English
Administrator's Office: +870 764 341 816

Tunisia (Tunisian Republic)
Capital: Tunis
Currency: Tunisian Dinar (TND)
Religion: Muslim, Christian
Language: Arabic, French
British Embassy, Tunis: +216 71 108 700

Turkey
Capital: Ankara
Currency: New Turkish Lira (TRY)
Religion: Muslim
Language: Turkish, Kurdish
British Consulae, Izmir: +90 (232) 463 5151

Turkmenistan
Capital: Ashgabat
Currency: Manat (TMM)
Religion: Sunni Muslim
Language: Russian, Turkmen
British Embassy, Ashgabat: +993 (12) 363 462/63/64

Turks and Caicos Islands
Capital: Grand Turk
Currency: US Dollar (USD)
Religion: Christian
Language: English, some Creole
Governor's Office: +1 (649) 946 2309

Tuvalu
Capital: Funafuti
Currency: Australian Dollar (AUD), Tuvaluan Dollar (TVD) (coinage only)
Religion: Church of Tuvalu, Bahá'í
Language: Tuvaluan, English, Samoan, Kiribati
refer to British High Commission, Suva, Fiji: +679 322 9100

Uganda Republic
Capital: Kampala
Currency: Uganda Shilling (UGX)
Religion: Christian, Muslim
Language: English (official national language), Luganda, Swahili
British High Commission, Kampala: +256 (31) 231 2000

Ukraine
Capital: Kyiv (Kiev)
Currency: Hryvna (UAH)
Religion: Ukrainian Orthodox, Ukrainian Greek Catholic, Jewish, Muslim
Language: Ukrainian (official), Russian, Romanian, Polish, Hungarian
British Embassy, Kyiv: +380 44 490 3660

United Arab Emirates
Capital: Abu Dhabi
Currency: Dirham (AED)
Religion: Muslim, Hindu
Language: Arabic (official)
British Embassy, Abu Dhabi: +971 (2) 610 1100

United Kingdom
Capital: London
Currency: United Kingdom Pound Sterling (GBP)
Religion: Church of England, although all other faiths are practised
Language: English, Welsh (in Wales), Gaelic (in Scotland)
Foreign & Commonwealth Office: +44 (0) 20 7008 1500

United States of America
Capital: Washington, DC
Currency: US Dollar (USD)
Religion: Protestant, Roman Catholic, Latter-day Saints, Jewish, Muslim
Language: English, Spanish
British Embassy, Washington DC: +1 (202) 588 6500

Uruguay
Capital: Montevideo
Currency: Peso Uruguayan (UYU)
Religion: Roman Catholic, Protestant, Jewish, Atheist
Language: Spanish
British Embassy, Montevideo: +598 (2) 622 36 30/50

Uzbekistan, Republic of
Capital: Tashkent
Currency: Som (UZS)
Religion: Sunni Muslim
Language: Uzbek, Russian, Tajik
British Embassy, Tashkent: +998 71 120 1500/1516 (consular/visa)

Vanuatu, Republic of
Capital: Port Vila
Currency: Vatu (VUV)
Religion: Presbyterian, Anglican, Roman Catholic, Seventh Day Adventist
Language: Bislama (offical), English (official), French (official), plus over 130 vernacular languages
refer to British High Commission, Suva, Fiji: +679 322 9100

Venezuela, The Bolivarian Republic of
Capital: Caracas
Currency: Bolivar Fuerte (VEF)
Religion: Roman Catholic
Language: Spanish
British Embassy, Caracas: +58 (212) 263 8411

Vietnam, The Socialist Republic of
Capital: Hanoi
Currency: Vietnamese Dong (VND) (US dollar widely accepted)
Religion: Buddhist, Roman Catholic, Protestant, Cao Dai, Hoa Hao
Language: Vietnamese, minority languages also spoken
British Embassy, Hanoi: +84 (4) 3936 0500

Yemen, Republic of
Capital: Sana'a
Currency: Yemeni Rial (YER)
Religion: Muslim
Language: Arabic
British Embassy, Sana'a: +967 (1) 302480-5

Zambia, Republic of
Capital: Lusaka
Currency: Kwacha (ZMK)
Religion: Christian, Muslim, Hindu, indigenous beliefs
Language: English (official language of government), plus six further official languages
British High Commission, Lusaka: +260 (211) 423200

Zimbabwe, Republic of
Capital: Harare
Currency: Zimbabwean Dollar (ZWD)
Religion: Christian, indigenous beliefs, small communities of Hindu, Muslim and Jewish
Language: English (official), Shona, Ndebele
British Embassy, Harare: 0772 125 160-167

Index

C

D

E

I

J

K

L

M

N

O

P

Q

R

S

T

U

V

W

X

Y